D1260732

TITUS OATES

By the Same Author:

Biography

KING JAMES THE LAST

Fiction

PARCEL OF ROGUES

LONDON GOES TO HEAVEN

HIS FIGHT IS OURS

GIN AND BITTERS

HE STOOPED TO CONQUER

ENGLAND FOR SALE

YOU CAN'T RUN AWAY

SIR DEVIL-MAY-CARE

COME TO THE MARCH

PRELUDE TO KINGSHIP

KING'S CRITIC

BE VALIANT STILL

UNDAUNTED

R. White ad vivum delin et Sculp.
TITUS OATES.
Anagramma
TESTIS OVAT.
This is the true Originall taken from the Life
done for HEN: BROME and RIC: CHISWELL. All others are Counterfeit

TITUS OATES

by

Jane Lane

ANDREW DAKERS LIMITED
LONDON

First published in 1949

Printed in Great Britain by
The Camelot Press Ltd., London and Southampton

"How can we think any thing, that moves by the Agency of a bad Man, to be good? Or that a good natured virtuous Man can be the Author or Mover of barbarous and wicked Purposes? In a Word; a just knowledge of Men goes a great Way in testing the Truth of History itself. So important is the Justice of the Characters of Persons there."

North's *Examen*, p. 31.

This book is dedicated to the many kind persons, too numerous to name, who, by patiently answering questions, offering advice and criticism, and making suggestions, have enabled me to write it; and particularly to Father Basil FitzGibbon, S.J.; to Mr. J. Manwaring Baines, B.Sc., F.R.S.A., F.Z.S., Curator of the Public Museum at Hastings; to the Right Rev. Mgr. Edwin Henson, Rector of the English College at Valladolid; to the Rev. E. J. Tongue, D.D., Librarian of the Baptist Historical Society; to Mr. Robert W. Oates; to the Rev. Leslie Hook, B.A., Rector of All Saints', Hastings; and to the unfailingly courteous and helpful staffs of the British Museum Reading Room and London Library.

CONTENTS

LIST OF ILLUSTRATIONS

All the above illustrations are reproduced by courtesy of the Directors of the British Museum

BOOK ONE

THE WEAVER'S SON

(1)

THE England of sixteen hundred and forty-nine suffered two national tragedies: the execution of King Charles the First, and the birth of Titus Oates. The first was the result of a violation of the Law and Constitution. The effect of the second was the writing of the darkest chapter in the history of English justice. The death upon the scaffold of the king, the supreme authority, followed upon a trial in which there was not one shred of legality; the birth of the obscure baby preceded a series of judicial murders without parallel in the story of these nations.

The paternal ancestry of Titus was solid and respectable.[1] Oates or, as they often spelled it, Otes, was a name well known in Norfolk, as L'Estrange, himself a Norfolk man, ruefully admitted.[2] Little Titus's great-grandfather, and likewise his great-uncle, had held the living of Marsham; his grandfather, another Titus, had combined the trades of weaver and brewer in the city of Norwich. But his father, Samuel, came to manhood in troubled times; when he reached his late twenties a great upheaval was shaking England; troops of horse and companies of foot, friend indistinguishable from foe save for their different slogans and 'field-marks', startled a peaceful countryside and dismayed the sober merchants of the towns. The weaving of worsted or 'Norwich-stuff' became all of a sudden a tame occupation, and about the year 1643 Samuel suddenly forsook his father's work-shop and the parental hearth.

But the young ex-weaver was not to be found among the raw recruits who drilled for the Parliament, nor yet among those who enrolled themselves under the standard of King Charles the First. Samuel's talents, inclinations, and sound business instincts drew him towards an occupation more congenial than that of soldiering, and when first he appears upon the page of history he is Brother Oates, a leading-light in a conventicle known as Lamb's Church, in Bell Alley,

Coleman Street, London.[3] He has forsaken not only his trade but his religion; he is now an Anabaptist; he disputes, preaches, holds forth, and in general is a thorn in the side of the Established Church which, in this topsy-turvy world of civil war, has become the Presbyterian.

There is no more common error than that of confusing the Dissenters of the seventeenth century with those of the twentieth. The very word 'Puritan' has become entirely divorced from its original meaning. Modern advertisement is fond of grave young men and women in starched collars and clothes of an attractive simplicity; the Puritan of these advertisements stands for honesty, solidity, sobriety, dependableness. Hence, when the student of history comes up against such facts as the Puritan massacres of Drogheda and Wexford, the slaughter in cold blood of the Royalist camp-followers after Naseby, or the appalling murder of old Archbishop Sharpe, he regards them as isolated incidents out of character with the Puritan philosophy. Similarly, we do not expect the Quaker of to-day to appear stark-naked in the market-place smeared with ordure, and we would be startled (to say the least of it) to hear a Baptist minister proclaim from the pulpit that he was Jesus Christ.[4] But our ancestors of the seventeenth century were not at all startled by such phenomena, which were everyday occurrences and the practical results of the Puritan philosophy.

The Baptist of to-day would have little in common with the Anabaptist, who yet was his spiritual ancestor. This sect came into existence at the time of the Reformation; it was a kind of offshoot of the main revolt against the ancient Church. John of Leiden, one of the fathers of the sect, laboured under the delusion that he was a direct successor of King David; he took possession of the town of Munster in Westphalia, deposed the magistrates, and himself took four wives, one of whom he beheaded in the market-place.[5] He and his brethren "would not allow Christians to recover their own by Law, nor to take an Oath, nor bear the office of Magistrate, and they pulled down Magistrates by way of fact where they had strength, and gave the power of the sword to their Ministers and Prophets, who decided all differences, and judged of all cases by Scripture, and undertook to kill all the Princes of the World, and cut off all the ungodly with another sword than that of the Spirit: They taught that all in their Church were holy, that none can be saved that will not make his private goods common, that it is lawful to have many wives, that all learning is prophane, and that mean ignorant men are the fittest to expound Scripture, that there must be no ordinary calling in the Church, but every one may speak as he is inspired by the Holy Ghost; that Christ may reign over all the World, and therefore all other Kings and Princes, and their adherents must be slain, till there be none left to reign but Christ; and what they taught they went really about to practise."[6]

A study of the Interregnum, the period between the execution of Charles I and the Restoration of his son, reveals that, a hundred years after the founding of the sect, the Anabaptists were still as fiercely fanatical. Their main doctrine was an insistence on 'total immersion' when the age of reason was reached, but apart from this, the most varied and peculiar tenets were preached by individuals among them. For instance, there was a certain Mr Nichols who preached "that God was the Author of all sin, and that all lyes came out of the mouth of God"[7]; some denied the divinity of Christ, others contended against the divine revelation of the Scriptures and the immortality of the soul. They ran the whole gamut of fanaticism, from the addressing of their Creator as "Right Honourable Lord God", to the contention that, sleep being a kind of natural death, it was lawful for a husband or wife to take another bedfellow while their partner was asleep; and that even incest and rape were not sinful when practised by the Saints (themselves). Into this whirlpool of private judgment gone mad, did young Samuel Oates plunge with zest; on one occasion he informed the congregation at Lamb's Church "That the Doctrine of God's eternal Election and Predestination was a damnable Doctrine and Error; and in the same place since the Disputation should have been between Mr Calamy and the Anabaptists, this Oats preached, That their Disputation should be forbidden by the Civil Magistrate, was the greatest affront that ever was offered to Jesus Christ, since the forbidding of Peter and John to speak in the name of Christ."[8]

Samuel and his confreres would have regarded the services in a modern Baptist chapel as tame in the extreme. At Lamb's Church, the younger members of the congregation "make a noise while they are at their Exercises, and them of the church will go to make them quiet, and then they fight one with another."[9] The services were lively, to say the least of it; "in their Church meetings, they have many Exercisers, in one meeting two or three, when one hath done, there's sometimes difference in the Church who shall Exercise next, 'tis put to the Vote, some for one, some for another, some for Brother Tench, some for Brother Bat, some for Brother Oats . . . in this Church 'tis usual and lawful, not only for the Company to stand up and object against the Doctrine delivered when the Exerciser of his gifts hath made an end, but in the midst of it, so that sometimes upon some standing up and objecting, there's pro and con for almost an hour, and falling out among themselves before the man can have finished his Discourse."[10]

In a word, the original Puritan was a red-hot revolutionary, sincerely convinced of his mission to impose by "another sword than that of the Spirit", his peculiar and private doctrines upon the rest of mankind.

(2)

It was customary for Mr Lamb to send his brethren forth into distant parts of the country, preaching and baptizing, or, in the expressive parlance of the day, "dipping". In 1644, Samuel Oates "went his progresse into Surrey and Sussex",[11] and it is probable that it was on this particular progress that he took unto himself a wife. There is, of course, no record of the ceremony, since undoubtedly it was performed by some member of his sect, and therefore the maiden name of this most unfortunate woman remains unknown. The parish books of All Saints', Hastings, in which are recorded her children's baptisms, reveals only the fact that her Christian name was Lucy;[12] she was a Hastings midwife, and she was "look'd upon by all that knew her to be a very Pious and Vertuous Woman in her way".[13] Probably she was one of Oates's candidates for dipping, for young women succumbed very easily to this thrill, the dippers "tempting them out of their fathers houses at midnight to be baptized, the parents being asleep and knowing nothing."[14] It was apt to be a dangerous kind of thrill, since the custom was to dip the candidate stark naked in a river at dead of night, and it is scarcely surprising to learn that "where Oats hath been dipping, that it was spoken of by many, that some young women who having beene married divers yeeres, and never were with child, now since their dipping are proved with child."[15]

In 1645, Samuel appeared in Essex, and Mr Edwards, the Presbyterian minister, received fresh complaints from his colleagues in that county. "A base and bold sectarist named Oats, a weaver in London comes down, and vents a gallimanfry of strange opinions, and draws great flocks of people after him, without all controul. The Constables of Bocking did on Lord's day last disturb them, going among them to presse Souldiers, and they used them dispitefully, bad them get to their steeple houses, to hear their Popish Priests, their Baals Priests."[16] At Billericay, Oates and his company having quarrelled with the local minister during service, informed the congregation that their pastor was Antichrist, and then they "came up through the Town in a body together, divers of them having swords and carrying themselves insolently; and upon this occasion some of the Town meeting them, and they falling out there was a Ryot committed, and some of them being brought to Chelmsford at a Sessions it was found a Ryot, and they were proceeded against according to the Statutes in that case."[17]

But not only had the Anabaptists a contempt for the civil magistrate, they were likewise aware that at this date they could brave with impunity such officials. "Oates whom you mention in your Book," complains another Essex minister, "hath been Sowing his Tares, Boolimong, and wild Oates in these parts these last five weeks without any controul, hath seduced hundreds, and dipped many in Bocking River, and when that's done he hath a Feast in the night, and at the end of that the Lords Supper. All *opera tenebrarum*. No Magistrate in the Country dare meddle with him, for they say they have hunted these [fanatics] out of the Country into their Dens in London, and imprisoned some, and they are released, and sent like decoy

Ducks into the Country to fetch in more; so that they go on in divers parts of Essex with the greatest confidence and insolencie that can be imagined."[18]

Secure in the protection of the Independent Army, which was rapidly assuming control over its creator, the Presbyterian Parliament, Samuel went merrily upon his midnight way, for besides the pleasure of dipping naked young women, he was making his fortune. A minister indignantly informed Edwards that " 'tis commonly reported that this Oats had for his pains 10. shillings a peece for dipping the richer, and two shillings sixe pence for the poorer; he came very bare and mean into Essex, but before he had done his work, was well lined and grown pursie."[19] Or, as an admirer of Samuel puts it, "His labours were abundantly blessed."[20] And when it is considered that the pound of his day was worth at least five of the pre-1940 pound, it will be seen that dipping was an occupation by no means unprofitable. It would be presumptuous to speculate as to whether or no it was profitable to the soul of the dipped, but there can be no doubt that upon occasion it must have been extremely uncomfortable for the body. "There's a Story pleasant enough, and Every Body has it, of a Woman that he [Oates] had under the Ordnance of Dipping, that still fell to Squalling and Screaming so soon as ever they had her above Water; Down with her again (cries Otes) 'Tis her Concupiscence. Now the Matter in Truth was This, The roguey Boys had sunk a huge Bundle of Brambles and Thorns in the Dipping-Place, and the poor Womans body, it seems, did not like that way of Discipline."[21] Since Samuel "was not content to give those of his Tribe common Washing, but souced and douced them", the predicament of the unfortunate woman, stark naked as she was, can be imagined.

In 1646, Samuel went a little too far in his contempt for the law, and gave the despised magistrates the chance for which they had been waiting. Hitherto, neither his constant disturbance of the peace, nor his addiction to blasphemy (he was the friend and admirer of the notorious blasphemer, Boggie) had allowed the civil authorities to take action against him, so lawless had the kingdom grown under the rule of the Saints. But now he found himself brought before the magistrates of Chelmsford in connection with the death of one, Ann Martin; "the Coroner laid to his charge, that in March last, in a very cold season, he dippeing a young woman, she presently fell sick, and died within a short time,[22] and though the Coroner had not yet perfected his sitting upon her death, all witnesses being not yet examined, nor the Jury having brought in their verdict (so that the full evidence was not yet presented) yet the Bench upon being acquainted with the case, and other foule matters also being there by witnesses laid against him, committed him to the Jaile at Colchester: It was laid to his charge then, that he had preached against the assessements of Parliament, and the taxes laid upon the people, teaching them, that the Saints were a free people, and should do what they did voluntarily, and not be compelled; but now contrary to this they had assessement upon assessement, and rate upon rate. Some passages also in his prayer are repeated, as that he prayed the Parliament might not cart the Ark, nor meddle with making lawes for the Saints, which Jesus Christ was to doe alone. Since Oats commitment to Colchester Jaile, there hath been great and mightie resort to him in the prison, many have come down from London in Coaches to visit him. . . . Oates the Anabaptist hath had great resort to him in the Castle, both of Town and Country; But the Committee ordered the contrary last Saturday."[23]

Samuel was tried for his life at the next assizes, "but the jury, consisting (as it was believed) of pickt rascalls of his owne gang, found him not guilty."[24] Nor was this an isolated incident; a trooper accused of a similar offence in Radnorshire was released by order of the Army, for by this year the power of the military Saints was approaching its zenith.[25] Samuel "was bound by the Judge to his good behaviour, and made to find Sureties that hee should neither preach nor dip; and yet notwithstanding the very next Lords day hee preached at Chensford, and goes on still in Essex preaching his errors".[26]

But the melancholy fate of Ann Martin had roused the resentment of the husbands and fathers of Essex to the point when they were resolved to take the law into their own hands. It might be their wife or daughter next time, and something had to be done. Even among the credulous, this recent tragic disproval of the Anabaptists' contention that the Lord was with their converts in fire and water, had caused uneasiness and anger. "The people of Wethersfield hearing that Oats and some of his companions were coming to their Town, seased on them (onely Oats was not in the Company) and pumped them soundly. And Oats coming lately to Dunmow in Essex, some of the Town hearing of it where he was, fetched him out of the house, and threw him into the river, throughly dipping him."[27]

This dose of his own medicine gave Samuel a sudden distaste for Essex, and "finding himselfe somewhat ympayred in his reputacion" as Wood quaintly puts it, he quitted his old haunts, and in 1647 appears in Rutlandshire.

Immediately the same complaints are heard. "Abel Barker to his much honoured friend Sir Thomas Hartopp, Knight, at Leicester. Sending a declaration concerning one Samuel Oates, a weaver, 'who preacheth constantly in this country', for the consideration of the judges, who may see fit to issue a warrant for his arrest and conveyance to the Assizes at Okeham. Hambleton. March 19, 1646/7."[28] "Letter from Robert Horsman to the High Sheriff. About the seditious action of a 'dangerous Schismatick' preacher, namely, Samuel Oates. Stretton, October 6, 1647."[29] "Warrant (signed Robt. Horsman) to the constables of Stretton, for the arrest of Samuel Oates on a charge of 'gathering together of unlawful and disorderly assemblies'."[30] "Letter from Robt. Horsman to the High Sheriff. Announcing the writer's satisfaction at delivering the same disturber of the Church into the High Sheriff's hands. Stretton, October 8, 1647."[31] He did not, however, remain in those hands very long. "Dec. 11. Petition of sundry of the ministers of the county of Rutland, and the parts adjacent, accusing Samuel Oates of Arminianism, Anabaptism, etc., and praying for his apprehension."[32] But he was still at large in the May of the following year, when the ministers of Rutland appealed to the House of Lords that he might be proceeded against for blasphemy.[33]

Such was Samuel Oates, the ex-weaver of Norwich; a rebel against all authority, by nature a sensualist, but cloaking his animal instincts with a convenient religious cant. To him and to his wife Lucy there was born, on some unrecorded date in the year 1649, a man-child; they called him Titus.

(3)

At Oakham in Rutlandshire there is, or was, a house pointed out to the curious as the birthplace of Titus Oates. It stood opposite the Crown Hotel, and, not inappropriately, close behind the pillory.[34] Of the exact date on which Titus first saw the light there is no record, but a description of the birth itself was given, many years later, to one, William Smith, and that by no less a person than Mrs Samuel Oates. "This", wrote Smith, "is verbatim what his Mother said of him, for I took special Notice of her Words . . . 'You know, Mr Smith, I have had a great many Children, and by my Profession I have skill in womens concerns. But I believe never woman went such a time with a child as I did with him. I could seldom or never sleep when I went with him, and when I did sleep I always dreamt I was with child of the Devil. But when I came to my Travail, I had such lard Labour that I believe no woman ever had; it was ten to one but it had kill'd me'."[35]

The child whose birth had cost his mother so dear was not attractive. He was afflicted with a very repulsive running at the nose, which earned him, among his playmates, the nickname of "filthy mouth"; he was also abnormally dull at his books, a fact which was to be a sore point with him throughout his life.[36] "I thought he would have been a natural", his mother confided to William Smith, "for his Nose always run, and he slabber'd at the mouth, and his Father could not endure him; and when he came home at night the Boy would use to be in the Chimney corner, and my Husband would cry take away this snotty Fool, and jumble him about, which made me often weep, because you know he was my child."[37] His mother's affection for him (an affection deepened by the fact that as a toddler he "was much troubled with convulsion-fits and small hopes of life"[38]) was not returned by this unpleasant infant, who grew up to abuse her and call her names;[39] it was the father who "jumbled him about" who absorbed any affection of which Titus was capable.

In this year 1649, Samuel Oates became chaplain to the

regiment of Colonel Thomas Pride, once a Sedgemoor swineherd, then drayman to a London brewer, now one of the military potentates, a fanatical Anabaptist, famous for his "Purge" of December 6th, 1648, when he and his soldiers had prevented two hundred and forty Members of the House of Commons from taking their seats. During the whole of the year 1649, Pride's Regiment remained in London, and presumably Samuel divided his time between the capital and his domestic hearth at Oakham. There are no more complaints about him from the Rutland ministers, for he was now attached to the all-powerful Army, but he was as ready as ever to dispute on matters of doctrine, and during one of his visits to Oakham made a journey into Lincolnshire on purpose to point out the error of his ways to a Mr Robert Wright, minister of a Baptist congregation in that county. It proved a sad waste of time, for not only did Mr Wright persist in his Popish practice of laying-on of hands, but, despite all Samuel's eloquence, even went so far as to introduce to his scandalized flock the ceremony of washing the feet.[40]

In the following year, Samuel accompanied his regiment to Scotland, there to aid in the crushing of a Scottish army which had rallied to the standard of the young King, Charles the Second. So wonderful an opportunity of converting the Presbyterian Scots (for there was much fraternizing between the two armies while they remained in camp) should surely have satisfied Samuel's energetic nature; but it was not so. By the end of 1654 he was involved in the rather vague conspiracy known as Overton's Plot, and though very little regarding this affair was allowed to get into the licensed news-sheets, from the little that there is it would seem that Samuel was among the principal conspirators.[41] In February, 1655, several of these, Samuel among them, were tried by court-martial, and were either cashiered or imprisoned or both. Samuel himself was examined on the 21st, "but there being some additional Articles against him, he had time given till Friday to put in his Answer".[42]

There seems to be no record either of his answer or his punishment; Echard says that he was imprisoned till the Restoration,[43] but a contemporary life of Titus states that when, after he had passed his fifth birthday, the child grew stronger, he was brought by his father from Oakham to London.[44] Either with or without his father, Titus seems to have moved to London at this time, and here he attended the Baptist meeting-house in Virginia Street, Ratcliffe Highway.[45] It is possible that he was sent to Westminster School; the contemporary life of him mentioned above says so definitely, and though the Records of Westminster are silent regarding him, the admission-books of the period are not by any means complete. Moreover, some complimentary verses adorning a portrait of Titus at the height of his fame, contain the lines:

> "*Westminster taught him, Cambridge bred him, then,*
> *Left him instead of books to study Men.*"

If this is a mistake, it is curious that Titus himself did not correct it; and if he went to Westminster at all, it must have been at this period.

But now a great change was to take place in the life of the Oates family, a reflection of that greater change which was due to take place in the national life. The people of England, weary of a succession of tyrannies, began to murmur dangerously loud, and the Government, rent with internal dissensions, crumbled. Monck, that cunning trimmer, saw his opportunity, and, judging the exact moment to a nicety, decided to call home the King. Upon the twenty-ninth of May, 1660, King Charles the Second rode into an exultant and feverishly Royalist London; and in the self-same year, Samuel Oates put off his Geneva cloak and bands and donned the garments of a Church of England parson.

(4)

The Baptist historian Taylor, who admired Samuel, explains the turning of his coat thus: "Such, however, was the respect which even his enemies had for his character and abilities, that, some time after the Restoration, he was offered 'a great place' by the Duke of York, on condition to his conforming to the church of England. In an evil hour the temptation prevailed; he conformed; and was presented to the benefice of Hastings in Sussex."[46] One cannot help regarding the last sentence as an anti-climax, for by no stretch of the imagination can All Saints', Hastings, be termed "a great place". Moreover, Mr Taylor was mistaken in saying that the benefice was presented by the Duke of York; Samuel's patron was, in fact, a Mr John Injames.[47]

The church of All Saints is a large solid edifice, standing on the site of one destroyed by the French in 1378. While to-day it bears within it the unmistakable marks of nineteenth century 'restoration', in Samuel's time it displayed the ravages of the iconoclasts of the Reformation. But one glorious fresco escaped destruction on both occasions, and may be admired to this day; it is the Doom painting, of late fifteenth century date over the chancel arch. It is interesting to speculate upon the nature of Samuel's feelings when, Sunday after Sunday, he was obliged to view the Blessed Virgin kneeling on the left of Christ, and St Peter standing at the gate of Heaven to receive the souls of the Blessed.

Hastings itself was in those days but a large village, though one of the Cinque Ports, with no proper harbour and a broken-down pier, the proposed re-building of which had been stopped by the outbreak of the Civil War.[48] It is possible very vividly to visualise the Hastings of Samuel's day by a walk round the Old Town, for All Saints' Street and the High Street are little changed. A house (at present, 1948, in the process of being restored) is believed to have been that occupied by the Oates family; it stands at the top of the High Street, a little beyond the junction of this and All Saints' Street.*

One of the first cares of Samuel when he got his benefice was to baptize his growing family according to the rites of the Church of England. The merry days of dipping were behind him; a mere sprinkling must now take the place of total immersion, a stone font and squalling infants must serve as substitutes for rivers and naked young women. Nevertheless, now that the Oateses were gathered into the bosom of the Established Church, her ceremonies, inferior though they were, must be observed. Upon November

* A photograph of this house appeared in *The Times* of July 29th, 1947, but was wrongly described as Torfield House. The latter, a mansion of much later date, stands southwards of the other, in the High Street.

20th, 1660, "titus otes an[d] constant otes sons of small and Lucy otes ware baptised",[49] and to make this double christening the more impressive, Samuel invited "some principal People of the Town for Godfathers and God-mothers".[50] The question as to whether Titus Oates ever was baptized was of deep interest to his contemporaries in the days of his fame, *The Loyal Protestant and True Domestick Intelligence* for December 3rd, 1681, even going to the trouble of applying for information to the inhabitants of Oakham, who affirmed that "They remember his Birth, and that he never was Baptized". Apparently nobody thought of consulting the parish registers of All Saints', Hastings.

Upon the following 2nd of February, a daughter was baptized; the name is scarcely legible in the register and looks like "hanehe"; possibly it was Hannah. Titus and Constant had an elder brother, Samuel, who, in 1658, had gone to sea. In June of 1662 this lad paid a visit to his home, and was promptly subjected to his father's zeal for the sacrament of baptism, that worthy combining the christening of Samuel junior with that of a new daughter, Anne. There are no more baptismal entries during Samuel's stay at Hastings, which was to last for another fourteen years or so; therefore it is safe to conclude that his family consisted of three sons, Samuel, Titus, and Constant, and two daughters, "hanehe" and Anne.

It was now high time that something should be done about young Titus's education; if he ever was at Westminster, he had certainly left it before this, for in 1664, at a very advanced age for those days, he was sent to Merchant-Taylors' School in London, the headmaster of which was at this time John Goad, B.D. William Smith, the man to whom Titus's mother later confided the details of her second son's birth, was a master at this school, and described the coming of the new boy, Titus Oates: "In the year 1664, he was brought to Merchant-Taylors-School, as a Free Schollar, by Nicholas Delves Esq., now living; he happening to be in Books that were taught in my Forms, I was sent for down to receive him into the School, which I did in an unlucky hour. And truly, the first Trick he Served me, was, That he Cheated me of our Entrance-Money which his Father sent me, which the Doctor [Titus] generously confest in his Greatness at Whitehall, and very Honestly paid me then."[51] What other tricks Titus played we do not know, but they must have been serious ones, for in the following year he was expelled. In the time of his fame, Merchant Taylors' was proud to own this son of hers, and under his name in the Probation Book there is the following description: "The Saviour of the Nation, first discoverer of that damnable, hellish popish plot in 1678." But another and a later hand added a disillusioned postscript: "Perjured upon record and a scoundrell fellow."

Titus's enforced exit from London proved fortunate for him, for it was thus he escaped those two great calamities which were now to fall upon the capital, the Plague and the Fire. Meanwhile, he was sent to pursue his studies at the small village of Sedlescombe, six miles from Hastings. Since local authority is positive that there was never anything but the village school here, which in those days would consist of a handful of children learning their horn-book in the schoolmaster's parlour, it seems curious that the Rev. Samuel should send his son, at the age of fifteen (an age when many youths were entering the university) to such a scholastic establishment. Possibly Titus was in disgrace, either because of his expulsion from Merchant Taylors' or for some other cause unknown to us; or perhaps it was that his backwardness made him unfit for anything except a village school. On the other hand his father may have boarded him out in this remote village from that same sense of exasperation which had caused him, when Titus was small, to "jumble him about".[52] At all events, to Sedlescombe he went; and there he remained for two years, that is until he was turned eighteen years of age.

On a June day of 1667, he went up to Cambridge to finish the education he can scarcely be said to have begun.

(5)

"In the year 1664", wrote one, Adam Elliot, who later was to have cause to remember his early encounters with the subject of this biography, "I was admitted into Cajus Colledge in the University of Cambridge, where I continued until 1668. . . . During my stay there, I remember Titus Oates was entered in our Colledge; by the same token that the Plague and he both visited the University the same year. He was very remarkable for a Canting Fanatical way conveyed to him with his Anabaptistical Education, and in our Academical exercises, when others declaim'd Oates always preach'd; some of which Lectures, they were so very strange, that I do yet remember them."[53] The authorities at Caius did not take kindly to Titus, and after two terms he was "spew'd out". Yet he managed to get himself admitted a servitor at St John's; and it was here he gave the first example of what he could do in the gentle art of lying.

He bought a coat of a poor tailor, and when it came to the question of payment, Titus affirmed that he had already paid. "The tailor, concerned less about the coat than about his honour lest he be thought to claim money not due to him, sought everywhere for the coat, and at length found it with a dealer in secondhand clothes, to whom Oates had sold it."[54] Armed with this evidence, the tailor brought his case to the notice of Titus's tutor, Dr Thomas Watson, who thereupon called Titus before him and demanded an explanation. Titus assumed the role of outraged innocence; he asked for a Bible, and offered to swear upon it that he had paid. But how had he come by the money? enquired Dr Watson, seeing that all money passed through his, the tutor's hands. His mother, replied Titus without a blush had sent him some money privately, by the hands of such-and-such a carrier. The carrier in question was called, and not only denied the story, but swore he did not so much as know Oates. It was the end; and Titus was sent down.[55]

This incident of the tailor and the coat, trivial though it seems, is full of interest in a study of Titus Oates. The records we have of his childhood are unpleasant, but up till now his bad conduct may be excused by his fanatical upbringing, his native stupidity, and early physical weakness. Now, however, he is a man; his character is formed; and the first glimpse we have of that character is a readiness to lie, wantonly, recklessly, audaciously, to the injury of the innocent. His first serious excursion into the realms of untruthfulness brought him no good, it is true; yet, far from halting him, it seems merely to have whetted his appetite for falsehood for its own sake. In the story of the tailor and the coat is the shadow of coming events.

Titus left Cambridge as he had left school, in disgrace. He left no reputation behind him for parts or learning, says the historian Echard, though he was capable of a "plodding Industry and an unparallel'd Assurance"; Echard records one other trait, which becomes ominous in the light of later events: "he seem'd distinguish'd for a tenacious Memory".[56] Dr Watson told Baker, the antiquary, that Titus was "a great dunce", and that he ran into debt, though he "does not charge him with much immorality". Latin he never mastered; "I will be a bond Slave for ever," exclaimed Lord Castlemaine, years later, "if he can Translate six Lines into Latin, without a Solecism";[57] and L'Estrange has the following passage in one of his *Observators*:

"*Whig*. Well! If other men will do amiss I cannot help it. *Non est MEUS* Culpa.

"*Observator*. How, How, How? Whig! *MEUS* Culpa?

"*Whig*. Yes, I say *MEUS Culpa*: and I'le shew ye Good Authority for't. Doctor Oates had fal'n foul in Language upon his Senior, in Cambridge; and was Condemn'd to ask his Pardon in a Copy of Verses, as a Composition.

"*Observator*. And a Copy of Verses, let me tell ye, in those days, went as hard with the Dr as Fifteen, or Twenty Thousand Pound did after ward. . . . But where's the Doctor's Authority all this while for *MEUS Culpa*?

"*Whig*. '*Non Sectare Meum, sed Contra Corrige Culpam.*' Now the Doctor has an Affection, I suppose, to the Masculine, because it is more Worthy than the Feminine.

"*Observator*. Right. The Doctor's was a HEE Culpa."[58]

It was in 1669 that Titus left Cambridge; and very shortly afterwards, apparently through the influence of the Duke of Norfolk,[59] he contrived to "slip into orders", and became curate of a church in Sandhurst, of which the Rev. Walter Drury was rector. Here it was, if we may credit Titus, that he received the first warning of the dire intentions of the Papists. He tells us that "the Acquaintance I had with some considerable Papists in the Year 1670 made me Suspect a Design carrying on by them to advance their own Religion, and to pull down ours; but I little thought that they had a Design for murdering the King, which in process of time I found out. . . . There was one Cotton at Mr Guilfourd's in Kent, that was often very pleasingly tempting me to come over to their Church; for, saith he, it will not be long before you must either burn or turn, therefore come over in time, that your coming over may be looked upon as meritorious."[60]

On March 13th, 1673, he was presented to the living of Bobbing in Kent, by Sir George Moore of Bobbing Court, who had the advowson of the vicarage.[61] Sir George had obtained this manor in right of his wife, and Hasted thus describes it as it was in his day: "The mansion of Bobbing-court, which was situated exceedingly pleasant, having a fine prospect on every side of it, stood almost adjoining to the south side of the church-yard. It has been many years since pulled down, but by the foundations remaining, the walls of the garden, and the out-houses belonging to it, which are yet standing, it appears to have been a building of a very considerable size."[62] Titus, living just across the way in his vicarage, must often have looked upon this pleasant mansion and envied it; for many years later he endeavoured to buy it with money he expected from the public purse.

But his residence at Bobbing was destined to be a short one, for the bad habits which had compelled both school and university to expel him, had not been laid aside when he put on his parson's gown. "He has been observ'd, wherever he has fortun'd to make his residence, to sow dissension among neighbours, even where he hath pretended to be a Minister of peace, a perpetual Make-bate."[63] There were perpetual complaints from his parishioners; on one occasion he was so drunk that he could not conduct the service; he stole his neighbours' pigs and hens;[64] and he was "complained of for some very indecent expressions concerning the mysteries of the Christian religion".[65] For these and other misdemeanours he found himself silenced by the Archdeacon of Canterbury and turned out of the living by Sir George Moore; Sir George died in 1678, fortunately, perhaps, for himself, since Titus's memory was remarkably tenacious of such affronts, and Smith the schoolmaster says that he endeavoured to make the Archdeacon a victim of his Plot, "as he will justifie for me, having very hardly escaped his snares, all honest and good Men being ever the greatest mark of his malice".

So, at the end of 1673, Titus shook the dust of St. Bartholomew's, Bobbing, off his feet, and turned up again, like the proverbial bad penny, at All Saints' Rectory, Hastings. Whether the Rev. Samuel was glad to see this oft-returning offspring it is impossible to say; at all events he seems to have decided to make the best of a bad job, and installed Titus as his curate.[66]

The ex-dipper was exceedingly unpopular with a large section of his congregation. But the ex-dipper's son had not been installed as curate for more than a few weeks before he made himself infinitely more detested than ever his father had been. Upon occasion he officiated for Samuel, and, "having neither Wit nor Learning, presently became the Scandal of the Pulpit, insomuch that the Fisher-Women pulled him out of the Pulpit; during his abode at Hastings, he was always quarrelling, and by Lies and False Suggestions, setting Neighbours by the Ears".[67] The Rev. Samuel's own position was being made impossible by this difficult son of his, and some other post must be found for Titus. Looking round for a likely job, Samuel's predatory eye fell upon a mastership in a generously endowed local school, a position at present occupied by one, William Parker.

(6)

The name Parker was one well-known and honoured in Hastings. A Reverend William Parker, early in the century, had bequeathed upwards of one hundred acres of land, in the parish of Ore, towards the maintenance of a schoolmaster for the free school mentioned above, the master himself to be elected by the jurats of All Saints'.[68] The present master, young William Parker, whose post Samuel Oates began to covet for his son, had a father, Captain Parker, a magistrate, one of Samuel's principal parishioners, and an ex-mayor of Hastings. He is described by contemporary writers as the "Governor" of Hastings, but as there never seems to have been such an office, it is probable that he commanded the local trained bands. This Captain Parker was the most distinguished member of that section of Samuel's parishioners who held their rector in disesteem, and almost certainly it was by his advice that at last the Bishop was applied to to restrain Samuel's "intolerable unjust dealings". The Rev. Oates grew apprehensive, and begged such friends as he had among his flock to make his peace; but his hopeful offspring had a better idea. One day "a certain person who had been very instrumental in endeavouring a reconciliation amongst them, by accident meeting Tytus Oates, in conference (amongst other things) demaunded of him how now at last matters were like to goe betweene his ffather and his parishioners, who presently answered 'it was no matter for there were now irons in the fire which if they tooke a right heat would doe the worke' ".[69]

Of the irons in question there were two. At Eastertide, 1675, Titus betook himself to the Mayor of Hastings; very solemnly and confidently he informed his worship that upon such and such a day, at such and such an hour, he going into his father's church, had discovered in the South Porch (a commodious erection, swept away in the nineteenth century) young William Parker the schoolmaster in the act of committing an unnatural offence with "a young and tender man-childe". The Mayor, good man, was profoundly shocked; young Parker's reputation made the story sound incredible, and yet the rector's son was so positive, and had made his charge so detailed. The schoolmaster was arrested, and, finding bail, was bound over to the next Sessions.

While William Parker junior was incarcerated and awaiting his trial, Titus again approached the Mayor. He had a further accusation to make, it seemed, this time against William Parker senior. He charged Captain Parker with having uttered treasonable and seditious speech. It is important to note the gravity of both these charges. By a post-Restoration Act, treasonable words were identified with High Treason, the penalty for which was the hurdle, the noose, and the quartering-block; while sodomy was now, and for a long while afterwards, a crime punishable by death. Upon April 17th, the Mayor and Jurats of Hastings wrote to the Secretary of State, Sir Joseph Williamson, as follows:

"By letters from Mr Samuel Otes we understand that his son, Titus, is expected to attend and make good his late information against Capt. William Parker, senior, exhibited to us and enclosed to you in our late letters, before the Privy Council next Wednesday. But, because he is bound to give evidence on an indictment against William Parker, junior, son of the above, for an unnatural offence, whose trial is unavoidably to be at the goal delivery at this town next Thursday, which we are all necessarily to attend, we pray that another day of attendance may be appointed for the said Titus Oates and others concerned in the said information."[70]

On the appointed Thursday, therefore, Titus appeared for the first time in the role in which he was to become so famous, and in this his debut as accuser in a court of law he had the benefit of his father's backing: "old Oates swore as to circumstances, but the young one point-blanke as to fact". But his hour was not yet come, and this first essay in the art of perjury proved a dismal failure. For the schoolmaster had been able to marshal witnesses of credit, and on the other hand Titus's love of being definite and detailed in his lies proved his undoing. It was established, first that there were masons at work on some repair of the church at the very hour of the supposed offence, and that they had seen nothing. Next, that at that very hour on that very evening, young Parker had been treating the parents of his pupils "with a select Gaudy-day Dinner" at his own house, which was a full half-mile from the church; the said parents testified that the schoolmaster had not stirred from their company the whole evening. Lastly, the alleged victim of Parker's offence could not be produced; and he could not be produced for the very good reason that he did not exist; there was no such person.

Young Parker was set free, "to the infinite gladness of the spectators"; and immediately declared his intention of bringing an action for damages against Titus to the tune of one thousand pounds. Poor Titus's stars shone darkly over him at present, for very shortly afterwards the Privy Council dismissed the charge against Captain William

Parker as a false and malicious prosecution, and the intended victim returned to Hastings, which signified its opinion of the whole affair by lighting bonfires and ringing bells.[71] Then, on May 27th, the Mayor and jurats of Hastings added insult to injury by deciding against Titus in his case against Francis Norwood, one of his father's churchwardens, whom he had accused of threatening to beat him. They declared that "the said Titus had voluntarily and corruptly committed perjury", and he was bound over in the sum of forty pounds to appear at the next Sessions to answer for his crime.[72]

With two such accusations hanging over his head, Titus felt that Hastings had grown a trifle too hot for him, and that it behoved him to leave it in a hurry. Having nowhere else to go, he did what many another "wanted" person did in those days: he went to sea.

(7)

How Titus managed to get himself appointed a naval chaplain is not known, but it cannot have been very difficult. He had a brother in the Navy; and, moreover, at this period naval chaplains were not required to produce anything in the way of a reference or a testimonial of good character. Many of them were parsons forced to flee from creditors; it was not until 1677 that the Lords of the Admiralty resolved that "no persons shall be entertained as Chaplains on board His Majesty's Ships but such as shall be approved of by the Bishop of London".

It must have been at the very end of May, or the beginning of June, that Titus embarked on board the *Adventure*, commanded by Sir Richard Rooth, bound for Tangier.[73] Of Rooth himself, little is known, but his being repeatedly trusted with a command speaks well for his character and abilities. Since the Restoration he had commanded in turn the *Dartmouth*, the *Harp*, the *Dartmouth* again, the *St. David*, the *Garland*, the *Lion*, and the *Swiftsure*.[74] In April of this year, 1675, he had been knighted for "good and faithful services";[75] his last command was that of the *Monmouth* in 1678. The object of his present voyage was to carry to Tangier its new Governor, Lord Inchiquin; on April 27th,

Hugh Salesbury wrote to Williamson that "*The Adventure*, Sir R. Rooth commander, is at Spithead waiting for the Earl of Inchiquin";[76] since Titus was still at Hastings on May 27th, it would seem that he had to wait some time.

Most vivid details of a naval chaplain's life are to be found in the diary of the Rev. Henry Teonge, who, in this very year, was driven to such employment through the attentiveness of duns. He arrived at his ship in such a destitute condition, that he was delighted to accept "from Providence", a "rugged towell on the quarter deck", "a peice of an old sayl, and an earthern chamber pott; all very helpful to him that had nothing".[77] We may take it his brother-chaplain, Titus, was in much the same straits when he embarked on board the *Adventure*. However, though the pay was not large (it was that of an ordinary seaman, nineteen shillings per lunar month, with the addition of a groat out of every seaman's monthly wage), the duties were not heavy, if we are to judge by Teonge's diary. The excuse of bad weather could always be used for the omission of a sermon, and when he did preach, Teonge frequently made do with the same text for three or even four Sundays in succession. The most arduous task was that of burying the dead, entries of which occur in this diary with a sinister frequency. Indeed, the Rev. Henry Teonge had so little to do that he employed much of his time writing execrable verse.

But the Rev. Titus Oates employed his spare time in less innocent recreation. There now occurs the first definite mention of his addiction to that vice of which he had accused young Parker. "And then for his Employment under Sr Richard Ruth; If his Coat had not Pleaded for his Neck, he might have Stretch'd for Buggery while he was under his Command."[78] "I have heard those who were abroad with him report, that he has committed such crimes a-ship-board, as have oblig'd the Captain, a Gentleman of very fair conditions, to wave all Civility usually bestow'd upon his Quality, and to order him to be drubb'd, and ty'd neck and heels, and after to be set ashore."[79] "Caught in the crime of sodomy, he narrowly escaped a hanging at the yardarm."[80] "As for his Brutalities of Lust; His Tangier-Adventure Rings of it."[81]

The subject is an unsavoury one, but it is essential to an understanding of Titus's character. There can be little doubt that he was a pervert, though this is the only instance in which he was actually punished for that vice. More than one accusation of sodomy was to be brought against him in the future, but as these were made after the year 1678, when he became immune from justice, he always escaped. When he went to school again, as a grown man, his superiors deemed him dangerous to the society of boys; and in his latter years, when it was safe to criticize him, there was scarcely a squib or a broadsheet published concerning him which did not contain a mention of his unnatural vices.

The *Adventure* reached Tangier towards the end of June,[82] and while the ship remained in port (which seems to have been for some little time), Titus had the opportunity of exploring this new British possession. An ambitious scheme of improvement was in progress; the castle was being enlarged and fortified, and builders were at work on the great Mole. It was a scheme dear to the heart of Charles the Second, but it was in continual danger of frustration for lack of money, and it would not be many years before King Charles's loving Parliament withheld supplies to a degree which forced him to give order to blow up his fine new works and abandon the port. Meanwhile, in intervals of admiring foreign parts, the Rev. Titus Oates was busy listening to Popish confidences.

It was a most extraordinary thing, but no sooner did this young parson come into contact with Papists, than they rushed to tell him their horrid secrets. He had had already one experience of this, at Sandhurst; and now, at Tangier, they were at him again. "I went and served his Majesty at Sea as a Chaplain", wrote Titus, "where I found many Difficulties by reason of sickness of Body. I refreshed my self at Tangire: There was one Gerard an Irish Dominican, that upon the first sight of me, required of me, Whether the Catholick Religion was established in England? . . . and I told him No: Why then, said he, the Dutch War is to no purpose."[83] In Titus's account of this period of his life, there is of course no mention of any little difference with his commander; but for the matter of that, there is not a word about the Parker scandal either, Titus wafting himself straight from the vicarage of Bobbing to the deck of the *Adventure*.

In December, the majority of King Charles's men-of-war were making for home on account of bad weather; the *Gazettes* of that month are full of accounts of shipwrecks. In the absence of any information to the contrary, we may take it that the *Adventure* was among them; at all events, early in 1676, Titus appears in London. He had been expelled the Navy after one voyage and, as has been seen, had been lucky to escape with his neck; two actions for perjury awaited him at Hastings, so in London he remained for the moment, most probably lodging with his father. For after the Parker scandal, Samuel likewise had found Hastings too hot for him, and had exchanged his snug rectory for obscure lodgings in Bloomsbury, and his new religion for his old one. "But neither the dignities nor the emoluments of his new situation", writes his admirer, Mr Taylor, referring to the benefice of All Saints', "could stifle the voice of conscience. He felt that he had acted wrongly, and resolved to retrace his steps. He, accordingly, resigned his preferments in the establishment, and returned to Mr Lamb's church, in which he continued, probably as a private member, till his death."[84] Samuel did not, as it happens, resign his "preferments"; he remained the absentee rector of All Saints' to the end of his days, as the parish books of that church are there to testify.

Whether or no Titus returned to Lamb's Church in company with his father, his religious views at this time were certainly unorthodox. One, Archibald Gledstanes, gives a most interesting account of an encounter with the newly expelled naval chaplain:

"Robert Cuningham and I, on a Sunday in the beginning of 1676 met Mr Oates in Coleman Street at the foot of the stairs, as we were coming down from the Socinian meeting-house. He asked where we had been and why we came down. We said we were disappointed of hearing Mr Knowles preach, whom we had heard to be a great asserter of the Socinian errors and we were bound to hear sermon somewhere else. He said he was very sorry Mr Knowles did not preach that day, and that he was more disappointed than we, as he heard he was a man of his principles. We asked what might be these principles of Mr Knowles so agreeable to him. He answered, he was informed he denied the Trinity and the satisfaction of Christ. Much astonished, we asked if that was his faith and if he really denied these things. He said he did really. We asked if he was not a Churchman (so his habit speaking him). He said he was and a prebendary of Gloucester (but we understood afterwards from prebendaries of that cathedral there was no such man of their number). He said he had signed the Thirty-nine Articles, whereon we upbraided him with perjury. Then, because of the noise in the street and the observation we had from persons drawing near to hear the clamour betwixt us, we were carried back upstairs to the meeting-house by some belonging to it, where we dealt with him very earnestly to explain himself in terms not so offensive to Christian ears nor so scandalous to his own profession. But instead he spoke most blasphemously in denying the Trinity, the Divinity and satisfaction of Christ and most ignominiously of the whole doctrine and mystery of our salvation to our very great horror and the no small offence of those of the meeting, though Socinian and professing to differ from what we held, yet they utterly disassented from what he owned, so gross and blasphemous he was all along. We were with him afterwards in Mr Ward's alehouse in the same street, where again he most pertinaciously adhered to all he had said at the meeting-house."[85]

Late in August, Titus encountered an old friend, no less a person than William Smith, his schoolmaster at Merchant Taylors'. When this school perished in the flames of 1666, Smith had got himself appointed master of the Lady Owen's Free School at Islington, the patrons of which were the Brewers' Company. It proved no easy post, for apart from the fact that the salary was of the smallest, after he had been there two or three years several gentlemen, Dissenters, came and set up rival schools without a licence. (Among these gentry was Robert Ferguson, afterwards known as the Plotter.) Smith, however, "bore all patiently," and in the evening, after his work was done, he would go into the City to take a glass of ale and chat with his friends at some tavern or club. It was in this manner that he now came face to face with his old pupil.

"The first time I saw Titus Oates, after he went from Merchant-Taylors School . . . was about Bartholomew-tide 1676. He was brought to me by Mr Matthew Medburne (who had picked him up in the Earl of Suffolk's Cellar at Whitehall that day he came to me) undoubtedly under a fatal Position of the Heavens." (Smith means fatal for himself, and so indeed it proved to be.) "Titus was in his Canonical Garments: I knew him not, till he told me who he was. To the Sun-Tavern in Aldersgate-Street they had me. Truly I was very melancholy, though I knew no cause for it. May be it pleased the Almighty Providence in that little prelude to give me some forebodings of the miseries that were ordained me from this unfortunate renewing of our old acquaintance."[86]

It must have been very shortly after this that Titus was at last tracked down and arrested, for on September 16th he was in prison at Hastings, pending his trial for perjury at the suit of young Parker. Between this date and the thirtieth of the same month, he was removed to Dover Castle, then the principal prison of the Cinque Ports.[87] Here, as in so many other periods of Titus's early life, it seems impossible to trace his exact movements; the Records of Dover, both those of the town and the castle, are barren of references to him, which is the more curious because somehow or other he contrived to escape. Rumour had it that he corrupted his guards; another contemporary version says that he "at last got a *Certiorary* to be removed to Dover one of the Cinque Ports (he pretending he could have no justice there [in Hastings], because the Parkers were the chief Magistrates of the Town) thereafter some time got out, and it is generally reported that he broke the prison and got to London."[88]

In November, a Mr Stirgin, "at the Instance of a Near Relation", came forward and offered to be answerable for Titus's appearance in court when he should be wanted. In return for this kindness, Mr Stirgin required both Titus and his father to sign a bond, which later came into the possession of L'Estrange, who reproduced it in his *Observator*, Vol. 2, No. 20: "The Condition of this present Obligation is such, that if the above bounden Samuel Otes, and Titus Otes, their Executives and Administrators, and every of them, do and shall save Harmless, and Indemnify the above-named John Stirgin, of, and from, all Costs and Damages, that he may sustain, for, or by reason of, his becoming bound for the said Titus Otes'es Appearance, in an action in his Majesties Court of Exchequer, wherein William Parker is Plaintiff; and also pay all other Costs and Damages that he may sustain, for, or upon the account of, his being Bound as aforesaid: Then this obligation to be Void, and of None Effect; Or else to remain in Full Force and Virtue."

Fortunately for the kind Mr Stirgin, young Parker, to save time and money, let the suit fall, "And", says L'Estrange, "there's an End of the Story."

Meanwhile Titus, once more skulking about London, had renewed his acquaintance with Matthew Medburne. This Medburne was an actor, a comedian, and seems to have been a most kind-hearted fellow, ready to be friends with anybody. He introduced Titus to a club in Fuller's Rents, Holborn, which met on Thursday and Sunday nights, and was kept by a Mr Mekins. Not a few of the members, including Medburne himself, were Catholics, but, says William Smith, "I never heard any Disputes about Religion or State Affairs it being a particular Article of our Club, that all such Discourses should be forbidden upon the penalty of sixpence forfeit for every default of that nature by any Member of the Society".[89] The intimacy between Medburne and Titus made William Smith uneasy, for he had not forgotten the boy who was expelled from Merchant Taylors'. "And truly, for my part, I had that very indifferent opinion of him, That I sometimes advised Medburne not to repose any confidence in him, remembering his perverse and wicked pranks, when he was a School Boy; which, indeed, was all I knew of him then: for his Suspension and Misdemeanours in Sussex and Kent were then unknown to us both."[90]

Titus's introduction to the club in Fuller's Rents had for himself, and for the whole of England, the most weighty consequences. For his association with Catholics there resulted in his appointment, in the new year of 1677, to the post of Protestant chaplain in the household of the Catholic Duke of Norfolk, at Arundel House in London. The result of that appointment was the bloodiest hoax in history: "The Popish Plot."

BOOK TWO

THE POPISH PROSELYTE

(1)

THE story of Titus Oates and the part he played in history is quite incomprehensible unless it is seen against the background of the times in which he lived. Particularly is it essential to understand the position of the English Catholics, with whom Titus was now for the first time to become intimate.

Because there was no active persecution during the reign of Charles I and the first eighteen years of that of his son, it is sometimes imagined that the penal laws, instituted by Elizabeth, were no longer in force. This is an error. It was still, officially, death for a man who, having taken Holy Orders overseas, returned to his native England; and it was death likewise for those who gave him harbourage. All persons above the age of sixteen years must attend the Anglican service on pain of a fine of twenty pounds a month; the hearing of Mass incurred imprisonment of one year and the fine of one hundred marks. Anyone informing the authorities of a priest saying Mass was entitled to the third part of the forfeiture of the said priest's goods, if it did not exceed one hundred and fifty pounds. The reconciling of any person to the Catholic Church was accounted High Treason, and any man knowing of this offence and not revealing it within twenty days was adjudged guilty of misprison of treason. All those taking office as schoolmasters, magistrates, sheriffs, etc., or degrees in a university, were required to take the Oaths of Allegiance and Supremacy; and, if he thought fit, the Lord Chancellor was empowered to tender these Oaths to any person whatsoever; those refusing to take them were guilty, for the first offence, of premunire, for the second, treason. The parents of any child sent to be educated in the Catholic seminaries abroad, were liable to a fine of one hundred pounds. And so on.[1] These laws remained upon the Statute Books, and could be put into execution at any moment.

There were two reasons why, since 1625, they had

remained more or less in abeyance. The first was the dislike of both Charles I and his son for religious persecution; the second was the gradual simmering down of that hatred against the Catholics which had been bred by the Gunpowder Plot. Moreover, the noble part played by so many of that religion in the concealment and escape of Charles II after the Battle of Worcester in 1651 (L'Estrange in one of his *Observators* lists no less than fifty-one Catholic men and women instrumental in that escape) had helped their cause considerably. The young King himself, when he came to the throne, had endeavoured, though without success, to persuade his Parliament to confirm the promise of toleration made in the Restoration Treaty of Breda; it is important to understand why he failed.

Many of the aristocracy, together with the squires and rich merchants, retained a strong hostility to the Catholics, not on religious grounds, but because a vast number of them owed their fortunes to the rape of Church lands at the Reformation, and they believed, or pretended to believe, that toleration was only the first step towards a general restoration of all this wealth to its former owners. Moreover, although the King had been restored by the unanimous consent of all parties, yet the victors of the Civil War (now the Opposition) were determined to retain what power they had filched from the Crown; from the Restoration onwards their purpose, to "clip the wings of the Prerogative", became clearer and clearer, culminating at last in their triumph at the Revolution. One of several ways in which they could hamper and oppose the King in his duty of governing, was to frustrate his efforts for religious toleration by stirring up the old "No Popery" mania; and the persistence with which they used this trick can be seen in the number of addresses and remonstrances made to Charles by both Houses throughout the first eighteen years of his reign whenever he endeavoured to frame measures of toleration, addresses and remonstrances which forced him, on one occasion, to break the seals of his Declaration of Indulgence in the presence of his Council. His necessity to give way was caused by the peculiar species of blackmail which had been used against his father: his Parliament would vote him no supplies until he did.

Two years after his Restoration, Charles married a Catholic princess and the old fear of Popery stirred a little among all classes, especially as it was rumoured that the marriage had been solemnized in secret with Catholic rites before the public ceremony. Seven years later, a more ominous rumour excited the realm; there were whispers that James, Duke of York, the King's brother and the Heir Presumptive (for it was clear by this time that Queen Catherine could have no children), was turned Papist. The Opposition did not neglect this golden opportunity; their murmurings against Popery rose to a shrill clamour, and in 1673 a reluctant Charles gave his assent to the Test Act, whereby all persons refusing to receive the Anglican Sacrament were debarred from holding public office. The Duke immediately laid down his post of Lord High Admiral, thus confirming the rumours of his conversion; and henceforward his religion formed the favourite weapon in the Opposition armoury. Next year, his marriage with the Catholic Mary of Modena gave the Oppositionists the excuse for openly addressing the King to exclude his brother from his presence. But the Duke was still popular with the mass of Englishmen, who had not forgotten his gallantry in naval battles against the Dutch; many saw the campaign of bills and addresses for what it really was, an oblique attack on the Crown itself; and though Charles was forced to order that the penal laws be strictly enforced, there was still no active persecution.

But in his desire for liberty of conscience, King Charles was hampered, not only by the Opposition, but, ironically enough, by a section of the Catholics themselves. The subject is a large one; it has never been thoroughly investigated, nor is this the place for such investigation; yet no true understanding of all that was to follow can be reached unless some mention of it is made. Very briefly then, and at the risk of over-simplification, the situation may be described in this way:

Persecution in any age, especially when it touches the daily lives of the persecuted, is wont to become intolerable to a large section of these unfortunates, who yet remain true in their hearts to the beliefs for which they are made to suffer. We have seen it in our own day. A man is not necessarily a "Quisling" if, forced to live under an alien rule which he is incapable of shaking off, he consents to make certain terms with his oppressors—terms which will enable him to pursue his daily life in peace. On the other hand, there is always a minority who will give way on nothing, who refuse to sacrifice the least fraction of principle for the sake of expediency, who are ready to undergo privation, persecution, torture, even death itself, rather than deny one of their beliefs, let those beliefs be spiritual or political.

So it was with the Catholics of the reign of Charles II. A section of the laity, headed by a body of secular clergy known as the English Chapter, were ready to compromise if they might pursue their religious life in peace. Opposed to the Chapter-men were a considerable number of the secular clergy, the regulars in general, and the Jesuits in particular, who would give way on nothing. It must be noted that the point on which the Chapter-men were prepared to compromise was one so vital that upon it had turned the original quarrel between Henry the Eighth and Rome. It was demanded of Catholics that, in return for the privilege of practising their religion in security, they take the Oaths of Allegiance and Supremacy; in other words, they must acknowledge the King of England to be the Head of the Church.

This question of compromise or no compromise led to a widespread and disastrous split in the ranks of English Catholics. There was a good deal of excuse for the laity, for they were far removed from the central authority at Rome and could obtain little direct guidance; many saw themselves as likely to be ruined by fines and to lose all that was dear to them, including, probably, their lives, if persecution should become active again. Moreover, the chance to compromise might never be repeated; if anything untoward happened to the Duke of York, the next monarch might well prove a persecutor. What made the situation worse was the fact that the Chapter-men were deeply impregnated with the schismatical views of the Gallicans and Jansenists, views which had come drifting over from France; and these clergy impressed upon their flocks that a Catholic could be, as one contemporary put it, "of the

Church of Rome, but not of the Court of Rome". The determination of the regular clergy (and again particularly the Jesuits), to uphold the pure faith without compromise bred in their opponents amongst those of their own religion so bitter an hostility that when, in 1661, the King had succeeded in appointing a committee to investigate the penal laws with a view to their abolition, the Chapter-men actually petitioned that the Jesuits be excluded from the toleration promised. The immediate result was that the discussions petered out and were never resumed; the ultimate result was not to show itself until the year 1678, when the Catholics of England, suddenly attacked, presented to the enemy a broken front.

It has been mentioned that the former hatred of Popery on the part of the common people had somewhat simmered down. The Fifth of November was observed, of course, as enthusiastically as ever, but it is probable that the relish shown for these anniversaries of Gunpowder Treason had its roots in the affection of Londoners for bonfires and fireworks, rather than in any real Protestant zeal. Yet the old hatred remained; the fire smouldered though it no longer flared; and it took very little to make it blaze once more. A tradition had grown up that Catholics were dangerous people; when a house caught fire, or a man was found murdered, the common people were wont to say, "You may be sure there's a Papist at the bottom of it", very much as their descendants make that observation, substituting Jew for Papist, and only half believing it in the individual case. The credulity of the uneducated is always profound; and the credulity of the common people of England of the seventeenth century in regard to the wickedness of Popery was shared by their betters. Cultured men like Evelyn and Pepys reveal in their diaries how readily they accepted the most fantastic rumours of Popish misdeeds.

In addition to a large section of the upper class who either feared Popery because they possessed Church lands, or used the No Popery slogan as a means for embarrassing the King, and the mass of the people who had by this time a traditional bias against Catholics, there were, of course, just as there are to-day, serious anti-Catholics, whose hatred of that religion was entirely genuine and disinterested. This hatred still blazes in many a ballad and tract of the times, as in Dr Walter Pope's vicious and exceedingly irreverent *Room for a Ballad: or, A Ballad for Rome*, and in the anonymous *The Pope's Great Year of Jubilee 1675*. Especially bitter was the feeling against the Jesuits; the following advice was delivered by John Oldham in all seriousness:

> "... *Or let that wholesome statute be reviv'd,*
> *Which England heretofore from Wolves reliev'd:*
> *Tax every shire insted of them to bring*
> *Each year a certain tale of Jesuits in:*
> *And let their mangled quarters hang the Isle*
> *To scare all future Vermin from the Soil.*"[2]

The question inevitably arises: What was the proportion of Catholics to the rest of England during this period? It is a question exceedingly difficult to answer. The England of the Restoration has been calculated to have contained from five to five and a half million souls, and of this total London had 390,000. Carte in his *Life of Ormond*[3] says that in the whole of England "there was scarce one Papist to a hundred Protestants". One contemporary states that "Protestants in number compared to Papists are in London above two hundred to one,"[4] but this was after a vast number had been driven out of London during the heat of the Plot of '78; and another, writing of Titus Oates's mythical army of 60,000 Papists, observes that it was "twice as many as there are Men, Women, and Children of Romanists in the whole Kingdom."[5] Lord Shaftesbury, writing in the spring of 1680, describes the Protestants of "London and England" as being forty to one of the Catholics.[6] Again, speaking of Titus's tales of a general rising of Papists, Higgons in his Continuation of Baker's *Chronicle*, asks: "How could it be thought that forty thousand effective men should be ready in London for such a design, when probably there are not that number of papists to be found in the city, though we take in women and children?" Many more quotations leading to the same conclusion could be cited, and it is safe to say that the proportion of Catholics, especially of those ready to sacrifice life or property for their religion, was small.

Nevertheless, stories of Popish plots could always be

relied on to find credence and arouse indignation. Some of these tales lived only a few days and were believed in only by the uneducated; others ran like wildfire through the realm and were accepted without question by high and low alike. Among the latter scares, that known as Habernfeld's Plot, which had made its appearance on the eve of the Civil War, had been particularly popular as a sensation; the narrative of it, under the title of *Rome's Masterpiece*, was published by Prynne in 1643 and in modern parlance proved a best-seller. In this, as in the printed narrative of the Gunpowder Plot, the high-lights were the murder of the King, the firing of London, the presence of a Papist assassin in the King's immediate circle, Popish dignitaries cognisant of the design, a Scottish rising to take place simultaneously with the English one, and the plot revealed at the last moment by a repentant conspirator. These were the conventional items on the programme; and it will be seen how faithfully Titus Oates followed them in 1678.

One more thing remains to be noted: it is that under cover of these scares there went on, all through the reign, terminating at last in the Rye House Plot, a series of genuine conspiracies against the Crown, engineered by the Opposition, undertaken by the fanatics among the Dissenters, chiefly old Commonwealth-men. Seditious books and pamphlets, inciting the people to rise for the Good Old Cause, warning the King of the fate which had befallen his father, and accusing him of being a secret Papist, poured forth from secret printing-presses; occasionally the malcontents did not stop at seditious tracts, as, to take only an instance, in the Yorkshire rising of '63. All this was to be expected. For the reign of Charles the Second was merely an armed truce between two irreconcilable political philosophies; it was the last stand of Monarchy against the power of gold. The Civil War was only yesterday; the Revolution was to-morrow. The men who had fought and bled under Cromwell were willing to do so again in the same cause, impeded only by the fact that the nation as a whole was as reluctant as the average man always is to have trade disorganized, husbands and fathers impressed, and the countryside laid waste by rival armies.

Because some of Cromwell's ablest lieutenants were

become Charles the Second's peers in Parliament, it does not follow that they had undergone any change of heart; and because Colonel Pride's chaplain, Samuel Oates, had hastened into the bosom of the Established Church we must not thereby jump to the conclusion that he had discarded the peculiar beliefs he had held prior to the year 1660. Neither must it be imagined that his son Titus was drifting towards Rome, just because he had become attached to the household of the Catholic Duke of Norfolk. Titus was in need, in very desperate need, of those prosaic things known as bread and butter, and in even greater need of a position and protection to secure him from the law which he had several times most deeply offended. As for his faith, that he was never a Catholic at heart we have on the best of authority—his own.

(2)

"In the Year 1675", says Titus, "I had obtained an Interest with Henry Duke of Norfolk, then Earl of Norwich, and Earl Marshal of England, who was very kind to me upon the Account of my contending earnestly for his Right of Presenting to a Living in the Diocese of Chichester to which Living the then Bishop (a turbulent Man) pretended the Right of Collating: And in the Year 1676, I was made his Chaplain; and I call the whole Family of the Norfolk Howards to witness my Fidelity to him and his Children, tho I am but churlishly used by some of them for my Truth and Fidelity to my Lord and Master."[7]

This account of how Titus came under Norfolk's patronage may or may not be true; unfortunately it is the only one extant, unless some clue to the extraordinary association is to be found among the Norfolk Papers, which are not accessible. Undoubtedly Titus was at Chichester, for however brief a period, prior to his appointment as chaplain to Norfolk, for he appeared as a witness at the marriage of a relation, Robert Hitchcocke, to one Alice Wattes, at St Peter's, in that city,[8] and long afterwards his former landlord there dunned him for money owing for lodgings. In regard to his appointment as Protestant chapain, it is almost certain that he obtained it through his meeting with Catholics at the club in Fuller's Rents. It was a very humble position in such a household, ranking with that of the upper servants; but Titus was not in a condition to pick and choose.

His new patron, Norfolk (he succeeded to the dukedom in this year, 1677), was a dim personality, leaving practically no impression upon his times. He was a man who definitely disliked unpleasantness, and desired nothing better than to live at peace with all his neighbours of whatever creed. He had lived in total seclusion during the Interregnum, largely abroad; and again, after the death of his wife in '62, he had retired to Flanders, where he built himself a small house in the neighbourhood of Bruges, contiguous to the old palace of the sovereign counts of Flanders, which had been turned into a convent by a community of Franciscan nuns. In 1664, he had accompanied the Emperor's ambassador to Constantinople, returning to England the following year. A lover of the fine arts and a prominent member of the Royal Society, he shrank from the hurly-burly of politics; and though he was sincerely attached to his religion, he seems to have inclined towards the party of the Chapter-men; it was his maxim that only patience and caution could wear out hostility. When persecution did break out, he straightway retired to Flanders, and there he remained until the heat of it was past. Such was the vague figure who now had the honour to have as chaplain to the Protestants in his household, the Rev. Titus Oates.

Whenever Titus managed to get himself a job, he straightway became arrogant and troublesome. One of the many roles in which he saw himself as a genius was that of preacher, and indeed his peculiar behaviour in the pulpit, reminiscent of the holders-forth of his father's youth, seems to have impressed many of his auditors, including the Lord Keeper Guilford, who "much admired his theatrical behaviour in the pulpit".[9] But there was at least one occasion during this period of his life when his preaching gave offence; the story is told by William Smith the schoolmaster, who was still seeing a good deal of his old pupil. Titus had dined with Smith at Islington, and they were then to go into the City to meet Matthew Medburne, "But in our way, passing by Sadler's Musick-House we met Dr

Slater, the Vicar of Clerkenwell, who complemented his Seeming Brother Clergy-man very gravely, and desired him to except [*sic*] of a Glass of Ale with him, upon which, growing more familiar, he desired him to give him a Sermon next Sunday, which Oates after much entreaty promised. But I took the Dr aside, and besought him not to accept of it, for some private Reasons I knew, which I did not particularize to him. But he thinking it might be only an Excuse, resolved to accept Oates's proffer, and accordingly Oates preach'd; and in his Sermon speaking all along very bitterly against Calvin, he call'd him always Jack. This Sermon gave very heinous offence to Two great admirers of Calvin, Mr Barker, and Mr Walsh, then in commission of the Peace. Who therefore sending for the Dr gave him a very severe Reprimand, for suffering such a Fellow to appear in his Pulpit. The Dr to excuse himself, acquainted their Worships, 'Twas I that introduced him; which story, though false, proved very prejudicial to me, these persons being my utter Enemies ever after."[10]

During Titus's stay in Norfolk's household, he must have heard much talk about an affair which had excited the whole of England during the past eighteen months. This affair, though it lies outside his personal history, must be described, because undoubtedly it had great influence upon his future. It was the affair of Luzancy.

There was a certain young Frenchman, whose real name is unknown, but whose mother was Beauchateau, a French actress. He was one of those unfortunate young men who find it hard to discover their true vocation; he was in turn a schoolmaster, a novice in a monastery, a servant to a bishop, an assistant to an itinerant missionary, and so on, all without satisfaction either to himself or his employers. Then a little matter of a forgery compelled him to leave his native land and cross to England; and here an idea occurred to him. He gave himself a good, long, high-sounding name: Hyppolite du Castelet de Luzancy; he made his way to the French Protestant Church in the Savoy; and there, having prevailed upon its clergy to allow him to mount their pulpit, he publicly objured the Catholic faith in which he had been bred, and treated his hearers to a picturesque account of the reasons which had compelled his apostacy.

This was in July, 1675; and he was instantly dubbed, by his enthusiastic audience, the French Jesuit.

To his pleasure, Luzancy discovered that he was in a fair way to make his fortune by this simple means; donations flowed in, not only from his fellow Frenchmen, but from the pious Protestants of England. But Luzancy was not without foresight. Things were all very well for the moment, but the excitement was bound to die down, and contributions would, alas! die with it. So, in October, he applied himself to some of the lords of the Opposition, and to them he told an even more affecting story. It seemed that, a month previously, Father St Germain, "confessor of the Duchess of York", had surprised him at his lodgings, and holding a dagger to his devoted breast had demanded an instant recantation and a return to his native land as the only alternative to death. The Oppositionists were jubilant; Lord Holles gravely communicated the matter to the King in the House of Lords; with equal gravity did Lord Russell bring it to the notice of the House of Commons; and London seethed with indignation and horror at the audacity of the bloodthirsty Papists. Persecution, already advocated by the Opposition, seemed about to blaze up into its well-remembered flames; the King published a proclamation for the arrest of St Germain (who escaped to France); the Lords rushed through a Bill for the encouraging of monks in foreign parts to leave their monasteries and follow the noble example of Luzancy; the Commons sent for the Lord Chief Justice and ordered him to issue warrants for the apprehension of Catholic priests, meantime recommending Luzancy himself to the care and bounty of King Charles.

But the convert, his head turned by so much success, now made a mistake. Examined by the Privy Council, he stuck to his former tale, but added that he had heard from some French merchants that in a short while the streets of London would run with Protestant blood, that there were infinite numbers of Jesuits and priests in London who did "good service to God", and that the King, at heart a Papist, had framed his Declaration of Indulgence with the express purpose of introducing Popery.

This story was at the same time too vague and too crude. The man was not an artist in lying. It is true that the blood of London was accustomed to curdle at the mere mention of Popish plots; but to make London really hysterical it was essential that there should be details, definite statements, something the good folk could bite on. Besides, the hit at the King was too dangerously direct, for the King was exceedingly popular. Not only this, but Luzancy lacked imagination; he was too apt to repeat the idle rumours that were always circulating through the coffee-houses; his tales had no real novelty. Finally, a French Protestant clergyman, one Du Maresque, of the Savoy, had the honesty to publish a pamphlet setting forth the details of Luzancy's previous adventures in France, including that awkward little matter of a forgery.

It was the end. Compton, Bishop of London (an Opposition stalwart), might severely reprimand Du Maresque for his tactless interference, and bestow upon the injured Luzancy the sacrament of Ordination and the living of Dover-court in Essex; the Privy Council might threaten the publisher of the damning pamphlet; still, the thing was dead, and nothing could revive it. But to the Oppositionists it had given immense food for thought, for it might so easily have been successful. It was talked about over tankards and coffee-cups for quite a while by the common people of London; and there can be no doubt that it was discussed in all its bearings among the group of priests in the household of the Duke of Norfolk. Neither is there any room for doubt that it provided matter for reflection for another young man who, like Luzancy, found it difficult to make a successful career for himself, the young man who now, after a few short months, was once again out of a job, Norfolk's ex-Protestant chaplain, Titus Oates.[11]

(3)

Titus had arrived at a stage in his career when it was obvious that nothing more was to be expected from the Church of England. He had lost one living after another; he had been dismissed from his chaplaincy in the Navy; and now, for some unknown reason, he had lost his humble ecclesiastical post in the household of Norfolk. The atmosphere in which he had passed his youth, and his extraordinary views on religion when he came to manhood, combine to assure us that he left the Church of England without regret. She was to be useful to him later, very useful indeed; for a brief period he was to pose as her champion. But it is clear that he never liked her; he was never of her; he was spiritually at home only in the bosom of extreme Dissent, for he was his father's son and a born rebel against all authority. The only thing he must have regretted on leaving the Established Church was the necessity to put off his parson's gown, for dearly did he love that garment. Later, he was to stick to it through thick and thin, even when he apostatised a second time from the Church of England; it gave him dignity.

Meanwhile, upon Ash Wednesday, March 3rd, 1677, he put it firmly aside, and was received into the Catholic Church by a mentally unbalanced priest named Berry.

Titus himself gave the reasons which induced him to take this momentous step, reasons which will be noted in their proper place, though they are unworthy of serious consideration. But in one thing he spoke the truth: he was never a Catholic at heart. A study of his whole career is sufficient to show that whenever he changed his creed he did it from hope of material gain, and there is no reason to believe that this occasion was any exception to the rule. As an Anglican parson he had collected neither money nor preferment, but had covered himself with disgrace; as for the Dissenters, his heart might dwell with them, but his head told him plainly that there was no future for him there. There remained the Catholics; and though they were officially proscribed, there were certain reasons why Titus may well have imagined that here at least he would have a chance to gain a livelihood without too much trouble to himself.

For at least one Catholic, poor Matthew Medburne, had been very kind to him, treating him to drinks, and in all probability providing the necessary introductions which had led to the Norfolk chaplaincy. Next, during his time in Norfolk's household, Titus must have heard a great deal about the dissensions among the Catholics, and about the intense dislike of a certain section for the Jesuits; this, taken in conjunction with the fact that the members of the Society of Jesus were the most vulnerable in case of persecution, suggested the chance of a little blackmail. Lastly, it is quite likely that amongst other things Titus learnt about the Jesuits was the fact that they were always ready to assist convert clergymen, especially those who professed an inclination to study for the priesthood. It must be repeated that the sincerity of his conversion need not be examined, because Titus himself was to repeat *ad nauseum* that he underwent no change of heart, and it would be unfair, at least in this instance, to doubt his word.

Father Berry, *alias* Hutchinson, the priest who had the doubtful honour of receiving Titus, was a peculiar man. Burnet calls him lightheaded and weak;[12] Lingard says that it was generally understood that he was deranged;[13] the author of the contemporary tract, *A Vindication of the English Catholics*, makes no bones about the matter, but states that Berry "was once stark mad: and is ever since cracked."[14] He had been a Protestant clergyman, had turned Catholic and entered the Society of Jesus, had secured his release from the obedience of the Society and become a secular priest, later returned to the Church of England (when on one occasion he preached for Burnet in London), and lastly turned Catholic again.[15] He was pitied by his former brethren, the Jesuits, who seem to have allowed him a small pension to enable him to maintain himself. But he was definitely sympathetic towards the views of the Chapter-men, and he had contacts among those Protestants who, like Compton, Bishop of London, hoped to absorb this section of the Catholics into the Church of England.

According to Titus, the Jesuits lost no time in admitting to their most secret counsels this most valuable and important convert:

"Upon my being reconciled", he writes, "I was brought to Mr Strange, the then Provincial of their Order, who admitted me into the Society of Jesus: when I was admitted, it was resolved by the Jesuits that I should pass the time of my Novitiate abroad in dispatching Business for the Society, which I chearfully accepted, and therefore accordingly they provided for me."[16] Note the beautiful simplicity of this course of events. He is received into the Catholic

Church and the Society of Jesus almost simultaneously; and without for one moment wasting time in testing the sincerity, fidelity, or ability of the new convert, the Jesuits decide that he shall transact their business abroad (business which, if made public, would send them all to the gallows), as a good way of spending his noviceship. There is not one single word, of course, about the long years of training which must be passed in the novice-house before the would-be Jesuit could be professed.

Before pursuing further the career of Titus the Popish proselyte, a new actor in his story must be introduced; for it was now, if not earlier, that Titus came under his influence. This was a Dr Israel or Ezreel Tonge, who had what is often described as a bee in his bonnet; the bee in question was the Society of Jesus, and in his determination to expose its machinations, Dr Tonge was convinced of the propriety of that sin which formed his favourite accusation against the Jesuits: he was content to employ bad means for a good end.

Tonge might have passed for a mere eccentric, but for this one thing. There was really no harm in his dabblings in alchemy and astrology, nor in his concoction of childish anagrams; but when it came to the Society of Jesus he was mad, really and dangerously mad. He dreamed dreams and saw visions; and in all those dreams and in all those visions there were Jesuits, gliding mysteriously from place to place, receiving dispensations to swear falsehoods, bloodily plotting against the lives of Protestants, sanctifying daggers for the slaughter of heretical kings, and gloating over the prospect of a London in flames. It was a mania. His life was devoted to the inventing, or, as he sincerely believed, the detecting, of Jesuit plots.

He was now in his late fifties, a Yorkshireman, born at Tickhill, near Doncaster; during the Civil War he had combined the profession of clergyman with that of schoolmaster, and it is amusing to read that he instructed his pupils "by the Jesuites' method of teaching; and boyes did profit wonderfully, as needes they must, by that method".[17] During the first few years of the Restoration he moved restlessly from place to place, from Durham to a school at Islington, from Islington to the English garrison at

Dunkirk, from Dunkirk to the living of Leintwardine in Herefordshire, from Leintwardine to St Mary Stayning's in London, from London to Tangier, and from Tangier back to London, where at last, in 1668, he settled down. He was married, with one son, Simpson, and he was now rector of the parishes of St Mary Stayning and St Michael's Wood Street, united after the Fire; with these he held the rectory of Aston, Herefordshire. All this while he had been writing anti-Jesuit tracts, assembling a vast mass of manuscripts which did not sell, for the market was sadly overstocked. By 1675 he had become a widower; and having no relations except his son, who was at the university, and one brother, John, an officer in the Guards, he moved into the house of a wealthy patron and bitter anti-Catholic, Sir Richard Barker, a physician in the Barbican. Here, if not earlier, he became acquainted with the Rev. Samuel Oates, and through Samuel, with his son, Titus.

(4)

Some six weeks were to pass between Titus's reception into the Catholic Church and the next important event in his life; and once again his movements become elusive. All we know for certain is that he was out of a job and forced to beg his bread, probably from Tonge,[18] indubitably from the Catholics. In Somerset House, the residence of the Queen, there were many priests;* to Somerset House did Titus betake himself, and, in the role of convert clergyman who had lost his livelihood for conscience' sake, solicited charity. The fathers there helped him as best they could, and Titus repaid their kindness in a manner very typical. One day while on a begging mission at Somerset House, "he found an appertunity in the sacrist and thence stole away a box of breads which in derision he cal'd a 'box of gods' and said he used them to seal his letters for halfe a yeere after".[19] He applied himself also to a Jesuit, Father Fenwick, who later testified that Titus "came once to me in a miserable poor condition, and said, I must turn again, and betake myself to the Ministry to get Bread, for I have eaten nothing these two days: And I gave him five shillings to relieve his present necessity".[20]

* There were only two Jesuits in the Queen's household, both Portuguese.

When we come to the trials during the Plot period, we shall find that, in order to prove that he was in London during the April and May of 1678, Titus called several witnesses who described encounters with him during that period. Some at least of these encounters may have taken place; but as Titus was in fact in Flanders during the period in question, they must have occurred, not in 1678, but in 1677. What lends colour to this theory is that their description of Titus's behaviour and appearance agrees very well with the condition he was in during the month of April and the first few days of May, 1677, when he was out of a job, newly turned Catholic, and forced to live on the charity of his co-religionists on the one hand, and on that of Dr Tonge on the other.[21]

First among these witnesses was an elderly minister, a Mr William Walker. He deposed to having seen Titus, wearing secular dress ("a gray Searge Coat, and I think a Gray Hat"), between St Martin's Lane and Leicester Fields, the latter end of March or the beginning of April; Titus, added Mr Walker, "was just like a Vagrant, a very Rascal." The minister did not at first recognize him, but on thinking it over during the night he became convinced that it was Titus Oates whom he had seen, and he said as much next day to a Mrs Ives, who kept a chandler's shop. Mrs Sarah Ives herself confirmed this, though she was vague about the time; she thought it was the middle of April. On Walker's telling her that he had seen Titus, she informed him of the dreadful news of the latter's turning Papist, and added that he was "lurking about the Town". Just then, Samuel Oates senior came into the shop to eat "some new thin Cheeses"; Mrs Ives asked him whether he had seen his son, and he replied no, not of late, but had heard from him.

Next there was a batch of witnesses from the domestic staff of Sir Richard Barker. These may, of course, have been drilled in their evidence. A Jesuit, Father Keynes, who actually lived in Barker's house under an assumed name and character (Barker little suspecting his identity) during the heat of the Plot persecution, says that "I observed that whilst I lived here the Protestants were accustomed to hold a sort of secret conclave, or council, assembling twice or thrice a week, and there, together with Oates, they concocted and arranged what evidence should be brought against our Fathers; what questions were to be asked of the Judges in the court, and there other matters were concocted amongst themselves".[22] Nevertheless, it is entirely possible that, while these witnesses were obeying orders in giving a false date, they really had seen Titus in the manner they described.

Mrs Mayo, Sir Richard Barker's housekeeper, had had Titus pointed out to her, "either the latter end of April or a week before Whitsun or a little after", by a servant of her master's, since deceased. She had never seen Titus before. He was dressed in a "Whitish Hat and colour'd Cloaths", and wore a periwig. On this occasion he had dined with Barker, the latter's two daughters, his sister Mrs Thurrel, her two sons, and a Dr Crocket (but none of these persons ever appeared to confirm Mrs Mayo's statement). Philip Page, Barker's servant, remembered to have seen Titus at about the same time, and described his appearance; he wore "a light-coloured Campaign Coat", an old black hat, strapped, and a pair of Spanish-leather shoes; "He had his Hair cut short almost to his Ears . . . and a small Stick in his Hand, walking melancholy about the Hall." He had enquired for Dr Tonge, and then for Barker. Butler, Barker's coachman, swore positively that he had seen Titus at Sir Richard's house the beginning of May. (Previous to this, he had seen him "before he went to sea", which would be, he believed, about a year or two before the occasion he was describing.) His description of Titus's dress was as detailed as Page's: "His Hair was cut off, close cropt to his Ears, and an old White Hat over his Head, and a short gray Coat over like a Horse-man's Coat." He had come into the gate-house where Butler was cleaning his master's coach, had asked for Dr Tonge, and had seemed very discontented at hearing he was out. But he had made no comments, and had gone away again.

There were two other witnesses called to testify to having seen Titus in London during this vital period; both were proved later definitely to have perjured themselves in the matter of dates. One was an old priest named Clay, who swore that he had met Oates in Mr Charles Howard's lodgings in Arundel House; he thought it was once in

April and once in May. Howard himself, who was brave enough to appear for the defence, denied encountering Titus at this period, though he admitted seeing him in May, 1677, and after July, 1678. The other witness was the schoolmaster, poor William Smith, who, as will be seen, was bullied by Oates into swearing that the latter had dined at his house in Islington the beginning of May, 1678, dressed in a "summer-suit, and a coloured Ribbon, and a great Knot on his Shoulder". It may well have been that in the beginning of May in the previous year, Titus appeared thus smart and prosperous; for it was at this time that he was again befriended, and his material needs provided for.[23]

(5)

Some time in April, 1677, Titus obtained an introduction to Father Richard Strange, an elderly man, Provincial (that is, Superior) of what the Jesuits termed the "English Province". The Jesuits in England were missionaries; as in the days of the Elizabethan persecution, so, ever since, it had fallen to their lot to keep alive the Catholic faith in this anti-Catholic country. England, or the "English Province", was divided by them into fourteen districts; St Ignatius or the London District, of which Father Harcourt *alias* Waring was superior, was served at this time by seventeen priests, some of whom lived within the liberties of the foreign embassies, others, at extreme peril, under assumed names, elsewhere. Feared and hated by the mass of Englishmen, to whom the very name Jesuit was synonymous with assassin, intensely disliked by some of their fellow Catholics, with the rope and the quartering-block for ever overshadowing them, the Jesuit Fathers of the English Province, a highly organized body of men, trained to obedience, continued to pursue their dangerous work.

At the time of Titus's introduction to Father Strange, the latter was about to start on the annual visitation of the Jesuit seminaries overseas undertaken by all Provincials. He was an old man, he was in a hurry, he knew nothing of Oates except that he was a convert clergyman, practically starving, and professing a desire to study for the priesthood. The Jesuits have been blamed for not investigating

Titus's past before befriending him, and if they were guilty of indiscretion in this, they paid the price of their folly to the uttermost farthing. But it must be remembered that, in this lack of discretion, they were in good company. The patrons of the Anglican Church, the officials of the Navy, and the Duke of Norfolk, all had accepted Titus without informing themselves of his record. Indeed, it was next to impossible to inform oneself of a man's record at this date, when there were no police, and news travelled at a snail's pace; one was more or less bound to take a man at his face-value (and Titus, when he wanted something, could be plausibility itself), and hope for the best. The Jesuits saw only a convert in dire need of help; they were incapable of delving into that great mind and discovering there the true reason for Titus's associating with them, the reason disclosed by Titus himself thus:

In the days of his greatness he was asked, " 'What was it, Doctor, that Mov'd you to run so many Risques, and Hazzards, of Soul, Body, and All (or to this Effect) for the Service of the Crown, upon this Instance?' (speaking of his running among the Jesuites, swearing, Sacramenting, Idolatrizing, and other Difficulties of that Adventure). Titus turn'd his Cane in his Hand; Advanc'd the Head of it to the Tip of his Nose; Laid his Head upon one Shoulder; and then smiling opened his Mouth and said (with a Tone and Accent peculiar to himself) 'I have heard (says he) that the Jesuites are a Subtile sort of People. Are they so! (said I to my self) But I shall go near to be too Cunning for 'em: For Nothing (an't please ye) but a Diamond can cut a Diamond; and so I went among 'em.' "[24]

In order to provide for his material wants, and to give him the opportunity to study for the priesthood (for which he professed the most earnest desire), it was arranged that this interesting convert, who was at this time described as "of a low Stature, thick shouldred, Brownish hayr, his beard more reddish then his head, about thirty yeares old",[25] should be sent to the English College at Valladolid in Spain, a seminary for higher studies, philosophy and theology. Naturally it was taken for granted by his new patrons that a man of his age, and one who, for seven years, had been a clergyman of the Church of England, was educated. At Valladolid he would have his material wants provided for, and could concentrate in peace upon his higher studies, at the same time familiarizing himself with a Catholic atmosphere.

Accordingly, he embarked at the Downs in *The Merchant of Biscay*, the master of which was one Lucas Roch, and arrived at Bilbao, May 16th, 1677. He was now Titus Ambrose, or Ambrosius (an *alias* was necessary since his going to this Catholic seminary was an offence against the penal laws), a poor student, owing the clothes on his back, the fare for his journey, his board, lodging, and education, to the charity of his new friends, the Jesuits. At Bilbao he stayed ten days, passing his time by calling on the Rector of the English College there, Father Juan de Clizonda, for a letter of introduction, and successfully begging some money from two English merchants, Michael Hore and John Grace.[26] Then, accompanied by a muleteer named Espinosa, he set out for Valladolid, and arrived there between four and five in the afternoon of June 1st.[27]

The English College at Valladolid, dedicated to St Alban, had opened its doors in 1587, and ever since had suffered from lack of funds, periodic visitations of the plague, and the unwavering hostility of the Spanish population of the town. The English students desired English superiors; the Spaniards, from Philip III downwards, were determined that they should have Spanish ones. The result of all these unfavourable circumstances was that for long periods together the College had very few students, and even sometimes none at all. It was passing through one of these depressing phases when Titus Oates arrived, and for a while he seems to have been the only student. A few Spanish Fathers, who could speak no English, were in charge; if Titus attended lectures at the University (which would have been closing down with the annual examinations and for the long vacation), he cannot have understood very much of them, since they were delivered in fluent Latin. Altogether if, as was afterwards maintained, Titus was persuaded by Tonge to accept the Jesuits' offer to go to Valladolid, in order that he might spy out the land, Tonge had chosen the wrong man and the wrong place.

Titus was bored to distraction. It was hot; he had no

Spanish and very little Latin; he was marooned in a deserted seminary; and he discovered to his disgust that he was expected not only to work, but to keep the college rules. Always before, in whatever circumstances, he had been able to get into some sort of mischief; denied this pastime at Valladolid, it would seem that he fell back upon his own imagination, which, in its peculiar way, was very vivid. The more he was disgraced, shunned, exposed, and expelled, the more did he depend upon his own good opinion of himself. Kicked out of the Navy, he had astonished two acquaintances with the statement that he was a prebendary of Gloucester Cathedral; very shortly to be sent away in disgrace from Valladolid, he was to startle other friends with the news that during his short sojourn there he had made a journey to the University of Salamanca and had been admitted doctor of divinity.

Apart from the fact that none but priests were admitted to this degree in the Catholic Church, there are extant the attestations of many respectable witnesses that, during his stay at Valladolid, Titus did not leave the College. Salamanca, which was the Oxford of Spain, remained for a long time blissfully ignorant of the degree it had bestowed upon Titus; five whole years were to pass before the preposterous lie filtered through to the University authorities, nor is this surprising, for the little world of Salamanca was very remote from the London of the Popish Plot. Upon receipt of the news, the authorities hastened to draw up a certificate, couched in terms of high indignation, attested by fourteen doctors and three notaries, and afterwards reproduced by L'Estrange in one of his *Observators*, declaring that "the said Titus Oates never received any Degree, either of Doctor, Licentiate, or so much as Batchelor, in this University of Salamanca; Nay, that there is no such Name to be found in the Matricula; which is the Registry for the Entrance of all the Scholars that come to this University." Well might Lord Castlemaine observe "if his Learning promoted him, (and you must remember, That Doctors at Salamanca do defend in the open Schools, a whole Course of Divinity against every body that will oppose them) let any Man that knows Oates, judge of his Doctorship by it."[28] Against all this, there is nothing but Titus's statement, sublime in its simplicity: "I was admitted Doctor of Divinity at the said University of Salamanca, and did all my Exercises for the said Degree that was required of me."[29] And to the end of his days, seriously among his admirers, derisively among the rest of his contemporaries, he remained the Salamanca Doctor.

(6)

Apart from the comfort he derived in bestowing degrees upon himself, Titus, while still marooned in a deserted college during the summer vacation, had one small adventure to relieve the appalling boredom of his new life, though it is to be doubted whether he appreciated it, at least at the time. At some date in September, there called upon him two of his fellow countrymen; their names (though they were at the time very much incognito) were William and James Bedloe, brothers.

Of this precious pair, William was not only the elder, but the natural leader. Though handicapped by a mean birth and lack of education, he had contrived to get into the household of Lord Bellasis, an English Catholic, where he conducted himself so adroitly that he was able to obtain the trusted position of letter-carrier to foreign parts. By using this employment to get himself acquainted with the names and concerns of persons of quality, he raised his fortunes several degrees higher, and off he went, travelling over Europe, appearing as Lord Somebody here, Sir Someone there, and obtaining lodgings, board, clothes and credit on the strength of a borrowed name and any amount of brazen self-confidence. A career of this sort is bound to lead to a jail sooner or later, and William Bedloe was not unacquainted with the insides of several prisons when he arrived at Valladolid in 1677. But he treated these vagaries of fortune with a very pretty indifference: tall, dark, and sufficiently handsome, with something of a military air about him (he had never seen a battle, but had managed to obtain the rank of captain by fraud from the Prince of Orange, and liked to live up to every part he played), he was always ready, in lieu of higher game, to take whatever fate offered him in the shape of victim, even when the shape was that of a poor English student named Titus Oates, *alias* Ambrose.

At this particular moment, "Captain" Bedloe was down on his luck. He had passed the summer pleasantly enough in his old fashion, with his brother James posing as his servant. In August, he visited Spain, and at Bilbao, under the name of Lord Gerard, he successfully "touched" a merchant, Mr Frankland, for three hundred doubloons. He was proceeding merrily upon his way when, at Lamorra, he was overtaken by a serjeant of the Chancery of Valladolid, sent in pursuit of him by the said Mr Frankland, who had discovered his true character and wanted his money back.[30] The brothers Bedloe, on their arrest, asked to be carried to Valladolid, because "they had a countryman there in the English College, who would furnish them with the money or get them credit. So he carried them to Valladolid, where their friend came to them, and, as soon as the deponent [Frankland] saw him, he knew him to be Titus Oates, having seen him several times at Bilbao".[31]

This implies some previous acquaintance between Oates and Bedloe, and it is very possible that they had met in England while the former was in Norfolk's household and the latter in the employ of Bellasis. According to Frankland, during the eight days that the two brothers were kept prisoner at Valladolid, Oates was every day in their company. They had a favourable trial, owing to the kindness of the Rector of the English College, and the merchant was able to recover part of his stolen property.[32] Next year, when Bedloe reappeared in England, there were to be vague "informations" that he and Titus talked over the latter's famous Plot at Valladolid;[33] and if they were much in each other's company at this time, it may well be that Titus bragged of his intimacy with Jesuit secrets, and of his being admitted to their inner counsels. But it is certain that when the time for parting came, Titus had no cause to regret the departure of William and James Bedloe. For on their farewell visit to him, he "left them in a chamber whilst he went to get them a dinner, and they the meanwhile were not idle, for finding ten pieces of eight in a drawer, they took them away, as appears by a letter from Oates to Father Suiman, in which he laments the loss of his money, and much more that of a book which they stole from him at the same time. Thence they went by Santiago to Corunna (la Groin) where they embarked for England."[34] Little can Titus have guessed, as he cursed the thieving William, how useful that worthy was to be to him later.

At Michaelmas some more students arrived at the English College, and one of them, Richard Duelly, has left us a description of Titus's behaviour at this time: "he was wont to express great resentments at the course of study he had undertaken, complaining exceedingly of the strict observances, and discipline of the sayd Colledge, and of the recollected manner of living there, which he was not able to endure; and also that he was not preferred before the rest of the Collegians by several exemptions, which he pretended to, by reason of his age, and advances in learning, as he thought, and especially of his great preferments, which he sayd he had left in the Church of England".[35] It was the same old story with the same old ending; in October, after he had been at Valladolid a little over four months, he was expelled.[36]

Accompanied by a post-boy, Titus set off on mule-back for Bilbao, October 30th. In the archives of the English College at Valladolid is the attestation of the post-boy himself, one Juan de Sandoval, made before a notary-royal in the city of Valladolid, and this most minutely describes their journey. Its importance lies in the proof it gives that Titus lied when later he swore that during this period he was travelling about Europe, interviewing Jesuit plotters and high personages connected with what was to become known as the Popish Plot. Apart from this, several details in the account are so typical of Titus that they deserve quotation. On Sunday, October 31st, at Torquemada, he refused to hear Mass and remained in the inn; on Tuesday, November 2nd, stopping to dine at a wayside hostelry called the Venta Blanca, between Pancorvo and Saracha, he asked the innkeeper "if one could say mass in the hermitage in front of the inn, as he wanted to say mass" (note that he is already masquerading as a priest, if not as a doctor of divinity); "and the declarant replied: how could he say mass after he had his breakfast and dined? and the said collegian declared 'that does not matter; in my country we say three or four masses after having eaten' ". Next day they arrived at Bilbao, and here Titus, who had been given the money for his journey by the Rector of the English College at Valladolid, refused to give the post-boy the piece of eight he had promised him if they made the journey in five days, but "he gave him no more than seven or eight quartos [a small brass coin worth about a halfpenny] and sent him away with a letter for the Father Minister of the said St Alban's College, saying he had written that he should give to the declarant half a dozen reales [a coin worth the eighth part of a piece of eight] while in fact he had written nothing of the kind".

Titus stayed at Bilbao for just over a week; the evidence of three merchants of that town proves that he did not leave it until he embarked for England.[37] William Frankland, the merchant robbed by Bedloe, stated afterwards that Titus tried to borrow money from him, but he refused, though he gave him one or two pistoles.[38] On the 11th or 12th of November, Titus sailed in *The Merchant of Bilbao* bound for Topsam, near Exeter, returning from his excursion into the realm of higher studies, as L'Estrange expressed it "as great a Noddy as he went".

(7)

Once again was Titus without a livelihood or prospects; but he was also without shame, and scarcely had he landed in England ere he went whining to his Catholic benefactors. "After he came into England he began to be very troublesome to his Romish Acquaintance, still pretending great Zeal, and that he had miscarried at Valladolid only because he did not understand the Humour of the Spaniards, who were Superiors of that Colledge."[39] At the selfsame time, he was telling another pitiful story to his fanatical friend, Dr Israel Tonge. "When I came from the University, in the Year 77", says Tonge's son, Simpson, "I found Otes with my Father, in a very poor Condition, who complain'd he knew not what to do to get Bread; who went under the name of Ambrose. My Father took him home, and gave him Cloathes, Lodging, and Dyet, saying he would put him into a way."[40] It is obvious, from what we know of Tonge, what that way was. Here was a young man, a Catholic and a protégé of the Jesuits, but on his own confession insincere in his conversion, and destitute of the means of livelihood; what better candidate for the post of informer about Jesuit plots—plots, let it be remembered, which Dr Tonge genuinely believed existed?

It is probable, therefore, that it was by Tonge's advice that Titus now applied to the Jesuits to be sent to St Omers College in Flanders. On his return from Valladolid his knowledge of the Jesuits, let alone their "plots", was about the same as it was before, and Tonge wanted to see some return for his money.[41] Titus for his part needed board and lodging; and though he must have viewed a stay in another Catholic college with extreme distaste, he was not in a position to refuse Tonge's advice. And at St Omers he would be at least among his own countrymen.

Writer after writer has repeated the erroneous statement (first made by Titus himself), that he became a Jesuit, and this mistake is due very largely to the fact that the writers in question believed St Omers to be a seminary for priests. It was, in fact, nothing more nor less than a boys' school, and its lineal descendant is Stonyhurst; it had been founded in 1593, for the benefit of Catholic parents who could not have their children brought up in their own faith in England. When Titus made his request to Father Strange, the English Provincial, the latter cannot have failed to point out to him the difficulties he must encounter, he, a man nearing thirty, and one used to some authority as a clergyman of the Church of England, sitting on a school-bench in the company of boys; but to this Titus may well have replied with truth that he lacked education, and that he was so enthusiastic for the chance to make up for lost time that he was willing to undergo any humiliation. At all events, permission was given, the die was cast; and on December 10th, 1677, between three and four o'clock of a winter's afternoon, Titus, now calling himself Sampson Lucy, presented himself at St Omers College, armed with letters of introduction from his Jesuit patrons in London.

The school authorities must have experienced something of a shock when they viewed this strange "new boy", for in appearance and manner Titus Oates was very strange indeed. He was squat, short, bull-necked; one leg was shorter than the other, which gave him a peculiar gait; some contemporaries speak of him as being bandy. By this date he had shaved off the beard he had worn at Valladolid, thus exposing to his startled schoolmasters a full view of his extraordinary visage. His complexion is variously described as "rainbow-coloured", "vermilion", "coffee-colour", and "purple"; the truth would seem to be that he suffered from high blood-pressure. His eyes were abnormally small and sunken, and on one eyebrow was a large wart. But his most striking feature was his chin; it was so long that his mouth, says L'Estrange in one of his *Observators*, was four inches above it. North's description is well-known: "His Mouth was the Center of his Face; and a Compass there would sweep his Nose, Forehead, and Chin within the Perimeter."[42] That enormous chin of his was to feature in every broadsheet, wood-cut and lampoon connected with him, from the failure of his Plot to the end of his days.

For the rest, his conversation was offensive, for he delighted in coarse oaths, blasphemy, and general grossness; his voice was somewhat high, and he affected a most peculiar diction. His attachment to the letter A was such that he made it do the work of the I and even of the O. Thus "My lord" became "Maay laard", and "I, Titus" was pronounced "Aye, Taitus". Whenever he spoke, it must have sounded like something between a bray and a bleat.

Apart from his unattractive appearance, the fathers at St Omers were not very pleased to see Titus; the fitting of a man of unknown character, and in his late twenties, into a boys' school is a task no schoolmaster would relish. Nor had he been there very long before he gave them cause to regret the Provincial's decision to send him to them. "In his relations with others he was very quick to give offence, but wholly impatient in bearing it himself. Those, whom he held in any regard, or rather feared, he constrained with blandishments or soothed with flattery, whilst those, whom he held at enmity, he tore to pieces in most outrageous fashion with sharp words. He was wont to praise himself and everything connected with himself, boasting like a lying crier of his own wares, of how much he had suffered and what loss of substance he had sustained in the cause of the faith. Meanwhile he performed his religious duties with negligence, and studied only his own convenience. Among the boys he was overbearing, but towards equals he bore himself timidly, whilst in dealings with superiors he was querulous, when not wholly without spirit.

"If during the day, he considered himself injured by some word, when he went to rest at night, he would chant aloud at harmless lads, whom he had provoked first by his great offensiveness, the sayings which the Royal Psalmist sang against the enemies of Christ and the Church, and call upon them the avenging hand of God. If this behaviour was not past bearing, it certainly was intolerable that he should exclaim against the Royal Family of the Stuarts, as stained with bastardy and tyranny. When it came to his ears that the son of the Duke of York had been cut off by sudden death, he said that the event caused him no more distress than if he had heard of the death of the Duke's dog.

"On account of this and similar misbehaviour, he was often given reprimands, with added threats that if he did not alter his manners and frame of mind he would be expelled from the College, but as often would he throw himself at the feet of superiors and beg forgiveness, saying humbly that the bad habits, which he had acquired from tender years, could not be thrown off in a moment, and that he would do all in his power by way of amendment. Frequently bewailing himself over these happenings, and with tears, which, as was discovered afterwards, he had at his command, he prevailed upon the Fathers to persevere in their search for his good qualities."[43]

On his first entering the College, he "was put to study among the Rhetoricians". (In these Catholic schools, the highest class was called "Rhetoric", and those below it "Poetry", "Syntax", "Grammar" and so on.)[44] "He went there [into Rhetoric]", explains one of his schoolfellows, Henry Thornton, "by reason of his Age, and upon no other account; he might have gone elsewhere with us who were of a lower Form, for any great store of Learning he had."[45] Titus certainly had cause to be grateful for the tact and consideration of his superiors; not only was he put into the highest form, though his learning did not justify it, so that he might be with the elder boys, but in the dining-hall he was given a little table by himself, where he sat in solitary state. Either it was this delicacy of feeling on the part of the school authorities which encouraged him to look for greater favours, or else he was resolved to carry out the advice of Tonge and search for Jesuit "plots"; at all events, scarcely had he arrived at St Omers than he began to badger the Fathers to admit him to the Society of Jesus.

Probably with a view to putting off an obviously unsuitable candidate by letting him see something of the training he would have to face, his superiors allowed him, about Christmas-time, to visit the Jesuit novitiate at Watten (which lay some two leagues from St Omers), for the week-end. The Rector of Watten formed the worse possible opinion of the would-be postulant; "he was found to be of a bad, and hypocondriacal humour, rash, indiscreet, turbulent, and vindictive, a great flatterer, boaster, and Lyer. In so much as reflecting on his little Devotion, and bold and inquisitive humour, some suspected him to be sent as a spy by some enemy to Religion. His greatest friends thought him to be but half a Catholic, all suspected in him a secret aversion to Monarchicall Government, and to the Royal Family of England; for which he being reprehended by the Deponent, he excused it by alleaging his breeding among the Puritans."[46] This accurate summing up of Titus's character, was not, unfortunately, acted upon as it should have been by his immediate expulsion; he was told merely that he was not a suitable candidate for admission to the Society.

Back at St Omers once more, Titus was allowed to enter into the Sodality, a pious congregation among the elder boys, and was appointed Lector by the Prefect of Studies; his duty was to read aloud every Sunday morning at 6 a.m. This privilege he immediately abused by reading a "ridiculous book", or, in Titus's opinion, "a pleasant Book, called the Contempt of the Clergy". Indeed, he seems to have taken pains to make himself as conspicuous as possible; unable to boast in his present company that he was a Doctor of Divinity of Salamanca, he informed the Jesuit Fathers that he had been Bursar of St John's College,

Cambridge, and doubtless bragged to his schoolfellows of other fine posts he had thrown up for conscience' sake. They were not, however, impressed, for his dullness and oddity were obvious to the youngest, "the Boyes for his folly and stupidness flocking about him as small Birds do about an Owle, so that he was judged by all very unfit to go on to higher Studies, not being able to speak two words of true Latin, as is evident by . . . his own essaying to read the Year of our Lord out of figures into Latin words".[47] This ignorance of Latin was noted by a schoolfellow named Clement Smith when, in April, Titus spent a few days in the Infirmary; "he proposed a question to the Physician about himself in Latin, and spoke a Sollecism, which was this, he said, *Si placet Dominatio vestra*".[48]

On April 19th (O.S.) a visitor called at the College; he was an Englishman, and had come to solicit charity from the boys. "I was the Person," said one of them, Clavering, "that made the Collection for him in the House; and I remember he did ask if there was anyone that was a student there that had been in Spain: We told him there was one, and described him, upon which he [said] he knew the Gentleman in Spain; upon that I told Mr Otes, that there was one there that knew him, but he deny'd to come and speak with him." And with reason, for this begging gentleman was none other than our old friend "Captain" William Bedloe, down on his luck again. Titus told a boy named Haggerstone "that there was a craving Englishman had been there to beg an Alms, and there was a Collection made for him among the Scholars, but he said he would give him nothing, for he told me he had been cheated by such an one of some Pieces of Eight in Spain".[49]

A couple of days later, a new scholar arrived at St Omers, one Burnaby, and it was observed by several of the boys that Titus immediately forced his company upon the newcomer in a manner which was much resented (there is a hint in the account of Oates's predilection for unnatural vice). Next day, Burnaby and another boy, Henry Howard, were amusing themselves in the garden by throwing stones at one another's shins. This displeased Titus so much that he threatened that unless they desisted he would go and tell the Father Rector. The reaction of his schoolfellows to such a threat can be imagined; Howard offered to beat him, and when Titus, very much upon his dignity, dared him to do it, Howard "throws up Mr Oates his Heels. With that Mr Oates look'd very fretfully upon him, and withdrew himself into the Infirmary, as we thought to speak to the Rector."[50] On the same day, another boy, Robert Beeston, had cause to notice Titus; there was a play acted, and Beeston had to sing in it; when, after the performance, some of his friends were congratulating him, Titus came up and informed him that "If I had paid for learning to sing, I had been basely cheated".

These and other incidents, trifling though they were, were to assume later a peculiar importance. It was to be Titus's contention that at this very time, when he was actually at St Omers, making himself unpopular with his schoolfellows, he was in London, attending a treasonable conference of the Jesuits. The date of this conference was, said Oates, April 24th (O.S.), and for once he spoke the truth. There was a Provincial Congregation held upon that very date in London; but it was not treasonable; it was not held at the place Titus named; and Titus himself was not there. He was at St Omers; and upon that very date he had a conversation with one of his schoolfellows, the boy named Clavering, upon that very subject: the Provincial Congregation of the London Jesuits.

There was nothing in the least unusual or exciting about such an assembly; Provincial Congregations were called every three years in each Province of the Society, and they were common all over Europe. Their business was to choose a Procurator to go to Rome in order to inform the General of the Jesuits about the individual affairs of each province. When chosen, the Procurators proceeded to the Congregation of Procurators, held at Rome. The only difference between the English Provincial Congregation and those in other countries was that the former, being in a hostile kingdom, was necessarily invested with a certain secrecy as to the place of meeting, and so on. An affair of this sort can have held no more interest for the average St Omers boy than a meeting of headmasters would have for the schoolboy of to-day; but it had, it seemed, an interest for Titus Oates. "I was talking with him", said Clavering, "and said he to me, Know you nothing what the Business is that they are to do at the Congregation? Said I, Mr Lucy, I know not what they do; I think not much: For I hear at those Meetings many times they stay an hour or two, and have done when they have chosen their Procurator."[51] It is probable that the conversation was suggested by the fact that the gouty old Rector of St Omers, Father Ashby, was absent from the College, and there was gossip that he had gone to combine attendance at the Provincial Congregation in London with a visit to the waters of Bath.

Upon the Feast of St Augustine, Titus was presented in company with many others to receive the Sacrament of Confirmation from the hands of the Bishop of St Omers. When Titus approached to be anointed with the sacred chrism, "his Lordship stopt . . . until he heard, he belonged to the English Colledg, and was presented by its Rector. The stop was noted by all present. The reason of it he was pleased to declare afterwards: viz, that he doubted whether Oates's hart was prepared to receive the Holy Ghost, the Spirit of Love, in whose face he perceived signes of great malice."[52] Two boys confirmed with Oates testified later to the truth of this story.

Besides all these small incidents, there were more general things by which his schoolfellows remembered Titus Oates. The dining-room of the College seated one hundred and fifty, religious and scholars, and, as has been noted, Titus was given a little table all to himself; it was placed next to that at which sat the fathers, and to this latter table all the boys must make a reverence ere they sat down. Every day, affirmed John Hall, the Butler or Refectorian, during the whole time of Titus's sojourn at St Omers, except for the week-end at Watten and a few days spent in the Infirmary in April, he had laid that little table with bread and beer. Had Titus disappeared for a week or ten days in April, as afterwards he swore he had, it would have caused a sensation; when any St Omers boy left for his native land, said young William Parry, a schoolfellow of Oates, "the whole College rings of it".[53] How much more would the whole College have rung with it had it been Titus Oates who had left for England in the middle of term, this man of twenty-nine sitting on a bench with lads in their teens, this man of the strange face and affected speech, this man who, as it seemed deliberately, had made himself, throughout his stay, so very conspicuous?

Boy after boy testified to this conspicuousness; "he was very Absurd, and always quarrelling"; "his Conversation and Canting Stories after Dinner and Supper, and times of Recreation, made him so remarkable, that no body could miss him all the time he was there"; "he was so Remarkable by his Stories and ridiculous Actions, and falling out with every one in the College, that if he had been absent, we must needs have missed him"; "he was like a Silly Person, as I may call him, that us'd to make sport, and no body could be miss'd as soon as he: And I saw a little Boy in the College beat him up and down with a Fox's Tail . . . all that knew him must miss him, if he went away."

Inevitably the time arrived when they did miss him. It had been obvious from the first that, sooner or later, away he must go, and for good. He had had a very fair trial, and had proved himself incorrigible as always. In June, the new English Provincial, Father Thomas Whitebread, came to the College to make his Visitation, and was informed by the Fathers there that, in regard to Titus, "time was lost in washing white the Ethiopian". Father Whitebread not only agreed, but insisted that Titus be immediately expelled. "The unhappy man shuddered at the bad news, as one who saw himself by this decision thrust back into his former state of misery, with no safe refuge on sea or land to make for owing to his former misdeeds. He was at a loss to know where to turn to beg for a living. Hence he tried on every side to find a way out, fawning upon the fathers and promising a serious reform of his ways, though among his companions, he broke out in words full of despair, openly asserting among other things that he knew not whither he would be driven by the burden of poverty, which he found unbearable; he must needs be, if not a Jesuit, a Judas.

"The Provincial, in no wise moved by these and other devices of this crafty man, ordered him to make himself ready to depart forthwith. The night before his departure, he was found in the Sodality Chapel, with his elbows resting upon the altar in the attitude of the priest at the moment of consecration. Asked what he did there, he answered that he was bidding farewell to Jesus Christ. Though these words are patient of a favourable interpretation, the character of this evil man, his bodily posture so smacking of studied insolence, caused them to be taken in an ill sense, so that several said at the time 'Oates has in such wise bidden farewell to Christ, that he will have no further dealings with Him'."[54]

How soon that terrible interpretation was to be justified, no man knew then, not even Oates. Upon June 23rd, 1678, Titus, in secular clothes, left St Omers for ever, and set out for England. "In the latter end of June, this Year, full fraighted with Materials of Names, Places, etc., he return'd to London, to his Friend and Assistant, Dr Tongue."[55]

(8)

Titus returned to London, and certainly renewed his acquaintance with the fanatical Dr Tonge; but there is no real evidence for Echard's implication that he did so with the express intention of collaborating with the doctor in the great "Design". There was a good deal of the animal in Titus, and of the savage animal at that; it is there in his portraits, and especially in his eyes. He was ready to snarl and bite and maul, but his chief concern was always his own material welfare. He had threatened Whitebread, before he left St Omers, that he would be revenged for the insult of his expulsion;[56] he had raged to his schoolfellows that he must needs be, if not a Jesuit, a Judas; and now, on his return to England, he mingled similar threats with a renewed whining for alms. No doubt, at the back of that tortuous mind of his, was Tonge's continual babbling of Jesuit plots, and the opportunities for gain and for revenge open to the discoverer of them. But it is clear from his behaviour, from this date right up to the end of September, that Titus only half believed in the success of such a course of action as Tonge had in mind. Titus had lived among Jesuits; he knew very well that their plots had reality only in the crazy head of Israel Tonge; he was aware of the King's hatred of persecution, and his common sense; he remembered the failure of Luzancy. The chances against a successful "discovery" were about a hundred to one; if it misfired, it would bounce back like a boomerang upon its sponsors. Meanwhile, there were the old imperative necessities to find: bread and butter, a roof over his head, some sort of a job, some sort of prestige to save from the shipwreck he had made of his career.

He was nearly thirty: he had tried everything, and at everything he had failed. The same dismal tale of disgrace and ignominy had followed him from his schooldays onwards. Expelled from school, sent down from the university, convicted of perjury, kicked out of the Navy, dismissed from two Catholic colleges; it was always the same story. Small wonder that the Jesuits in London regarded him as a worthless weakling whose threats were beneath contempt; for the positive evil in him, the deep-rooted, savage malice, which slumbered beneath his animal nature, had not yet disclosed itself, save in the case of young Parker, of which they were unaware. "After he came into England again he went sculking up and down the Town among the Romanists, and was very troublesome, being perpetually begging something for a poor Student and converted Minister, who had voluntarily left a great Benefice to Embrace the Catholick Faith . . . he made great complaints, and threatned them sore; he told some of the Jesuits . . . that if they would not such a time furnish him with such a sum of Money, they should all repent it; they knowing their own Conscience, looking on him as a mere Vagabond and Scoundrel, took no notice of what he said, knowing his Majesties Clemency, and never suspecting that he [Oates] would take such a Diabolical Course as swearing of Treason, but only inform of them as being Priests."[57]

Desperate for want of bread, shunned by the Jesuits, reluctant to put himself wholly in the power of the crack-brained Tonge, Titus was driven to the most extraordinary shifts to keep body and soul together. "I have heard it credibly reported, that this profane Wretch, made it his business to go about fidler-wise, amongst places of publick resort, and ridicule preaching, by a Presbyterian Cant, and as the Fidlers us'd to press in to companies, and say, Gentlemen, will ye please to have a Lesson of Musick, this Montebank us'd to say, Gentlemen, will ye have a Sermon; and when the reckoning came to be paid, there was usually twelve pence left for the Fidlers, and six pence for the Doctor. This they say was one way he had of Living, after he was turned from St Omers, before he laid hold of the Plot."[58] Another way was to beg from lay Catholics, and in this he was occasionally successful, as with the kind-hearted comedian, Mathew Medburne, "who was instrumental in obtaining him some assistance for his relief from persons of quality of the Romish Religion . . . one thing was remarkable, That about that time that we had an account of the Battel of Mons, he met Medburne, and Mr Thomas Hughes (who is now living, and a member of the Church of England, and ready to attest it) and complaining of his extreme necessity, he told them, He had not eaten a bit of Bread in Three Days; upon which, they carryed him into the Cock in the Haymarket, and made him Eat and Drink, giving him also some Money."[59]

Exactly when it was that he resigned himself, in sheer desperation, to the influence of Israel Tonge, it is impossible to say, but the probability is that it was some time in July. He could not continue to support himself by occasional doles; the Jesuits, warned by the Rector of Watten "to have a care of dealing with him, because of his murmurations, calumnyes, and threates",[60] would have nothing more to do with him; and Tonge's scheme, mad as it must have sounded, was the only alternative to starvation. Thus it was that "in the conclusion he betook himself to his old Councillor in the Barbican; and there they fell to the Hammering of their First Project over again".[61] From this time onwards, until the crisis, we have glimpses of the pair, a busy couple, Titus nervous, Israel confident, Titus wolfing food at his patron's expense, Israel in his element, shuffling papers, noting down lists of names, pressing for details of the Jesuit seminaries overseas, "hammering out" that project which was as real to him as the sun in heaven. Titus had a poor lodging in Cockpit Alley, off Drury Lane, whence he issued at frequent intervals to meet Tonge for these ominous little conclaves at the Flying Horse in King Street, Westminster, at the Golden Horse Shoe in the Strand, at the Bull in Great Queen Street, or at York Buildings, where lived Titus's father, the disreputable ex-parson, Samuel Oates. All this while Titus remained

TITUS OATES, D.D.

Wisdom instructing him to discover this Hellish Popish Plot.

incognito, retaining the *alias* he had adopted at Valladolid, Titus Ambrose.[62]

Contemporaneously with his aiding Tonge in an invention of a plot by the Catholics, Titus was actually still begging from the Catholics, perhaps hoping against hope that someone of that religion would give him a job and so save him from the probable disgrace and punishment which might follow the plans of Tonge, perhaps merely spying at his patron's behest. He chose a Catholic doctor, Fogarty, to cure him from an attack of venereal disease;[63] he pestered the Jesuit Provincial, Whitebread, to grant him either a pension or admission to the Society of Jesus, offering in return to "give up to him an Accusation consisting of above fifty articles, which at the next Parliament would be exhibited against the Jesuits";[64] and early in August, on the very eve of the Plot's appearance, we find him being entertained by Catholics whose names are not disclosed. The incident is related by a Father Coniers, who "went to wish a good journey to two Gentlemen of my acquaintance, then in London: there I found a third Gentleman also of my acquaintance, and a Fourth, whose face I had never seen. After the ordinary civilities, and declaration they had no business together, I made one of the Conversation. The Discourse was common and Innocent: where this Fourth person brought in something out of Scripture concerning the tribe of Benjamin, so far from any thing of what was talked of, that I entertained this opinion of him, that he was a weake, and froward Man. That discourse being soon ended, I afterwards learnt he had been a Parson, was turned Roman Catholick, had been some time at S. Omers: his name, Oates. To my knowledge I never had heard of the name of Oates before."[65]

Nor indeed had a great many other people; yet it was destined that in a little over a month, that name was to be on the lips of every man in London.

(9)

The month is August; the year is 1678; the scene is London.

The weather is extremely hot, with threat of thunder.

Parliament is in recess. King Charles, who has just had the satisfaction of seeing the Opposition deprived of their most fruitful source of attack by the Peace of Nymegen, is about to take a quiet holiday at Windsor. The Earl of Shaftesbury, leader of the Opposition, has not very long come out of the Tower and begged pardon for his faults at the Bar of the House of Lords. The Earl of Danby, that shrewd Yorkshireman, having successfully negotiated the marriage of the Duke of York's daughter, Mary, with the Duke of York's nephew, William, Prince of Orange, reigns supreme. King Louis of France, disgruntled by being continually fooled by King Charles of England, views with displeasure the general pacification of Europe, and continues to hand out his bribes to anyone among the Oppositionists or elsewhere who can make life difficult for that tiresomely clever statesman, Charles Stuart. In Scotland, the Covenanters threaten fresh strife; but Scotland is a long way off. The common people of London have more interesting matters to think about. There are the fashions, the pleasure-gardens, the play-houses, trips in the cool of the evening to Barn Elms or Chelsea, the excitement of St Bartholomew's Fair; the summer, hot as it is, has not brought back the dreaded plague; the havoc wrought by the Great Fire is disappearing as the ring of hammers and the voices of workmen tell of a brand-new London slowly pushing its way upwards amid the charred timbers and heaps of rubble left by that unforgettable conflagration.

Outwardly, then a very peaceful, contented London, this of August, 1678. The crowds of foot-passengers who push and jostle their way along the narrow streets remain blissfully unaware of the significance of the small, gnome-like figure with a hairy face who walks arm-in-arm, and deep in talk, with the squat, bull-necked, abnormally long-chinned young man, his companion. Here and there a rude boy calls after them, as rude boys will; now and again a hackney-coachman flicks with his whip their absorbed backs as a gentle hint to them to get out of his way. In the coffee-houses, and in the taverns, where this oddly assorted couple pursue their endless talk, it is the same. The hum of gossip rises round them while they sit unnoticed; the latest murder is discussed; merchants babble of their gains or their losses at sea; pity or contempt is expressed for the neglected Queen, juicy stories are exchanged about the King's newest fancy in mistresses; relief is shown that England will not, after all, have to aid young William of Orange in his struggle against Louis of France; arguments arise for and against the merits of the Heir Presumptive, James, Duke of York.

Sometimes these arguments grow heated. Say what you like about the Duke, he is a Papist, and what is worse, an open one. It would not be so bad if he had the grace to conceal his Papistry (say those who, if he did so, would be the first to talk about wicked dissembling). He is so zealous a Papist that he has chosen his religion in preference to his naval service, he who used to be so fine a patriot. He has his hordes of priests around him there at St James's, some of them Jesuits, if all the tales be true. What kind of king will he make? He'll do whatever the Pope bids him do, mark my words. At this point, heads are shaken darkly, and the old stories circulate once more: Gunpowder Treason and Plot, the persecuted Protestants of France, Bloody Mary, the Great Fire.

The gossipers finish their coffee, or their ale, and out they go again, brushing past the gnome-like old man, the long-chinned young one, whispering together in their corner. London is busy, trade is brisk, men and women are good-humoured, though perhaps a little jaded with the long, hot summer. Only beneath the cheerful Cockney surface the old fears lie slumbering, hibernating, fatted with the rumours of a century, but, if awakened, avid for more. Crude, reasonless hatred of the thing known as Popery lies like a fuse in the mind of London, waiting to be fired.

It is through this London that there walks, unnoticed, obscure, and threadbare, the busy couple with their heads together, the little old man with the eyes of a fanatic, the thick-shouldered young man with the eyes of a savage beast. And concealed between them is a lighted match.

BOOK THREE

PART I

THE PLOT IN THE BALANCE: AUGUST 13TH–OCTOBER 17TH, 1678

(1)

AT noon on Monday, August 12th, Dr Tonge had an interview with a man named Christopher Kirkby. This Mr Kirkby, who appears with the utmost abruptness for the briefest possible time during this period, was a bankrupt merchant who had managed to get himself attached, as a kind of tax-gatherer, to the Lord Treasurer, Danby. He was also an amateur chemist, occasionally employed in the royal laboratory, and therefore known, at least by sight, to the King. Into the startled ear of Mr Kirkby, Tonge poured a wondrous tale; he did more; he showed him a sheaf of papers, and after a hasty glance at these, Kirkby gave it as his opinion that the whole matter should be laid before the King without delay. Either at his own or Tonge's suggestion, he undertook the approaching of his Majesty, and "about two of the Clock in the Afternoon he went to Whitehall, but could not all that Afternoon meet with an opportunity of seeing the King, except in Company of His Royal Highness; so he returned to the Dr and advised what to do, and how to proceed, Mr Kirkby writ a few lines to present to His Majesty the next morning as He should walk in the Park, signifying that if His Majesty would be pleased to give him a quarter of an hours Audience, he should make known something, that as it was of the greatest importance, so it was only proper for his Royal Ear, and not to be delayed without eminent danger."[1]

Next morning, King Charles set out as usual for his vigorous promenade in St James's Park. He was cheerful, for to-morrow he would go to Windsor, and there he would see the improvements made since his last visit, the fresco paintings of Verrio, and the wood carvings of Grinling Gibbons. As he came through the Outward Gallery to go down into the Park, a man whom he recognized as Christopher Kirkby stepped forward, and hissed in conspiratorial tones that he was in danger of his life, and must take care to keep within the company. "The King, more surprised with the strangeness of the News, than any Apprehension of the Danger, only ask'd how that could be? To which the other answer'd, That it might be by being shot at; but to give a Particular Account required more Privacy."[2]

Used to fanatics of all kinds, and anxious only to continue his walk in peace, Charles ordered the excited chemist to await his return in his Closet; and presently was listening with ill-concealed impatience to a long, incoherent, and most unlikely story about one Grove, and one Pickering, who were lurking in the Park with intent to shoot him, and of how Dr Israel Tonge, rector of St Michael's, Wood Street, had accidentally discovered the design. Possibly Charles had heard of Tonge; it was, curiously enough, on this very day that the doctor's brother, John Tonge, received his commission of captain in the Coldstream Guards.[3] At all events, the King bade Kirkby bring this friend of his to the Red Room in the palace that same evening between nine and ten o'clock.

If Charles had hoped that Tonge would prove more coherent and less fanatical than Kirkby, he was disappointed. He took one look at the strange figure of Israel Tonge, and another at his mass of papers, and asked the gentlemen to excuse him; he was bound for Windsor tomorrow, and must be up betimes. The pair of them should have an interview with the Lord Treasurer in the morning; meanwhile, he would keep the manuscript. This did not please Messrs Kirkby and Tonge, who exhibited great anxiety concerning the precious papers, imploring the King to keep them "secret and safe; otherwise the full Discovery would be prevented, and their lives in hazard; further proposing, that under the notion of Chymists, they might have access to His Person to prevent all suspicion"; to this proposal, Charles, who intended to enjoy his holiday at Windsor, gave a decided negative.

Next day, August 14th, the pair were forced to possess their souls in patience until four o'clock in the afternoon, for the Lord Treasurer's son, Dunblane, had been taken ill in the night, and the anxious father, having sat up with him, had risen at a very late hour. When he did arrive, however, Danby was brisk and business-like, and displayed a pleasing solemnity which must have gone far in soothing his impatient visitors. Producing the papers, given him by the King the night before, he asked, were these the originals? No, replied the cautious Tonge, they were copies. Then where, he was asked, were the originals? And who was the author of them? Israel Tonge was now in his element; the originals, he said, had been thrust under the door of his chamber by an unknown hand; as for the author, he did not know him, "only he fancy'd it must be one that had some time before held Discourse with him tending to such Matters".[4] This was a downright lie, since the author was none other than himself; and when, in reply to Danby's further question, did he know where to find the mysterious unknown, he said, "No, but he had seen him lately two or three times about the Streets", it was certainly a prevarication. But Tonge was a genuine fanatic; he honestly believed in his fantastic plots and his mythical Jesuits; and it is only fair to give him the benefit of his abnormality, and to say that in all probability he believed he spoke the truth.

Danby's reaction to these ridiculous tales was uncharacteristic. At any other moment in his career, the hard-headed Yorkshireman would almost certainly have dismissed Tonge, his papers, and his plots, and packed Kirkby after him. But Danby was passing through a crisis in his political life; he had made himself odious to the Opposition by the way in which he had pulled the country through its financial troubles, and though a threat to impeach him in '75 had failed, a new attempt was to be made, he knew, at the forthcoming session of Parliament, an attempt which, owing to certain indiscretions of his own, and his general unpopularity, might well prove successful. The French King hated him, the Duke of York disliked him, Charles II, though he valued him as a clever financier, felt for him no personal regard. Therefore, what Danby needed above all else at this moment was an object with which he could divert Parliament's attention from himself, and what could be better than the ever popular scare of a Popish plot?[5] So Danby turned a sympathetic ear to Tonge's ravings, gravely accepted his tale of mysterious papers pushed under his door by an unseen hand, and, stressing the necessity to keep all secret (he was not going to trail this red herring across his enemies' path before he judged the moment ripe), asked for more.

Two or three days later, probably on the 17th, he got it. Dr Tonge had new "informations". He had learned, he said, the very day when Grove and Pickering would be following the King to Windsor, to execute upon him their fell design. Further than this, in case they proved as unsuccessful as formerly, four Irishmen, names unknown but henceforward always referred to as the Four Irish Ruffians, had been hired to go in a stage-coach to Windsor as understudies. To all this Danby listened with his former seriousness, and said that as he himself was bound for Windsor, he would leave one of his gentlemen, Mr Floyd, in London, who, directly he heard further details from Dr Tonge, would ride post to carry them to his master.

But a series of small accidents seemed fated to frustrate the designs of all these assassinating gentlemen far more effectually than the efforts of the zealous Israel. It had been so all along, according to the mysterious papers, which told how Grove and Pickering had "dogged" the King for eight mortal years with intent to kill him, and always something had prevented them. On one occasion Grove failed because he had a cold;[6] another time Pickering had forgotten to load his pistol; once he had missed his target in the Park, and this was particularly mysterious, for neither the King nor any of his attendants had been conscious of this lurking villain, though he had "flashed in the very Pan". Nevertheless, the Jesuits, their employers, were very patient with Grove and Pickering, and as late as April of this year had declined to find substitutes. And now the Four Irish Ruffians were experiencing the same sort of minor accidents. They missed the coach to Windsor; they would come next day, "but no News of them; and Mr Floyd brought Word they could not come, for one of their Horses was shoulder slipt, or some such frivolous Excuse".[7] Small wonder that King Charles refused to lay the matter before his Council. "It would only create alarm", said that shrewd gentleman, "and may perhaps put the design of murdering me into the head of some individual who otherwise would never have entertained such a thought."[8]

Frustrated by his Majesty's incredulity, Tonge, on August 26th, started a fresh hare. He sent word to Danby, who was now in Oxfordshire, that a packet of letters, containing the most fearsome treason, could be picked up at the Windsor letter-office, addressed to Father Bedingfield, confessor to the Duke of York. On receipt of this interesting information, Danby rode post to Windsor, and was probably not a little annoyed to find the letters already in possession of the King. For it had chanced that Bedingfield, taking an early morning walk, had encountered the post-boy, and enquiring if there were any letters for him, had been handed a mysterious packet. On opening it, he found the signatures of friends, but in a handwriting quite unknown to him, and contents which had caused him straightway to carry the letters to the Duke of York, who had handed them to the King.

The Forged Letters, as they came to be called (and with reason) seem to have been the result of Danby's perpetual urging of Tonge to produce some tangible proof of his wild tales. The "author" of the original papers was still lying low, "for fear the Papists should murder him", explained Tonge; but in those papers mention was made of a whole host of letters which had passed through his hands. Surely, then, said Danby, something of that nature could and should be produced.[9] So here were five letters, smelling to high heaven of forgery, so much so that they were never produced as evidence against the future victims of the conspiracy. When called upon to "make a state of the evidence" before the trials, Sir William Jones, Attorney-General, who later was to welcome with open arms the most questionable witnesses in his case against the victims of the Plot, commented thus upon these letters: "If they can be so proved as to be believed to be the hands of the several persons by whom they are said to be written, they do fully make out the guilt of the writers, and do much confirm all the rest . . . but against the truth of the said letters there are many objections, some from the prisoners, others from the letters themselves, and the way of their coming to light: the particulars thereof, as they are many, and some resulting from the inspection of the letters themselves, so I doubt not but the same are fully remembered by your Majesty."[10]*

The Forged Letters had gone the way of Grove and Pickering and the Four Irish Ruffians. The King remained incredulous, and looked straight through Mr. Kirkby when that anxious gentleman put himself in the royal path; even Danby was coming to the reluctant conclusion that he must look elsewhere for an object to divert Parliament when it settled down to his attack. Dr Tonge's wonderful firework had gone off like a damp squib. But Dr Tonge was tenacious, and madly sincere. While the King, exasperatingly aloof and tranquil, continued to enjoy his holiday at Windsor, Dr Tonge settled down determinedly to drill into his part an actor he had kept hidden up to now, an actor whose ability he rather doubted, and who seemed to be suffering from a chronic attack of stage-fright. But the time was come when the whole cast must pull together to save the play; the mysterious pusher of papers under doors had done well enough off-stage; now he must brave the limelight, and earn his salary, and play the part for which he had been chosen.

Little did the author-stage-manager know that the part this unknown actor was to play was destined to be that of leading man.

(2)

Some three weeks had passed since the Great Design had been laid before the King. Dr Tonge and Mr Kirkby had been vastly busy, chasing imaginary assassins, arranging for the conveyance of the Forged Letters, interviewing the Lord Treasurer of England, and generally striving with might and main to convince King Charles of the existence of a Popish Plot. But all this while the supposed author of Tonge's manuscript, the source of all his information, was occupied with the old sordid problem of how to get enough to eat. Whether Tonge was poor or merely mean, it is impossible to say, but despite all his grand promises of a pension to anyone who would collaborate with him in exposing Jesuit machinations, Titus Oates was still living

* These Forged Letters came, long afterwards, into the hands of Sir Roger L'Estrange, and may be read in full in his *Brief History*, 2, 7–9.

in his miserable lodging in Cockpit Alley, still scrounging, begging, and whining for aid.

It is most curious and ironical that, not only on the eve of the Plot, but during the initial stages of the Plot's "discovery", Titus remains a vague figure, and that the only notices we have of him show him in his old character of vagrant. On Friday, August 30th, he paid his landlady eight or nine shillings for his board, at sixpence a meal, and showed her three shillings more, bemoaning himself that this was his whole estate, "Clutching his Fist, and Swearing without Book, that he would not be kept at that rate. By the Token, that same Day, he would have borrow'd Twenty Shillings of Mr Wilson, the next Neighbour."[11]

A day or two afterwards, he again encountered Father Coniers, the Jesuit who had formed so poor an opinion of him soon after his return from St Omers. "About the beginning of September . . . walking alone in Grays-Inn Walkes betwixt 11 and 12, this Mr Oates thrust himself alone into my Company: when having given the same character of himself, he fell, in my Judgment, to downryght begging: for having told me, he had lost 4. or 500 *l.* a year in Benefices for his Religion, what considerable Preferments My Lord Bp. of London had offred him, to return to the Ch. of England: how he wondered no better Provision was made in the Roman Church for Persons so well qualified as himself; that his Faculty in Preaching was much taken notice of, his Cheife employment having been to preach before the Judges. He told me, he was reduced to that necessity, that he was forced sometimes to take a walk instead of his dinner: and desired me of all kindness to preferr him to some Gentleman to teach his children: meat, drink, lodging, and 10 *l.* a year would satisfy him. . . . You cannot doubt how willing I was to ridd myself of such a Man, who for ought I knew, myght be anything, as well, as what he represented himself to me, or others, with whom he found more beliefe then with me, or a better opinion of his parts, and vertu: and so with the Ordinary Civilities, I dismist myself of him."[12]

During the first week of September, Titus is still to be found in the company of Catholics. Smith, the schoolmaster, records a very curious and significant argument with Titus, which occurred during that week. "Medburne and John Philips brought him to me at Islington: we went to the Catherine-wheel, where we drank a Bottle or two of claret, and my Boy brought me some new Acts of Parliament, then newly publish'd. Upon reading them there happened a very great Debate between Medburne and Titus Oates, concerning the Three Estates; Titus affirming, the King to be one of the Three Estates, and answerable to the other Two which he called the Lords and Commons. Medburne contradicted him, and told him he lied; insomuch that they grew to very hard words; Philips justifying Oates and I Medburne: I showing my reason in one of the preambles of the Acts, wherein 'twas exprest; *Be it Enacted by the King's most Excellent Majesty, with the Consent and Advice of the Lords Spiritual and Temporal, and Commons assembled in Parliament, etc.*, urging, That if the King had been One of the Three Estates it would have run thus, Enacted by the King, Lords and Commons, etc. Here 'tis Observable, The very time when Oates was just upon Discovering a Plot in Zeal for the Preservation of His Majesties Life, he was nevertheless talking Treason against his Prerogative."[13]

It was only now, in these first days of September (dry, hot days after a dry, hot summer),[14] that Titus ceased to be occupied with the sordid problem of how to obtain his bread. Upon Monday, the 2nd, he "came to Mr Kirkby's Lodgings in Fox-Hall, where he first saw him, or heard him named, and there he furnished him with money for his necessary Expenses, appointing to meet him the day following at the Pheasant in Fullers-Rents, to receive farther Informations, and to give less suspicion by being often seen in the Company of Dr Tonge, and so all be discovered".[15] Tonge's Diary gives a few more details; Titus "came to Dr Tonge to St Mary Overies after Sermon-time, and so all Three went by Water to Fox-Hall; but Otes in a Boat by himself, and following at a Distance for fear of Discovery, which was the first time Otes was made known to Mr Kirkby. Upon this Occasion, Otes was furnish'd with Mony, a Suit and Gown, and other Necessaries".[16]

Titus remained at Vauxhall until Saturday, September 7th, and Tonge stayed to bear him company and drill him into his part. The tenant of the house was one Lambert, a bell-founder, who was glad enough to sub-let some of his rooms, for he was in debt to his landlord for rent. Here Titus and Israel could be private, and here they were vastly busy; for they were elaborating, revising, and generally trimming up that plot which so far had very miserably misfired, the conspiracy known to history either as the Popish Plot or the Oates Plot, whichever side you happen to be on. In point of fact it was neither; it was Dr Israel Tonge's.

The historian Oldmixon, who knew Oates and firmly believed in the Popish Plot, scoffed at the idea that Oates could have invented it, because he was so dull and stupid. This was very true; but the point Oldmixon missed was that Tonge was neither. The Plot, crude though it was, was clever, for besides being sensational, it was extremely detailed and circumstantial. For these latter qualities in it, Tonge was indebted to Titus, whose contacts with Jesuits at home and abroad enabled him to supply names of persons and places, and details of Catholic ceremonies sufficient to impress the average Protestant. Note how even now Titus is still skulking in the background while Tonge manages all. From Kirkby's bald Narrative, it is easy to form a picture of Titus as he was at Vauxhall, reluctant as ever to apply himself to any task which meant hard work, though pleased to be in his parson's gown again, and to have money in his pocket and food in his belly. L'Estrange, who knew more about the back-stage business of the Plot than any man outside the circle of conspirators, describes the situation with his usual vividness: "Tonge made the Musique all this while, and Otes only Drew the Bellows. . . . He, poor Devil, swore to anything that came next, without either Feeling, or Foreseeing the Conscience, or the Consequences of Things. A False Oath in his Mouth was no more then an Invenom'd Tooth in Mouth of a Mad Dog. He snapt at every thing that was in his Way, and no Remedy for the Wound, like a Piece of his own Liver. . . . Otes'es Part was divided betwixt a Malicious Humour that he brought into the World with him, and an Habitual Course of Wickedness that made his Sins as Familiar to him as his Daily Bread: but the Invention, the Contrivance, and the Conduct, was altogether Tonge's."[17]

The one mistake L'Estrange made was in underrating the extent of that "Malicious Humour". It was the mistake of the normal man tolerant of weakness in himself and others, but always sceptical of positive evil. Titus's malice, the one trait in his character which made him really sinister, had risen above the surface of his weakness several times in the past, but so far had brought him no reward. Now, upon the eve of his enormous power, it displayed itself again, but it was still petty, lacking opportunity to be anything else. It was at this very time, when Titus was being kept hard at work by his patron Tonge, that he made two attempts to involve in the conspiracy a man who had been consistently kind to him, his old schoolmaster, William Smith.

Two or three days after the argument about the King's Prerogative, says Smith, Titus "came to see me again in the Evening, and desired me, with all intreaties imaginable, to write him a Paper of Verses, in Latin, upon our Blessed Saviour and the Virgin Mary, which he intended, as he said, to carry to the Jesuites as his own, to demonstrate his Learning, and try if thereby they would re-entertain him, and get him into some Catholick Family, where he might teach some Children, he being then totally destitute of any livelihood. The Verses I made for him, and he fetch'd them the next morning, forcing upon me, as a gift, a pair of Tweezers, which he said he brought out of Flanders. He particularly desired me, in the aforenamed Verses, to make a long Narrative in the praise of the Virgin Mary, pretending it would very much please the Jesuites. But truly I thought not fit to do so, and omitted it. The next, and last time he came to me was on a Saturday, some few days after in September: on a Saturday which happen'd to be the day before the great noise of the Popish Plot broke out; and I invited him to the Katherine-wheel, where he pull'd out a handful of Money, which seem'd to be about 30 or 40 shillings, offering me the acceptance of it, in return of the many Reckonings I had paid for him, and the Treats I had made him; but I refused it. Then he ask'd me if I had heard any thing of a Plot; I told him, No: upon which, he said, There had been great complaints at Whitehall about a Plot of the Jesuites, against the King. He promised to come and

Dine with me the next day, but I saw him no more till the First day of November, when he appear'd at the Lords Bar, and swore falsely against me. The reason why I mention these two passages is this: He told me, after I was got into his favour, That he came both those times to trapan me."[18]

Meanwhile the zealous but futile Kirkby, who was still busily pursuing imaginary assassins, had enjoyed a long talk with Titus at Vauxhall on September 3rd, "and having received from him what he had to communicate, appointed to meet the next morning at Heaven in the old Pallace-Yard, Westminster". ("Heaven" was a tavern, and in the same vicinity was another called "Hell".) Titus kept the appointment, and had a pathetic tale to tell his new friend. He had been to see Father Whitebread, who had told him that he had heard rumours of the betrayal of the Jesuits' schemes to the King, and that he suspected the betrayer to be Titus himself. Whitebread had beaten the poor young man, and had boxed his ears, ordering him immediately to return to St Omers. Upon receipt of this news, Kirkby proposed to Tonge, "that seeing Mr Oats was discovered, and in danger . . . Dr Tonge would be pleased to get Dr Oats his Information sworn before some Justice of the Peace: and the sooner it was done, the better".[19]

Accordingly, upon September 6th, after Kirkby had made another vain attempt to speak to the King at Windsor, Dr Tonge, "as he expected more encouragement from the public, than from the King or his Ministers, he thought proper, before he was presented to the council, to go with his two companions to Sir Edmundbury Godfrey, a noted and active justice of peace, and to give evidence before him of all the articles of the conspiracy".[20]

(3)

Justice Godfrey's entrance in the tragedy called the Popish Plot is almost as mysterious as his abrupt exit from it. For why did Tonge select this justice, among all the justices of the peace in London, to take Titus's affidavit?

Sir Edmund Berry Godfrey was a man of fifty-seven, very deaf, very melancholy (his father had died suicidally mad), somewhat eccentric in his habits, conscientious to the point of fussiness in his public duties, knighted for his courage in entering a pest-house during the Great Plague and fetching from thence a notorious thief, possibly (but only possibly) sharp in business. He was a bachelor, living in Hartshorn Lane, near Charing Cross; his trade was that of wood-monger, and he had a wharf at the end of the lane where he lived. His lugubrious appearance masked a very real courage; he had defied the King himself, dunning his Majesty's physician for a debt in the Verge of the Court; and early in the present year, as foreman of the Grand Jury of Middlesex, he had not hesitated to bring in an indictment for murder against the homicidal maniac, the young Earl of Pembroke, who was a close friend of the Opposition leader, Shaftesbury. This was an exceedingly dangerous thing to do; and when Pembroke's peers brought in a verdict of manslaughter only, and, on claiming benefit of clergy, Pembroke walked from the court a free man, Godfrey had deemed it prudent to take a long holiday abroad. But he was now returned, and was attending to his public duties with all his old strictness; the only laws he did not rigorously enforce were those against religious dissenters of all denominations, including the Catholics.

Though a staunch Protestant himself, Godfrey was genuinely tolerant; not only this, but he had friends who were of the hated religion. "No man", says Burnet, "lived on better terms with the papists than he did." Hence the question, never yet answered, why did Tonge select this particular justice to take Titus Oates's affidavit concerning an alleged conspiracy of the Catholics? Why not select a justice known to be definitely anti-Papist? There were enough and to spare of these in London. There was one in particular who was afterwards to be Titus's chief ally. His name was Sir William Waller; he was the son of a rebel commander of the Civil War, and his Protestant zeal was famous. He was "a great Inquisitor of Priests and Jesuits, and Gutter (as the Term was for Stripping) of Popish Chapels. In which he proceeded with that scandalous Rigor, as to bring forth the Pictures, and other Furniture of great Value, and burn them publicly; which gave Occasion to suspect, and some said positively, that, under this Pretence, he kept good Things for himself. In a Word, he was called the Priest Catcher."[21] Here, surely, was the very man for Tonge's purpose; yet he chose instead a justice known to be tolerant in his religious views, and friendly with individual Catholics, Sir Edmund Berry Godfrey. Why?

The correct answer to that question might go far in solving the whole mystery of Justice Godfrey, a mystery which has excited speculation from that day to this. An attempt to find it is not relevant to a life of Titus Oates, for, as has been seen, Titus was at this time little more than a puppet in the hands of Tonge, and can have had little say in the choice of the justice before whom he was to lay his information. The following tentative suggestion may not, however, come amiss, since, to the present writer's knowledge, it has never been offered before. In his choice, it is possible that Tonge was guided by the advice of certain great persons who may already have taken him under their protection. For in *Florus Anglo-Bavaricus*, the account of the Plot in Latin, there is a curious statement. Describing the contriving of the Plot at Vauxhall, in the house of Lambert the bell-founder, the anonymous author of the tract adds: "Further men of rank came thither in their coaches, and when they could not attend these conferences in person, sent their instructions by footmen and servants in their varied liveries, so that the authors of this invention could be traced with little difficulty by an observer well acquainted with English conditions." It is obvious that these "men of rank" are to be identified with certain of the Opposition lords who afterwards used the Plot as a means to their ends. One at least among these lords had a grudge against Godfrey—namely, the acquitted murderer, the Earl of Pembroke. The forcing of Godfrey to take an affidavit of this nature made him vulnerable, which was what Pembroke desired.

Tonge himself does not seem to have been entirely convinced of the wisdom of choosing this particular justice, for, if we are to believe Kirkby's Narrative, the doctor used the most extraordinary caution at the interview. He "would not permit [Godfrey] to read the particulars of the Information, telling him that His Majesty had already a true Copy thereof; and that it was not convenient that it should be yet communicated to any body else, only acquainting him in general, that it contained Matter of Treason and Felony, and other high Crimes . . . whereupon Sir Ed. B. Godfrey rested satisfied without reading them, and under-writ Dr Oats his Affidavit, that the matter therein contained was true; and at the same time Dr Tonge made Oath that it had been made known to the King". Some of this is obvious nonsense. We cannot seriously imagine a man of Godfrey's character and experience "resting satisfied" with such mysterious and dangerous informations without reading them. But while it is probable that Tonge used all his endeavours to prevent Godfrey reading the informations, it is probable almost to the point of certainty that Godfrey, having read them, treated the whole thing as a ridiculous story, and that, having done so, and finding later that it was received as gospel by the world at large, he fell into that strange panic which was the prelude to his death.[22] For he did not inform the King as he should have done, and misprison of treason was a very serious offence.

It is a relief to turn from these dark and mysterious regions back-stage to the wings in which the seeming clown, Titus, nervously awaits the moment when he must face the limelight. On Saturday, September 7th, while Kirkby was making fruitless efforts to speak with the Earl of Danby, poor Titus was undergoing a most humiliating adventure under the auspices of the Comic Muse. He returned to his old lodging in Cockpit Alley, probably for some belongings left behind when he moved to Vauxhall, and "about bed-time, that Night, one Stratford, the very next Neighbour (that was gotten most confoundedly drunk) fell to Disciplining some Damsels that were then in his House . . . the Noise, and the Hurry, brought Otes to the Window. . . . Stratford falling on so unmercifully upon the poor Wenches, Otes squeaks out to him to hold his hand: which gave the Enemy a short Diversion; for what with his [Oates's] Napkin-Night-Cap (like a Christian Turbant) and his fine Pipe (Peculiar to himself), the drunken fellow presently chang'd his Battery, and took the Reverend Doctor for a Reverend Matron, Call'd him all the Bawds, and Jades and Bitches, in Nature; and fell on upon the Windows with Brick-bats. . . . The next day . . . [Oates] went away . . . about Ten a Clock, he took his Morning

Draught with his Landlord; told him, he would stay there no longer: Threatned to be revenged of Somebody; And so departed."[23] The clown's paint was scratched, and beneath it was revealed malice personified; as poor drunken Stratford was to find to his cost.

All this while, King Charles had remained incredulous, and by September 9th the three conspirators were become exceedingly depressed. Kirkby returned from Windsor to London, reported the King's continuing scepticism to his confederates whom he met at the Flying Horse in King Street, and advised Titus to return to his lodging in Vauxhall, "as well for his security, as that he might have Company to chear him in his then sad Condition, to which he agreed";[24] here they all remained from the 9th to the 28th, endeavouring to raise one another's fallen spirits. All three were "much perplexed with fear of failing; and they had Reason, for no Mortal could dream such Things should happen, as did, to lift up the falling Engine".[25] "Dr Oats," says Kirkby, "imploy'd himself to write out Copies of his Information; and Dr Tonge to enquire after the Lord Treasurer, whom he sought for at Wimbledon [where Danby had a house] several times, to give in the needful and occurring Informations, which are now under his hands, before the private Committee, being all three much perplexed both in regard the danger they were in, and the seeming neglect of the Discovery they had made." Kirkby means, danger from the Jesuits; but actually they were in danger from the law. False witness was an offence held in particular horror by our ancestors, and its punishment, which included branding, was heavy.

But in the meantime, unknown to the conspirators, the efforts of the Duke of York had persuaded the King to lay the whole matter before the Privy Council. James has been blamed for this, but his action was natural and honest. The dreadful accusations made by Tonge and his colleague against the Duke's fellow Catholics, and in particular against his own confessor, Bedingfield, were quite intolerable to a man with so strong a sense of justice as James; he wanted the whole matter investigated and exposed. Upon the 27th, therefore, at night, Mr Floyd, Danby's gentleman, came to Vauxhall to fetch Tonge to the Council (the Court being by this time returned to London). Tonge and Kirkby scarce able to believe in their good fortune, went at once, but by the time they arrived at Whitehall, the Council had risen, and they were ordered to attend at ten o'clock next morning.

Tonge, meanwhile, had bethought himself. It was possible that the Privy Council might prove as sceptical as the King; in order, therefore, to ensure that his "informations" should be submitted to the judgement of the public, he got Titus out of bed at an early hour on the morning of Friday, September 28th, and, accompanied by Kirkby, once more knocked upon the door of Justice Godfrey in Hartshorn Lane, "carrying the first Depositions, sworn the sixth of September, and two copies written by Mr Oats, to have them sworn, That each might have an authentick Copy";[26] the original depositions had been added to very considerably in the interim.

Having ensured publicity for their precious Plot, Tonge and Kirkby went to keep their appointment at the Council-board, sending Titus back to Vauxhall; but, on being admitted, they were informed that Tonge's original informant, the mysterious pusher of papers under doors, was wanted for interrogation. Tonge at once returned to Vauxhall to fetch his protégé. The great moment was now arrived; the stage was set, and the inexperienced actor must play his role. Hastily was he dressed for the part in a new silk gown and white bands, with a fair woolly periwig soon to be famous in many a woodcut; and, no longer Titus Oates the weaver's son, no longer Titus Ambrose or Sampson Lucy the convert parson dependent upon Jesuit charity, but Titus Oates, D.D. of Salamanca, he was thrust by his stage-manager's hands into the full glare of the limelight, to face an audience composed of the King's Privy Council, and to say the piece he had been learning off by heart in the seclusion of the Plot House at Vauxhall, his famous *Narrative*.

(4)

In any biography of Titus Oates, his *Narrative* is bound to present a problem. For while on the one hand it is too long and too dreadfully complicated to be reproduced in its entirety, even in an appendix, it is so essential to his story, forming as it did the basis of his Plot, that it must be laid in some shape or form before the reader. Those possessed of sufficient patience and interest may read it in full in its two printed versions, *The Discovery of the Popish Plot* and the *True Narrative*, both in the British Museum. The *True Narrative* was published by order of the House of Lords, who ordered likewise that it be printed "at large" in their journals, to the embarrassment of their noble posterity. The original *Narrative*, sworn before Godfrey, September 6th, contained forty-three articles, but by the 28th these had grown to eighty-one; the drawing up of the *Narrative* into articles is interesting, for Prynne in his *Rome's Masterpiece*, the printed "Narrative" of the Habernfeld Plot, had used exactly the same device.

The following is an attempt to summarise, very shortly, each article, sufficient, it is hoped, to give the reader not only the gist of the Plot, but some example of Titus's inimitable impudence and malice (to say nothing of his curious ignorance concerning the most ordinary matters of etiquette observed among the Jesuits), of the extent of his patron Tonge's fanaticism, and of the credulity of the nation which swallowed the whole monstrous story at a gulp.

1. A letter, seen by Titus, from certain English Jesuits to an Irish one, Father "Sinman" (possibly Father Sweetman) in Madrid, containing news of plotting in Scotland "under the Notion of Presbyterians".

2. Ten pounds bestowed on Titus to enable him to carry the above letter to Madrid. He broke it open at Burgos.

3. Treasonable sermon preached at Valladolid, in which Charles II declared to be a bastard, and the Oath of Allegiance "Heretical and Anti-Christian, and Devillish".

4. The Duke of York to be dispatched in the same way as his brother, unless he answers the Jesuits' expectations, in order to which they have sent Bedingfield to him as confessor. This news Titus learnt from letters he saw at at Valladolid.

5. False report by Father "Sinman" that Charles II was poisoned (and that James to be served with the same sauce

unless he brought in Catholicism) received with great joy at Valladolid, Titus again seeing the letter.

6. Great diligence being used to murder the King. Titus read this in Father "Sinman's" room in Madrid, in August, '77 (when actually he was at Valladolid).

7. Apologies by Father "Sinman" for false report, but "Honest William" (the nickname of John Grove), faint-hearted although he had been promised £15,000 to do the deed. Letter seen by Titus same place and time as above.

8. Fathers Strange and Keynes promised £10,000 by Provincial of New Castile if they would slay Charles II. Titus brought the letter to Strange in London on his return from Valladolid, and he not being able to read Keynes' letter, which was in Spanish, Strange kindly gave him his own to read, it being in Latin.

9. Titus given letters to carry to the Rector of St Omers from the English Jesuits, when he was sent to that College. These he naturally read *en route*, and found that they reiterated the writers' determination to slaughter Charles II by poison if not by stabbing.

10. Letters, enclosed in above, to Père la Chaise, the French King's confessor, in Paris. Titus given these letters to carry to Paris, and presumably broke them open as usual. They stressed the importance of destroying all Protestants "root and branch".

11. Presbyterians in Scotland to be stirred up to rebellion, and 40,000 "Black Bills" to be sent to arm the Irish. The French King to land an army in Ireland. Apparently no letters to this effect read by Titus, but he "heard" it.

12. Father Coniers ordered to preach on St Thomas of Canterbury's Day in the Sodality Church at St Omers against the Oath of Allegiance. Strange removed from Provincialship, and Whitebread put in his place.

13. Detailed account of a letter concerning new resolve against the lives of Charles II and his brother, which Titus ends naïvely thus: "which Letter, he, the Deponent, saw in the hands of Richard Ashbey [the Rector of St Omers], and desired to read it, but the said Ashbey would not read it to him, Jan. the 2. 1678". We are left in the dark, therefore, as to how he knew the contents of the letter.

14. Fathers Ashby and Blundel to share the office of

Ordinary of Newgate Prison, in order to seduce the prisoners from their religion and loyalty, and parents to be bribed to do the same by their children.

15. Charles II's intentions towards Spain are not to assist her against France, "but to stand a looker-on", and in reprisal for this the King of Spain advised by the Jesuits to seize the estates of English merchants.

16. Horribly treasonable words heard by Titus in the Library of St Omers College, regarding the dispatch of the Black Bastard, otherwise Charles II, and the certainty of the Duke's passport to Eternity if he failed the Jesuits.

17. Letters sent to the Emperor's confessor, saying that Charles II had underhand stirred up the Hungarian rebellion against his Imperial Majesty, and had sent the rebels money.

18. More about the landing of a French army in Ireland. The General of the Jesuits to contribute 500,000 crowns towards this enterprise, and the Pope would not be behind-hand in generosity if he saw some progress.

19. Parody on the King's Speech at the opening of Parliament sent to St Omers "for the Fathers and Scholars to Laugh at, and then translated into French, and given to the Governor of St Omers, who sent it to the French King his Master". Pickering has again attempted to shoot Charles II, but the flint of his pistol was loose. He is to have 300,000 masses for the health of his soul as a reward for the deed when done.

20. Titus going to enquire of his confessor whether he might keep January 30th, the anniversary of the execution of Charles I, as a fast, was told that Charles I was no martyr, but an heretic; his confessor "withal added, that he was not King James's Son, but a Bastard, begotten on the Body of Queen Anne of Denmark by her Taylor".

21. Two Jesuits sent to Ireland with £2,000 as a bribe to the natives to rise, and empowered to offer them £4,000 more.

22. English Catholics to be encouraged to contribute to the Irish and Scottish rebellions.

23. Catholicism must be brought in by the same method as that used by the Jesuits for the ruin of Charles I—namely, by the effusion of blood—and the Jesuits at St Omers therefore implored their brethren in England to

waste no more time in giving the first blow, i.e. the slaughter of the King. These letters composed by Titus himself, and signed in his presence, February, 1678.

24. Answer to above said "that they had found, that although the Duke was a good Catholique, yet he had a tender affection to the King, and would scarcely be engaged in that concern, and if they should once intimate their designs and purposes unto him, they might not only be frustrated of their design but also might lose his favour".

25. Coming and going of letters between St Omers and the English Seminary in Ghent, and between Ghent and England. Jesuits in London refused advice of those of Ghent to treat with the secular clergy about the design, the latter being "rascally fellows" and "inclined to live in peace and obedience to their Prince". (This is an interesting touch. Titus evidently had not forgotten the internal dissensions of the Catholics, about which he must have learned a great deal while in Norfolk's household.) The "fatal blow should be given to the Black Boy [Charles II] at Whitehall with all the speed that might be". All these letters read by Titus.

26. In March, several attempts to assassinate Charles II made by "Honest William" and Pickering, but with no more success than previously, for which failure William "chidden" and Pickering had twenty lashes.

27. News from Ireland that the Irish ready to rise at ten days' warning, with 20,000 foot and 5,000 horse, and with a further 15,000 horse in the north. Secret commissions sent out by the General of the Jesuits, and Irish resolved to cut all Protestant throats. A "General Consult" summoned by Provincial to meet in London, and Titus among those ordered to attend it "as a Messenger from Father to Father." (It is curious that Titus should describe the Provincial Congregation as the General Consult, for at St Omers he had learned the correct name for this assembly. Possibly "General Consult" sounded more sinister.)

28. Description of the "General Consult". Titus had come over from St Omers with nine or ten others. "At which Consult, thus held in the Month of May [April 24th, O.S.], the Deponent was present to attend the Consulters, and delivered their Concerns from Company to Company;

and then a little after they left the White-horse Tavern, and divided themselves into several Clubs or Companies. Some met at Mrs Saunders house in Wild-street; other at Mr Ireland's in Russel-street near Covent-Garden, and in other places; all which, though in several Companies, 5 or 6 in a Company, did contrive the death of the King: In order to which there were Papers sent from Company to Company, which the Deponent carried, containing the opinions of the timeing their business, and the manner how it was to be done: And within 3 or 4 days after, the Deponent went to S. Omers with the Fathers that came from the other side of the water." (This article is given here in more detail than the others, because it was the most important, and at the same time the most impudent, accusation made by Oates. On the date in question, he was actually, as has been seen, at St Omers, as the defence proved during the trials. Yet it was upon this very article that the prosecution based its case.)

29. On a visit to St Omers in June, Whitebread told the Rector (and, of course, Titus) that the Society might shortly expect to see Charles II "laid fast enough", and that if James would not behave himself, "his passport was made to lay him to sleep".

30. Bribe of £50 accepted by Titus to assassinate Israel Tonge, author of *The Jesuits Morals*. Other anti-Catholic writers to go the same way.

31. Titus called to the Rector's room at St Omers on purpose to receive the interesting information that the late Chancellor, Lord Clarendon, had been reconciled to Rome on his death-bed.

32. Titus sent to England, June 23rd (note the clever spicing of a mass of falsehood with grains of truth), "to attend the motions of the Fathers in London", with £4 for his charges, and £80 promised for his past and future services.

33. Sir George Wakeman, the Queen's physician, to be offered £10,000 to poison Charles II. The Bishop of Hereford to be slain likewise.

34. Titus treated to a detailed account of the firing of London in 1666, by Father Strange, who had taken a principal part in it. (The failure of the Jesuits to cut all

Protestant throats once they had achieved the Fire, the former being the avowed motive of the latter, seems to have been a most singular oversight on their part.)

35. New efforts to be made to promote a Scottish rebellion.

36. Ashby desired by Harcourt, Rector of the London District, to "make a Progress in Somersetshire, to inform those of the Society of the intended Design", after he had finished his course of waters at Bath.

37. Wakeman's £10,000 to be increased to £15,000; whether or no Wakeman apprised of this, "the Deponent cannot inform here in this Article".

38. Twelve Jesuits sent by Whitebread from St Omers to Holland, to foment a rising against the Prince of Orange.

39. Whitebread blames the Fathers in London for being dilatory in the matter of Wakeman. Both this and the previous information in letters shown to Titus.

40. Letters from Whitebread (suddenly and belatedly cautious and using ciphers) prophesying that Westminster shall lie as low as London did in '66, and declaring that until this happened, and Charles II slain, the Catholic faith could not prosper.

41. Oates gratuitously informed that the Jesuits have £60,000 a year in rents and £100,000 in the bank, though their spy system costs them £4,000 a year.

42. General resolve to "raise a Commotion" in England and Wales, made by various Jesuits in Titus's presence.

43. Two new messengers, disguised as Dissenting ministers, sent to Scotland to stir things up.

(These 43 articles formed the original *Narrative*, as it was sworn to before Godfrey on September 6th.)

44. Edward Coleman, the Duchess of York's secretary, gives away State secrets to the Jesuits in return for money, through one Smith "who daily lurketh about White-Hall".

45. Under the guise of merchants, scriveners, and tobacconists, the Jesuits "take an estimate of the strength of the Nation".

46. Letters from Whitebread rejoicing that Wakeman has settled for £15,000, but urging the old assassins, Grove and Pickering, to continue their efforts.

47. On the same day (August 9th, 1678), £10 offered to Titus to kill Berry (the priest who had received him into

the Church), because he had written in defence of the Oath of Supremacy.

48. Pleasant conversation concerning Charles II's illegitimacy and speedy end.

49. Titus taken by Grove (who surely ought to have been more gainfully employed) into the garden of Wild House and regaled with the story of the firing of Southwark in '76.

50. August 11th, letters from St Omers urge the slaying of the Duke of Ormonde as the correct prelude to the Irish rebellion. This article is interesting because it gives the first direct, though cautious, hit at James. Fenwick, says Oates, told him that "one that was a Catholick should play such a Game, as never was played since the Conquest". Titus enquiring the identity of this mysterious person, was informed that "It was the Duke of York".

51. More conversation in code at Father Keynes', all about Mum and Chocolate, Barley-Broth trade, the Order of Magpies, etc., which, deciphered, turned out to be the old tale of the assassination of eminent Protestants, this time including the Duke of Monmouth, illegitimate son of the King and the pet of the Opposition.

52. Charles II to be dispatched, definitely, while at Windsor. (Considering the number of assassins hired to stab, shoot, and poison him, the fact that he had survived up to this date, August 12th, was little short of a miracle.)

53. Edifying conversation between Titus and the traitor Smith, who shared Oates's lodging and had £50 a year from the Jesuits in return for daily information. Also speculation as to whether the Catholics could or could not cut the throats of 100,000 Protestants in London.

54. Information against William Smith the schoolmaster, Matthew Medburne the actor, and several other humble objects of Titus's malice, for treasonable talk heard by him at their club, for which they were to be thanked by the Jesuits.

55. If Charles II did not become R.C. (Roman Catholic), he would soon cease to be C.R. (Charles Rex).

56. August 20th, letters arrive from St Omers to Fenwick giving news that the twelve Jesuits have landed in Holland, and that "Appletree Will" (William of Orange) shall not be great.

57. Fenwick writes to St Omers the same day that Charles II has gone to Windsor, and that the Fathers and "Honest William" will follow him thither.

58. Titus accidentally present at a sermon preached by Keynes to "twelve persons, Men in poor Habits, yet men of quality, as the Deponent doth suppose by the whiteness of their hands", in which the lawfulness of deposing and destroying heretical princes insisted on.

59. Unknown gentleman (Oates had forgotten his name) persuaded by the Jesuits to move from his lodgings in Westminster, "lest God should destroy him with the Sinners of that City".

60. Oates informed that the Benedictines (who since 1661 had had a convent at the Savoy, next door to Somerset House), had promised to assist the plotters with £6,000. Number of persons employed in the assassination of Charles II evidently considered insufficient, for Titus now implored to join their ranks, but excused himself on the plea of never having fired a gun in his life. Several days before this, he had heard Father Coniers lay a wager with a gentleman in the Savoy that the King would not eat any more Christmas-pies. Twenty thousand Catholics, "substantial persons and fit for arms", ready to rise as soon as the King is slaughtered. Titus advised Keynes to let Wakeman do the actual killing, "and then the people would not apprehend it so much".

61. Titus taken by Keynes to meet some Dominicans, who, however, could not spare any money for the Design; nor could the Carmelites, but they promised prayers.

62. Conversation about slaying the King at Windsor; poor "Honest William" has a sore throat and cannot go, but Coniers and Anderson will go next morning. (This was Father Munson, *alias* Anderson, O.P., of the Duke of Norfolk's household.) Later, meeting Coniers, Oates had a merry conversation with him on the subject.

63. Wednesday, August 31st, "Consult" of Jesuits and various Benedictines about letters from Archbishop Talbot of Dublin concerning the killing of Ormonde (Dr Fogarty the best person to undertake this), and a general Irish rising.

64. Fogarty deep in the whole Plot, and present when Wakeman agreed to poison the King. It was he who had

hired the Four Irish Ruffians to "mind the King's postures at Windsor".

65. Sir William Godolphin, English Ambassador at the Court of Madrid, in the Plot. Titus has seen Godolphin at mass in Madrid, knows he is a Papist, and swears that he "hath perverted a Kinsman of his own".

66. August 22nd, Oates sees £80 counted out and dispatched by Harcourt, in the name of the Provincial, for the hire of the Four Irish Ruffians.

67. First mention of the Forged Letters. Oates shown by Fogarty a letter written by him to Bedingfield, and told of eighty others written to the Jesuits in England on the same subject—that is, the slaughter of the King and a general design against the Protestants.

68. Meeting Coniers by accident at 6 p.m., August 22nd, after failing to meet Tonge by appointment, Titus informed by Coniers that the latter has not been able to go to Windsor after all because his horse is lame and he himself has sciatica. However, he is as resolute as ever, and (in the publicity of Grays Inn Walks), shows Oates a knife, which is a foot long in the blade and half a foot in the haft, with which he intends to slay Charles II through his (Coniers') cloak.

69. Same day, Titus shown (apparently in the open street) a bag of "Tewsbury Mustard-balls, a notable biting Sawce", intended for the firing of Westminster.

70. August 24th, Oates told by Blundel in Fenwick's chamber to be of good cheer, for the Protestant religion "was on its last legs".

71. Oates shown a plan of the proposed firing of Westminster and Wapping, and has it explained to him in detail.

72. Same day (August 30th), he is shown a Bull issued by the Pope, disposing of the chief ecclesiastical posts in England; in this are the names of two archbishops, nineteen bishops, two abbots, and five deans.

73. September 2nd, Oates shown letters from Scotland announcing the fact that 8,000 Catholics are ready to rise there.

74. Also letters from St Omers concerning the Jesuits disguised as dissenting ministers sent to Scotland, and news of £1,000 bestowed on them by Père la Chaise.

75. Letter from Whitebread, seen by Oates, in which former speaks of being informed of some betrayal of their

plans (this was on September 3rd), but nevertheless orders Blundel not to desist from the business, and adds that thanks should be tendered to Fogarty for his zeal.

76. Whitebread arriving in London next day, orders Oates to appear at his lodgings the following morning.

77. Oates, attending Whitebread as ordered, is struck three blows with a stick and has his ears boxed for blabbing to the King. However, if he will disclose the name of the minister who has been with him to the King, Whitebread will forgive him, but he must return immediately to St Omers, and Blundel will "take care of carrying on the Fire in Wapping in the Deponent's room".

78. Titus informed by Pickering that Coniers has gone to Windsor. This was on September 6th.

79. About to attend the Provincial that night, Oates, that most fortunate of eavesdroppers, overhears Whitebread and others plotting to torture him, once they have got him overseas, till he has confessed who went with him to the King.

80. Venturing to return to his old lodging in Cockpit Alley that night, he narrowly escapes assassination at the hands of one Stratford, a stranger, who "endeavoured to break open the house where the Deponent lay; and did break down a door to get in to his lodging, but was forced to Retreat. . . . And when he saw he could not come to Assassinate him (as the Deponent verily believes) he Reviled him, and broke several Quarries of Glass in a Window, under the lodging of the Deponent." (Observe the malice which draws into the Plot the poor drunken Stratford, whom Oates admits was a stranger to him.)

81. September 8th, Sunday, while Oates is going to attend public worship (dare one ask of which denomination?), Father Nevil meets him, warns him that the Jesuits are out to destroy him, and enquires where he lodges. But Titus "suspecting this Person to be a Trappan", does not tell him.

To the *Narrative* was added a list of the conspirators, viz. 9 Benedictines, 3 Carmelites, 2 Franciscans, 10 Dominicans, 51 Jesuits by name and 12 "whose names I know not, but I know their persons", 14 secular priests (names obtained from Father Whitebread), 2 lay brothers, 8 "secular persons", and 4 "other persons"; and when the *Narrative* was printed a further list was added of "such Noble-men and Gentry as are in this Conspiracy, whose Names occur at present". This ominous phrase "occur at present" was to form a notable feature of Oates's evidence during the entire Plot period. From the beginning to the end, he insisted on his right to hold back informations and accusations as he thought fit, bringing them out only when it suited him, an example followed by the whole bevy of informers who came to be known as the "King's Evidence".

Such, then, was the masterpiece of falsehood and nonsense now lying on the table of the Privy Council in Whitehall Palace, when, upon this twenty-eighth day of September, 1678, Titus Oates made his first entrance in what was to be one of the bloodiest melodramas in English history.

(5)

He was introduced by the Clerk of the Council as "Mr Titus Oates", and this must have annoyed him, for, since his return from St Omers, he had been careful to inform his Protestant friends that he was Titus Oates, D.D. of Salamanca. But on the other hand, he was probably too nervous to feel more than a passing irritation at this insult to his dignity; if there had been a former occasion on which he had appeared before this august assembly, it must have been at the examination of Captain William Parker, an episode he had done his best to forget. And here on the table before him was that long, complex, wild *Narrative* of his, painstakingly composed, re-written, corrected, and improved upon under the fanatical eye of Dr Tonge in the Plot House at Vauxhall, that monstrous tissue of lies he now must back up by word of mouth. One circumstance favoured him; the shrewd and sceptical Charles II was not present; his Majesty had left for Newmarket to enjoy his hunting and his racing, though he had attended the morning session. Also, it was obvious that Titus had an ally in Danby, who saw with dismay the imminent re-assembling of Parliament, and who would be ready with an unobtrusive prompt should Titus hesitate.

But he did not hesitate. That high, affected voice of his

spoke at great length and with astonishing glibness, reeling off lists of names from memory, accusing high personages without the least embarrassment. The Council was impressed—nay, awed—to hear him repeat the very words written down in his *Narrative*.[27] Here and there he spiced the story with a new and juicy detail; he had heard Sir William Godolphin absolved by the Archbishop of Tuam; the cutler who had made Coniers' knife had made four more, intended, of course, for the Irish Ruffians; the Jesuits had even attempted to preach their hellish doctrines in the conventicles of London, "but the London people are too knowing".[28] These grave and learned men, the King's most trusted advisers, shuddered as they heard the fearsome details; they seemed hypnotised by this strange young man in his parson's gown, and only one mild doubt clouded the tranquil morning of their credulity. Titus "had been trusted with a multitude of treasonable letters at different times: his only object was to detect and defeat the conspiracy: undoubtedly then he must have secured some of these papers as evidence against the traitors. He confessed, however, that he stood there without a single document; but promised to produce evidence in abundance if he might be furnished with warrants and officers to arrest the persons, and seize the papers of the individuals whom he had accused. To this proposal the council gave its assent."[29]

When Titus had withdrawn at last, the Councillors looked at one another in a state bordering upon bemusement. It was impossible, said one of them, voicing the sentiments of the rest, that one young man could have invented so detailed, so complex, a conspiracy. "If he be a liar", added Mr Henry Coventry, "he is the greatest and adroitest I ever saw." It was a just verdict on Titus Oates, but unfortunately it was neither taken nor intended to be taken seriously. When the meeting broke up, Danby sent a courier galloping after the King, imploring his Majesty to put off his holiday at Newmarket and return post haste to London. Very reluctantly, Charles complied.

While the King's coach-horses drew his bored and irritated Majesty back towards his capital, Titus Oates was enjoying his first taste of power. Accompanied by a strong guard of soldiers, and armed with warrants signed by

Danby himself, he was setting forth merrily to arrest his former benefactors, the men who had saved him from starvation, who had given him free board and lodging and education, who had forgiven him his faults so many times. That night he arrested Father William Ireland and Father John Fenwick, both Jesuits, and Pickering, the Benedictine lay brother. The weather had broken at last; there was now continual rain and a high wind;[30] through the wet night Oates waddled on his bandy legs, rousing the neighbourhood with his hammering on doors, dragging his victims from their beds, routing in drawers and cupboards for letters, account-books, private papers.

Next day he was summoned to an extraordinary meeting of the Privy Council, and was examined both morning and afternoon; at both sessions the King was present. Those shrewd black eyes, melancholy and humorous all at once, used to sizing up all conditions of men, stared appraisingly at the odd figure which bowed and scraped at the foot of the table. But, the first plunge taken, Titus faced his Sovereign squarely, and informed his "maist Graacious and Glaarious Maajesty" that, having ventured "may lafe" for him at sea, and "may saul" for him on land (the first referred to Titus's short and disgraceful career as a naval chaplain, and the second to his feigned conversion to the Catholic religion), he was now come to save his life by making known a hellish conspiracy.[31]

He then embarked upon his story as confidently as yesterday, and, lest those who had heard it once before might find the tale a trifle wearisome, invented some new details. He had made a practice of going to confession to as many of the Jesuits as possible, that he might get to know them. He had been sent to Spain on the excuse of fetching over the body of Sir Francis Cottington (a former English Ambassador who had died there), and Mr Fox, *alias* the Duke of Norfolk, had given him ten pounds for the purpose.* His audience was a little more disposed to be

* This is the only instance I can find of Oates's trying to involve Norfolk in his Plot. The omission of other attempts to ruin a former benefactor, who was also a prominent Catholic, admits of the possibility of blackmail on the part of Titus, though there is no concrete evidence for it. The reader will remember that directly persecution broke out, Norfolk left the kingdom and remained overseas until it was safe to return.

critical to-day, influenced, probably, by the presence of the King, and even ventured to ask questions. How, for instance, did Coniers propose to escape after stabbing his Majesty? "If he can but escape being knocked on the head, he doubted not of his pardon," replied Titus cryptically.[32] The Forged Letters were resurrected for his benefit, and the Council was greatly impressed when, having been shown a line of each, he answered correctly whose it was, according to the signature. (It was not until a comparison had been made between these letters and the writing in the confiscated papers of Fenwick and Ireland, that it was discovered that there was not the least similitude. Sir William Jones and Sir Robert Southwell told the Duke of York afterwards that "upon comparison of the narrative and the letters, they were perswaded Oates writ every one of them himself".[33]) On the other hand, there were some doubts about Father Ireland. Oates had said that Ireland went to St Omers a week or a fortnight before Bartholomew-tide. Yet the letter produced as proof of it was dated St Omers, August 1st.[34]

But such slight criticism was as nothing to the ordeal Titus was now to face. King Charles, sitting there with his hat on at the head of the table, surrounded by his bareheaded Councillors, maintaining that deceptively indolent demeanour of his, seemingly bored by the whole business, suddenly began to ask questions. Mr Oates had stated that, among other great personages, he had interviewed Don John of Austria, in whose presence he had seen paid out the money for the bribing of Wakeman. Now, would Mr Oates be good enough to describe Don John's appearance? Titus replied without hesitation that Don John was tall, lean, and dark; it was the conventional idea of a Spaniard. Then was the Council affronted to hear the King laugh, as he exclaimed: "I know him very well. He is fat, short, and fair." Before Titus had time to recover himself, Charles shot another question at him. Mr Oates had interviewed Père la Chaise, had he not? Indeed he had. Where had this interview taken place? At the Jesuits' house just by the Louvre, was the answer. "Man", cried Charles Stuart, who had spent many weary years of exile in Paris, "the Jesuits have no house within a mile of the Louvre."[35]

But there was growing in Titus that stupendous audacity, that astonishing self-assurance, which were to carry him triumphantly through every threat to his credit as a witness. He replied, probably with something of a sneer (for he knew he had convinced the Council), that his Majesty was too good a Protestant to know about Jesuits' houses, and that his Majesty's own innocence and virtue might well prevent him from guessing the depths of wickedness to which these Papists were sunk. The King himself, perhaps content to have caught the informer out in two such manifest falsehoods, perhaps merely nauseated by the whole business, rose and left the Council Chamber, muttering: "For my part, I call the fellow a lying knave." But his Councillors stayed on; some were genuinely convinced of the truth of Oates's fairy tale; others scented the chance to bring down political enemies by the aid of it; all of them were only too willing to equip Mr Oates with fresh warrants and to order him a strong guard of soldiers for another long night of arrests.

So for the second night in succession did Titus drink the heady wine of power, and the first name on his list was that of Father Thomas Whitebread, against whom, probably because it was he who had ordered Titus's dismissal from St Omers, he entertained a very particular grudge. The Provincial and his Socius, or secretary, Father Mico, *alias* Hervey, were lodged within the liberties of the Spanish Embassy in Wild Street, and both were at this time confined to their beds with a severe fever; Whitebread indeed was so ill that he had received the Last Sacraments. Titus, however, regardless alike of the rights of asylum or of the dictates of common humanity, forced his way into their lodging, and ordered them to be dragged from their beds to prison. The Spanish Ambassador, aroused by the tumult, hurried to the scene, and persuaded the soldiers that the priests in the residences of foreign ambassadors were entitled to the immunity of the law. Nevertheless, the soldiers, probably egged on by Oates, struck the two fathers with the butts of their muskets, and carried off all their papers.[36]

From here the party of armed men, headed by Titus in his parson's gown and bands, went to the lodging of Father

Harcourt, Rector of the London District, and to that of Father John Keynes, but both these priests had received timely warning and had absented themselves. Next they searched the house of the Earl of Powis for Father William Morgan, but he was not in London at the time. "They also selected here and there Catholics of lesser note against whom Oates entertained a private grudge, and threw them into prison."[37] Father Thomas Jenison, a Jesuit whose brother was later to join the ranks of the informers, was among those arrested on this night, and was sent by Titus on foot through the pouring rain to Newgate, while Titus himself took a coach at the public expense. It had been hoped to arrest Edward Coleman, sometime secretary to the Duchess of York, but he was not at home; certain papers were discovered in his house, however, and these were sealed up and carried away. There will be more to say about both Coleman and his papers when he and they were examined before the Privy Council.

Titus, rolling homeward in his coach in the small hours of the morning, must have congratulated himself upon the work accomplished in two strenuous nights. He had feasted upon revenge, drunk deeply of power, and he had obtained a fine haul of papers, now sealed up and awaiting examination by the credulous gentlemen of the Privy Council. Surely among such a mass of documents there must be something which would lend colour to his tale, even if it were but a few lines in cipher or a cryptic sentence, for these Jesuits lived in England in defiance of the law and were fain to take what precautions they could when they were obliged to put pen to paper. In any case, he was Dr Titus Oates (and very soon he was going to insist on being addressed so); and, by the entreaties of his Council, King Charles had just assigned him a pension of six hundred pounds per annum, a suite of apartments in Whitehall Palace, and a guard for his precious person. Fickle fortune had smiled on him at last. He, but a week since, the half-starved pauper, living on the charity of a crazy fanatic, with a shady past and a hopeless future, was now suddenly rich, courted, deferred to, dining off silver plate in the palace of the King of England, with a guard of his Majesty's soldiers whenever he walked abroad.

It was true that Dr Israel Tonge was housed in Whitehall likewise, but with a smaller pension and less sumptuous apartments. Already, in Titus's mind, Tonge, his benefactor, was shrinking to minute proportions; the ladder which had thrust him up to greatness was being kicked away; and Titus, seeing the mad scheme successful beyond his wildest dreams, had no trouble in convincing himself that he and he alone had discovered and exposed the Popish Plot, that he and he alone had the right to that title, soon to be bestowed on him by an England gone mad, "The Saviour of the Nation".

(6)

While Titus basked in the unaccustomed sunshine of success, and the taverns and the coffee-houses began to hum with wild rumours, and Charles II went off to his jockeys and his race-horses at Newmarket, there was one gentleman who turned upon the infant Plot a gaze which became steadily more interested. His name was Anthony Ashley Cooper; his title, Earl of Shaftesbury.

It was thought by some in Shaftesbury's day, and by others since, that my lord himself was the real author of the Popish Plot, the inventor of the whole story. This is almost certainly untrue; but that he used the Plot for his own ends, took it under his care, and became, so to speak, its general manager, no one can doubt. Indeed, he himself has left no room for doubt, for he remarked to an acquaintance: "I will not say who started the Game, but I am sure I had the full Hunting of it."[38] Dryden's lines, so often quoted, sum up the situation very well:

> "*The wished occasion of the Plot he takes;*
> *Some circumstances finds, but more he makes.*
> *By buzzing emissaries, fills the ears*
> *Of listening crowds with jealousies and fears*
> *Of arbitrary counsels brought to light,*
> *And proves the king himself a Jebusite.*"[39]

But it was Roger North who supplied the shrewdest commentary:

"I find nothing of his Lordship's Midwifry in the bringing forth that Discovery; for that seemed left to a lower

Order. But it is more than probable, he was behind the Curtain, and in the Depths of the Contrivance, and, after the chief Throws were over, he was the Dry-Nurse, and . . . took Charge of leading the monstrous Birth, till it could crawl alone. . . . The Reason, why I say he was in the dark Contrivance, is, that he was too cunning ever to work in a Wheel, of which the active Principle was not perfectly understood, if not entirely commanded, by him. One may guess as much from this Passage. A certain Lord, of his Confidence in Parliament, once asked him what he intended to do with the Plot, which was so full of Nonsense, as would scarce go down with *tantum-non Ideots*; what then could he propose by pressing the Belief upon Men of Common Sense, and especially in Parliament? Its no Matter, said he, the more Nonsensical the better; if we cannot bring them to swallow worse Nonsense than that, we shall never do any good with them."[40]

Anthony Ashley Cooper, soon to become Oates's chief patron, was born at Wimborne St Giles, in Dorset, in 1621. From his mother he inherited the very ancient name of Ashley and that family's diminutiveness of build; from both sides of his family he derived an excellent awareness of the value of money, for Great-grandfather Cooper had founded the Cooper millions on the rape of the monasteries, and Grandfather Ashley had been imprisoned for peculation after the capture of Cadiz by Essex and Effingham. Anthony's father died when the lad was ten years old, leaving him to fight for a rich inheritance with a pack of grasping relatives, and to the care of a tutor, one Mr Strong, a Nonconformist minister, "whom afterwards, in gratitude, he got preferred for his Excellent Talent in haranguing the People against the King and the established Government both in Church and State, to be placed at St Margaret's in Westminster. . . . From this Minister he received those early prejudices against Episcopacy, which stuck by him to his last."[41]

In 1639, having left Oxford without taking a degree, he married the daughter of the Lord Keeper Coventry, an excellent match. When the Civil War broke out, he raised a regiment of foot and a troop of horse at his own expense for the King; and he deserted the Royal Cause in the spring of '44. It is interesting to note the state of that cause at the precise moment when young Cooper chose to leave it. The Parliament had just contemptuously rejected the King's overtures for peace; a Scottish invasion on the Parliament's behalf was imminent; the King's resources were dwindling, Cromwell's star was rising, Newark was closely besieged and even Oxford, the royal headquarters, threatened, Waller had defeated Hopton in the West, and Fairfax Byron at Nantwich. It was, in short, the psychological moment for changing one's coat.

In the year of the King's execution, Anthony Cooper lost his wife. In the following April, when a Royalist reaction looked like a certainty, he married Lady Frances Cecil, sister of the loyal Lord Oxford. She had the tact to die in 1654 before her connections could do her anxious husband any harm, and two years later he married into the immensely wealthy family of Spencer. All through the Interregnum he managed to keep in with whatever faction happened to be on top for the moment, and when the Restoration became inevitable declared himself a Royalist, and was one of the commissioners sent to Breda to invite the King home. On his way thither, his carriage overturned, and he received an injury from which he was to suffer for the rest of his life.

Made a Privy Councillor by the restored Charles, Cooper had the bad taste to sit on the commission which tried his old friends, the regicides. For the next few years he was engaged in engineering the ruin of Hyde, Earl of Clarendon, the leading minister, in amassing a huge fortune, and in striving by every means in his power to make himself the power behind the throne. In '72 his industry was rewarded by the prize he had coveted all along—namely, the Great Seal—and at the same time he was created Earl of Shaftesbury.

So far he had but followed the prevailing fashion of his age, an age which saw the gentle art of trimming carried to a height which would have astonished the simple politicians of the preceding centuries. But Shaftesbury was essentially of his class, the class of squires whose fortunes had been made by the rape of the ancient Church. Money had acquired a new value; whoever held the purse-strings held the power, and power was thus a concrete thing, rapidly ousting authority—even the old sacred authority of the Crown. Shaftesbury's nickname of Shiftsbury was really not quite fair; certainly he had turned his coat any number of times, but the heart which beat beneath it remained stoutly anti-monarchical, and it is obvious that he was a great deal happier, and in his proper element, when, in 1673, he trimmed for the last time and became leader of the Opposition. Not only was he anti-monarchical on principle, but he had a bitter personal grudge against Charles II because that king was his one superior in the art of statesmanship.

It was obvious by this date that King Charles could have no legitimate children, and that his successor would be his brother James. It became Shaftesbury's aim, therefore, to ruin James and prevent his coming to the throne. For if he could do this, he could put in place of the hereditary heir a puppet, a figure-head, who would owe his position to Shaftesbury and his class and so must dance to their tune. There was an excellent candidate to hand, the King's favourite bastard, the Duke of Monmouth. For Monmouth was handsome (which would please the people); he was weak, vain, beloved of his father, jealous of his uncle, and could be relied on to do what he was told when it was manifestly to his own advantage. As for James, he had given the Opposition a mortal weapon against him: he had turned Papist.

In January, 1674, Shaftesbury led an address in the Lords for a proclamation banishing all Papists and reputed Papists from London, solemnly declaring that he knew of the existence of sixteen thousand able-bodied men of that religion who were ready to rise at the Pope's order and cut all Protestant throats. It was the kind of thing that had been said before, and would be said again; and no one except the populace and the fanatics took it very seriously. A more fruitful source of attack upon the King was to keep him short of money; or, rather, to promise him unlimited supplies in return for a statement that he had married Monmouth's mother, and that Monmouth, therefore, was his legitimate heir. Shaftesbury knew very well that Charles had a doting affection for his eldest natural son, and was a little contemptuous of his own brother James; what my lord could not get into his head was that, despite his readiness to use the tricks of the politician, and his weaknesses as a human being, Charles II, on certain matters, could be as adamant as his father. Therefore was Shaftesbury most unpleasantly surprised when the King took advantage of his rashness in declaring that the prorogation of Parliament for fifteen months was illegal, and clapped him and some of his Opposition friends into the Tower. The feel of the iron hand under the velvet glove is always a daunting experience.

It has been mentioned earlier that when Shaftesbury came out of the Tower at the end of February, 1678, after having been forced to eat humble-pie and beg the King's pardon, he found Parliament prorogued, the stolid Danby (whom he hated) supreme, peace in Europe, and the Opposition languishing. Even the old game of blackmailing the King was not worth playing, for the astute Charles had found a secret source of supply in his cousin, Louis of France. Shaftesbury, therefore, had not a single card left in his hand, and luck was so against him that it scarcely seemed worth while to pick one up. But he was a born gambler, and he did pick one up. When he looked at it, he found that fate had dealt him the joker, *alias* Titus Oates.

(7)

On September 25th, Parliament, which was to have reassembled on October 1st, was prorogued by Royal Proclamation to October 21st;[42] for, to the disgust of his Privy Council, King Charles was determined to treat the Plot as the hoax it was, and to enjoy his Newmarket holiday in peace. It is only fair to record Titus's own version of the way in which he dealt with this doubting-Thomas attitude of mind in his Sovereign, though it is necessary to spoil the touching little story by stating that it was not told until after the death of the King, and the triumph of the Opposition in 1688, had made it safe to tell such picturesque lies.

It seems that Titus, appalled by King Charles's attitude towards the Great Design, insisted on some private audiences, and in the privacy of the Royal Closet did not hesitate to let his Majesty know that he was aware of Charles's being secretly reconciled to Rome, and that the real reason why the Papists designed to murder him was that he had not kept his promise to drag a reluctant England to the feet of the Pope. The King, says Titus, quailed before this forthright speech, begged Dr Oates not to make it public, and hastened to assure him that he was now entirely convinced of the authenticity of his disclosures. "Good God, said the King, is this the Kindness that is to be shewed me for all the Favours I have shewed that People? At which his Majesty wept."[43]

On September 30th, several of those already arrested for the Plot were examined by the Council, including Father Ireland and Edward Coleman. The first denied the charges against him and swore that he did not know the mysterious Smith, said by Oates to have shared the latter's lodging and to have received £50 a year for daily information. Smith himself appeared to deny these accusations.[44] In the afternoon, Coleman, who had voluntarily surrendered himself to Sir Joseph Williamson, one of the Secretaries of State, was brought up for examination. He was a Catholic convert, son of a Suffolk parson; he was one of those busy, meddling, over-zealous proselytes who are a liability to their cause and themselves. With a genuine zeal for his religion he combined an unpleasant material greed, and it was plain that he could not distinguish between the two. For several years past, he had been endeavouring, with very little success, to procure money from the French King and his confessor, Père la Chaise, by offering his services in furthering the Catholic cause in England, and in '77 had informed Father St Germain that he could prevent the marriage of the Princess Mary with the Prince of Orange, if a sufficient reward were forthcoming.

In this intriguing with foreigners, Coleman was but following the example of his betters; there was scarce a lord, in the Opposition or out of it, who was not a recipient of Louis's bribes. The Duke of York had rebuked him for his meddling, but he had paid no heed. By the King's command, he was recently dismissed from the service of the Duchess of York, whose secretary he had been, "so that he appear'd seldome at Court, but being known to depend on the Duke, Sir Edmond Bury Godfrey made choice of him, to send his Highness an account of Oates' and Tongue's depositions as soon as he had taken them. The Duke, perceiving Oates had named Coleman [in his *Narrative*], bid him look to himself, for he was sure to find no favour, and therefore if he had any papers that mighte hurt him, to secure them immediately";[45] this friendly hint was acted upon only partially, with the result that the raid on Coleman's house resulted in the seizure of certain papers which bore upon his intrigues with the French.

The failure of Luzancy to make good his accusations against him, and his genuine innocence of the crimes of which Oates accused him now, enabled Coleman to face the new informer with a contempt which seemed justified by a blunder of the first magnitude made by Titus at the outset of the examination. Pointing to Coleman, the Clerk of the Council enquired of Titus: "Do you know this gentleman?" Titus looked at the gentleman (who stood but a few feet away from him), and answered positively that he had never seen him before.

Then, not noticing the curious hush which had fallen, Dr Oates went on to speak of other matters. He was bursting with informations, accusations, denunciations; his memory was growing better every moment. In the midst of his harangue, his ear caught the name Coleman, and to his horror he discovered that the person addressed was the gentleman he had just denied knowing. A lesser man would have lost his nerve; not so the brazen Titus. He knew Coleman perfectly; of course he did. The candle-light which illumined the Council Chamber on that dark afternoon had got into his eyes; that was how he had not recognized him at first glance. The battery of his accusations, intensified by spite, turned full upon Coleman; this was the man who had given away State secrets, as they would find when they came to examine his papers, and it was he who had paid the money to Wakeman to poison the King. The Council, now committed to a belief in Oates's story, though perhaps a little dismayed by that positive "I never saw him before", placed Coleman in the care of a messenger, and made a note to examine his papers without delay.

There is this to be added: That on the self-same day, in the self-same place, Titus, confronted with Sir George Wakeman, the Queen's physician, returned to the question,

"Do you know this gentleman?" the self-same answer, "I never saw him before". It will be seen at the trials of Coleman and Wakeman how Titus attempted to excuse these two extraordinary lapses of a memory so famous for its retentiveness.

An examination of Coleman's papers enabled the infatuated Council to ignore any such lapse for the moment, for at long last here was something concrete in the way of evidence. An impartial reader of these papers must be convinced at once of one outstanding fact: Not one of them contained a single syllable relative to the Plot "discovered" by Oates. But the Privy Council was not composed of impartial readers; it was hot on the scent of this damnable conspiracy, and when it read expressions merely foolish or fanatical it had no hesitation in declaring them to be proofs of Oates's story. From the bundle of papers seized at Coleman's house on the night of September 29th, five were selected, later to be produced at his trial. The first was a long letter from Coleman to La Chaise (unsigned, but Coleman freely owned it as his), asking that priest's help in persuading Louis to send money to Charles II in order that the latter might, despite Parliament's opposition, restore the Duke of York to his command of the Navy, and bring in liberty of conscience. The second was a short, courteous, but wholly noncommittal reply from La Chaise. The third was a "declaration", drawn up by Coleman, but made to seem as though dictated by the King, setting forth the reasons why Parliament should be dissolved. The fourth was a letter, written as it were by the Duke of York, but really by Coleman (as the latter confessed later to the House of Lords), adding his Highness's persuasions to Coleman's to obtain a loan from France. The fifth and last was another letter from Coleman to La Chaise, giving the latter the key to a cipher for future correspondence, and respectfully lamenting that his Most Christian Majesty had not yet sent any money.

A bare summary of these letters shows their folly; but the expressions used in them made them a thousand times more dangerous to the writer. "We have here", wrote Coleman, "a mighty Work on our hands, no less than the Conversion of three Kingdoms, and by that the utter subduing of a Pestilent Heresie, which has domineered over great part of this Northern World a long time; there were never such hopes of success since the death of our Queen Mary, as now in our days." And again: "Success would give the greatest blow to the Protestant Religion that it has received since its birth." Taken in their context, the meaning of these extravagant words was obvious: Coleman hoped for the conversion of England to the Catholic faith through the known toleration of the present King, and the succession of the Catholic Heir Presumptive, a succession which the Opposition was doing its best to prevent and which required, therefore, financial aid from France. Needless to say, they were not taken in their context; and while poor Coleman himself admitted them to be foolish and indiscreet, the Council had no hesitation in declaring that they proved the reality of the Plot.[46]

On October 7th there were some new arrests, among them that of Mr Richard Langhorne, an eminent Catholic barrister, whose sons had been fellow students with Titus at Valladolid. He was thrust into Newgate without any previous examination, and there remained, in close confinement, till his trial in the following June. Two days later, an unknown correspondent wrote to Sir Francis Radcliffe, giving an account of the Plot which shows how garbled were the versions of it even among the educated, for, while Parliament remained in recess, no official statement concerning it had been made. It is to be hoped for Titus's sake that he did not read this particular version:

"Oates, a Jesuit, meeting lately in Italy with the General of that Order, was set on by him to destroy the King and the Duke of Monmouth, either by gun, pistol, or poison. In order thereto, the King being lately at Windsor, he presented a gun or birding-piece against him at a dark window as he was passing by, which certainly would have had its effect, but by a miraculous providence and mercy, the flint always flew out as he was about the doing of it. As to the other way of poison, as the King was in his return from Windsor to London, he was taken with a great thirst and calling hastily for wine, which being presented to him in a glass looked somewhat troubled, whereon he was advised to forbear it, but going on to drink it, he first dipped a piece of bread into it and threw it to one of his dogs, which having hastily eaten it died presently thereof. These are miraculous deliverances. On this plot Oates is taken, which confessed all in a letter to his Royal Highness, who immediately went to his Majesty with it, the fellow, it seems, being struck with amazement and horror of conscience."[47]

This, and other rumours, kept tongues clacking over coffee-cups and tankards during the first two weeks of October, and London gave symptoms of that dread disease called mass hysteria. Yet there was still time to prevent it, for even the mob, though excited by the swinging of lanterns in the dark, the tramp of soldiers' feet, the hammering on doors at dead of night, and the sight of half-dressed gentlemen, rumoured to be Jesuits, being hustled to Newgate, had not yet entirely succumbed to the mania. The King, good-humoured and cheerful as ever, was enjoying himself at Newmarket; Shaftesbury held his hand, intending to make every ounce out of the Plot once Parliament met; and sober men like Evelyn and Burnet looked askance at the informer, Titus Oates.

"While the King was gone [to Newmarket]", wrote Burnet, "Tonge* desired to speak with me. So I sent to him at Whitehall, where both he and Oates were lodged under a guard. I found him so lifted up, that he seemed to have lost the little sense he had. Oates came in, and made me a compliment, that I was one that was marked out to be killed. He had before said the same to Stillingfleet of him: but he made that honour that he did us too cheap, when he said Tonge was to be served in the same manner, because he had translated the Jesuits Morals into English. He broke out into great fury against the Jesuits, and said, he would have their blood. But I, to divert him from that strain, asked him, what were the arguments which had prevailed on him to change his religion, and to go over to the church of Rome? He upon that stood up, and laid his hands on his breast, and said, God and his holy angels knew, that he had never changed, but that he had gone among them on purpose to betray them. This gave me such a character of him, that I could have no regard to anything he either said or swore after that."[48]

* "I had met him at Sir Robert Murray's." Burnet, 281.

Here, then, was the situation in the middle of October, 1678. The symptoms of hysteria were there, but the disease was not yet dangerous; the fuse was lit, but there was still time to stamp upon it ere it reached the gunpowder. If anything, the balance was on the side of health and sanity; the Plot "began a little to cool, and was sinking in its credit."[49] It was at this precise moment that some unknown hand flung into the scales a murdered corpse, and the sanity of London was blown to pieces.

(8)

Ever since he had taken Oates's depositions, Sir Edmund Berry Godfrey had been observed by his acquaintance to be in a state of melancholia extraordinary even for him. He muttered to himself as he paced his chamber or roamed the streets; he burned a mass of papers, and took care in settling all his trifling debts; and now and again he would let fall some disjointed remark which, while it showed distraction of mind, gave no clue to the cause of his uneasiness. "We have not sounded the bottom of this business yet." "Upon my conscience I believe I shall be the first martyr." "Have you heard that I am to be hanged?" "Oates has forsworn himself; Oates is a liar."

There was one reason plain enough (though it was unknown to his friends) why he should be troubled. He had sent a warning to Coleman to burn his papers, and if the papers Coleman had neglected to burn were pronounced treasonable by the Council, the man who had advised him to destroy such evidence of his folly was in no inconsiderable danger. There was also the general position of Godfrey in this crisis. He was an experienced and conscientious justice of the peace, and as such was the nearest approach to a senior police official to be found in those days; and the setting of the Plot, the White Horse tavern, Wild Street, Drury Lane, and so on, was in his own area, which he knew intimately both as a tradesman and a magistrate. It is impossible to imagine a man of his character refraining from making some private investigations after taking Oates's first depositions; and the fact that he came to the conclusion that the whole thing was a malicious fabrication is proved by his warning to Coleman. His friend Mr Robinson later made the interesting disclosure that Godfrey consulted the Lord Chief Justice about his two examinations of Oates; on the other hand, though he had only the bare word of the informers that the King had been made cognizant of the Plot, Godfrey had neglected his duty as a magistrate of assuring himself that this was so, though he had conveyed a private warning of what was afoot to the Duke of York through Coleman. He was, therefore, in a cleft stick, and in this almost certainly lies the meaning of his mysterious words to another friend, Mr Mulys: "Some great men blame me for not having done my duty, and I am threatened by others, and very great ones too, for having done too much."[50]

Whatever it was that was troubling Godfrey, it seems to have come to a head on Friday, October 11th, when a private messenger delivered a note at his house in Hartshorn Lane. The note itself was never found, the identity of the messenger never disclosed; but that evening, at a vestry meeting of his parish church, St Martin's-in-the-Fields, Sir Edmund was observed to be in a state of mind bordering upon distraction. Again he insisted on settling some small private debts, and when he went home he burned a whole armful of papers on his hearth. The following morning, Saturday, October 12th, he rose earlier than usual, and was observed by his clerk to put into his pocket a very large sum of money: seven guineas, four broad-pieces, and four pounds in silver; in modern terms, something in the nature of seventy pounds. Then he went out into Hartshorn Lane.

At intervals during the course of that Saturday morning, he was seen in various parts of the town. He could not but be recognized, for he was "a Man, so remarkable, in Person and Garb, that, described at Wapping, he could not be mistaken at Westminster. He was black, hard-favoured, tall, stooping, wore a broad Hat, and sometimes a Gold Hat-band, and went commonly wiping his Mouth, and looking on the Ground"; "His Daily Custom was to go about alone, creeping at all Hours, in Lanes and Alleys, as his Fancy, or Occasions led him".[51] A friend of his, seeing him pass by in the Strand at dinner-time, invited him in, but Godfrey replied that he was in great haste. This was the last time he was ever seen alive by a friend.

Even before the day was over, a curious rumour that Godfrey was missing had filtered through the town, and the news-letters of this very Saturday carried the rumour into the country. This fact is of great significance, for one may well ask with Roger North: "What a Matter was it, that a Justice of Peace did not dine at home, to raise such a Hubbub as this? A Thing that must, sometimes, happen to everyone, as Business or Friendship may engage them Abroad."[52] Of even greater significance is the fact that the rumour was spiced with the additional report that the Papists had murdered him, for not only does it give the best commentary on the state of London's nerves, but it suggests its being put about by someone who knew the fate designed for Godfrey, knew that he was about to be missing in sober earnest, and already had decided on whom the blame was to be cast.

Godfrey did not return home that night, but even in this there was no real cause for alarm, since it was his custom from time to time to visit his aged mother in Hammersmith. Next day his clerk went thither to enquire, but without result. And now the rumours grew in volume and diversity; Godfrey had been seen at the Earl of Danby's lodging; at the Duke of Norfolk's at Arundel House; at St James's Palace; even at Whitehall. He had eloped with a lady of fortune; he was lying low to escape creditors; he had been discovered in bed with a whore. Monday, Tuesday, and Wednesday passed without news, and the excitement mounted with every hour. On Thursday, at midday, the Reverend Adam Angus, curate of St Dunstan's-in-the-West, was browsing in a bookshop in St Paul's Churchyard, when he was tapped upon the shoulder by a strange young man in a grey suit, who informed him that Godfrey's body had been found in Leicester Fields, "by the Dead Wall", with his own sword run through him. The young man in the grey suit then left the shop, and was never seen again. A search of Leicester Fields revealed no Godfrey.

That same afternoon, the corpse of Sir Edmund Berry Godfrey was found in a ditch near old St Pancras Church at the foot of Primrose Hill, at that time an exceedingly lonely neighbourhood; his own sword was run through the heart. Immediately, the cry which had been merely excited during the past few days swelled into a roar of stark panic, a roar which soon was to shake all England and rock the very throne:

"Godfrey has been murdered by the Papists!"[53]

PART II

THE HEAT OF THE PLOT: OCTOBER 17TH, 1678–JULY 18TH, 1679

(1)

THE death of Sir Edmund Berry Godfrey, one of the most fascinating of unsolved historical mysteries, can be noticed here only in so far as it concerned Titus Oates.

It was to be, against all reason, the chief foundation-stone of his Plot, and as such is part of his story. But the perennial question, Who killed Sir Edmund Berry Godfrey? is not relevant to a life of Oates, and his biographer is denied the pleasure of investigating in detail any one of the many solutions which have been put forward from that day to this. At least twelve different theories have been offered during the last two hundred and sixty years, including one which suggests that Oates himself was the murderer. Though the last-named suggestion was made by such eminent authorities as Lord Birkenhead and Sir James Stephen, it need not be seriously considered, for not only is there lacking the least shadow of evidence to back it up, but a crime of that nature was not in keeping with Titus's peculiar temperament. It is true that his violent temper often expressed itself in bodily assault, as there will be occasion to notice during the course of his history. But he was not a man to run unnecessary risks by killing his enemies with his hands when he could do so with his tongue. Nor was he the type of criminal capable of planning or executing so perfect a murder (for murder it undoubtedly was) as that perpetrated upon Godfrey.

For the rest, it is sufficient to mention that the theory of suicide was thoroughly investigated by L'Estrange in the seventeenth century, and by Mr Alfred Marks in the early years of the twentieth; and the theory of murder, with a variety of different assassins, by many able pens, ancient and modern. Perhaps the most interesting of these solutions is that offered by Mr J. G. Muddiman—namely, that Godfrey was murdered, for reasons of private revenge, by the homicidal maniac, the Earl of Pembroke. Yet, when all is said and done, but two concrete facts have been established; first that the only persons who benefited by Godfrey's death were the managers of the Plot, the Opposition leaders and their tools; secondly, that the three men hanged for the murder were innocent.

On October 18th, the day after the discovery of Godfrey's corpse, the Duke of York, writing to his son-in-law and nephew, the Prince of Orange, added a pathetically casual postscript: "There is another thing happened, which is, that a justice of peace, one Sir Edmundbury Godfrey, was missing some days, suspected by several circumstances, very probable ones, to design the making himself away. . . ."[1] While these words were being written, the cry rose louder yet in every coffee-house, in every tavern, at every street-corner, on 'Change, at the play-house, in the market-place: "The Papists have murdered Sir Edmund Berry Godfrey!"

We may well believe that Dr Titus Oates, living on the fat of the land in Whitehall Palace, was not backward in echoing that cry. He himself, in one of his tracts, was afterwards to admit that the Papists "by that silly and impolitic Murther of Sir Edmund Bury Godfrey rather pour'd oyl then water upon the Fire, and fed that into a blazing Flame, which else they might have easily quench'd, and puft away the Smoke".[2] But that it was "silly and impolitic" on the part of the alleged assassins was not now allowed to be the point. The spectacular appearance of Godfrey's corpse had saved Titus's Plot from extinction, and he and his friends (and he was soon to discover that he had very great and noble friends) were set upon working it up for all it was worth. "This business happen'd well for Oates", says Smith the schoolmaster, "as he afterwards told me: He would usually say, I believe not a Word on't; but my Plot had come to nothing without it; It made well for me; I believe the Council would never have taken any farther notice of me else, if he had not been found: He was a cowardly Rascal, for when I went with my Depositions to him, he was so frighted, that I believe he beshit himself; for there was such a stink I could hardly stay in the Room. This Character he would frequently give of that pretended

Proto-martyr to Popery; and the very person, whose misfortune, even by his own confession, was the very support of his pocket."[3]

Why the Papists should murder the justice who had distinguished himself by his reluctance to persecute them was not, of course, a question the unthinking mob paused to consider for a moment. The more intelligent members of the community explained it vaguely thus: "The common Place was that this daring Fact (an odd Sort of Daring, to kill a Man in a Corner, and hide him three Miles off in a Ditch) was to hinder a farther Search into the Bottom of the Plot. After this, every new Witness, that came in, made us start; now we shall come to the Bottom: And so it continued from one Witness to another, Year after Year, till at last it had no Bottom, but in the Bottomless Pit."[4] In point of fact, it was no longer safe to deny that Godfrey had been murdered by the Papists, since a denial entailed the risk of being implicated in the Plot; so any explanation would serve.

The inquest took place on October 19th, and the verdict of murder was brought in by the testimony of two surgeons who had viewed and opened the body. Other medical practitioners, deeming this testimony unsatisfactory, solicited permission to examine the corpse; but Godfrey's brothers, rich City merchants, successfully opposed the suggestion, for they were afraid of a verdict of *felo de se*, which would deprive them of the succession to Sir Edmund's estate.[5] Next day, the Coroner appeared before the Council; and it is interesting to note that several things mentioned by him on this occasion were afterwards suppressed, as, for instance, the fact that the dead man had eaten nothing for two days before his decease.[6] On the same day, and again on the 24th, the King issued proclamations for the discovery of the murderers; the sum of five hundred pounds and a free pardon were offered to anyone coming forward to make such a discovery. Meantime, the body of Godfrey was conveyed in solemn procession to his own house, the doors of which were flung open so that the populace might enter and gaze their fill upon the mangled corpse of the Protestant martyr.

This public exhibition of the body continued until the funeral on the last day of October.

(2)

Meanwhile, the Council had been busy in putting the final touches to its case of the Popish Plot before the reassembling of Parliament. On the 18th the judges were called in, and the Attorney-General handed Titus's *Narrative* to the Clerk of the Council, having, it would seem, drawn up the complicated rigmarole under heads.[7] A fine legal point was not yet settled: was the evidence of one witness sufficient to indict and convict in cases of High Treason? Two days later, the judges gave it as their opinion that a single witness was not sufficient, "but if one witness swear fully to the point with one or more witnesses concurring in material circumstances to the same fact, it is sufficient to indict or convict for such treason [as compassing the death of the King]".[8] Likewise was there a slight difficulty in the case of Edward Coleman; the judges were called upon to answer: "If the contriving, endeavouring to subvert the Protestant religion, and the restoring the authority of the Pope, by combining with foreign powers, be treason, etc., or, if it be not treason, what crime is it?"[9]

Parliament reassembled on the 21st, and after listening with suppressed indignation to the King's casual reference to the Plot, and his statement that "I shall leave the matter to the law", both Houses combined in appointing November 13th as a solemn fast, and the Commons set about the examination of Titus Oates. They were entirely obsessed by the Plot, and such trifling matters as the preservation of the peace in Flanders, the King's pressing need for supplies, and so on, must be sternly set aside. On the 23rd they had the privilege of a first sight of the now famous Dr Oates at their Bar, and an opportunity of hearing that peculiar voice give in "his Information touching the Plot and Conspiracy mentioned in his Majesty's Speech";[10] he added a description of the Benedictine monks at the Savoy, whereupon the House issued its warrant for a thorough search of those premises, and others for the apprehension of individual monks accused by Oates.

Titus was called in again next day, "and having given in a further Information to the House, touching the said Plot and Conspiracy: *Ordered*, That the Justices of the Peace for the County of Middlesex, and City of Westminster, do withdraw and take the examination of Mr Oates upon Oath".[11] On both these days, the House observed with what must have been something approaching awe the almost miraculous improvement in Mr Oates's already famous memory. New "informations" were continually forthcoming; the General of the Jesuits, by order of the Pope, had drawn up patents for all the chief civil and military posts in England under a Catholic régime; most, if not all, of these patents had been seen by Dr Oates, and many had actually passed through his hands. It is possible that the less credulous among the Members shied a little when they heard the names of the commanders of the new Catholic Army—the gouty old Lord Bellasis, that fiery rebel general, John Lambert, who had lived in prison since the Restoration and was grown senile, Lord Petre, who had never held any military command, Sir Francis Radcliffe, who was wedded to a life of ease; and so on. But the House was not in a mood to be critical, and, sending for the Lord Chief Justice, bade him issue warrants against all the persons named in Titus's latest information. Those to hand—namely, the five Catholic peers, Bellasis, Petre, Powis, Stafford, and Arundell, who were already in the Gatehouse—were committed to the Tower.[12] Impeachment, the customary procedure in such a case, would have given them time to prepare their defence, consult with their friends, and engage legal aid. Besides, this abrupt clapping-up of five peers had the advantage of giving the people the impression that something really dreadful had been discovered concerning them.

On the second day of his examination, Titus was asked if he knew anything further about the Plot, or could name any other persons implicated in it. "He solemnly answer'd He did not; and about nine at Night, the House sent for the Lord-Chief-Justice Scroggs, who took his Examination on Oath, and in the House seal'd twenty six Warrants against several Lords and others, that he had sworn against."[13]

Next day, October 25th, Titus was examined before a full House in the morning, and in the afternoon his place was taken by Dr Tonge. On the 26th, Lord Castlemaine was committed to the Gatehouse; and on Monday the 28th, Titus again regaled the House with his wondrous disclosures. These, the examination of Coleman's papers and of Coleman himself in Newgate, and the searching of the houses of several of Coleman's friends, kept the Commons fully occupied during the next few days. Meantime, Titus was to appear before a more august assembly.

(3)

On the last day of October, the Bishop of Rochester rose in his place in the House of Lords, and informed their Lordships that that very morning, while he was presiding at the Committee for Examinations, newly set up by the Upper House to investigate every ramification of the Plot, the Earl of Peterborough had informed the Committee that the Lord Annesley, son to the Earl of Anglesea, Lord Privy Seal, having had discourse with Mr Titus Oates the previous evening, could apprise the Committee of something of great concern. Annesley, duly called in, had related how Mr Oates had said to him that if he could be heard in the House of Lords, he had something to say which would in a manner clear the Duke of York from the suspicion under which he had fallen as a result of Coleman's letters.[14]

Titus was summoned accordingly; and this was what he had to say. He understood that "Mr Coleman had highly impeached the Duke of Yorke by Letters; to which, he said, he thought the Duke was wholly innocent", and this for the following reasons. First, the Jesuits had a counterfeit seal of the Duke's, and he, Oates, had been sent into Spain with credentials under this seal. (Asked where it was, he replied that it was in the custody of Father Strange.) Next, in February or March last, a criticism had been made by the Jesuits at Ghent that James was not made cognizant of their designs; the reply to this had been that the Duke, though a very good Catholic, had so great a love for the King his brother that he would never prove true to them in a design which included the assassination of Charles. Thirdly, because there was a letter to Father Blundel, seen by Oates, which expressed the longing of the Jesuits to see James trepanned into the business. Fourthly, a certain

Meredith Lloyd had told Titus that there was a parcel of letters to be delivered to James at Windsor, "that he might burn them, thereby to draw the Duke into the Plot". Lastly, because the plotters had drawn up patents and commissions for offices both civil and military without consulting James. Having thus said what he had to say, Titus was commanded to withdraw.[15]

The question immediately arises: Why did Oates concoct and volunteer these elaborate lies in defence of the Catholic Duke of York? And was it his own idea, or was it suggested to him by others?

We cannot be certain whether, in matters connected with his Plot, Titus was already receiving advice from someone knowledgeable in public affairs. The chances are that he was not. But what is quite clear is that his head was completely turned by the unexpected success of Tonge's wild scheme, and that he had come to look upon it as his own invention. Tonge and Oates, heretofore as Simeon and Levi, were already at loggerheads as to which of them had "discovered" the Plot, and were shortly to quarrel violently upon the subject at a public dinner. It had become an article of faith with Titus, not only that it was his Plot and his alone, but that every detail of his *Narrative* was true.

Now, in the *Narrative*, Titus (or Tonge) had made the Jesuits affirm that they were uncertain of the Duke as an ally, and that unless he would put himself wholly under their influence, he must go the way of his brother. Only in one article is there any hit at James, and that a very vague one. It is evident that Titus's accusation of Coleman was a lucky stab in the dark; Coleman was an obvious target, known to everyone as a meddling and indiscreet Catholic convert, and one previously accused by Luzancy. When an examination of Coleman's papers showed a constant use of James's name, and when it became clear that the Opposition was going to make use of this as a handle against the Duke, Titus may have taken fright, lest, instead of backing up his *Narrative*, these papers disproved it; there is the probability likewise that he was scared by the fact that he might be called on to make an accusation against the King's brother, the Heir Presumptive.

But there is another possible explanation of Titus's

unexpected defence of James at this juncture. It is given by Sir George Sitwell thus: "Great care had been taken [by the Opposition] not to alarm the Court. If the Duke of York had been accused at the outset of a conspiracy to kill his brother . . . the Plot would probably have been smothered. . . . But the first sketch of the Plot seemed to offer the King, whose life had been aimed at, an opportunity of maintaining his army, which was to have been disbanded on the 26th August; to the Duke, who was also to be despatched, the Jesuits not being sure of him, a means of recovering his popularity and credit in the country; and to the Lord Treasurer a way of turning the wrath of Parliament into another channel."[16] This is assuming that Titus, when he came forward to clear the Duke on October 30th, was acting on the advice of the Opposition lords who later were to manage the entire Plot. Though this assumption is, in the present writer's opinion, unlikely, it may well have been that Titus, in his decision to clear the Duke, was influenced by the failure of Luzancy, an episode which clearly had stuck in his mind. For it was Luzancy's direct hit at the King which had been the principal cause of that young man's failure.

This much is certain: that when, later, Titus ate his own words by a definite accusation of the Duke, he did so at the instigation of Lord Shaftesbury; Schoolmaster Smith affirms this, and says that Titus told him so.[17] L'Estrange pithily comments upon this right-about-face: "He over-shot himself most Damnably too, in the Bus'ness of the Duke of York in his True Narrative. He goes and Acquits him of the Plot, there, hand over head, before he's aware: And then when he would have given all the Shoes in his Shop afterward to have made a Traytor of him, the Basket was already Pinn'd, and there was no getting of him into't."[18]

(4)

Next day, the last of October, the corpse of Sir Edmund Berry Godfrey was at long last borne to the grave, accompanied by every possible display of pomp and solemnity. It was preceded by seventy-two clergymen in their gowns, and followed by more than a thousand gentlemen, all in deep mourning; many Members of Parliament attended. The fanatical Dr. Lloyd, Rector of St Martin's-in-the-Fields, appeared in the pulpit to preach the funeral sermon; he was escorted thither by a bodyguard of two stalwart gentlemen dressed as parsons, whose business it was to see that no attempt upon his life was made by any lurking Papist. He took as his text the words "As a man falleth before the wicked, so fellest thou", and proceeded first to a statement that Godfrey had been murdered for his attachment to the Protestant religion, and then to a violent denunciation of the Catholics. As the hot words fell upon the excited congregation, and the bells tolled over the heads of the thousands who overflowed into the streets, an ache for vengeance filled every breast, and London's dangerous malady approached its crisis.

Dr Titus Oates was not, it is regrettable to have to say, amongst the mourners. He was fully occupied in the Lords' House, whither he had been summoned immediately after Prayers, and directed to "proceed in giving an Account of the Commissions given to several Lords, and other Persons, for offices Civil and Military: Upon which, he proceeded in a particular Narrative thereof, with some Circumstances tending to make out the Truth thereof. And then was commanded to withdraw, but stay without. Then, upon Consideration had thereof, The Lord Chancellor, by Directions of the House, caused him to be called in again; and told him, 'That the Lords expect not his entering into Particular Circumstances; but, if there be particular Persons concerned, of what Quality soever they be, the House expected he should name them.' But he named none, but those he had mentioned in his Narrative; nor could name no other Person."[19] Later he was complimented by the Lord Chancellor on all he had done, and informed that the House had recommended to the Duke of Monmouth the care and safety of his person, to the Lord Chamberlain of the Royal Household the provision of better accommodation at Whitehall, and to the Lord Treasurer of England the supply of his necessities.[20]

On the same day, the Lords gave order for the arrest of four schoolmasters, including William Smith, and two booksellers, all on the accusation of Titus, and directed that they should be brought to the Bar of the House next day.[21] Later it transpired that Titus's object in having Smith arrested was to induce him to appear as a witness against Matthew Medburne the actor (against which humble benefactor Titus had conceived a most bitter hostility), and Smith therefore was merely to be frightened. At the schoolmaster's examination, his former pupil said he did not know him, but had heard a Mr Kirkby of the Guards say that he had heard Smith swear he would "dismember the King".[22] Even in their present state of infatuation, the Lords could not stomach such hearsay evidence; but although they did not imprison Smith, they revoked his licence to teach.[23]

As for the other victims, Oates was reckless enough to accuse one of the schoolmasters, Mark Preston, of having heard his confession, whereas Preston was able to prove that he was a married man with a family; Glisson, another of them, accused by Oates of instilling Popish principles into his pupils, turned out to be a staunch Protestant and produced a licence from the Bishop of London's Chancellor to keep a school; and the charges against both the booksellers were dismissed as trifling. These two, and Glisson, escaped scot-free, but the unfortunate Preston was committed to Newgate, and was still there in the following April;[24] Smith was placed in the custody of Black Rod and set free three days later minus his livelihood; and young Richard Langhorne, accused by Oates of having received, in the latter's presence, one of the Popish commissions intended for Lord Arundell, was returned to the prison from whence he came.[25]

On November 7th, Titus was called to the Bar of the House of Lords to identify one John Blundel, but was kind enough to admit that he did not know him, adding that the person named in his *Narrative* was one Nicholas Blundel. On this day their Lordships ordered that the King be petitioned to grant Oates a pardon, a warrant for which was issued on the 10th;[26] and on the 16th they further addressed the King, "That His Majesty will be pleased to give Leave, that Tytus Otes may name to His Majesty Two Persons such as His Majesty shall approve of, to be with and attend the said Tytus Otes upon his necessary Occasions;

and that His Majesty will be pleased to give Order to the Lord Treasurer, that such allowances of Money may be made to the said Tytus Otes as his necessary Occasions shall require".[27] On the 18th, his Majesty agreed to allow Oates two servants, but ventured to draw their Lordships' attention to the fact that he had already provided money for Titus's "necessary Occasions".[28] The Lord Treasurer gravely informed the House next day "That Mr Otes had sent to him for Two Hundred Pounds, whereas there hath been paid him already One Hundred and Twenty Pounds, to supply his Necessities". The House, finding itself like to be involved in a question of some delicacy, "left it to His Majesty".[29]

Meantime, Shaftesbury had launched his first direct attack upon the Duke of York. On November 2nd, he had declared in an impassioned speech that the only way to save the country was to dismiss James from the Council; Russell moved the same in the Commons. On the 4th, an address to this purpose was presented to the King. On the 9th, James obeyed his brother's command, and from his seat in the Lords announced that he had resigned from the Privy Council; on the same day, the King made a speech which, considering his disbelief in the Plot, was extremely unworthy of him, asking both Houses to pass laws to curtail his brother's power, and to "think of some more Effectual Means for the Conviction of Popish Recusants."[30] Though no blood had yet been shed, persecution hung darkly over the Catholics of England; already many small tradesmen had been ruined by the recent proclamations against Papists, and the London jails were overcrowded with members of that religion, many of whom were destined never to be brought to trial.

The Commons, unsatisfied, pressed for the passing of a Bill which would expel James from the Court. A Bill of this nature was passed on the 20th, but, while it laid still harsher penalties on Catholics in general, it contained a proviso that these should not extend to the Duke. Despite the efforts of the Opposition to reject this proviso, and their frenzied cries of "Coleman's letters! Coleman's letters!" it was carried by a majority of two. On the last day of November, the royal assent was given to the Bill; and by it the Duke of Norfolk, the Earls of Shrewsbury, Berkshire, Portland, Cardigan, and Powis, Viscounts Montague and Stafford, and Lords Mowbray, Audley, Stourton, Petre, Arundell, Hunstan, Bellasis, Langdale, Teynham, Carrington, Widdrington, Clifford, and Gerard of Bromley lost their birthright of a seat in the House of Lords, which unjust proscription must extend to their descendants.[31]

Baffled for the moment in their direct attack on James, Shaftesbury and his friends concentrated on other and more oblique ones. Before noticing these, it is necessary to greet the dramatic reappearance of an old friend of Titus Oates.

(5)

On the last day of October, the Secretary of State had received a most peculiar letter. It contained the request that the writer, who signed himself William Bedloe, should be taken into custody in the city of Bristol, whither he was travelling after a spell in one of the London jails, and brought back under a guard to London.[32] Accordingly, on November 5th, a warrant for his own apprehension had been sent to Bedloe himself, with directions to deliver it to the Mayor of Bristol, and to repair to London "in the privatest manner you may".[33] Mr Bedloe chose instead to have himself arrested in the most public manner possible, and travelled under a guard to a London which already hummed with rumours regarding him. The key to the mystery was very simple: Mr Bedloe, down on his luck again, had heard of that five hundred pounds' reward offered to the discoverer of the Godfrey assassins.

On November 7th he was examined in the presence of the King by both Secretaries of State.[34] He knew nothing, he said, of the Plot, but everything about the murder of Justice Godfrey. He had seen the corpse at Somerset House; Godfrey had been stifled (this was an unfortunate slip, as afterwards transpired) by two Jesuits, Walsh and Le Faire, who were assisted by one of Lord Bellasis' gentlemen and a waiter in the Queen's Chapel. He himself had been offered two thousand guineas if he would help remove the body, but most nobly had refused. It had been carried out of

Somerset House at nine o'clock on the night of Monday, October 14th, by three persons unknown to him, but retainers at Somerset House.

Next morning he was brought to tell his story to the House of Lords, and it was wonderful what a good night's sleep had done for his memory. He still knew nothing of Oates himself, but he had been told by Walsh and Le Faire of the commissions received by Lords Bellasis and Powis, and of the authority given to Lord Arundell to appoint other officers. This provoked the King to exclaim: "Surely the man has received a new lesson during the last twenty-four hours!"[35] By the twelfth, Bedloe's memory had improved to such a degree that he was able to give quite a long account of the Plot, with the exact number of troops appointed to land in England, the names of their commanders, the victims marked out for assassination, and so on. Also, he had remembered that Godfrey had not been stifled (for he had learnt by this time the findings of the inquest), but strangled with a linen cravat. All sorts of new details had come back to him about the actual murder, and he did not spare his own character in the recounting. "I heard him", said Bramston, "when he came into the House of Commons first to make his narrative standing at the barr. He begann thus: 'Mr Speaker, I have binn a great rogue; but had I not binn soe I could not have knowne these things I am now about to tell you.' "[36]

The Opposition leaders welcomed Bedloe with open arms; and this for two special reasons. Up till now, they had been quite unable to make an arrest for the murder of Godfrey, and this had displeased the mob, who were in the mood for blood. And, secondly, they were minded to make an oblique attack against James through the Duke's good friend, Samuel Pepys. They had in custody Pepys' young clerk, Samuel Atkins, and their plan was to frighten Atkins into accusing Pepys, and Pepys into accusing James. So far, however, they had been baffled by the unexpected obstinacy of young Atkins; not one word would he say against his master. [37] The advent of Bedloe offered a solution to this difficulty; all they had to do was to hint to that co-operative gentleman that another improvement of his memory, on the lines that he had seen Atkins in the group about Godfrey's corpse at Somerset House, would be welcome to them.

Mr Bedloe was only too ready to oblige; but again there was a check. Atkins, for a young man of slightly debauched character (he had been in trouble with his master more than once for his love of wine and women), continued to be most irritatingly dumb. Far from admitting his guilt, he was occupying his time in Newgate in an endeavour to remember how he had spent the crucial days between Godfrey's disappearance and the discovery of the corpse; and he believed that, given time, he could do so. Meantime he said stoutly: "No fear of death shall make me tell a solemn lie to the prejudice of anyone." The only thing to do with a man like that was to keep him in close confinement, and trust to prison conditions and the shadow of the noose to bring him to his senses.

Failing to make good use of Bedloe, at least for the moment, Shaftesbury turned in another direction for aid in the next move in his game. There is no room for doubt that, if he had not done so already, this was the moment when he took into his unofficial employ, and under his powerful patronage, the original informer, the "First Discoverer", Titus Oates.

(6)

On the evening of November 23rd, a Mrs Lloyd,[38] sent by Tonge, but obviously acting on the instructions of someone far greater, went to Whitehall to solicit a private audience with the King for Dr Oates. After some hesitation, Charles agreed to see him next morning; and on the 25th that braying voice once more startled the Council with brand-new "discoveries". They were the most dangerous he had made up to date, yet he seems to have voiced them without any trepidation, notwithstanding the fact that he had now to give himself the lie and accuse yet another victim, and a very great one, whereas, as has been noted, he had sworn before the Lords on October 31st that he knew of no other persons concerned in the Plot.

His new information was a direct attack upon no less a person than the Queen. Previous to this, on November

13th, he had made a few evasive hints about her Majesty to the Council. Catherine, he had said on this former occasion, had sent several sums of money to the Jesuits, who had offered her in return 500 masses, 650 pairs of beads, and 1,150 mortifications, and she had two Jesuits "at her elbow", but he dared not say "they have any plot".[39] Now, however, but twelve days later, he had no hesitation in informing the Council that, in July last, he had seen a letter in which it was affirmed by Sir George Wakeman that the Queen had given her consent to the murder of the King her husband. Moreover, in August, he had accompanied several Jesuits to Somerset House, and, when they were admitted to the Queen's presence, he was left in the ante-chamber. But they had most obligingly left the door ajar; "he had the curiosity to listen"; and he distinctly heard a female voice exclaim: "I will no longer suffer such indignities to my bed! I am content to join in procuring his death, and the propagation of the Catholic Faith!" Soon afterwards, the Jesuits came out of the Presence Chamber and went away, leaving Oates to follow at his leisure. So he took the liberty of looking into the room they had vacated, and there saw "no other woman than the Queen".

Now, all this was very dangerous ground, and the Privy Council was flustered and uneasy. Why had not Mr Oates mentioned this important information earlier? He had kept it to say privately to the King, replied Titus, ignoring the fact that according to his story it was in July he had first heard about the Queen's assent to the murder. Did he know the Queen? Had he ever been in her presence before? He had seen her, answered Titus vaguely. Then, as usual, he went on to invent some new details. He remembered now that the incident he had described had occurred just after High Mass (Titus loved these Popish terms, well calculated to bring a shudder to good Protestant frames). There had been some persons with him in the ante-room, whose names he did not know, but none save himself had had the curiosity to listen at the half-closed door. The Jesuits who had taken him to Somerset House were Fathers Fenwick, Keynes, and Harcourt, and one other whose name he had forgotten. The Lord Treasurer gently prompted him: Langworth? That was it, agreed Titus, Langworth. Why, he was asked, did the Jesuits go to Somerset House on this occasion? They were sent for by the Queen; she had sent a messenger to bring them, one Sir Robert, or perhaps Sir Richard, a nimble man of ordinary stature about forty-five years old. Titus could not swear to this person if he saw him. Do you know Mr Bedloe? asked someone. Titus immediately turned evasive. It was like he had seen him but he did not know him by that name. Again the question, "Why not say all this earlier? And why answer heretofore, being asked, That he had nothing more to say against any great persons?" If he had, replied Titus airily, he must crave the Council's pardon, but he had just not understood the question. Had he any notes or papers on this business, such as he had all along said he had handled when employed by the Jesuits in the Plot? Titus answered firmly, No, he durst not trust such a thing to paper.[40]

The reaction of the King to this story was very different from that expected by Oates's mentor, the Earl of Shaftesbury. The trouble with Shaftesbury was that he knew men's weaknesses, but not their strengths. He was aware that the King had no love for his plain little Portuguese wife, and that he longed for an heir. He had calculated, therefore, that Charles would jump at the excuse provided by this tale to divorce Catherine, and marry a woman who could provide him with one. Shrewd men like Shaftesbury are sometimes very simple; they take it for granted that because a person is weak in one direction, he will be so in all. Charles was an adulterer; therefore it was impossible for him to be loyal to his wife. But it was not impossible. The Council was flustered by Oates's story; Charles was frankly furious; and the resolution he displayed in defence of his neglected wife astonished the Opposition.

The first thing he did was to order the Earls of Ossory and Bridgewater to conduct Titus to Somerset House next day and compel him to point out to them the room and the ante-chamber he had described. Titus did not relish this at all, for in actual fact the only occasions when he had been to this vast, rambling palace were those on which he had begged from the Catholic priests there in the days of his destitution. As he dared not commit himself, he was forced to suffer a sudden lapse of memory; the situation would have been comic had it not been so tragic, for the little procession spent hours wandering up and down and round and round searching for a non-existent pair of stairs and a couple of mythical rooms. "In all the Search he made for a Pair of Stairs, he said, the Stairs he sought for were a light Pair of Stairs, and the Rooms they [the conspirators] went to had great Folding Doors, and were high large Rooms."[41] Lord Ossory, writing to his mother, the Duchess of Ormonde, on November 30th, related with satisfaction how "in matter of fact as to the house, wee found him in a manifest lye, which will appear under our hands".[42] The second part of the King's counterattack took the form of an order "gating" or confining Titus within his apartments at Whitehall, with instructions to his guards that no one was to converse with him in private. But in this sad plight he was soon to find an unexpected friend; the way in which this good news was conveyed to him is thus described by his servant, John Lane:

"About the time when . . . Mr Titus Oates did impeach the Queen, and was therefore confined to his Chamber, and no body suffered to speak to him in private, his Father and I coming about Eight a Clock at Night from Westminster-Hall, he bid me, if possible I could speak to his Son, deliver him words from him to this purpose, that he should not fear, nor be daunted, but chear up, and Impeach the Woman, since he so well knew that Mr Bedlow was resolved to assist him in his Evidence against her (which Woman old Mr Oates, Father to Mr Titus Oates, did explain afterwards to me to be the Queen).* This was written by me, and copied by George Neal, who then served Mr Titus Oates, and who told me he delivered those words in writing under a Dish of Meat to Mr Titus Oates, who privately put it in his Pocket. This I took notice of, because we all then thought, and Mr Oates told us, that he had no body to assist him in his Evidence against the Queen."[43]

Old Samuel's good news was true. When Titus was called to the Bar of the House of Commons on November 28th, he beheld his old acquaintance, William Bedloe, secure in a newly acquired pardon for all offences committed up to

* Titus's own nickname for her Majesty was "Dame Short-Arse".

date,[44] and ready and willing to back up Titus's dangerous accusation against the Queen of England. The doubtful acquaintance of Valladolid had turned into a friend indeed. Bedloe had his lesson off pat; he had overheard the Queen give her consent in October (according to Titus, she had already given it in July, but such little discrepancies were really beside the point); she and the conspirators had had a conference regarding the murder of her husband in one of the galleries of Somerset House, with Mr Bedloe listening underneath it. She had been reluctant at first, but the persuasions of Lord Bellasis, Mr Coleman, two French clergymen names unknown, and several Jesuits, had worn down her resistance. To the question, Why had he concealed this vital information when he had been examined about the Godfrey murder, Mr Bedloe answered with sublime simplicity that it had escaped his memory.

The Members were now to have a great thrill. They beheld the figure of Dr Titus Oates, in all the glory of silk gown and bands, take Bedloe's place at the Bar; and they heard that strange, high voice raised to a pitch which echoed round the Chamber, as he gave vent to the memorable words:

"Aye, Taitus Oates, accause Caatharane, Quean of England, of Haigh Traison!"

The state of English politics at this date cannot be better illustrated than by the reaction of the Commons to such an accusation. On the bare word of an obscure informer, they immediately voted an address for the removal of the Queen and her household from Whitehall, making no bones about treating their Sovereign's consort as a convicted traitress, she, a foreigner in a strange land, and a woman known to be loyal to her husband and to her adopted people, and one who, from her first coming over, had stood aloof from politics. A message was sent to the Lords soliciting their immediate concurrence. The Lords, who had not yet lost all sense of decency, replied with dignity that Oates and Bedloe should be examined by them next morning.[45] Titus, meanwhile, submitted a complaint to the Committee for Examinations regarding the restraint laid upon him. He could speak to no one in private, he said, "not so much as his own Father", he was bereft of his servants, and all his letters were read by the King's order. He desired the Committee to move the Lords to order him his former freedom, and also "some Supply of Money, in regard he is out of Purse about Fourscore Pounds on his own Account, about this Business, since the 11th of August last".[46] He added a request for the renewal of his pardon; for there was the unpleasant possibility, that, despite the protection of Shaftesbury and the credulity of the Commons, he had gone too far in accusing the Queen.

On the 29th, he and Bedloe appeared at the Bar of the House of Lords. Titus, before coming to the business in hand, made a personal appeal to their Lordships on the subject of his restraint, which he prayed might be taken off, that he might give his evidence "more chearfully". The Lords, however, were in no mood to listen to such grievances; what they wanted to know was, Why had he said, in this very place, upon October 31st, that he had no other person to accuse than those he had already named? Titus's reply was feeble even for him. What he had meant was, " 'That he had no more to name, meaning of this House, before whom he then was.' " Ignoring this for the moment, the Lords shot at him another question almost as embarrassing; why, when he had made his first accusation against Sir George Wakeman, had he said nothing about the letter in which he now said Wakeman had affirmed that the Queen had given her consent to the murder of the King? The best that Titus could manage in the way of explanation was that on that occasion he had been up two whole nights priest-hunting, and was so weary that he had forgotten it. In how many hands could he himself write, asked one of the Lords significantly. Titus, not at all put out, made the naïve admission "that, when he saw a Hand that pleased him, he endeavoured to imitate the same". The earls of Ossory and Bridgewater then made their report of conducting Titus over Somerset House in a vain search for the apartments he had described to the Council.[47]

Bedloe having done no better at his examination, their Lordships, after wringing from him an admission "that he had no more to say of any Persons either in or out of this House than he had already charged", resolved to refuse their concurrence with the Commons' address for the removal of the Queen from Whitehall; this despite the vigorous protest of Shaftesbury and two of his fellow Oppositionists. All they would do was to vote for an address for the apprehension of all Papists within the realm; and the impeachment of the five Catholic lords in the Tower was carried. Shaftesbury had failed again, and the charge against the Queen was allowed to be buried in silence. There remains only to be added a most curious "information" concerning it, volunteered, long afterwards, by Titus's brother, Constant Oates, a glazier in Southwark:

"About the accusing of the Queen Dr Tonge told me in Dr Oates' chamber at Whitehall that there would be a sudden blow given, meaning a rising, and therefore advised me to get certain houses for him and the Doctor to fly to to preserve themselves and also desired me to persuade all my friends and acquaintances to get arms to defend themselves for the Papists had great interest at Court. He further told me to prepare grenadoes, as he called them, made of glass bottles with holes in them like grenado shells, filled with powder and wildfire, saying they would do more mischief than ten men could, being flung into a body of men or houses, and that it was good to have half a dozen of them in an house. To this end, he said, he had taken several houses, both above and below Bridge, for them to fly to, and that the place I propounded was the fittest of all for them to fly to, it being a meal shop and a Presbyterians. He intended to disguise himself, and that, if they did not stand by him now, meaning the Protestants, they deserved to perish with the Doctor. He said, they were resolved to go through with it now, although they were in great danger, and that he feared that, when the Doctor accused the Queen, he would be hanged."[48]

(7)

The initial stages of the Plot were now concluded; there were to follow the trials of the victims, a series of trials which form the blackest page in the history of English law, and which, for a blatant and cynical disregard for even the rudiments of justice, have not their equal in the records of judicial butchery.

By this date the London jails, and especially Newgate, were filled with men of all conditions, who were now to face packed juries, judges who did not even pretend to be impartial, a parcel of accusers drawn from the most degraded of mankind, and a howling mob which, denied the spectacle of the quartering-block and disembowelling-hook at Tyburn, undoubtedly would have stormed the jails and lynched the victims. From the moment of their arrest, the prisoners were kept in solitary confinement, denied legal aid, debarred from all communication with the outside world, and left to make what defence they could against the accusations of Titus's and his comrades' elastic memories from the knowledge of the charges levelled against them at their examination before the Council; one at least of the victims, the barrister, Langhorne, was never examined at all. During the course of the next few months, many of these unfortunates succumbed to the horrors of contemporary prison conditions, and so escaped the mockery of a trial; among these were Fathers Bedingfield and Mico, Dr Fogarty, and the poor comedian, Medburne. The rest awaited their ordeal, heavily fettered, denied sleep through the continual howling of the mob round the prisons, and given at most a week's notice of their trial ere they were placed in the dock.

When judges and juries alike behaved in so indecent a manner, it is difficult to apportion blame. The real responsibility rested with the Opposition leaders, who so inflamed the mob that any other verdict than that of "Guilty" would have resulted in a riot. "That incredible fictions should ever pass in courts of justice, without the courts making just observations upon them, was extraordinary: But care was taken to terrify the judges with shouts and acclamations on the one part, and hissings on the other, by which they were to be persuaded, not only by the sense of the people, but of their violent desires, whereby they might imagine dangers to themselves if they should appear to check the stream."[49] The judges could argue with some justice that "if an apostle had spoken against [the evidence], no impression had taken place, nor had it done the prisoners any service".[50] The hysteria which had seized upon the nation had affected high and low alike; to deny the reality of the

Plot was to be suspected of participation in it; fear, hatred, and credulity were the ruling passions of the hour, and held sway over the Lords of the Privy Council as over the meanest beggar in the streets. Worst of all, the King himself, though continuing completely sceptical, swam with the tide.

The best that can be said for the conduct of King Charles the Second during the Popish Terror has been said by Mr Arthur Bryant. To wait till the storm had spent itself, to let the law take its course, was all he could do to save his country from a renewal of civil war. It may be so. It may be that as a statesman his conduct was brilliant; but there can be no doubt that as a king, as the father of all his people, his conduct was despicable. None knew better than he what "letting the law take its course" meant at that precise moment; none knew better than he that the victims were innocent. In riding out the storm to avert civil war, he sacrificed a section of his subjects to mob violence and party hate; he was responsible, not only for the victims who died upon the scaffold, but for all those unfortunates, known and unknown, who perished in the jails, for the hearts that were broken, the families divided, the livelihoods lost in this dreadful persecution. If he averted civil war, he allowed instead the utter degradation of his country, an England bankrupt of integrity. His conduct during the Popish Terror can be explained only by his famous maxim: "I intend never more to go upon my travels." Anything, even dishonour, was preferable to the exile he had endured for nineteen mortal years.

The person who embodied the King's justice at the ensuing trials was one well fitted for his sinister task. His name was William Scroggs; he had been knighted in 1676, and in May of this year, 1678, had been made Lord Chief Justice. He was popularly supposed to be the son of a butcher, though actually his father was an Oxfordshire squire. North sums up his character thus: "He was a Man that lay too open; his Course of Life was scandalous, and his Discourses violent and intemperate. His Talent was Wit; and he was Master of Sagacity and Boldness enough; for the setting off of which, his Person was large, and his Visage broad. He had a fluent expression, and many good

Turns of Thought and Language. But he could not avoid Extremities; if he did ill, it was extremely so, and if well, in Extreme also."[51] His well-doing was not in evidence during the Plot trials, for he was a frank careerist, and since it was clear that the nation, from Parliament downwards, desired the blood of the victims, his verdicts were a foregone conclusion.

On the other hand, the Attorney-General, Sir William Jones, "was a man of excellent parts and learning in the laws, a courteous and fine speaker, and with good manners. . . . No man had a more clear head, and of a polite behaviour."[52] He seems to have had singularly little to do at the trials, the Lord Chief Justice taking upon himself the case for the prosecution. As for the juries, they were shamelessly packed, particularly during the later trials, when they were impanelled by the two Sheriffs, Slingsby and Bethel, fervent Oppositionists.

A word must be added regarding the printed accounts of the trials. There was no official reporting; short-hand writers were present in court, and these were engaged by the informers or the Plot-managers; their reports had to be submitted to the censorship of the judges and the Attorney-General before they were printed, and it followed as a matter of course that a great deal of evidence was suppressed. The printed trials formed a perquisite of Oates and his colleagues; in December, 1678, Titus petitioned the Lord Chief Justice "for the power of taking and printing the trials as shall be tried on account of the late plot discovered by him",[53] and we may be sure that he was careful to allow no really damning refutation of his "evidence" to appear in such versions. Lord Castlemaine was later to complain that his own and his witnesses' answers were "strangely mangled and lamed" in the printed reports; and the curious reader may get some idea of this "mangling" from a tract entitled *Some of the most Material Errors and Omissions in the late Printed Tryals of the Romish Priests at the Old-Baily*, published in January, 1679.*

* In the following pages, the quotations are from the 1719 edition of the *State Trials*, as being the oldest. It is not possible to give page references, as the pages in this edition are so often numbered incorrectly.

A TRUE NARRATIVE OF THE HORRI

HELLISH POPISH PLOT, THE SECOND PART

(8)

The first victim to be brought up for trial was a Catholic goldsmith, or, as we should say, banker, William Staley, on November 20th. It was, so to speak, a dress-rehearsal for the main drama, and the object of it seems to have been chiefly to inspire terror; as Oates did not appear as a witness, a very brief account of the business will suffice.

Staley was accused by a man named Carstairs of saying to a friend of the former's, a Frenchman named Firmin, that the King was a rogue and persecuted the people of God, and that he, Staley, would stab him if nobody else did. These words Carstairs swore he overheard in an eating-house in Covent Garden. He went next morning to Staley and demanded money in return for his silence; Staley, aware of his own innocence, refused. He was immediately apprehended, and five days later tried and found guilty. Firmin, his friend, though not tried, was charged with the same offence, and therefore could not give evidence in rebuttal. While under condemnation, Staley was asked if he knew anything of the Plot; he answered no, and continued to the end to deny the words sworn against him. "He was executed at Tyburn, where he behaved himself very decently."[54] Carstairs, his accuser (of whom Burnet gives the most odious character), died not long afterwards, ordering that his corpse be cast into some ditch like a dog's, because he said he was no better.[55] In this repentance he was, as will be seen, almost unique among the gang of informers. In the following year, hearing that Staley's relatives had had a mass said for his soul, the Lord Chief Justice ordered the goldsmith's corpse to be dug up, his quarters displayed on the City gates, and his head stuck on one of the poles of London Bridge.

Staley suffered on November 26th, and next day Edward Coleman took his place in the dock at the Old Bailey. The King had promised him that if he made a satisfactory confession he should have a pardon; such promises seem to have been made by Charles at the outset of the Terror in an effort to prevent the effusion of blood, but undoubtedly they were made later by the Opposition with the object of inducing one or other of the victims to turn evidence against his friends and so corroborate the far from satisfactory testimony of "Dr" Oates. Coleman, while he freely and frankly acknowledged that he had acted foolishly, and while he voluntarily yielded up the cipher to his correspondence, which contained evidence of his pecuniary transactions with France, to the Committee of the House of Commons ordered to visit him in Newgate, continued stoutly to deny all knowledge of the conspiracy. The charges against him fell under two heads: his proposing a rebellion against Charles II entailing his death; and his effort to procure "aids and assistances" from the French. If aids and assistances could be interpreted as arms, instead of what they actually were, money, this constituted High Treason.

Titus was the first witness.[56] No sooner was he risen on his bandy legs than he was addressed by the Lord Chief Justice in a very solemn and respectful manner. There was no reason in the world why Mr Oates (when he remembered, Scroggs even called him Dr Oates) should say anything not strictly true. "I would not have a tittle added for any advantage. . . . You have taken an Oath, and you being a Minister, know the great regard you ought to have of the sacredness of an Oath; and that to take a Man's Life away by a false Oath is murther, I need not teach you that." (As circumstances were to prove, more ironical words were never spoken.) In regard to the manner in which he gave his evidence, Dr Oates was to "take your own way and your own method".

Thus encouraged, and secure in the knowledge that the Bench, the jury, and the entire body of spectators were with him to a man, Titus launched upon his evidence. In the previous November, Coleman had entertained in his house one John Keines or Keynes, confessor to several converts, of whom Oates was one. Going to visit Keynes there, Oates was seen by Coleman, who enquired who he was. Keynes replied that he was one who was about to be sent to St Omers, whereupon Coleman gave him a letter to the Rector of that college. Needless to say, upon his way thither Titus opened it, and found it to contain treasonable expressions. Prompted by the Attorney-General, Oates then described the "Grand Consult" of the Jesuits at the White Horse tavern in the Strand, adding that the resolution to murder the King, officially adopted on that occasion, had been communicated to Coleman in his hearing at Wild House. Likewise that it was mentioned by Coleman in several of his letters; not one of these letters could Titus produce, and indeed it did not seem to occur to the Court to ask for them.

So the solemn lies continued. Coleman had been present at that other "Consult" between the Benedictines and the Jesuits in August, at which the murder of the Duke of Ormonde was planned and 40,000 "Black Bills" ordered for the rebellion in Ireland. Oates had been in Langhorne's chamber and had seen Coleman's commission from the General of the Jesuits to be Secretary of State. Coleman had been orderd to approach Wakeman about the poisoning of the King, and was instrumental in hiring the Four Irish Ruffians. And so on. Obviously he was enjoying himself, was Titus; here he stood in his smart silk gown, chief witness for the Crown, with the judges of England deferring to him, the Attorney-General beaming approval upon him, the mob in the public galleries hanging on his words. But when at last the prisoner was permitted to cross-examine, things became not quite so pleasant.

For Coleman immediately began on that awkward moment when Titus had denied knowing him in the Council Chamber. Mr Oates had said then, definitely and positively, that he had never seen the gentleman before, whereas "he is extremely well acquainted with me now, and hath a World of Intimacy". Titus stood on his dignity and made his former excuse: "my sight was bad by Candle-light, and Candle-light alters the sight much". This had been good enough for the Council; it was not, apparently, quite good enough for the Lord Chief Justice. Gently but firmly, Scroggs required to know of Dr Oates how it was that, apart from not seeing Coleman properly, he had not laid more to his charge on that occasion. Titus fell back on what was to become a favourite and famous excuse: "then was I so weak, being up two nights, and having been taking prisoners, upon my Salvation, I could scarce stand upon my Legs". But it was clear that Scroggs was not altogether satisfied, and, perhaps because he sensed this, Coleman pressed his accuser hard.

"*Coleman.* Pray ask Mr Oates, whether he was not as near to me as this Gentleman is, because he speaks of his Eyes being bad.

"*Mr Oates.* I had the disadvantage of a Candle upon my Eyes; Mr Coleman stood more in the dark.

"*Coleman.* He names several times that he met with me in this Place and that Place, a third and fourth Place about Business.

"*Mr Oates.* He was altered much by his Periwig in several Meetings, and had several Perriwigs, and a Perriwig doth disguise a Man very much; but when I heard him speak, then I knew him to be Mr Coleman." To the further question, why, having recognized Coleman by his voice, he had not accused him of the crimes he now laid to his charge, Titus replied with sweet reasonableness: "Because I was not asked."

He was followed by his principal lieutenant, William Bedloe. This gentleman was now as conversant with the ramifications of the Plot as Oates himself, and had been almost as active in it; he had carried over a large package of treasonable letters from Coleman to Père la Chaise, had heard two French abbots and several English monks discussing the Plot, and had carried back letters to Coleman and Father Harcourt. And he had been called into the latter's room specially to hear Coleman say that "if he had a hundred Lives, and a Sea of Blood to carry on the Cause, he would spend it all to further the Cause of the Church of Rome, and to establish the Church of Rome in England: And if there was an hundred Heretical Kings to be deposed he would see them all destroyed".

The five documents selected by the Council from among the papers seized at Coleman's house were then produced, read, and commented upon. After this, the prisoner desired that Oates be recalled; the latter, pleading fatigue, had withdrawn to refresh himself, and probably was not too well pleased to be brought back, especially as Coleman was now being tiresomely persistent on the subject of dates. He wanted to know on what days of the month in April and May Titus had been with him. Mr Oates was immediately at his vaguest. He could not be sure, but he believed it was within two or three days of the "Grand Consult".

And what was the date of the other "Consult" between the Benedictines and the Jesuits, at which Coleman was supposed to have been present? Titus did not know, except that it was some time in August; then, probably remembering that he had stated positively in his *Narrative* that it was on August 21st, he added that he "thought" it was that date. He could prove, cried Coleman with pathetic triumph, that he himself had been in Warwickshire all that month, and he did actually call one witness who testified to that effect. Given time, he pleaded, he could produce others; but the Bench was singularly uninterested.

With a candour and humility which were to remain with him to the end, the prisoner went on to admit that his letters had been foolish and extravagant, but he insisted that his whole object in thus intriguing with France had been "to make the King and the Duke (as far as I thought in my power) as great as could be". As for Oates and Bedloe, "My Lord, I never saw Mr Oates but in the Council-Chamber, I never saw him in Rome, in other parts I never saw the face of him, or knew him in my whole life; nor did I see the other till now in Court, as I hope to be saved. . . . Positively I say (and upon my Salvation) I never saw these Witnesses, Oates but once, and Bedlow never before." He drew attention to the fact that Oates and Bedloe did not swear to the same thing; but this the Lord Chief Justice swept aside with the utmost contempt; and Sir Francis Winnington, the Solicitor-General, summed up the case for the Crown. He ended thus:

"Our Execution shall be as quick as their Gunpowder, and more effectual. And so, Gentlemen, I shall leave it to you, to consider, what his Letters prove him guilty of directly, and what by Consequences; what he plainly would have done, and then, how he would have done it; And whether you think his Fiery Zeal had so much Cold Blood in it, as to spare any others. For the other part of the Evidence, which is by the Testimony of the present Witnesses, you have heard them.—I will not detain you longer now the day is going out."

Mr Justice Jones added a solemn admonition:

"You must find the Prisoner Guilty, or bring in two Persons Perjured."

The jury had no difficulty in choosing between these alternatives, and after a very short absence brought in the required verdict. Next day, the prisoner was brought into court to have sentence passed upon him; he produced a diary showing that he had indeed been out of London all August, but it availed him nothing, and he was compelled to listen to an unctuous sermon preached to him by Scroggs, full of insults against his religion, and ending with a lurid picture of what he must expect in the next world. The Lord Chief Justice then passed sentence; and it was the sentence exclusive to the crime of High Treason. Coleman was to be drawn on a hurdle from Newgate to Tyburn, on which journey he was liable to be half killed by the pelting of the mob; he was to hang on the gallows for a space, to be cut down alive, stripped, mutilated, ripped open, disembowelled, and quartered. And his body was to be disposed of as the King thought fit.

He listened to that dread sentence with a steadfast mien; and afterwards, in a speech so humble and dignified that it went far to redeem his many weaknesses, he again denied all knowledge of the Plot, and thanked the Lord Chief Justice for his "charitable counsel". He suffered on December 3rd, behaving himself with courage and simplicity; and since this was the first of his victims, we can scarcely doubt that Titus Oates was among the crowds at Tyburn who gloated on the butchery.[57]

(9)

December came in frosty and dry, and was to continue so the whole month.[58] Dr Titus Oates, well-fed and warmly clad, had no pity to spare for his victims, lying in the stone dungeons of Newgate. "When the two great Discoverers, Oates and Bedloe, had once drawn blood, they assumed new Courage, and became more formidable to the Romish Party, and more estimable to the other."[59] On the 2nd, Titus marched into the House of Commons to listen to a message from the King restoring to him his full liberty, and granting him a pardon "of all misprisons and concealments of treasons from the beginning of the world to the 28th [of November] by himself alone committed or with any other persons".[60] On the 7th, he heard the welcome news that, by order of the King and Council, Catholics were prohibited from attending the Queen's or the Embassy chapels.[61] On the 13th, taking a leaf out of his leader's book, Bedloe complained to the Committee for Examinations that he was kept short of money. "The Earl of Essex and the Bishop of London are desired to acquaint the King with Mr Bedloe's complaints."[62] On the 17th, the first batch of Catholic priests, Fathers Whitebread, Fenwick, and Ireland, were brought to trial, together with John Grove ("Honest William"), a Catholic layman, servant to some of the London Jesuits, and Thomas Pickering, a Benedictine lay brother.

The destruction of Coleman had been pleasing to Titus because it established his credit and tickled his vanity; the accomplishing the ruin of his friends in need held a more personal satisfaction. They had doled out alms to him, and made him listen to dull sermons; they had kept him at his books and refused him admission to their Society; now they would see how Titus Oates, D.D., repaid such conduct. He mouthed his evidence with the utmost relish; the old lies were enlarged upon, spiced with horrid little details for the benefit of the mob; Grove and Pickering had been seen by him walking in St James's Park "with their Screw'd Pistols, which were larger than ordinary Pistols, and shorter than some Carbines. They had Silver Bullets to shoot with, and Grove would have had the Bullets to be Champt, for fear that if he should shoot, if the Bullets were round, the Wound that might be given might be cured."

He had the most piteous tale to tell about his being beaten by Whitebread on suspicion of having betrayed the Plot; "my Lord, I did profess a great deal of Innocency, because I had not then been with the King; but he [Whitebread] gave me very ill language and abused me, and I was afraid of a worse mischief from them. . . . And, my Lord, though they could not prove that I had discovered it, yet upon the bare suspicion I was beaten and affronted, and reviled, and commanded to go beyond Sea again; nay, my Lord, I had my Lodging assaulted to have murthered me if they could." And not content with "champing" bullets, Grove had collected Peter-pence for furthering the Plot;

Titus himself had seen an account-book in which this "Honest William" entered the sums thus obtained; moreover, this was the villain who had gone out of his way to relate to Titus how he had fired Southwark in '76.

Grove, questioned by the Lord Chief Justice, admitted having seen Oates two or three times, though never at Father Whitebread's, as Oates maintained. On one occasion, just before Titus's setting out for St Omers, Grove, out of the kindness of his heart, had lent the destitute convert eight shillings, and had been told by Titus that though the latter could not repay it, Grove could get it from Father Fenwick, which indeed he had done. Fenwick admitted this; and the following somewhat undignified little duologue then took place between him and the Lord Chief Justice:

"*L.C.J.* Why did you not ask Mr Oates for it?

"*Fenwick.* He was not able to pay it.

"*L.C.J.* Why did you then lay it down for him?

"*Fenwick.* Because I was a Fool.

"*L.C.J.* That must be the Conclusion always: when you can't evade being proved Knaves by answering directly, you will rather suffer yourselves to be call'd Fools."

In reply to Fenwick's offer to have a written declaration sent over from St Omers, sealed with the College seal, and signed by all the collegians, to the effect that, when he said he was attending the "Grand Consult" in London, Titus was really at school in Flanders, Scroggs retorted: "Mr Fenwick that will not do: for first if it were in any other case besides this, it would be no Evidence, but I know not what you can get from St Omers, or what you will call Authentick." If, however, they could prove by other means that Oates was not in London in April and May of this year, it should be remembered to their advantage; in the meantime, he added kindly: "Let Mr Oates sit down again, and have some Refreshment."

Whilst Titus enjoyed a little well-earned rest, Bedloe took his place. His main accusation was that in August, in Father Harcourt's chamber, he had heard Ireland, Pickering, and Grove discussing a new attempt to assassinate the King. To this Ireland replied that he could produce some twenty witnesses to prove that he was out of London all

August. There followed a slight unpleasantness. James Bedloe, called by the prosecution to back up his brother, denied all knowledge of the Plot; he did not know Ireland, and had only heard of Grove and Pickering. He could, however, he added brightly, testify to his brother's intimacy with Jesuits overseas. It is scarcely to be wondered at that William Bedloe, shocked by such a wretched performance on the part of his dear brother, wailed piteously: "My Lord, may I have liberty to withdraw? my head akes extremely, I cannot endure it." He was told that he might sit down, but must not leave the court.

The prosecution now produced with obvious pride the only material evidence it had been able to unearth. Among all the papers and accounts and letters seized from the Jesuits in London on their arrest, two letters only were ever produced at the victims' trials. The one brought in as evidence by Serjeant Baldwin at the present trial had been selected because it was from one Jesuit to another giving notice of the forthcoming Provincial Congregation (Oates's "Grand Consult"). As both letters played a more important part at a later trial, there is no need to do more than mention them here.

Since Bedloe's evidence was positive only against Ireland, Grove and Pickering, the other two prisoners, Whitebread and Fenwick, should now have been discharged, for in cases of treason the law required two witnesses. Instead of this, they were ordered to be carried back to Newgate. "Upon this occasion, the Court committed a most enormous and crying Act of Injustice. For when they saw these two must be cleared, they, by a Quirk in Law, pretended to discharge the Jury of them, and put off their Tryal to another Time; though they had pleaded to the Indictment, and the Jury was sworn, and the Witnesses examined. They pretended indeed they had Precedents for this; but as a Great Man observes, Precedents against Reason only prove that the like Injustice has been committed before."[63]

Whitebread and Fenwick having been removed from the court, the other three prisoners were now called on to make their defence. Ireland again insisted that, if he might have time to send for witnesses, he could prove that he was out of London all August. He had been given but one day's notice of his trial, and, like the rest, was ignorant of the charges to be made against him; yet his devoted sister, Anne Ireland, had already, in great haste and flurry, prevailed upon a Mr Charles Giffard and one Harrison, a coachman, to appear on her brother's behalf. ("I did it of myself," she explained piteously. "I never did such a thing before, and did not understand the way of it.") The first testified that Ireland had been in his company at Wolverhampton from a day or two after St Bartholomew's Day, until September 9th; the second that he had met Ireland at St Albans on August 5th, and had remained with him until the sixteenth. (Actually, as was afterwards proved, Ireland had an unimpeachable alibi for the whole of August.) The coachman was unmercifully bullied by Scroggs; and the Recorder, Sir George Jeffreys, replied with a sneer to Ireland's plea for time to send for other witnesses: "To save him that labour, the King's Evidence will prove, that he was in Town at that time." This particular "King's Evidence" turned out to be a Mrs Sarah Paine, who swore that on about the 11th or 12th of August she had seen Ireland at the door of his lodgings, a scrivener's, in Fetter Lane.

Since the verdict was a foregone conclusion, the Lord Chief Justice was getting a trifle bored with this farcical trial; and he now addressed the prisoners in that jocular fashion calculated to brighten the proceedings.

"*L.C.J.* Mr Pickering, what say you for your self; you relie upon your Masses.

"*Pickering.* I never saw Mr Oates, as I know of, in my life.

"*L.C.J.* What say you to Bedlow, he tells you he was with you in Harcourt's Chamber such a day.

"*Pickering.* I will take my Oath I was never in Mr Bedlow's Company in all my life.

"*L.C.J.* I make no question but you will. And have a dispensation for it when you have done. Well have you any Witnesses to call?

"*Pickering.* I have not had time to send for any."

Scroggs treated with contempt Ireland's suggestion that witnesses should be called to prove whether or no Oates was a man whose reputation entitled him to credit as an evidence; there were those, said Ireland, who could prove very ill things against him.

"*L.C.J.* Why have you not Witnesses to prove it?

"*Ireland.* We could have had them if we had time.

"*L.C.J.* See what you ask now, you would have time and the Jury are ready to go about their Verdict.

"*Ireland.* Why, we desire but a little time to make out our proof.

"*L.C.J.* Only you must tye up the Jury, and they must neither eat nor drink till they give in a Verdict.

"*Ireland.* Then we must confess, there is no Justice for Innocence."

But at this point, Anne Ireland excitedly informed the court that there had just arrived Sir Denny Ashburnham, who had something to say concerning the character of Oates. This gentleman, Member of Parliament for Hastings, gave his evidence with considerable reluctance; so much is clear from the printed trial. He had known Titus from his cradle, he said (a figure of speech, surely, for Titus was rising twelve when his father first went to Hastings), "and I do know that when he was a Child, he was not a person of that Credit that we could depend upon what he said". "What signifies that?" asked Scroggs hurriedly; but the witness had not quite finished. From his knowledge of Titus in youth, he went on, he would not have believed in the Plot if it had rested solely on the testimony of Oates, but naturally other circumstances had now convinced him. There was, however, a little matter of an indictment against Titus for perjury at Hastings; and he now handed a copy of that indictment to the Attorney-General.

This was decidedly dangerous ground. We can imagine Titus's sudden agony of doubt, the Bench putting bewigged heads together, the jurymen whispering in their box, the spectators, scarce able to believe their ears, shocked into breathless silence at this threat to the credit of their idol, Dr Oates; as Serjeant Baldwin, with the damning document actually in his hands, stood up and asked permission to read it. But Scroggs saved the situation. He saved it by pronouncing the memorable words:

"Truly I do not think it sufficient Evidence or fit to be read."

They were, perhaps, the most extraordinary words ever spoken by a Lord Chief Justice of England.

Then, sweeping aside the prisoners' efforts to record the loyalty of their respective families to Charles I and his son, Scroggs directed the jury to bring in a verdict of Guilty; for that is what his summing-up amounted to. For a really vicious speech, it has not its equal in the whole period of the trials, and it contained the famous denunciation of the prisoners, and of the Catholics in general: "They eat their God, they kill their King, and saint the Murtherer!" He ended thus:

"I return now to the Fact, which is proved by two Witnesses, and by the concurrent Evidence of the Letter and the Maid [Mrs Sarah Paine]; and the Matter is as plain and notorious as can be, That there was an intention of bringing in Popery by a cruel and bloody Way; for I believe they could never have prayed us into their Religion. I leave it therefore to you to consider, whether you have as much Evidence from these two Men, as can be expected in a Case of this Nature; and whether Mr Oates be not rather justified by the Testimony offered against him, than discredited. Let Prudence and Conscience direct your Verdict, and you will be too hard for their Art and Cunning. Gentlemen, if you think you shall be long, we will Adjourn the Court till the Afternoon, and take your Verdict then.

"*Jury*. No, my Lord, we shall not be long."

Nor were they. Scarcely had they left their box than they were into it again, with a verdict of Guilty against all three prisoners. The Lord Chief Justice beamed upon them. "You have done, Gentlemen, like very good Subjects, and very good Christians, that is to say, like very good Protestants: And now much good may their Thirty Thousand Masses do them."

A small hitch occurred ere sentence could be pronounced, Mr Jack Ketch not answering to his call to come and tie the prisoners' thumbs with whipcord according to custom. When eventually the hangman did arrive, and had been suitably rebuked by Mr Recorder, the latter first preached the prisoners a sermon, piously assuring them that all his insults against them and their religion were the outcome of Christian charity; and then pronounced that terrible sentence:

"*That you the Prisoners at the Bar*, *be conveyed hence to the place from whence you came, and from thence that you be drawn to the place of Execution upon Hurdles, that there you be severally hanged by the Neck, that you be cut down alive, that your Privy Members be cut off, and your Bowels taken out, and burnt in your view, that your Heads be severed from your Bodies, that your Bodies be divided into Quarters, and those Quarters be disposed at the King's pleasure: And the God of infinite Mercy be merciful to your Souls.*"

(10)

The year was dying, that memorable year of sixteen hundred and seventy-eight; Christmas was come, with its merry-making and its mummers, and its message of peace to men of goodwill. It was in the midst of the festive season that Mr William Smith, the ex-schoolmaster, living now from hand to mouth without a livelihood, received a summons from Dr Titus Oates, his old pupil, to come to the doctor's apartments at Whitehall. A Major Fisher, who brought the summons, added the warning that it would be the worse for Mr Smith if he came not.

Poor Smith durst not disobey, though he took the precaution of carrying a witness with him, his friend, Thomas Hughes; in the sumptuous apartments occupied by the man whom he remembered as a most unpleasant schoolboy, he found Dr Oates in company with Mr Thomas Smith, "a Counsellor". It transpired that Titus was still thirsting after the blood of poor Matthew Medburne, the actor (who, as has been noted earlier, was to die in prison ere he could be brought to trial), and he now told William plainly that he required him to appear as a witness against their mutual friend. "Counsellor" Smith, to impress the ex-schoolmaster, delivered a long harangue, pointing out that it was his duty as an honest man to disclose anything he knew concerning the Plot; to which William replied simply that he knew nothing.

"Then Otes desir'd me to step in with him into his Closet", says William, "where he privately told me, That if I would appear against Medburne, he could procure an Order from the King to the Brewers, to re-instate me in my School; which he promised to perform, upon the Condition aforesaid. The Answer I made him, to excuse my self was,

That the School would be little worth to me now, under my present Aspersions and Circumstances. Upon this, he offer'd me his Power and Interest, in promising me anything else I could find convenient; with reiterated Protestations of serving me, and Intreaties to accuse Medburne. All this I refused, with a Compliment, That I would consider of it: Upon which we return'd into the Chamber, to our Company again: And soon after, parted friendly."[64]

While Titus was thus busying himself with the pursuit of private grudges, his devoted lieutenant, Bedloe, was passing through a period of considerable anxiety. In Bedloe, Oates had the second witness necessary to convict his mythical plotters of treason; but in the matter of the Godfrey killing, Bedloe stood alone. Young Samuel Atkins was still lying in Newgate, as irritatingly unco-operative as ever, and in the background his master, Samuel Pepys, was working hard to clear him of the charges made against him. The Jesuits Walsh and Le Faire had not been found, and in any case would require a second witness to convict them of the killing; and Bedloe's patrons were showing signs of impatience. Godfrey had died in October; Bedloe had come forward in November; and here was Christmas come in and the mob was still howling in vain for the arrest, trial, and execution of the murderers of the proto-martyr of the Popish Plot.

It was now, however, that Bedloe's luck turned. There was a certain man named Miles Prance, a silversmith, whose shop was in Princes Street, a turning off Drury Lane. He was often employed by the Queen to make ornaments for her chapel in Somerset House; he was a Catholic, and had several friends among the Jesuits; in character he was timid and weak. In his house was a lodger, one John Wren, with whom Prance was not on the best of terms. There had been some unpleasantness over a tankard lost and never found again; and latterly there was the question of arrears of rent. Wren owed Prance fourteen months' rent, and Prance, whose income was modest, threatened eviction. Wren, who either could not or would not pay up, decided that the present state of public affairs offered him a way out of his difficulty, for his landlord, being a Catholic, was become exceedingly vulnerable. So Wren went and informed the authorities that, two or three nights during the week of the Godfrey murder, Prance had lain out of his house; Prance was immediately arrested.

On December 23rd, he was brought into the lobby of the House of Commons, and there put into a little room to await examination. Into this little room "several went out of Curiosity, and among the rest the Discoverer Bedloe;* who, staring about him, enquired privately, which was the Prisoner? and finding the Man, he immediately retir'd. After some Hours waiting, they carry'd Prance to an Eating-House call'd Heaven; and into a Room where Bedloe was purposely planted by Sir William Waller and others, when of a sudden he started up, and with a cursed Oath cry'd out, This is one of the Rogues that I saw with a Dark Lanthorn about the Body of Sir Edmund-Bury Godfrey; but he was then in a Periwig."[65]

The luckless Prance was hurried before the Committee for Examinations, and there submitted to the seventeenth-century form of the third degree. But timid man though he was, he put up a fight for it. He admitted the truth; he was acquainted with several Jesuits, and when he had heard of the arrest of Ireland and his companions, he had remarked, apparently in a tavern, that they were honest men, though he believed he was drunk at the time. Also, it was true that he had lain away from home two or three nights after this, because he had heard that some people threatened to complain of him for his rash words. But he was absolutely positive that he knew nothing about either the Plot or the Godfrey murder.

There was a way of dealing with men like Prance. They clapped him into a certain underground hole in Newgate, without light, air, or firing (and, remember, it was the depth of winter); and he was told plainly that if he did not confess he would be hanged out of hand. Twelve hours of this incarceration proved sufficient to break his spirit, and on December 24th he asked to be taken to Lord Shaftesbury, who was then at his palace of a house in Aldersgate Street. What was said at this interview is not known, but immediately afterwards Prance was conveyed to the Privy Council,

* Oates was present also, according to Bedloe in his evidence at the trial of Hill, etc.

where he accused five men of the murder of Justice Godfrey; two Irish priests, Gerard and Kelly, and three laymen, Robert Green, the cushion-keeper of the Queen's chapel, Lawrence Hill, servant to Dr Godden, or Godwin, treasurer of the Queen's chapel (Dr Godden was then in France), and Henry Berry, porter at Somerset House. It will be remarked that this was a different set of murderers from the bunch named by Bedloe, and the reason for this is obvious: Bedloe's murderers, after two months' search, could not be found. In the present mood of the nation, it would be quite simple to fit in the rest of Bedloe's story with that of Prance when the actual trial took place; meanwhile, the three laymen, Hill, Green, and Berry, were easy to pick up and confine in readiness for that event.[66]

The story of Prance, while it forms an essential part of the "Popish Plot", is only indirectly connected with the history of Titus Oates, and therefore cannot be followed in any detail here. It is a particularly ugly story, because of the very strong evidence which exists that Prance was tortured in Newgate. The poor man had a conscience, and on December 29th, having demanded to be taken to the King, retracted all he had said, and swore he knew nothing of the murder or the murderers.[67] He was returned to Newgate (surely an inexcusable weakness on the part of Charles II), and on January 11th performed yet another *volte-face*. We can but guess at the dark and dreadful scenes which took place while he was confined a second time in that underground hole in Newgate; all we know for certain is that on this date, January 11th, 1679, Miles Prance composed his "Narrative" of the murder, assisted in the composition by the Keeper of Newgate. It would be about this time that William Smith, the ex-schoolmaster, had his first sight of the new recruit to the disreputable band of informers:

"Coming one Evening to visit [Oates] at Whitehall, I found Bedloe and Prance with him; amongst other Discourses, they Talkt of Sir Edmundbury Godfrey; Oats laught at the business, and said, Here is Bedloe, that knew no more of the Murder than you or I did. But he got the Five Hundred Pound, and that did his work, and gave this Blockhead 30. *l.* of it. He pickt him up in the Lobby of the House of Lords [*sic*], and took him for a Loggerhead fit for his purpose; at which Bedloe laught heartily, and Prance seemed a little dull, and displeased."[68] Smith adds that Oates and Bedloe "used always to make the business of Godfrey a Ridiculous Story, and Entertain'd themselves when Private with the Jest on't".

On the last day of the year 1678, Sir Joseph Williamson, one of the Secretaries of State, made some very obscure and mysterious notes regarding Titus, which, since no clue to their meaning is anywhere to be found, must be given to the reader without comment: "As to Oates designing to escape. Warcupp called in. Oates expressed a fear of being in Whitehall and as if he were in danger in it and offered, that, if any of them would carry him with them to their houses, he would go with them. Spoken to him and Sir H. Bethell, and Sir Richard Everard etc."[69] It is evident that his fears, whatever their nature, were soothed away, for in Whitehall he remained, living sumptuously at the King's expense.

(11)

The Plot has now been chronicled from its birth, through its sickly infanthood, to its flourishing maturity; but, in order not to interrupt the sequence of events, a certain most important aspect of it has been neglected—namely, its background. No adequate picture can be formed either of Titus himself or of the dreadful national hysteria he created unless we can visualise the state of the kingdom in general, and of London in particular, during the Popish Terror. This mass hysteria was to prostrate the nation from the discovery of Sir Edmund Berry Godfrey's body on October 17th, 1678, till the late summer of 1681; we shall see the progress and gradual decline of the disease in the events of that period of time; but, in order to understand these events, an investigation must now be made into the symptoms of the national fever.

First, then, the rumours. These were no longer confined to the common people. The Committee for Examinations appointed sub-committees innumerable for the purpose of investigating the most fantastic tales. From October 28th to November 2nd, 1678, one of these sub-committees spent its time listening to accounts of a scheme to blow up both Houses of Parliament; mysterious noises had been heard in cellars in the vicinity, and Christopher Wren and Hugh Maio were kept busy searching the said cellars, while the luckless Sir John Cotton, who kept his coals and faggots in one of them, was ordered to remove these in order to facilitate the search. Officers of Ordnance attended with their bores, and sentinels patrolled nightly in this hunt for imaginary successors to Guy Faux. Meantime, the King was implored to keep away from Parliament till all was safe, and Northumberland House was got ready to accommodate both Lords and Commons.[70]

November 12th to the 14th was taken up with an enquiry into the fearsome business of Mr Choqueux's fireworks. This gentleman was a surgeon living in the Savoy, and rumour had it that dreadful Popish engines of destruction were stored in his house. They turned out to be rockets, "serpents", and "manacles"; the two former species of firework were proved to have lain in his house eighteen years, kept by him "against the King might have occasion for them for any show", and obviously left over from the celebrations of 1660; and as for the "manacles", they were nothing more exciting than holders for Roman candles. Choqueux himself escaped with a rebuke for daring to affright the Parliament's Committee.[71] On December 3rd, a man named Smith accused two acquaintances, Hoare and Beacon, of being in the Plot; he had heard them, he said, talking about blunderbusses. It transpired that Smith was drunk and that the "blunderbusses" were specimens of the large kind of drinking vessel vulgarly known by that name. The Commons even took into serious consideration the news that "combustible matter" had been found in Sir George Wakeman's stables. They were not so far gone, however, as to miss the chance of pointing out to the King, in connection with the menace of lurking conspirators in their cellars, that their roof wanted mending. Both Houses spent much time examining "priests" who turned out to be laymen with families, and "conspirators" who were able to prove themselves law-abiding citizens, and in searching for "murdered victims" who turned up alive and well with the most depressing regularity.

In December of '78 a really exciting story set the town

agog. The Lords, busy appointing yet another committee to investigate a report of "great knocking and Digging in the Earth, in some Cellars adjoining to this House", were interrupted by a yet more dreadful rumour; "there came up from Dorsetshire an Account, post, with the Affidavits of two Men, that the French were landed in the Isle of Purbeck, for they saw them drawn up in Line, with the Officers at their Posts in the Head of them, or to that Effect. The Earl of Danby, then Lord-Lieutenant of the County of Dorset, rode to London with such Precipitation, that, when he came to the Hyde-Park Gate, his Hat was lost. He rode with his Sword drawn, and, as he galloped along, called to the People, Arm Arm, the French are landed!"[72] He was soon, however, followed by expresses who brought word that the "line of battle" was nothing but a hedge, and the "French troops" some horses grazing in a meadow.

The City, that stronghold of the Opposition, was not behindhand in adopting panic measures. Nearly thirty thousand people, Papists or suspected Papists, were driven from their homes and employment, and ordered to retire ten miles from London; meanwhile, the London jails housed two thousand "traitors" awaiting trial. Posts and chains were fixed across the principal streets, in order to repel an attack of Popish cavalry. The trained-bands, militia-men, and volunteers paraded day and night, and pieces of cannon were planted in front of the Royal Exchange and other buildings. Sir Thomas Player, the City Chamberlain, voiced his brethren's sentiments in the immortal words: "I do not know, but, the next morning, we may all rise with our throats cut."

Needless to say, fashion did not fail to take advantage of the panic. The Countess of Shaftesbury started the rage for little pocket-pistols which ladies carried in their muffs. An enterprising merchant produced sets of Popish Plot playing-cards; the suit of spades dealt exclusively with the murder of Godfrey, the others ranged from the Great Fire to the most recent "discovery" made by the informers, and from Rome, via the White Horse tavern, to Whitehall. Titus figured conspicuously in this pack, looking young and handsome, with a normal-sized chin. Ladies had scenes from the Plot painted on their fans, and the *Protestant*

(*Domestick*) *Intelligence* advertised a "New set of very useful Buttons, for Shirt Sleeves or Ruffles, there being described upon them some of the most remarkable passages of the late Horrid Plot". The Green Ribbon Club, which met at the King's Head tavern near Temple Bar, and was the headquarters of the Opposition, introduced a striking new mode for gentlemen:

"There was much Recommendation of Silk Armour, and the Prudence of being provided with it, against the Time that Protestants were to be massacred. And accordingly there were abundance of those Silken Back, Breast, and Potts made and sold, that were pretended to be Pistol Proof. . . . This was Armour of Defence; but our Sparks were not altogether so tame as to carry their Provision no farther, for truly they intended to be Assailants upon fair Occasion; and had, for that End, recommended also to them a certain Pocket Weapon, which, for its Design and Efficacy, had the Honour to be called a Protestant Flail.* It was for Street and Croud-Work, and the Engine, lurking perdue in a Coat Pocket, might readily sally out to Execution; and so, by clearing a great Hall, or Piazza, or so, carry an Election by a choice way of polling, called knocking down. The Handle resembled a Farrier's Blood-stick, and the Fall was joined to the End by a strong nervous Ligature, that, in its Swing, fell just short of the Hand, and was made of *Lignum Vitae*, or rather, as the Poet termed it, *Mortis*."[73]

From this club there issued many of the wild rumours which were designed to keep London's nerves on edge. When the loyal apprentices of the City prepared to celebrate Restoration Day with that burning of the rump which had become traditional, the Green Ribboners put it about that this was a new branch of the conspiracy, and their pamphleteers published lists of those whose throats were to be cut by the young desperadoes. Men saw Jesuits everywhere, even in the street-hawkers. "They speak of one Jesuit that cry'd *work for a Cooper*; another that wrought upon the trade of shoo maker; Priests in Red coats innumerable: And it is observed that upon the bringing of the Late Plot to Light, all the little Frenchmen with their Marionets and Puppet-shows vanish'd in a trice: which gave a Suspition

* Oates carries one in the illustration facing p. 240.

that they were only a kind of Itinerant Agents for the Faction."[74]

The news-sheets had every day some new scare. A man could not be absent from his house overnight but it was whispered he was murdered by the Papists. A house on fire, a highway robbery, the murder by some drab of her bastard child, all immediately became the work of these villains. The lengths to which credulity could go is well illustrated by the following extract from the *Domestick Intelligence, or News both from City and Country* for July 31st, 1679:

"From Bristol they write, That upon Thursday the Twenty fourth of this Instant July, there were found in the feilds near that City, five sheep killed, with their bellies ript open, and nothing but the fat taken out of them, all the rest Carcass being left entire behind, which has put the People into great apprehensions and fears, considering that on the Thursday before . . . there were three sheep beside these found in the same manner and it has been observed that the like has been done, both in London, Northampton, and several other places in this Kingdom, some time before the dreadful burning thereof, the Consideration of which has made such a Consternation among the People that they are afraid to sleep in their Beds, and have appointed extraordinary Watches and Guards for their security; There has also within a few days last past, been sometimes Twenty Cows of a night milked for several nights together by some unknown Persons, upon what occasion or design cannot be imagined, upon which the owners watched their Cows for some nights, and then they gave their full meal next morning, all which tends to increase the fears of the People, that it is some damnable firing design carrying on by the Papists, and therefore all possible care is taken by Sr John Lloyd the Mayor of Bristol, Sr Robert Cann, Mr Alderman Yates, Sheriff Jackson and many other of the most Eminent Citizens of Bristol, if possible to seize and discover these cursed Conspirators, to which end they have advised with Captain William Bedlow who is at present in that City."

The opportunities for blackmail and for the satisfying of personal spite, in this national hysteria, can be imagined. The *Calendars of State Papers* are ugly with the accusations of those on the scent of revenge or reward. As for the

Catholics themselves, their plight was worse even than during the Elizabethan persecution, for during that era a lingering affection for the old Faith made the mass of the people sympathetic towards the victims. Now they were not only butchered, imprisoned, harried, and fined by the enforcement of the Penal Laws, but were execrated by the populace; the houses of the Catholic gentry were ransacked, and in some cases almost demolished, in the search for concealed priests, and those priests who succeeded in evading capture were forced to take to the woods and heaths, where they were hunted with dogs like wild game.[75]

Astride this nightmare England straddled supreme the figure of Titus Oates. Christopher Kirkby had vanished from the stage; Bedloe was merely his old friend's lieutenant; Tonge, so jealous of Titus that he had let fall in public the shocking admission that Oates knew nothing of the Plot but what he had learnt from him, was shut out of his protégé's apartments in Whitehall, and scarcely appears in the limelight again before his death in 1680. There was, it is true, a growing company of new informers, Turberville, Dugdale, Dangerfield, and others, but not one of them ever approached the fame of Titus. He was the man invited to their feasts by the great Livery Companies of London, admitted an honoured member of the Green Ribbon Club, where he consorted with earls and viscounts, implored to fill the City pulpits, deferred to by the judges of England, addressed as "Dr Oates" by King Charles himself. The terror of him was universal, for no one knew whom he might choose to accuse next, nor in what direction his famous memory might improve.

"Oates never would say all he knew; for that was not consistent with the Uncertainty of Events. For he could not foresee what sort of Evidence there might be Occasion for, nor whom (it might be thought fit) to accuse: All which Matters were kept in Reserve to be launched or not, as Occasion, like fair Weather, invited, or storms discouraged. . . . When Oates was examined in the House of Commons, and was asked if he knew of any farther Design against his Majesty etc. instead of answering that question, he told a Tale of a Fox and a Goose, that the Fox, to see if the Ice would bear him and his Goose, first carried over a Stone as heavy as the Goose. And neither then, nor ever after during his whole Life, would he be brought to say he told all he knew; and diverse of his witnessing Train had learned that of him, saying, as some did, that that (meaning what was then sworn) was all they thought fit to declare yet: Which was a Behaviour that would not have been endured in any Time or Country, but only in England, and at this Time."[76]

Those little sunken eyes, that monstrous chin, that bull neck, that squat figure became known, feared, hated, or adored by the highest and the lowest alike. The poor dunce, the "snotty fool", the shabby, slinking vagrant, already had deprived twenty-three peers of their seats, had put six lords in the Tower, had accused his Queen of being a poisoner, had sent an ex-secretary of the Duchess of York to the gallows, had sent hundreds of innocent men into exile, had deprived thousands of their homes and livelihoods, and had so held up public business in both Houses that for two years the records are completely barren of legislation. And there was worse to come. He was the man of the hour, a national figure; and he carried himself accordingly.

He kept a tame counsel, one Aaron Smith, a lawyer of most shady reputation, who "attended his Client with remarkable Diligence, and, at the Trials, stood in his Bar-Gown guarded with Black Velvet, conspicuously at his Elbow, to observe the whole Evidence, that he might be better able to give Chamber Counsel against the next".[77] In his apartments at Whitehall, he "commonly had two or three every day to wait upon him to dress him";[78] he had his petitioners who stayed upon his leisure in the anteroom; he had his physician, one Dr Jones, to whom was entrusted his health, and who did a little informing on his own account, accusing a rival, Dr Emanuel Smith, of trying to poison Mr Bedloe.[79] He was considered a most eligible bachelor, he with his reputation for unnatural vice; and match-making mothers fawned upon him. "Oh Christ! (says a Lady, in my Hearing) That I had but a Daughter, to throw her into the Arms of Otes or Bedloe."[80]

Like many an upstart before or since, Titus needs must find himself a pedigree. He "would needs be descended from some Ancient and worshipful Stock; but there were not so many nobles Families strove for him, as there were Cities strove for the Parentele of Homer. However, the Heralds were sent for, to make out his Pedigree, and give him a Blazon. They were posed at the first of these; but they made good the Blazon in a Trice, and delivered it *authenticamente*: And it was engraved on his Table and other Plate; for he was rich, set up for a solemn Housekeeper, and lived up to his Quality."[81] Schoolmaster Smith adds some amusing details. Two "Herauld-Painters, Mr Wright and Mr Blackmore . . . found out a Coat which they believed no body now could claim, *viz* a Chevron between three Crosses Croslet Fitchee. Being the Atchievement of Sir Otes Swinford, Husband to the Lady Katherine Swinford, afterwards married to John of Gaunt, Duke of Lancaster. This the Doctor believed, and joyfully received, and most Triumphantly Engraved it on all his Plate, and in a large Seal Ring".[82]

"Whenever I came to Westminster Hall", Titus is made to say in a skit on him, "or to the Old Baily, or to any well-affected Coffee-house in the City, the people ran in shoals to view my person, and made a lane for me as I passed along. . . . I had my Guard of Beefeaters to protect me from being insulted or assassinated, my ten pound per week duly paid without deductions, Venison Pasties and Westphalia-Hams flew to my Table without sending for, I was as much stared at, at the Amsterdam-Coffee-House and at Dick's, as a Foreign Ambassador, when he makes his entry through Fleet-street."[83] He himself tells us that the King offered him the bishopric of Chichester, and although this is probably untrue, he was certainly "big with Hopes of being made a Bishop, and much dissatisfied with the National Ingratitude in not making him one".[84] A versifying admirer went so far as to suggest that a statue of him be set up in some public place; but, fortunately for posterity, the suggestion was never acted upon.

Roger North's description of Titus at the height of his power is well known, yet it is so graphic that no apology is needed for inserting it here:

"He was now in his trine Exaltation, his Plot in full force, Efficacy, and Virtue; he walked about with his

Guards (assigned) for fear of the Papists murdering him. He had Lodgings in Whitehall, and 1200. [*sic*] *l. per Annum* Pension: and No Wonder, after he had the Impudence to say to the House of Lords, in plain Terms, that, if they would not help him to more Money, he must be forced to help himself. He put on an Episcopal Garb (except the Lawn Sleeves), Silk Gown and Cassock, great Hat, Sattin Hat-band and Rose, long Scarf, and was called, or most blasphemously called himself, The Saviour of the Nation. Whoever he pointed at was taken up and committed,[85] so that many People got out of his Way, as from a Blast, and glad they could prove their two last Years Conversation. The very Breath of him was pestilential, and, if it brought not Imprisonment, or Death, over such on whom it fell, it surely poisoned Reputation, and left good Protestants arrant Papists, and something worse than that, in Danger of being put in the Plot as Traitors."[86]

(12)

The new year of 1679 came in with frosts and some snow. The first glimpse of Titus is significant; Sir Joseph Williamson, Secretary of State, notes his fear of this monster who, but a few months previously, had been destitute and unknown. "Bedloe and Oates being in the outward room of the Council Chamber", writes Sir Joseph on January 3rd, "the first to ask a protection for his witnesses, the latter to give in the informations concerning the Prince of Orange etc., Mr Bedloe having the two nights preceding sent by my chamber keeper to speak with me, I, having appointed him to come this morning, went out to him, and he acquainted me with what he had said to the King on Wednesday morning coming from church, viz., of the unfitness to have the trials of the priests printed, unless they were first executed, the intentions of some in the City to assault the prisons, etc., a plot under a plot, etc. Several members had asked him, if he had nothing against Lord Treasurer or me. The first, he said, he knew nothing against, of me he could declare they looked upon me as an enemy—the same he had told me once before etc. *N.B.*—As I came out from speaking thus with Bedloe, Oates, having in the meantime been before the Council, chanced to come out as I came out with Bedloe following me, upon which passage it is not unlikely that this may by Oates be reflected upon etc. If so, let this [be] for the help of memory etc."[87] Williamson already had been confined in the Tower by order of the House of Commons, without reference to the King, for having countersigned commissions to gentlemen not considered good Protestants; but Charles who, though overwhelmed in the main struggle, was fighting desperately on small points, had released him forthwith.

Parliament, which had been prorogued on December 30th, was dissolved on January 24th, as the only means of saving Danby from impeachment (that lord, in order to placate his enemies, immediately joined in the clamour for the banishment of the Duke of York); and on the same day, Ireland and Grove were executed at Tyburn. The King, who knew perfectly well that it was judicial murder, had agreed only with the greatest reluctance to let the law take its course, impelled thereto by the organized mobs who paraded the streets—mobs which reminded him all too forcibly of the rabble which had howled round Whitehall for the blood of Strafford when Charles was a boy. "Great numbers of the rabble daily resorted to Newgate and the Recorder's house to know the time of execution to the putting some in fear of an outrage."[88] Either in hope of making him "confess", or because the King hoped somehow to save him, Pickering was reprieved till the 9th of May; Charles had a particular affection for the Benedictines because of his contact with them during his escape from Worcester.

In the interval between his condemnation and his execution, Father Ireland had employed his time in writing down an exact day-to-day account of his movements between August 3rd and September 14th of the previous year, the period when Oates swore he was in London; not because he had any hope of a pardon, but because he was determined to establish his alibi and so clear himself of the odious charges made against him. Both he and Grove were pelted by the mob all the way to Tyburn, as, bound upon their sledges, they were dragged over the unmade roads, and Ireland was interrupted continually by the Sheriff in his speech on the scaffold. This speech was moving, though very short;[89] John Grove was even briefer, saying merely: "We are innocent, we lose our lives wrongfully, we pray God to forgive them that are the causes of it." It is to be noted that the majority of the Plot victims forgave Oates by name upon the scaffold.

On the following Sunday, the murderer of Ireland and Grove "preached at Wood street and was sent to Whitehall in Lady Player's coach".[90] According to Luttrell, "there was great thronging" when it became known that the great Dr Oates was to mount the pulpit of Dr Tonge's church.

In February, London learned with indignation that one Captain Bury or Berry, and Alderman Brooks, had been approached by the Papists to "throw the plott upon the Presbyterians".[91] Bury's and Brook's depositions were printed in a pamphlet, *A True Narrative of the Late Design of the Papists to charge their Horrid Plot upon the Presbyterians*, the compiler of which is naïvely astonished to find two such staunch Protestants being approached by these villains; he explains the mystery by concluding that the Papists were "infatuated". On the 10th of this month, the whole of London flocked to the Court of King's Bench to witness the trial of the three laymen accused by Prance of the Godfrey murder.

Of all the Plot victims, these were perhaps the most pitiful. The Jesuits, by their profession and their entering England, knew that they risked the penalty for treason; men like Langhorne and Coleman were at least educated and able to conduct their defence, though it availed them nothing; but these three, Hill, Green, and Berry, were ignorant men of the servant class; one of them, Berry, was a Protestant, and another, Green, was old and very feeble. Their trial cannot be followed in detail here, for Oates played but a very small part in it; the printed account of it, bald and "mangled" though it is, is moving in the extreme, for not only is it obvious that the three victims were dazed and bewildered by the whole business, but the evidence of such witnesses as they were able to call harrows the reader's feelings by its homeliness and simplicity. To give only one example: old Green's landlady remembered a certain day because she had indulged in the unwonted extravagance of buying a dozen pigeons to make a pie for some guests.

The principal witness was Prance; Bedloe, because his murderers had disappeared, was kept well in the background, though even so the discrepancies in the respective evidence of these two informers was so glaring that at times it seemed to embarrass their friends upon the Bench. Titus's own evidence concerned the fears displayed by Godfrey before his disappearance. The former described making his original depositions before that justice, of how Godfrey had come to see him on (he thought) September 30th, and told him he had been threatened and affronted by "some great Persons (whose Names I name not now) for being so zealous in this Business", and of how several Popish lords had threatened him. "He was in a great Fright, and told me, he went in fear of his Life, by the Popish Party, and that he had been dogg'd several Days.

"*Mr Attorney-General*. Did he tell you that he was Dogg'd?

"*Mr Oates*. Yes, he did; and I did then ask him, why he did not take his Man with him, he said, he was a poor weak Fellow: I then ask'd him why he did not get a good brisk Fellow to attend him? but he made no great Matter of it, he said, he did not fear them, if they came fairly to work; but yet he was often threatned, and came sometimes to me to give him some Encouragement, and I did give him what Encouragement I could, That he would suffer in a just Cause, and the like: but he would often tell me, he was in continual Danger of being hurt by them [the Papists]."

This touching picture of Godfrey being dogged by Papists, and flying for encouragement to Dr Oates (who, up to the last three weeks of Sir Edmund's life, had been plain Mr Oates, the penniless vagrant, and, according to himself, very thick with the Papists), put the spectators in just the right mood to listen uncritically to the fantastic and embarrassingly contradictory stories of Messrs Prance and Bedloe; and the inevitable verdict was received by all with a great shout of applause.

During the course of the next few days, Oates and Bedloe thought fit to submit their expense-sheets, or accounts of "what Moneys they had for the good of the Publick, expended and paid out of their own Pockets; Oates beginning his when he was in a starving Condition, without

Money or Credit; and Bedloe, when he had just before been fed out of the Alms-Basket at the Marshalsea, and a little before at the Castle of Lincoln. The former amounted to six Hundred and seventy eight Pounds, twelve and sixpence: The Latter, being of a shorter standing, amounted to no more than two Hundred and thirteen Pounds, without any odd Money."[92] In his *Observator* for August 4th, 1683, L'Estrange included an itemised bill which he said was this of Titus's, though it is thought to be merely a clever skit. Whether fictitious or no, it makes very amusing reading; there are expenses for journeys to Salamanca and Madrid, eighty pounds "owed" Titus by the Jesuits, and presents (most of them, perhaps appropriately, of knives) to various clerics. If L'Estrange's bill is a true reproduction, it must have seemed a little hard to Charles II that he should be expected to pay Titus £50 for "My Manuscript of the Alexandrian Version of the Septuagint which I gave them [the Jesuits]", and one wonders about the nature of the "Necessaries for Winter" which cost what would amount in our money to over a hundred pounds. Two cases of spectacles, said to have been presented to Father "Sinman" at Madrid, gave L'Estrange the perfect cue: "But for all that, I would he had not parted with his Spectacles, for his Eyes are none of the Best; and he has been Two or Three times ready to spoil all for want of 'em."

On February 11th, young Samuel Atkins, who all this while had languished in Newgate, was at last, by his own insistence, brought to trial, and acquitted. It was really impossible to bring in any other verdict, for he produced good Protestant witnesses who proved conclusively that during the crucial period he was lying at Greenwich "soundly foxed"; though from the multitude of questions put to him regarding his religion it is plain that, could they have made him out to be a suspected Papist, they would have condemned him by hook or by crook, so anxious were they for the credit of the "King's Evidence". Even as it was, Bedloe was commended for his zeal, and the Attorney-General stated explicitly that the proving Atkins innocent did not in the least detract from the reputation of the Crown witnesses.

Ten days later, on February 21st, Lawrence Hill and

Robert Green were hanged at Tyburn; poor old Green's little speech is worth recording for its extreme pathos. He said merely this: "I desire all your prayers; and as for Sir Edmund Berry Godfrey, I know not whether he be alive or dead; for in my days I never saw him with my eyes, as I know of; and if false people will swear against me, I cannot help it. I pray to God to bless my King and all his people." Berry, the Protestant, was reprieved till the 28th; on that date, still steadily protesting his innocence, he followed his two companions on the road to Tyburn. In the same month, Father Francis Nevil, S.J., a man of eighty-four, was arrested in the house of a Catholic gentleman in Stafford, and flung downstairs with such violence by the pursuivants that he died of it.[93]

(13)

The next important trial in the series, that of the Five Jesuits (as they came to be called), was not to take place till June; but meanwhile, all through the spring of 1679, the great Popish Plot continued to hold the stage of public affairs, for it remained the Opposition's chief weapon against the Monarchy.

On March 3rd, the King again declared in the presence of his Council that he had never married any woman but the Queen, thus reaffirming Monmouth's illegitimacy; but next day he was forced to send his brother James to Brussels to get him out of the way before the new Parliament met on the 6th. The Oppositionists had swept the polls, and this new Parliament, for lack of higher game, immediately fell tooth and nail upon the luckless Danby; early in April, a Bill of Attainder was passed against him, and he was sent to the Tower. Titus himself had taken a hand in this attack upon the King's most useful minister; on March 21st, he and Tonge had been called before the Council, and Titus "gave in an Information, not only against Thomas Earl of Danby, but also against Sir John Robinson, Colonel Edward Sackville, and Captain Henry Goreing, all Three Members of the House of Commons, which rais'd a new Flame in that Place".[94] A day or two later, Titus declared to the House " 'That being one Day in the Privy-Garden, the Earl of Danby, passing by, reflected upon him and said,

There goes one of the Saviours of England, but I hope to see him hang'd within a Month.' And likewise at the same time Oates gave his Testimony against Colonel Sackville, a Member of the House formerly question'd, declaring that he said, That they were Sons of Whores, who said there was a Plot, and that he was a lying Rogue that said it. Whereupon the Colonel was immediately sent to the Tower, and order'd to be expelled the House, with a Petition to the King to be made incapable of bearing any office. But in a short time, upon his Submission, he was discharg'd from his Imprisonment, but not restor'd to his Seat in the House."[95]

It is a relief to turn from this stern Titus to the gentler one whose heart could always be touched by any species of that Nonconformity in which he had been bred. Though at present he posed as the champion of the Church of England, and wore her uniform, it was the company of his former Dissenting brethren which pleased him most, as will be seen in instance after instance throughout his life. At the moment he was minded to use his great influence on behalf of a Quaker, one Dewsbury, or Dewsborough, who had been making a disturbance in Northamptonshire somewhat on the lines of Titus's father's youthful pranks. A gentleman of that county wrote to Titus the ingenious suggestion that the trouble-maker should be made to appear a Jesuit (it was a common pretence that Jesuits moved about disguised as Quakers), when it would be easy to arrest him, and so give Northamptonshire a little peace. On March 13th, the all-powerful Dr Oates replied as follows:

"MR W[HITFIELD]

"Yours I received in which you mention one desbrough his Name is William Deusberry a Quaker, whom you wold doe well to discharge, hee is noe Jesuit, nor lyke one: I looke on it to bee our discretion not to meddle with any protestant dessenter in this day, but bend our forces against the common Enemy of protestant religion the papists and endeavour to win by argument those that are dessenters from us. Sr here is a Certificate from some that have knowne him these 20 yeares and upwards, who are Men of repute in their Generations and protestants. and pray did you ever know that there was such Correspondency betwixt Jesuits and Quakers as might render them Suspicious? or did you ever know any priests or Jesuits in their Meettings or there Suffer'd to preach? for I know the Jesuits and the Quakers; and there is such vast difference in points of religion, that it is as possible to reconcyle light and darkness as to reconcyle them though they may appeare different from us yet they are I think no Murderers as the Papists have been and are: I have no more but that I am yours though Unknown,

"TIT. OATES."[96]

While Titus was using his powerful influence on behalf of the Dissenters (a section of whom very shortly afterwards precipitated a bloody rebellion in Scotland), the state of his country was going from bad to worse. "The king was poor; the officers of the crown and the household were clamorous for their salaries and dues, which had not of a long time been paid, and no wonder, when Sir Robert Howard, one of the chief officers of the exchequer, declared in the house of commons, that there was not money sufficient for bread for the king's family; there were no stores anywhere, either for the sea service or the land; the garrisons were all out of repair, the platforms decayed, and the cannon dismounted; the army divided, for the Duke of York and against him, the officers of state the same; the parliament for the most part in a ferment, and glad of these public misunderstandings, as favouring their desire of clipping the wings of prerogative, reducing the height of monarchy, and furthering their private designs; the king also and his brother at variance, and so kept by those who promised to make his majesty quite easy, if he would but comply with them so far as to disinherit the duke; so that he was quite in suspense as to what resolution he should or should not take."[97] The only success gained by the King at this stage of his mortal battle with the Opposition was in getting a proviso into the Popish Recusants (Discovery and Conviction) Bill, exempting from the penalties of practising their religion the Catholic men and women who had saved his life after the Battle of Worcester.

In their efforts to keep the flames of the Plot brightly

burning, the Oppositionists did not, of course, neglect that most useful fuel, propaganda. Mr Dudley North, a merchant in the Turkey trade and brother of the Lord Keeper Guilford, returning home after twenty years' absence, "came with such an idolatrous respect for Oates and his plot, as if he had been truly, what Oates blasphemously arrogated to himself, the saviour of the nation. This was instilled into him by the merchants of the Turkey Company in England; who, being generally factious, in the flame of the plot, had sent accounts abroad which created such enorm imaginations in the factors. But when, after a long converse with his lordship [Guilford] (for a little time would not do) the mystery of iniquity was unveiled, and the merchant saw that his idol was such a heap of nastiness, he wondered sufficiently at the stupidity, or knavery, of his correspondents here." Even had Guilford had the time to have written him the truth of the matter before his return, "it had not been safe to have committed to a written despatch, such freedoms about the plot, as was needful to do right to it. . . . But the factious party made it religion to propagate the faith of the plot, all the world over, as far as they could carry it by their correspondence."[98]

On March 24th, however, there was laid before the Committee for Examinations the first attempt at a counter-blast. This was a French pamphlet, published in England, entitled *Lettre escrite de Mons d un Amy d Paris, touchant la Conspiration d'Angleterre, qui se plut dire un Factum, pour les Catholiques persecutés*. It appeared anonymously, but the author was really Father Warner, S.J., successor to White-bread as Provincial. It stated that Oates could not have been interviewing Père la Chaise, as stated in his *Narrative*, because he was at that time at St Omers, and it gave the depositions of fourteen students of that college in proof of this assertion. After describing other of his inconsistencies and lies, it added a rumour that when he accused the Queen, "the Duke of Buckingham then exclaimed 'This rascal [Oates] will spoil our business. He can't govern himself; it is not time yet to bring the Queen forward.' " "They tell me", continued the author, "that Oates is to have a statue at the Mansion House. Do write the inscription. I have given you sufficient materials."[99]

Oates, who next day was to hear both Houses of Parliament repeat that there had existed, and did exist, a horrid and treasonable conspiracy, contrived by those of the Popish religion, for the murdering of the King and the subverting of Protestantism, could afford to despise so feeble an attack upon his credit. But the English envoy in Paris, Henry Savile, was not so indifferent to the impression which the Plot proceedings was creating abroad. In a letter to his brother, Lord Halifax, he complained: "I have writt to Mr Secretary severall times to tell him the necessity of having something put out in print to give an account to the world of our proceedings since the discovery of the plott, which for want of some such treatise is wholly unbelieved here, and our nation upbraided with all the infamous reproaches the violence of angry fools can invent. I have made Coleman's tryall and Oates his depositions be translated, but cannot get them printed; I would therefore downright ask leave of this King to print them as a justification of my master and country, but I cannot get a line from the Secretary upon this Matter."[100]

On April 7th, the articles of impeachment against the five Catholic peers in the Tower were forwarded to the House of Lords; on the 15th, the victims returned their answers. Lord Petre gave a direct Not Guilty; the others pleaded that they could not be expected to answer a charge which contained no specific details of the alleged crime, and which did not, therefore, enable them to prepare a defence. The Commons protested that this was an evasion, and resolved to demand judgment in default of an answer. On the 25th, the four lords yielded to the inevitable, and, while saving to themselves the benefit of exception from the generality, uncertainty, and insufficiency of the articles, severally pleaded Not Guilty.[101]

On the day before this answer was returned by the lords, there had taken place the trial of Nathaniel Reading, a Protestant barrister, accused by Bedloe of having endeavoured to persuade that informer, in return for money, to whittle down his evidence against the Five Lords so as to render it insufficient to convict them of High Treason. The case of Reading has never been thoroughly investigated, but the strong probability is that the charge against him was manufactured in order to silence him as a witness for the defence. His conviction certainly suited Bedloe perfectly, for, having had other dealings with that informer, he knew rather too much about Bedloe's past for Bedloe's comfort, and the penalty of the pillory, to which Reading was subjected, disabled him from appearing as a witness in the future. Also, he served as a useful excuse for Bedloe's failure to give evidence against Whitebread at the first trial of that priest, for Bedloe could swear that his failure to do so was the result of Reading's bribes.

Between April 20th and May 27th, Shaftesbury and his colleagues launched their second direct attack against the Duke of York, now for the first time openly advocating his exclusion from the throne. The King's only means of defeating this was to prorogue Parliament for ten weeks, a course which, he hoped, would enable him likewise to save Danby and the Five Lords. Shaftesbury, losing his temper, declared that the advisers of this step should pay for their presumption with their heads.[102] On May 9th, Thomas Pickering was butchered at Tyburn. Oates had a particularly petty personal grudge against this man, because Pickering had turned him away when he came a-begging at the Savoy. The gentle and retiring lay brother prayed for his enemies and accusers on the scaffold, and, on the point of being turned off, pulled up his cap that all might see his smiling face as he enquired: "Is this the countenance of a man who dies under so gross a guilt?"[103]

Titus himself was occupying the period before he could appear in his favourite role of King's Evidence again, in a way which must have afforded him great satisfaction. On May 22nd an old enemy of his, Francis Norwood, once his father's churchwarden at Hastings, was hauled up before the Committee for Examinations to answer to a charge of "abusing" Dr Oates; and on the 24th, after having denied a further accusation that he had been with the Five Lords in the Tower, was committed to the custody of a messenger.[104] On the 23rd, Titus had taken a trip to Newgate to inspect some condemned priests, specially brought up from the provinces for this purpose, to see if he recognized any who had been concerned in the Plot. Next day he was able to inform the Committee that one of them, Lewis, was a Jesuit, and had attended the "Grand Consult".[105]

But the chief business occupying Titus at the moment was the collecting of witnesses who would swear, at the forthcoming trial of the Five Jesuits, that he, Oates, had been in London in April and May of the previous year; for he knew that the fact that he had been at St Omers during those months would form the chief plank in the defence platform. The personalities and evidence of these witnesses have been examined earlier in this work; it remains only, therefore, to describe the way in which one of them was bullied by Oates into perjuring himself, a method so typical of this degraded period, that it may well have been used with others.

William Smith, the ex-schoolmaster, was still keeping in touch with his old pupil, probably because he was afraid of him; and having failed to induce him to come forward as a witness for the prosecution of his own free will, Titus and his friends at last compelled him to do so by threats, though at first they told him only that he was to swear that Titus had dined with him the previous *summer*, which was true. Later, however, "they all prest upon me", says Smith, "that it must be in April or May; promising me, that if I would tell the Truth [*sic*], they would endeavour with the King and House of Lords, to have me restored to the place I lost, or a better; urging withal, That if I would not tell the Truth, things would be worse with me, and much more to that threatning purpose. I being apprehensive of danger, and having already suffer'd too much, considering too I was not upon my Oath, I ventured to say that truly I thought it might be about May; which Sir Thomas Lee [Chairman of the Secret Committee of the Lords] wrote down, and afterwards required me to subscribe to; which I not suspecting they would ever demand of me, was surprized into, and durst not deny them."[106]

The luckless Smith, with whose weakness, so honestly admitted, it is impossible not to sympathise,* was very soon

* He was so poor that he paid but threepence a week for his lodging, and he confesses he was terrified by the dismal reports he had heard of the state of the prisoners in Newgate. He bitterly repented his perjury, and in '81 submitted an account of his trepanning and former association with Oates to Secretary Jenkins, but it was not allowed to be printed till 1685. See also *Examen*, pp. 222, 237–40.

disillusioned on the last point. He found himself subpœnaed for the trial of the Five Jesuits, and when he appeared at the Old Bailey, the officer at the door told him "that I must go to the Fountain Tavern at Snow-hill; where coming, I found the two Oates's, Father and Son (that being the first time that I had ever seen the Father) together with Councellor Smith, and many other persons, strangers to me". After some civilities and a glass of wine, "Councellor" Smith got the victim alone with himself and Titus, and bullied him into a promise to swear that Titus had been at his house in May, 1678. "This I must averr, or there was a Jayl ready hard by to receive me; which truly would have been soon done, for the Court was then sitting, and undoubtedly that accursed and unlucky Paper [which he had signed before the Secret Committee], with the strength of Oates his credit and sway at that time of day, would have laid a bigger man than myself by the heels."[107]

There was now to take place that trial which would put to the test the credit of Titus Oates, for it was known that witnesses had been brought over from St Omers to prove him a liar. He was not, however, perturbed, for he knew he could expect the same protection from the Bench as formerly; he knew that the defence witnesses would be abused by the rabble out of court, bullied by the Bench and the Attorney-General in court, and disbelieved by everybody because they were Papists; and he knew also that he would have at his back, not only his faithful lieutenant, William Bedloe, but Miles Prance and a new recruit to the choice bevy of informers, Stephen Dugdale. Altogether he must have been at his most confident when he swaggered into the Sessions House of the Old Bailey on June 13th, 1679, with the officers of the court making a clear path for him, and the acclamations of the rabble resounding in his ears.

(14)

There were five men in that big dock which was decorated with rue and rosemary to protect the court from jail-fever. Father Thomas Whitebread was now in the sixty-second year of his age, and was still very weak from his illness, which the conditions of Newgate had done nothing to improve. Father John Gavan, the youngest of the five, was thirty-nine; he was a Londoner, remarkable for the beauty of his voice and for his eloquence. He had not attended the Provincial Congregation, for he had not then taken his last vows. Father Anthony Turner, a convert, aged fifty, was a Leicestershire man, and since being sent on the English Mission, had laboured chiefly in the neighbourhood of Worcester. He was a man so lacking in that guile popularly attributed to the Jesuits that, forced to go on the run at the outbreak of the Plot persecution, he had recognized his inability to hide himself and so had given himself up to a justice of the peace as a priest and a Jesuit. Father John Fenwick, who was the same age as Father Turner, was likewise of Protestant parentage. In prison he had suffered so grievously from the weight of his fetters that it had been debated whether to amputate his leg. Father William Harcourt, the senior of the five, was turned seventy; it is said that it had long been his habit to pray daily for the honour of dying for that religion in the cause of which he had laboured so long.

The customary proceedings commenced. The Clerk of the Crown directed each prisoner to be set to the Bar; each was required to hold up his hand while the indictment was read, and then was asked if he pleaded Guilty or Not Guilty. To the reply of Not Guilty was returned the question: "Culprit, how wilt thou be tried?" "By God and my Country", came the formal answer. "God send thee a good deliverance", intoned the Clerk; and all was ready for the prosecution to open its case. A slight departure from the smooth course of such legal ceremonies was caused to-day by Father Whitebread who, immediately after the reading of the indictment, protested against the illegality of his being brought to trial after the evidence against him, as given at the trial of Ireland, had been deemed insufficient. Scroggs and the Lord Chief Justice of the Common Pleas, Sir Francis North, could counter this only by legal casuistry. Whitebread's challenge of those jurymen who had sat at the former trial had to be allowed, however; then Mr Belwood, K.C., opened the case for the Crown, followed by Sir Creswell Levinz; and at long last Dr Titus Oates took the centre of the stage.

That old, old story of "consults" and conferences and the hiring of assassins must have grown a little stale by now, though Titus could always be relied on to add a few new and piquant touches. He was in an excellent humour, and condescended to explain unasked how it was that he had denied knowing Gavan on the latter's arrest: "but now I must speak a Word to this Gentleman, Mr Gavan, the Prisoner at the Bar, whom when I saw come into the Lobby, he had gotten on a Periwig; so there was one asked me, whether I knew him? I know him now, but truly then I did not well know him, because he was under that Mask, and I could not say any thing against him then, because he being under an ill-favoured Periwig, and being a Man that I knew had a good Head of Hair of his own, I did not well understand the Mystery of it, and so spared my Evidence at that Time, from informing the Council against him"; and so on. The way a periwig seemed able to disguise Oates's old friends was really quite remarkable.

Titus was in so bumptious a mood to-day that he did not hesitate to snub the Bench itself, when he felt a snub to be justified. Speaking of a meeting of the Jesuits at Wild House, he said there were some fathers there whose names he could not remember.

"*Gavan*. Was I there, pray Sir?

"*Dr Oates*.* No, no, Sir; I am not to talk to you still, I am to speak to the Court.

"*L.C.J. North*. We would recommend this to you, to name Persons when you speak of them.

"*Dr Oates*. Where I have Occasion I will name them, my Lord."

Permitted to ask questions, Gavan immediately tackled Titus on the subject of a letter Oates had sworn he had seen written by him.

"*Gavan*. Mr. Oates, you say you saw my Name to a Letter for the taking up of Money: To whom was that Letter writ?

"*Dr Oates*. There was a Letter from you, to Mr Ireland. And he did receive it by the Hands of Grove.

"*Gavan*. Where was that Money to be taken up?

* Hitherto the compiler of this collection of the *State Trials* has called him plain Mr Oates.

"*Dr Oates*. My Lord, I say, that Letter was received by Grove, who is out of the way, and can't prove it, and was delivered to Ireland [also 'out of the way', be it noted].

"*L.C.J.* I perceive your Memory is not good.

"*Gavan*. I perceive his Memory is very good.

"*Dr Oates*. This Letter did give an Account of the Business of Staffordshire, and the Particulars of that Mr Gavan did afterwards give an Account by Word of Mouth, and some other Things not fit to be named.

"*Gavan*. Pray, where was it, Sir, that I gave an Account of it; in London, or in the Country?

"*Dr Oates*. In London.

"*Gavan*. In what Month?

"*Dr Oates*. In July it was.

"*Gavan*. What part of July?

"*Dr Oates*. It was when Mr Ashby was in Town, the beginning or middle.

"*Gavan*. Just now, you said it was in the latter end.

"*Dr Oates*. My Lord, I beg this Favour, that if the Prisoners at the Bar ask any Questions, they may be proposed to the Court, for they are nimble in their Questions, and do a little abuse the Evidence. They put Things upon them that they never say.

"*Mr Just. Pemberton*. Propose your questions to the Bench, that you would have asked.

"*Gavan*. I will do so, my Lord, in whose Honour I have more Confidence than in whatsoever Mr Oates says or swears."

Soon there came what was for Titus the danger-point of the trial. Whitebread and Fenwick began to press him with questions concerning his visit to London for the "Grand Consult". Titus plainly disliked this subject; he hated ever being tied down to dates and he had a particular distaste for questions of that nature when they bore upon this crucial period. So he now suffered one of those convenient lapses of memory which had stood him in good stead on previous occasions. He had even forgotten the names of those who had come over with him for the "Consult", though as Fenwick pointed out, they were all in his *Narrative*. Lord Chief Justice Scroggs, always willing to give Titus a helping hand in such moments of embarrassment, suggested that "perhaps a Man will venture to Write more than he will Swear", to which Fenwick retorted: "It was sworn before a Justice of Peace, and will not, I suppose, be denied, and therefore he must make his Evidence agree with it, being part of his Narrative." Gavan followed this up by pressing Titus to say definitely what time it was in July when he said he had seen him in London. Feeling perhaps that he was not showing to his best advantage, Titus invented a pretty little story about remembering the occasion because Gavan "were a little illish, and there was a Cordial brought to you by an Apothecary, that went by the name of Walpoole.

"*Gavan*. My Lord, I never saw Walpoole in my Life.

"*L.C.J.* I believe he is known well enough, such an one as Walpoole the Apothecary. But ask what Questions you will.

"*Dr Oates*. I cannot say whether it was Walpoole himself, or his Man, that brought it."

Things were not going very well for Dr Oates, and when it transpired that Turner also had been unrecognized by Titus because of a "nasty Periwig", Scroggs seems to have decided that a round rebuke of the prisoners from the Bench might help matters along. "I see," he roared at them, "your Defence will be little else but Captiousness, to disprove him in Circumstances of Time, Place, Persons, and Numbers; now all these are but little Matters to the Substance." Having thus disposed of the case for the defence, Scroggs allowed Dr Oates to sit down.

Titus's place was taken by the new informer, Dugdale; he had been bailiff to Lord Aston, and had been dismissed for embezzling his master's rents. His evidence related to the consultations said to have been held between priests and Catholic laymen at Tixall, the seat of his former employer; since this was his first public appearance as a perjurer, he needed a great deal of prompting and encouragement from the Bench—"You may take your own way, and you shall be heard, you shall not be interrupted. . . . You deliver your Testimony like a sober modest Man, upon my Soul", and so on. It seemed that Dugdale had given the conspirators £400 towards the expenses of the Plot, and that in return for this generosity Gavan had promised to get him canonised. He had intercepted about a hundred letters concerning the conspiracy, in one of which he had learned that Godfrey was to be slaughtered; he called a witness to back up his statement that he knew on the Tuesday that Godfrey was killed, though his corpse was not found until the Thursday (which, one might have thought, looked a little suspicious for Dugdale). The witness in question mildly disgraced himself by wondering aloud why Dugdale had not given evidence at the trial of the three men executed for the Godfrey murder; and even the Bench seemed a little critical of the information that Whitebread had sent by the ordinary post a letter in which he had written in plain terms that he and his colleagues intended to kill the King.

The more experienced Prance followed; and then came Bedloe, who, like his great leader, was at his most brazen. As for his failure to give evidence against Whitebread and Fenwick at the former trial: "I did then say that I did see Mr Whitebread, and he hath been in several Consultations for the carrying on of the Plot; but then I did it with a Caution, that I never heard of Mr Whitebread, that he was so very much concerned; and indeed I had no Reason to say so, because I heard him myself, and could not well speak from the Hear-say of another." Having explained himself in this eminently satisfying manner, Bedloe retold all Oates's old stories about the Four Ruffians, the hiring of Grove and Pickering, and the bribing of Wakeman. To hear him so word-perfect, one would never have believed that at his first coming in as an informer he had known absolutely nothing about the Plot.

When Bedloe had finished, the prosecution produced the two letters selected from among the multitude of papers seized from the Jesuits on their arrest. Old Father Harcourt patiently explained the meaning of the first one.

"That Letter was writ to me, who had *Jus Suffragii*, a Right to come and vote in our Congregation, which, according to the Constitution and Orders of our Society, is within the Compass of three Years, where they meet about the particular Affairs of the Society.

"*L.C.J.* What was it [the Congregation] about?

"*Harcourt*. It was about choosing an Officer; choosing a

Procurator to send to Rome; that was the chief Point: And Secrecy was a Thing that was recommended to everyone, as it was fit it should be, we living in a Country, where every one's Eye was upon us, and we an Eye-sore to them, we ought to be cautious of meeting in such Numbers, as might give an offence, and this was the only Thing, indeed." Scroggs, of course, rejected this explanation without wasting time examining it; he then spent some time in pointing out to the jury that no innocent man could possibly have written such a letter.

The second letter had been selected by the Plot managers because it contained the word "patents", which suggested to minds unbalanced by the national hysteria the truth of Titus's story about commissions and patents issued by the Pope for the appointment of officers once the Plot had been successful. Actually, said Whitebread, the letter referred to his own appointment as Provincial in January, 1678; he added that every such patent was termed *Literae Patentes*, though it was designed for only one person. It goes without saying that this explanation also was swept aside with the utmost contempt.

The prisoners were now called upon to produce such witnesses as they had been able to call. Their main contention was that Oates was not *probus testis*, and that he was, in fact, a perjurer; in proof of which they called sixteen witnesses, chiefly students, from St Omers, who testified, one after the other, that Oates had not left the College from his first coming there in December, '77, to his final expulsion in June, '78, except for one week-end, about Christmas-time, at Watten. Incidentally, these witnesses bore testimony to the extremely bad opinion the Jesuits had formed of Titus directly he came under their care, which drew from the prisoners the pertinent question, often repeated: Is it likely we would have trusted such a man with a plot which, if betrayed, would have ruined us all?

Each of these witnesses (and the majority of them were but schoolboys) before giving his evidence was compelled by the Bench to admit that he was a Catholic, an admission which endangered his parents, since it was a penal offence to send boys to be educated in the Catholic schools overseas; and all had to endure a barrage of insults and sneers from the Lord Chief Justice. "I can swear that I saw him [Oates] at least till June," said one, "if I can believe my own Eyes." "Your Religion," wittily retorted Scroggs, "does not allow you to believe your own Eyes." In the words of Ailesbury, who was present, "that bloodsucker, Chief Justice Scroggs, rejected them all with such passion as that they could scarce get out of Westminster in safety, the mob rising upon them and crying, 'Away with them that slander the Saviour of the Nation'; which I remember very well, being accidentally in the Hall".[108]

Gavan, who insisted that his case was different from the others because Oates admitted that he was not at the "Grand Consult", but had put his signature to its resolutions, now again challenged Titus to state definitely when he had seen this. It was in June or July, replied Titus vaguely. Gavan immediately called witnesses to prove that during these months he was at Wolverhampton, lodging at the house of a Mrs Winford. This lady, who was present in court, testified to that effect; and one of the most disgraceful pieces of bullying to be found in these trials followed on the part of Scroggs, who cross-examined her.

The prisoners, though it was manifestly hopeless to expect justice from such a Bench, persisted in their attempts to catch Titus out. Whitebread and Harcourt offered to prove that he had perjured himself at Ireland's trial, when he had affirmed that Ireland was in London when actually he was in Staffordshire. It needed all Scroggs' ingenuity to support Titus under this barrage. The following is a specimen of the dialogue:

"*Dr Oates*. I never said such a Word.

"*Harcourt*. Here it is in the Trial.

"*L.C.J.* I stand not by the printed Trial, it is no Record in Law. In short, were Mr Ireland and Mr. Harcourt together at that time?

"*Dr Oates*. No, they were not.

"*Gavan*. He did then say, that he did receive of Mr Ireland, the 2d of September, 20s. that he borrowed of him; now the 2d of September he [Ireland] was at Boscobel.

"*Dr Oates*. My Lord, I was not positive as to the day; but as near as I remember (those were the Words I said) it was the 2d of September; but whether it was the 1st, 2d, 7th, 8th or 9th, I would not be positive in it." Against the bare word of Dr Titus Oates, the testimony of Sir John and Lady Southcott, their son and daughter, a Mrs Harewell (Ireland's hostess at Wolverhampton), her daughter, Penderel the landlord of the Royal Oak at Boscobel, his wife, a Mrs Giffard and her sister, and other witnesses called by the defence to prove that Ireland was away from London during the period in question, had no chance at all.

The prosecution retorted by again producing Sarah Paine, who repeated her extremely unconvincing and unsupported story about seeing Ireland at the door of his London lodging one day in August; also eight witnesses to prove that Titus himself was in London during the time of the "Grand Consult". Their testimony has been examined earlier in this work; but it should be added that Sir Richard Barker, Tonge's patron, who was one of them, could say only that he had heard from his servants that they had seen Titus during that period. To this testimony Whitebread replied that when he had been brought to trial the first time, and had pressed Oates to declare who had seen him in London in April and May of '78, Titus could not produce a single person. The Bench very naturally ignored this, and bade the prisoners say what they could for themselves. All five emphasized the unsatisfactory nature of Oates's evidence, and Turner summed up their defence thus: "All that I have to say, my Lord, is this, to ask whether it be reasonable that Bedlow and Oates should be looked upon as good Witnesses, that these Persons who have been such scandalous People should be admitted to an Oath, who are debarred from the Sacrament; for according to the Church of England, no man that is publickly scandalous can be admitted to the Sacrament."

Scroggs summed up with his usual gusto. He sympathized with the jury for having such a long and confused mass of evidence to remember, but reassured them with the statement that he did not remember it all himself, much of it, he said, being impertinent. He then remembered, with admirable exactitude, the testimony of Oates, Dugdale, Bedloe, and Prance. As for the St Omer scholars, "it is very doubtful and suspicious, to have such green, and flexible Minds thus imploy'd, and I must leave it to you, to consider how far these Young Men, train'd in such Principles, may be prevail'd on to speak what is not True". Having himself harried and badgered the prisoners and their witnesses on the subject of dates, he excused all Oates's inconsistencies regarding such things thus: "Examine your selves, how often every Day you do mistake Things that have been transacted half a Year ago, and err in Point of Time, taking one Week for another, and one Month for another; and tho' I must say it is considerable, yet too great Weight is not to be laid upon that." He complimented Mr Dugdale as a new witness for the King, and deplored the bad taste of the Jesuits who had "made Reflections on him for his Poverty". Chief Justice North was tactless enough to remind his brother judge that Dugdale had sworn he had given the Jesuits four hundred pounds, but Scroggs ignored this, and continued triumphantly:

"But I will challenge all the Papists in England, to satisfy any Man that hears me this Day, of one piece of Evidence, which will turn every Protestant's Heart against the Papists." This piece of evidence was, it transpired, the murder of Justice Godfrey, with which the prisoners were not charged. It was, however, asserted Scroggs, evidence of the Plot in general, and while it was a specimen of what the Papists had done, it was likewise a warning of what the prisoners would do unless condemned.

After this long harangue, Scroggs left the Bench, Mr Recorder remaining behind to take the verdict of Guilty, which was delivered in a quarter of an hour.

(15)

The very next day the dock was occupied by Richard Langhorne, the Catholic barrister, who, ever since his arrest in October, had been kept in the strictest confinement. The principal charges against him were that he had endeavoured to procure forces to invade the kingdom and to join with those raised in England by the Papists; and that he was to be Advocate-General in this Popish army. A great deal of the evidence, both for the prosecution and the defence, was almost exactly the same as that produced at the trial of the Five Jesuits, and need not, therefore, be given in detail.

A new note of caution was observable in Titus's testimony at this trial; the reason for this may have been that he knew the prisoner to be a man well versed in the law, or possibly he had taken fright at the pressing attack made upon his credit by the Jesuits on the previous day. At all events, he contrived to postpone appearing in the witness-box until his chief patron, Scroggs, had appeared upon the Bench, which was not until both Bedloe and Prance had given their evidence, and he showed a strong disinclination to particularize about the seven or eight commissions Langhorne was supposed to have shown him. He was far happier repeating treasonable conversations; and he was in the thick of describing how Langhorne had told him how disgusted he was by Wakeman's haggling over the price of poisoning the King (the prisoner had called Wakeman, said Oates, "a covetous man and a narrow-souled physician"), when he was affronted to hear Langhorne seek and obtain the court's permission to ask him some questions.

The first few innocent queries were enough to wring from Titus a bleat for help. "My Lord, I desire, if your Lordship please, that Mr Langhorn may ask the Court, and the Court ask me; for I know the Court will be so kind, as to ask me such Questions as are reasonable, and proper for me to answer." Scroggs agreed; but even so it was bad enough. Langhorne, like the Five Jesuits, was obstinately inquisitive about Titus's visit to London in April and May, 1678. How long had he stayed? Who had come over with him? Did he travel to London from the coast by coach or horseback? Where did he lie in London? And so on. Then, suddenly, Langhorne changed the subject.

"*Langhorne.* I remember he professed himself a Roman Catholick, I see he is a Minister [for Titus, as usual, was in his gown and cassock]: I desire to know of him when he left the Protestant Religion, and became a Convert, as he called himself; call it what you will, when he left being a Protestant, and became a Papist, that is what I mean.

"*Dr Oates.* He does it for nothing but to quarrel.

"*L.C.J.* When did you leave the Church of England?

"*Dr Oates*. My Lord, if it be the pleasure of the Bench to ask me that Question——

"*L.C.J.* You ought to answer it, tho' it be nothing to the Purpose.

"*Dr Oates*. Then I answer, it was either in February or March, 1676/7.

"*Lang*. My Lord, I desire to know whether he had any Benefice.

"*Dr. Oates*. Yes, I was sometime Vicar of Bobbing in Kent. But I suppose this is to make me accuse myself of something, whereby I might forfeit my Living: for, my Lord, I have a Right in a Point of Equity still to that Living, but only for going beyond Sea without Leave of my Ordinary, I am not now Vicar of [Bobbing].

"*Lang*. When did you come to your Vicarage?

"*Dr Oates*. In 1672.

"*Lang*. You became a Papist in 1677. I ask this question, whether he did leave his Living before he turned Papist?

"*Dr Oates*. My Lord, I am not willing to answer that question."

Indeed he was not. The shoals and quicksands of his past were all about him, the disgrace of Bobbing, the Parker scandal, the expulsion from the Navy. But there was no help for it; he had got to make some kind of an answer, for even the Lord Chief Justice seemed temporarily to have deserted him.

"*L.C.J.* When did you leave your Living? Did you leave it before you went away?

"*Dr Oates*. It was not very long before, but the reason why I am not willing to tell, is, when I left the Parish, I left it in the Charge of Mr Thomas Turner, Vicar of Milton, and I did go about Chichester, and served a Sequestration there. The Air was not a good Air in that part of Kent, and I had not my Health; and that was one Reason, and for other Reasons best known to myself."

He must have been sweating, must poor Titus, as he gabbled these incoherent explanations; but the prisoner himself saved him further embarrassment by most unwisely demanding whether, when he became a Papist, he became a Jesuit also. The Bench pounced like lightning upon so improper a question, observing that whether or no Titus had said in his *Narrative* that he became a Jesuit, narratives were not evidence, and that in any case it was a matter of doubt whether Dr Oates's pardon would cover admission to the Society of Jesus. The fact that Langhorne, closely confined since his arrest nearly nine months previously, had had to rely on the printed narratives of Oates and Bedloe for any knowledge of the charges to be brought against him weighed with the judges not at all. But they need not have troubled themselves by explaining why Titus was not obliged to answer such questions, for Titus flatly refused to answer, and that was that. Nevertheless, it must have been with enormous relief that he heard Langhorne say presently, that, at least for the moment, he had done with Mr Oates.

Bedloe was recalled to tell a new and intriguing story of the Irish invaders planning to land at Milford Haven disguised as pilgrims. When asked by the prisoner, via the Bench, whether he had now completed his charges against him, he replied in mild rebuke: "I cannot say, my Lord, that this is all I have to say against him; Things may occur to my Memory hereafter, which do not now." It was at this precise moment that Titus's memory underwent one of those sudden improvements so common to it. He had omitted, he confessed, something very material; this was to the effect that the Congregation in Rome had contributed 800,000 crowns towards the expenses of the Plot, and that this sum was known by Langhorne to have reached France in July or August. Bedloe's memory immediately caught the infection, and he remembered that Father Keynes went to see Langhorne and came out with a letter; and taking Bedloe into a tobacco-shop in Wild Street, told him the contents of it, namely, that Cardinal Barbarino had written chidingly to the prisoner because the latter did not go on faster with the business of the Plot.

After the prosecution had brought a witness to prove the Plot in general (he turned out to be the Duke of Monmouth's cook), Langhorne made what defence he could. This was necessarily confined to an endeavour to discredit the two principal witnesses against him, and he first demanded to know whether they were not guilty of the very treason with which they charged him, since, by their own admission, they had been active in carrying letters and so forth between the plotters. Bedloe replied with satisfaction that he had three pardons from the King; Oates made the odd statement, "I have two Pardons under the Broad-Seal, but I don't know what is in them." Langhorne turned next to the sordid subject of rewards; had the witnesses received any, and did they expect any more?

"I have received a Reward," snapped Titus indignantly, "by disbursing 6 or 700. *l.* out of my Pocket, and I don't know when I shall see it again."

The Bench itself was shocked beyond measure by Langhorne's question. Did he think that the King bribed witnesses? He had been told by a fellow prisoner, answered Langhorne, one Reading, that Bedloe had a reward of five hundred pounds. Reading, retorted the Lord Chief Justice, had stood in the pillory and therefore was disabled from being a witness. But really he was surprised at the prisoner for making these insinuations. "Mr Langhorn, whatsoever you object of this kind, does fly in the Face, and reflect upon the Integrity and Wisdom, of King, Lords, and Commons." Bedloe added plaintively that he also was seven hundred pounds out of pocket for his patriotism; which, considering that he was newly come out of prison when he made his "discovery", seems a little strange.

Langhorne now called the St Omer witnesses, whereupon Titus pretended fright. "My Lord," he cried, "here are Papists come into Court with their Swords on." "They will not draw them here," Scroggs reassured him; and the Lord Mayor added some soothing words: " 'Tis well enough, 'tis well enough, Dr Oates, you are safe enough here." Amid the frankly expressed boredom and contempt of the Bench, these ferocious Papists, most of them lads in their teens, were permitted to give their evidence. Then Mrs Grove, widow of John Grove, testified that Titus had not lain at her house, as he said he had, at the time of the "Grand Consult"; in answer to which, Sir Creswell Levinz explained to the jury that naturally Titus would then have been in a disguise. A few minutes later, Lord Castlemaine entered, and informed the Bench that some of the defence witnesses had been so threatened and abused by the rabble outside that they dared not come into court to give their evidence. There was one so manhandled, he said indignantly, that it was doubtful whether he would survive. The entire Bench lifted up its hands in pious horror. It was a dreadful thing, an unjustifiable thing; it was not to be suffered; it should be looked into. Lord Castlemaine had but to name the villains who had perpetrated this outrage, and they should be punished. His lordship not being able to give a name to that many-headed monster, the mob, the case continued.

The widow of the landlord of the White Horse tavern was called by the defence, and stated that there was no room in her late husband's tavern large enough to contain more than a dozen persons at a time. (Titus had sworn that at the "Grand Consult", which he said was held in this tavern, there had been fifty Jesuits present, though lately he had reduced the number to eighteen or twenty.) Three strangers in the court immediately stood up and contradicted the witness, saying that twenty or even thirty could be accommodated in the largest room. The appearance of these three strangers was so suspiciously timely, that one is left with the impression that the informers had got wind of the calling of the landlord's widow, and had brought these gentlemen into court specially to contradict her. The woman had shown considerable courage in coming forward, and her evidence was candid and simple. She had asked: "Is that Mr Oates?" and on being told it was, said she had never seen him before, and she thought she remembered all her customers. In regard to the White Horse tavern, she said: " 'Tis a small inconsiderable House, there is not a Room in it that will hold above a dozen, I never remembred so great a Company was in my House at one Time, but once, in all my Seven Years, and that was a Jury of the Parish, and they could not be together, but were divided into three Rooms." This gave the Lord Chief Justice his chance to explain to the jury that no doubt the conspirators had met there in several different companies on the same morning.

Denied the right to question Oates upon his previous statement that Ireland was in London during August, Langhorne returned to Titus's odd assertion that he was out of pocket over his discovery of the Plot. He would like to examine a couple of witnesses, said Langhorne, concerning Mr Oates's financial position previous to his appearance as an informer. The Bench dealt with this with admirable firmness.

"*L.C.J.* Look you, here is the Thing, he gives you an Answer, to which he was not in the least bound, nor is it to be charged by you; he says he is out Seven Hundred Pounds, but that is not Evidence, nor is the Jury to take any notice of it, nor is it to affect him. And would you have him give us an Account how he came by that Money?"

Since an answer in the affirmative would have been futile, Langhorne passed on to a question about Bedloe. He would like to know how it came about that Mr Bedloe, having told the Lords that he had no more persons to accuse than those he had already named, now brought these charges against himself; he offered in evidence a copy of the Record of the House of Lords. The Bench with some asperity refused to accept it; it was not evidence, and even if it had been, the probability was that Bedloe had omitted to accuse Langhorne only because of some understandable lapse of memory. "You see that now at these Trials," said Scroggs with dignity, "he says sometimes, this is all I can remember at present, but by and by he recollects himself; would you hinder him from saying then what he remembers?"

Plainly it was useless to attempt a defence. One of Langhorne's witnesses, a woman, affirmed that she dared not give her testimony because of the threats of the rabble; Mr Charles Howard, who was brave enough to come forward and state that the prosecution witness, Clay, had erred in saying that Oates was at Arundel House in May, '78, made no impression whatsoever upon the Bench or the jury; and the rest of the witnesses who testified to having seen Titus during the crucial period, though their evidence varied considerably from that which they had given on the previous day, yet were received by all as persons of the highest probity. Still, with temperance and calmness, Langhorne persisted in saying what he could in his own defence, though he admitted that circumstances had made it a poor one. "I have been a close Prisoner so long, and have had but one Week's time to provide, and therefore must be fain to take such Information as my Friends and Relations could pick up, to answer what he [Oates] hath said in his Narratives, supposing he would have said the same here; therefore I am not able to make any better Defence. . . . These Men have had time to get their Witnesses together: I never saw one of mine till they came into Court. I hope, my Lord, I shall find no Disadvantage in my coming here upon the account of my Religion, for that would seem as if you condemned me meerly for that: I disclaim all Principles of Disloyalty; and I do assure your Lordship, I do believe it is Damnation to any one that shall go about to kill the King, or deprive him of his Government: I shall leave the rest to your Lordship and the Jury."

His Lordship proceeded to direct the jury against the prisoner, taking particular care to discredit the St Omer witnesses. Young Papists, he said, were bred to believe that "a Lye does God good Service, if it be for the Propagation of the Faith". He dealt very tenderly and respectfully with the witnesses who had testified to having seen Oates in London during the time of the "Grand Consult", adding with what must have been unconscious irony: "Now must all these People be downright Perjured; it can be no Mistake, but they are all falsely forsworn, if there be not Truth in it. And when here are Seven or Eight Witnesses positively Swearing, against the Affirmation of so many others [the defence witnesses were not permitted to be sworn], we leave the Credit of both Sides to you, who are the Judges of the Fact."

Again the jury were absent for a very brief space, and again the verdict was that of Guilty. "Upon which there was a very great Shout." The Five Jesuits were brought into the dock to hear the dread sentence in company with Langhorne; and yet again, when it was ended, there was a thunder of applause. London, like a tiger, licked its lips at the thought of so much blood.

(16)

The Popish Plot had created such a madness in the nation as even its managers can scarcely have anticipated; and there seemed no reason why, after a little more skilful handling of it, it should not prove a mortal weapon against the Monarchy itself. Titus was already saying in private that the King was as arrant a Papist as his brother;[109] Titus would make no bones about saying the same thing publicly if ordered by his patrons so to do. It might seem hard to prove Charles an accessory to a plot to kill himself, but nothing was too difficult for men like Shaftesbury. He was in the Plot, they would say, but was unaware of the assassination part of it. The country was just in the mood to believe anything; the King was fighting with his back to the wall, his only weapon the continued prorogation of Parliament; the mob was at its most dangerous, goaded continually by broadsheets, lampoons, ballads, and rumours, excited to fever pitch by the butcheries at Tyburn, itching to satisfy its craving for mischief with something more concrete than the maltreatment of defence witnesses and the shrieking of insults at fettered prisoners.

There was only one thing needed to make the success of the Plot complete, and that was for one of the accused to "confess" to its reality in return for his life. So far, not one single victim had yielded to this temptation; the steadfastness, or obstinacy, of the victims, particularly of lowly ignorant men like Hill, Green, and Berry, was unnatural; and the Plot managers were determined to try again. So, on the eve of their execution, Shaftesbury approached Gavan and Turner in Newgate, and promised them a free pardon if they would acknowledge their guilt. The choice of these two showed cunning, for Gavan was young, and Turner had given himself up, which seemed to argue a certain timidity. But once again my lord was disappointed. Gavan answered very simply for them both, that "he would not murder his soul to save his body; for that to acknowledge the plot would be acknowledging what he knew not, and what he did believe was not".[110]

Therefore on Friday, June 20th, were all five Jesuits tied on hurdles outside Newgate, Whitebread and Harcourt on one, Gavan and Turner on another, and Fenwick on a third by himself. Thus strapped prone upon the wooden sledges, and accompanied by a drum and fife band and by a large force of soldiers, they were drawn to Tyburn-tree. A greater crowd than had ever been seen before accompanied the procession and swarmed about the gallows; yet, so incalculable is the mood of mobs, that the very hooligans who had yelled and execrated at the trial listened in silence to the speeches of the five victims on the scaffold. Whitebread spoke first, reaffirming his innocence, forgiving his enemies, praying for the King, and repudiating the favourite charge against the Jesuits that they had a dispensation to lie in the cause of their religion. Old Harcourt, who followed, was three times interrupted by Sheriff How. Turner, who came next, deliberately referred to the "Grand Consult".

"It is true," he said, "I was at the Congregation of Jesuits held on the 24th of April was twelve-month; but in that meeting, as I hope to be saved, we meddled not with state affairs, but only treated about the concerns of our Province, which is usually done by us, without offence to temporal princes, every third year all the world over." "You do only justify yourselves here," broke in the Sheriff. "We will not believe a word that you say. Spend your time in prayer, and we will not think our time too long." "I am, good people," continued Turner, ignoring the interruption, "as free from the treason I am accused of as the child that is unborn, and being innocent I never accused myself in confession of any thing that I am charged with. Certainly, if I had been conscious to myself of any guilt in this kind, I should not so frankly and freely as I did, of my own accord, have presented myself before the King's most honourable privy council."[111]

Gavan spoke with the eloquence for which he was famous, ending in this manner:

"And having discharged my duty towards myself, and my own innocence; towards my Order, and its doctrines; to my neighbour and the world, I have nothing else to do now, my great God, but to cast myself into the arms of your mercy. I believe you are one divine essence and three divine persons; I believe that you in the second person of the Trinity became man to redeem me; and I believe you are an eternal rewarder of the good, and an eternal chastiser of the bad. In fine, I believe all you have revealed for your own infinite veracity; I hope in you above all things for your own infinite fidelity; and I love you above all things for your infinite beauty and goodness; and I am heartily sorry that ever I offended so great a God, with my whole heart: I am content to undergo an ignominious death, my dear Jesu, seeing you have been pleased to undergo an ignominious death for love of me."[112]

Lastly came Fenwick, who had scarcely started to speak before Sheriff How began a series of interruptions, which ended by that worthy gentleman's giving the spectators an account of his own firm belief in the Plot and in the guilt of those hanged for the murder of Godfrey.

The hangman had adjusted the halters and had descended from the cart; the five victims were pulling down their white caps; when, suddenly and dramatically, there was a commotion in that vast crowd as a horseman came thrusting his way through it, waving a paper above his head and yelling at the top of his voice "A pardon! A pardon?"

The Sheriff, bewildered and incredulous, snatched the paper; it proved actually to be a pardon signed by the King, but attached to it was the condition that the Five Jesuits should "acknowledge the Conspiracy, and lay open what they knew thereof". The victims, smiling, answered that they thanked the King for his clemency, but that it was not in their power to fulfil the conditions, because they could not disclose that of which they possessed no knowledge.[113] They were immediately turned off; but, contrary to sentence, were allowed to hang until they were dead, and the butchery was perpetrated upon their lifeless bodies.

This failure of Jack Ketch (who treated his clients according to their popularity or otherwise with the mob) to carry out his duty, combined with the unusual patience, and even respect, with which the multitude had listened to the last speeches of the priests, seemed to argue a sudden fall in fevered England's temperature; moreover, the impression made by the printed speeches was such as seriously to alarm the managers of the Plot, particularly as these speeches had been most carefully edited before publication. The Opposition news-sheets took every opportunity of reminding their readers of the guilt of the victims; and the *Domestick Intelligence, or News both from City and Country* added to its description of the arrest of a Richard Blundel (who again turned out not to be the Blundel mentioned in Titus's *Narrative*), the remark that this arrest "may reasonably take off the impression that the last words of those Jesuits who have been executed, may have made upon some tender minds". But the effect of the speeches was even worse abroad, and poor Mr Henry Savile was seriously worried; "they have a terrible effect heer", he wrote from Paris to Secretary Jenkins, "people being soe possessed against us upon this occasion, that it will need some very exact narrative of ail has passed amongst us to convince the world our proceedings have not been soe barbarous as heer and everywhere southward they have been reported to bee".[114]

The Plot managers, determined to counteract the impression made by these speeches, made a really strenuous effort to induce Langhorne to "confess" to the Plot. When he refused, they made a second offer; he should have his life if he would disclose the amount of the property of the Jesuits in England. To this he agreed, and his books and papers were restored to him. But contrary to popular belief, the amount turned out to be anything but sensational, for the Jesuits, far from being rich, maintained their work by alms and economic management. So determined, however, was Shaftesbury to use Langhorne as a means to a complete restoration of the credit of the Plot, that, in a personal interview, he informed the barrister that he should have not only his life, but any reward he chose to name, if only he would admit the reality of the conspiracy. Langhorne, to his eternal honour, refused; and on July 14th he too started on that dolorous journey which led to the noose, the quartering-block, and the smoking cauldron.

He wore, we are told, a black suit and periwig,[115] and he carried with him on the sledge the manuscript of his last speech, which he had written in prison. This he gave to Sheriff How upon the scaffold, saying that the noise of the multitude prevented him from being heard, and desiring that the speech might be printed. In it he had enumerated the great preferments and estates offered him if he would have consented to acknowledge the Plot.[116] When the hangman placed the rope about his neck, he took it in his hands and kissed it. His last words were: "Blessed Jesus, into thy hands I recommend my soul and spirit; now at this instant take me into Paradise. I am desirous to be with my

Jesus. I am ready, and you need stay no longer for me." When the cart was drawn away, "the hangman having struck him on the breast, and pull'd his legs to dispatch him, he was stripped, and being quite dead was cut down and the sentence executed upon him".[117]

(17)

On July 18th, four days after the execution of Langhorne, yet another batch of victims was placed in the dock at the Old Bailey; they were Sir George Wakeman, the Queen's physician, and three Benedictine monks, William Marshal, William Rumley, and James Corker. The last-named had appeared with the Five Jesuits at their trial, but having pleaded that, given time, he could produce witnesses, had enjoyed the unusual favour of being remanded back to Newgate.

For some while the trial proceeded in the manner of its predecessors; the King's Evidence swore, evaded, embellished, and swaggered; the Bench bullied the prisoners, deferred to Oates and his colleagues, airily swept aside inconvenient testimony, and listened with indulgence to the most glaring inconsistencies on the part of the informers. Bedloe was particularly brazen, and made such choice statements as "I cannot directly at present call to mind the Person's name, I may by and by, perhaps", and Dugdale got himself into such deep water that the entire Bench had to come in a body to his aid. Prance, who came next, had recalled several new details, and Robert Jenison, a new informer, whose brother was a Jesuit, had a great deal to tell about an interview with Ireland in London in the previous August, during which Ireland had said it would not be hard to poison the King. It was plain that Jenison had been most carefully coached beforehand, and that his evidence was deemed of the utmost importance; for the completeness of Ireland's alibi had somewhat disturbed the managers of the Plot.

"But now, Gentlemen," said Sir Robert Sawyer, K.C., grimly to the prisoners, "it will behove you to take notes, for we shall come home to you, and we begin with Dr Oates."

Dr Oates's evidence was refreshingly different from that which he had given at former trials. The "Grand Consult", the Four Ruffians, the lurking assassins in St James's Park, all had grown a little stale; here was something to titillate the jaded appetites of his admirers. It seemed that Father Ashby, Rector of St Omers, had applied to Sir George Wakeman in London in the previous July for instructions for a cure at Bath. Wakeman had given him a prescription in writing, "a Pint of Milk in the Morning, and a Pint of Milk at Night, and should drink no Morning's Draught but Milk, and that he should have one hundred Strokes at the Bath, at the Pump"; the physician had added, presumably as a psychological tonic, the news that the Queen had agreed to murder the King. A day or two afterwards, Titus (who said he had no previous acquaintance with Wakeman), went to Ashby's lodging, and there he saw Wakeman "sit in a writing Posture, I saw him lay by his Pen, rise up and go away, and the same Hand that he left behind him in a Paper where the Ink was not dry, was the same Hand that writ the Letter to Mr Ashby".

There followed the old story, told by Titus to the Council at the time when he had accused the Queen, of his being taken by some Jesuits to Somerset House and of his overhearing her Majesty agree to poison her husband; but even here Titus was able to introduce a little novelty. Now his story was, that when the Fathers came out from her presence, he had expressed a great desire to see her, so they had brought him into her apartment, when she immediately had asked Father Harcourt (in this stranger's presence) whether he had received the £1,000. It was the very same voice, Titus assured the court, which he had just heard agreeing to the murder of the King. In the same month, Wakeman had been offered (of course in Titus's presence) ten thousand pounds to undertake the poisoning, but he had refused it. Letters were then sent to Whitebread, who ordered his brethren to add another five thousand to the price; and the physician had settled for this figure. Titus admitted that he had not himself witnessed this acceptance, because he was then sick of the stone, but he had seen the transaction inscribed in the "Entry Book" of the Jesuits at Wild House; the writing was Harcourt's, and with his own eyes had he seen Wakeman's signature, acknowledging the receipt of five thousand pounds on account. He could not tell what day in August, nor in what place, this money had been paid.

Asked if he had anything more to say against Wakeman, Titus replied with his usual caution that that was all he could recollect at present. This necessitated a gentle prompt from Sir Robert Sawyer; was there not a little matter of a commission? Yes, there was, replied Titus; there was a commission for Wakeman as Physician-General of the Popish army; he himself had seen it in Wakeman's hands.

Wakeman immediately challenged him on the letter to Father Ashby. Had not Mr Oates said previously that he did not know his handwriting? There was, retorted Titus, that occasion when he had seen him sit in a "writing Posture"; what was written then must have been written by the prisoner, for the only other gentleman in the room (presumably Ashby) "was lame of both Hands". Wakeman, leaving this point for the moment, referred to that awkward moment in the Council Chamber last September, when Titus had denied knowing him. But the Saviour of the Nation had met this one before, and was not abashed by it.

"My Lord," he brayed, "you may be pleased to know, when I saw Sir George Wakeman at the Council I had been up two Nights together, and the King was willing once to excuse me from staying any further Examination, and being so ill and indisposed for want of Rest, in respect both of my Intellectuals, and everything else, I might not charge him so home; but now I have a proper Light whereby I may see a Man's Face, I can say more to him."

"This," cried the prisoner, "is just Coleman's case, the Light was in your Eyes."

Pressed still further on this subject, Titus stood on his dignity and simply refused to answer. He must have been amazed and affronted to hear Scroggs say, with unwonted sharpness, that certainly he must answer if the question were lawful. However, added the Lord Chief Justice, Wakeman might call his witnesses presently, and meanwhile Dr Oates should state his charges against the other prisoners. This Dr Oates proceeded to do. Corker, he said, had a patent from Rome to be Bishop of London, and from

Lambspring in Germany had written a letter at the end of last August giving his consent to the raising of £6,000 by the Benedictines, of whom he was President, in aid of the Plot. Marshal and Rumley likewise had given their consent (though the latter was only a lay brother); this was about all Titus could recollect against the three monks "at present", except that when Fathers Hitchcot, Howard, and Coniers were laying wagers as to whether the King would live to eat any more Christmas-pies, Marshal had gone halves in a bet with Coniers that he would not.

Marshal immediately showed an embarrassing desire to find out just when had taken place this "Consult" of the Benedictines, of which Titus had spoken so much. It was in August, said Titus. But what date in August? Between the first and the middle. Marshal appealed to the Bench. How was it possible for him and his fellow prisoners to make their defence if their accusers would not be more definite regarding dates? "'Tis fit he should answer," returned Scroggs, who seemed to be in a bad temper, "if he can tell the Time, but if he cannot, we can't help it." Oates thereupon deigned to observe that if the prisoners could tell him the date of the Feast of the Assumption, he could fix the other date. August 15th, Marshal informed him.

"*Dr Oates*. My Lord, it was either the Day before, or the Day after [in his Narrative he had stated that it was August 21st].

"*Marshall*. Now he hath avouched this positively.

"*Dr Oates*. Nay, I will not be positive.

"*Marshal*. But you were so, that it was the Day before, or the Day after.

"*Dr Oates*. I appeal to the Judges of the Court."

It was an appeal which never yet had failed to produce the required protection, but on this occasion it was not quite so successful. Scroggs, mildly indeed, but with a new and alarming persistence, tried in vain to elicit a positive answer. After a few minutes of this, Titus could stand no more. "My Lord," he bleated, "I desire I may have leave to retire, because I am not well." "You must stay, Dr Oates," unkindly replied the Lord Chief Justice, "till after their Defence be over." Mr Recorder, evidently distressed by the plight of the Saviour of the Nation, hastened to add: "If you desire to have any Refreshment, you shall have it got for you."

It is to be doubted whether the recalling of Bedloe made Titus feel any better. For not only had Bedloe nothing against Rumley (a fact which ensured that prisoner's acquittal), but he had imperfectly rehearsed his piece against Wakeman. After the informer had finished his evidence against the other prisoners, and Wakeman was about to call his witnesses, the Lord Chief Justice startled the court by remarking to Sir Robert Sawyer that he did not think that Bedloe had said anything material against any of the prisoners; he then briefly rehearsed that informer's evidence. Sawyer demurring, Bedloe was again recalled, with a caution to have a care what he said; he took the hint, and this time said his piece correctly, which drew from Scroggs the exclamation, astonishing from those lips: "He says now quite another thing than he said before." Wakeman, on the other hand, who was ignorant when he came into court of what Bedloe's accusation against him would be, and therefore had no defence whatever, turning to his fellow prisoners, cried in despair:

"There is my business done!"

The best Sir George could do was to concentrate on disproving the evidence of Oates, and for this purpose he called a Mr Chapman (a Protestant, by the way), ex-Mayor of Bath. This gentleman testified that on July 17th last, a very feeble and infirm old gentleman who was really Father Ashby, but was then passing under the name of Thimbleby, had come to Bath for a cure, and had applied to him, Chapman, for lodgings. Chapman, by profession an apothecary, had been handed by this old gentleman a prescription from a doctor; he had torn off the Latin portion of the document, because it concerned him in his professional capacity, but the English portion he now produced in court. It contained not one word about the King or the Queen, except that he was desired to provide for the patient a lodging as near as possible to their Majesties' bath. This note was not in the hand of Wakeman, which he knew well, to prove which fact he produced several of Wakeman's prescriptions.

It appeared that on the day the prescription for Ashby, with its postscript about lodgings, was written, Wakeman had come home tired and unwell, and had bidden his man Hunt (himself an apothecary), write at his dictation; Hunt confirmed this, described how Wakeman had dictated the prescription to him, and how, early next morning, he himself had carried it to Ashby, who was to go that very day to Bath. Another witness, Elizabeth Henningham, testified that she had been present at the writing of this document, which she had seen and read. Lastily, Wakeman insisted that the prescription Oates swore to having seen contained directions such as no doctor would give; to order milk to be drunk with the waters, for instance, was quite unheard of. In reply to all this, Titus invented the feeble retort that the document produced was not the one he had described in his charge against the prisoner.

But Wakeman had not done with him yet. Mr Oates had described this mythical document at the Bar of the House of Commons, but, when he came before the Lords, had said positively that he did not know Wakeman's hand. Surely, insisted Sir George, if he had then such proof as now he had, "if he had seen me writing, and came into the Room where the Paper I writ was yet wet", he would have mentioned it when examined about his knowledge of the prisoner's handwriting. Called on by Scroggs to explain this mystery, Titus could muster up only the old puerile excuses.

"*Dr Oates*. My Lord, Sir George Wakeman had his Liberty because I was so weak, by reason of being up two Nights together, one whereof was very wet, and being hot, wet, and cold, all in a few Hours time, so that I thought it would have cost me my Life; not being used to such hard Services, I did not charge Sir George so fully: Tho' it may be objected to this Court, that I was bound to speak the whole Truth; and so I did, as Opportunity and Health would give me leave. And as to the Letter, and what I said about it in the Lords House, Sir George is mistaken. He says here that I said I knew his Hand no otherwise, but by seeing Sir George Wakeman subscribed to it."

At this, Sir George promptly called Sir Philip Lloyd, Clerk of the Council, who had been present when Oates was examined before the King on the last day of September, 1678. Lloyd described the whole scene, and especially how Oates, having said he had seen a letter from Whitebread to Fenwick in which it was stated that Wakeman had agreed to poison the King, was called in again and asked if he had anything definite against Wakeman other than that he had already deposed. "Mr Oates," continued Lloyd, "when he did come in again, and was asked the Question, did lift up his Hands (for I must tell the Truth, let it be what it will) and said, No, God forbid that I should say any thing against Sir George Wakeman, for I know nothing more against him. And I refer myself to the whole Council whether it was not so."

Driven into a corner, Titus went into a perfect orgy of self-pity. "My Lord, the Council did not press me to my Knowledge; I will not be positive, but if the Council did press me, and I did make that Answer, I do appeal to the whole Board, whether or no I was in a Condition to make any Answer at all, when, by reason of my being hurried up and down, and sitting up, I was scarce *Compos mentis*." "What!" snapped Scroggs, suddenly losing his temper altogether, "must we be amused with I know not what, for being up but two Nights? It did not require such a deal of strength to say, I saw a Letter under Sir George's own Hand." This was too much for Titus; he had been actually rebuked by his special protector, the Lord Chief Justice. He took refuge in insolence. "To speak the Truth," he sneered, "they were such a Council as would commit no Body." It was just about the worst thing he could have said; and the court listened in breathless silence while Mr Recorder delivered to the Saviour of the Nation a sharp rebuke for daring to speak thus of the King's most honourable Privy Council.

It was now the turn of Marshal and Corker to make their defence; Rumley, since there was only one witness against him, was relieved from that necessity. The other two defended themselves with skill and vigour, Corker asserting that "he that Swears against another, ought to be himself a Credible Witness; and then, secondly, strengthned by Probable Circumstances; Circumstances that bring along with them some Probable Evidence distinct from the Witnesses themselves: otherwise, I think that the Party

THE DEVIL, TITUS OATES AND THE POPE

accused, without any Proof of his side, ought to remain in the Possession of his own Innocency." In an endeavour to expose the absurdity of Oates's story in general, he produced a witness, Ellen Rigby, housekeeper to the Benedictines, who testified that Corker and Marshal were in bed in the same house in which Pickering was taken, and yet Oates had not arrested the two fathers, nor had he then accused them of anything at all. Marshal, for his part, boldly warned the Bench of the results of its notorious partiality:

"I do not fear Death tho' it should appear in far more frightful shapes, than that we may be like to suffer. So, my Lord, it is not so much a concernedness for my own Life, as for the Honour and Justice of the Court, that I plead for a Respite to have Witnesses that may positively and particularly disprove the Testimony of Mr Oates. . . . Every Judge is as much obliged to follow his Conscience, as any Formality in Law."

"Pray teach your own Disciples," angrily retorted Scroggs, "don't teach us: You come and talk here what regard we are to have to our own Consciences, as if we did not know that better than any Papist or Priest in the World."

But Marshal, nothing abashed, replied in a speech of great length and notable eloquence. He spoke of those already executed for the Plot, of their protesting their innocence with their latest breath, of the "Landskip of Horror" and the "Caves of Darkness" to which they must have condemned themselves if, upon the very brink of Eternity, they had lied. "Present Content," he cried, "where the Enjoyment is like to continue, works with a strong Influence upon humane Nature, and chains it fast to the present World. But, my Lord, with the approach of Death, Reformation of Conscience doth offer to advance, and we do observe those who have lived a very ill Life, frequently to make a good end; but, my Lord, it is a thing scarce ever heard of or known, that those who have lived all their Lives well, should die ill." Bedloe at least among the informers had owned himself a villain; was it so unlikely then that such a man should bear false witness, "while Preferment tickles him, Rewards march before him, and Ambition beckons to him, which he greedily follows, tho'

God and Conscience tell him 'tis unjust?" Lastly, he hinted that posterity would censure the notorious partiality of the judges in these trials; and at that Scroggs interrupted, and himself launched into one of his famous diatribes against the Catholic faith.

"I do believe," thundered the Lord Chief Justice, "it is possible for an Atheist to be a Papist, but 'tis hardly possible for a knowing Christian to be a Christian and a Papist. . . . Therefore never bragg of your Religion, for it is a foul one, and so contrary to Christ, that 'tis easier to believe any thing, than to believe an understanding Man may be a Papist. You have provoked me to this: and indeed I ought to do it, because you have so much reflected on the Justice of the Court. . . . Perhaps you have Tricks enough to gull your own Party, but you have not to deceive Protestants. . . . We have a Bench of Aldermen have more Wit than your Conclave, and a Lord Mayor that is an infallible as your Pope."

Marshal answered with a last appeal:

"Then, my Lord, for a Conclusion, I have been told, and I will only desire the Jury to take notice of it, that every Jury that finds a Man guilty of Death, upon the Testimony of Witnesses that come in against him, do take it solemnly upon their Consciences, that what such Witnesses swear is true."

"That they believe they swear true," corrected Scroggs; adding with a vicious sneer: "For we have no Infallibility with us: 'Tis one thing to say 'tis true, and another thing to say we believe it is true. Look you, the Jury may give a Verdict which is false, and yet go according to their Consciences. Do you understand that, Priest?"

The bitterness expressed in that last word is reflected in the first part of Scroggs' summing-up. No one who reads his speech can doubt that the Lord Chief Justice was in a thoroughly bad temper, riled beyond bearing by Marshal's hints at his partiality, and in all probability disgusted by the poor show put up by the King's Evidence. He was obliged to begin by directing the jury to acquit Rumley; his reply to the objection of the other prisoners, that there was nothing against them except the witness of those two doubtful characters, Oates and Bedloe, was that there was the

Plot itself, concerning which Prance, Dugdale, and Jenison had all given evidence. He touched upon the vexed question as to whether or no Father Ireland had been in London in August; and it is highly probable that the overwhelming proof formerly offered that he had not been, and that his death had been judicial murder, had much to do with the almost unbelievable pettiness with which Scroggs sneered at those already executed for the Plot. Evidently, he taunted, the men who had thus protested their innocence on the scaffold "did suppose a Purgatory, where you may be purged from such Peccadillos as this dying with a Lye in your Mouths".

But the second half of Scroggs' summing-up was a complete surprise. Whether as the result of a twinge of conscience, or because he was acute enough to have marked the gradual decline of the national hysteria, the fact remains that the Lord Chief Justice condescended, clean contrary to his custom, to display a measure of impartiality. "Look you, Gentlemen," said he, "we will shew ourselves what we ought to do, let them be what they will; we would not, to prevent all their Plots (let them be as big as they can make them) shed one Drop of innocent Blood. Therefore I would have you, in all these Gentlemen's Cases, consider seriously, and weigh truly the Circumstances, and the Probability of Things charged upon them." To the amazement of all present, he spoke with some asperity about the puerile excuses of Oates. "I tell you plainly, I think a Man could not be so weak, but he could have said, he saw a Letter under his Hand." His conclusion was shattering in its contrast with those of the former trials:

"These Mens Bloods are at stake, and your Souls and mine, and our Oaths and Consciences are at stake; and therefore never care what the World says, follow your Consciences; if you are satisfied these Men swear true, you will do well to find them Guilty, and they deserve to die for it: If you are unsatisfied, upon these Things put together, and they do weigh with you, that they have not said true, you will do well to acquit them."

Titus Oates was petrified into an outraged silence; but Bedloe found his voice in a *cri du cœur*:

"My Lord, my Evidence is not right summed up!"

"I know not," observed the Lord Chief Justice icily as he lumbered off the Bench to seek refreshment, "by what Authority this Man speaks."

The jury was absent a full hour. On its return, the customary procedure was gone through in an atmosphere of sudden suspense. As each prisoner raised his hand, the Clerk of the Crown intoned to the jury the familiar words:

"How say you? Is he guilty of the treason of which he stands indicted, or not guilty?"

But the answer to that question was new and shattering; hitherto it had not been heard in the whole course of these trials.

"Not guilty."

"Down on your knees!" cried the Keeper of Newgate to his four charges in the dock. "Down on your knees!"

"God bless the King and this honourable Bench!" four voices answered in chorus.

It was the first acquittal. It was the first symptom of returning health. England would remain for a long while dangerously sick, but at least the crisis was past.

PART III

THE PLOT IN DECLINE: JULY 18TH, 1679–AUGUST 31ST, 1681

(1)

THE acquittal of Wakeman and his companions infuriated two sections of the people: the Oppositionists and the mob who were their dupes. The first relieved their feelings by circulating a rumour that Scroggs had been bribed to sum up for the defence; by persuading Wakeman to flee overseas through the menace of a second prosecution; by getting the three monks re-committed to Newgate on a charge of priesthood only; by seeing that all manner of new legislation against the Catholics absorbed the attention of the Council; and by insisting on the immediate execution of some of the many priests imprisoned in the provincial jails. Accordingly, Father William Plessington suffered at Chester on July 19th, and on the 22nd Father Philip Evans, S.J., and Father John Lloyd were executed together at Cardiff. On August 7th, 12th, 22nd, and 27th, five more priests were butchered at several different places throughout the kingdom, one of them, Father Nicholas Postgate, being eighty-two years of age, and another, Father John Kemble, eighty.[1] The rage of the mob, on the other hand, expressed itself in a manner typical of an angry rabble; a half-hanged dog was flung into the coach of the Lord Chief Justice as he was leaving London to go on Circuit.

But the average Englishman, though he continued firmly convinced of the reality of the Plot, was become a little ashamed of his hysteria. The attitude of the educated man at this time may be summed up in the following extract from Evelyn, written on the day of Wakeman's trial, which Mr Evelyn himself attended:

"For my part, I looke on Oates as a vain insolent man, puff'd up with the favour of the Commons for having discover'd something really true, more especially as detecting the dangerous intrigue of Coleman, prov'd out of his owne letters, and of a generall designe which the Jesuited party of the Papists ever had, and still have, to ruine the Church of England; but that he was trusted with those great seacrets he pretended, or had any solid ground for what he accus'd divers noblemen of, I have many reasons to induce my contrary beliefe. That among so many Commissions as he affirm'd to have deliver'd to them from P[adre] Oliva and the Pope, he who made no scruple of opening all other papers, letters, and seacrets, should not only not open any of those pretended Commissions, but not so much as take any copy or witnesse of any one of them, is almost miraculous. But the Commons (some leading persons I meane of them) had so exalted him, that they tooke all he said for gospell and without more ado ruin'd all whom he nam'd to be conspirators; nor did he spare whoever came in his way."[2]

Meanwhile, the disgruntled subject of this criticism had taken his wounded pride to Hastings for a short vacation. "Dr Oates having obtained leave of his Majesty to go into the Country for his health sake, hath also a Commission directed to the Sheriff and Justices of the Peace of that County in which he shall reside, to furnish him with a Guard for the safety of his person, if he shall desire it."[3] But he had scarcely commenced his holiday ere he was summoned back to London in connection with Jenison's new "discoveries", that informer having just obliged his patrons by remembering the names of the Four Irish Ruffians, hitherto anonymous. "It is said that Dr Oats who had leave from his Majesty to go to Hastings in Sussex to visit his Friends and Acquaintances is ordered upon this new discovery to return again to London."[4] Dr Oates simply could not be spared. "Two Gentlemen taking Lodgings about Lymehouse, and continuing there for some time, they were suspected by the Inhabitants to be Dangerous Persons; whereupon they procured a Warrant to bring them before a Justice of Peace; and accordingly they were brought Yesterday before Justice Roycroft, and not being able to give a Satisfactory Account of themselves, they were committed to Newgate upon suspicion that one of them is one of the Ruffians, mentioned in his Majesties last Proclamation, it being designed that Dr Oats shall come thither to see whether he knows either of them."[5]

In the middle of September, however, Dr Oates did find time for a little recreation, though the sequel to it proved somewhat humiliating. The antiquary Wood, who was staying with his friend Ralph Sheldon at Weston, records the incident in his journal: "You must note that lord Lovelace brought Oats to a hors-race at Woodstock on Holy Roode day; and because he would have company there to the inriching of the towne, he caused [Oates] to preach on Sunday and Tuesday. This was partly to spite the Lord Treasurer and the King for taking away [Lovelace's] place of ranger. After the horse race was done, Oats sent word to the vice-chancellor [of Oxford] that 'he would come and wait on him, not surprise him, for his degree'. But they denied him—that is, if he was Doctor of Divinity at Salamanca they would incorporate him. . . . Hereupon he and the citizens say wee are Papists."[6]

The King's dangerous illness in August had brought the Duke of York hurrying home from exile to his brother's bedside, but on Charles's recovery the Duke was ordered into banishment once more, the pill being a little sweetened by a similar order to the Duke of Monmouth. The latter, on the eve of departure, had the comfort of an interview with the Saviour of the Nation:

"On Wednesday last, about Eleven of the Clock in the Forenoon, His Grace the Duke of Monmouth, attended by a great Number of Gentlemen, went to Arlington-Garden, where the King then was to take his leave of him. The King Received and Embraced him very affectionately; after which, He went thence into the Pellmell in St James Park, where the Duke met with Dr Oats, who took his leave of Him, with a speech to this purpose; That he wished him a prosperous and happy Voyage, and a quick and speedy Return: And that he hoped he would bear his departure from his Majesties Presence, suitable to that great Courage he always possessed; Especially since he carried the affections and Hearts of many of His Majesties best Protestant Subjects along with him."[7]

(2)

It was just at this time that Titus, smarting from the injury his credit had suffered by the acquittal of Wakeman, hatched a little plot which, had it proved successful, would have afforded him some small consolation.

There was a certain man named Adam Elliot; it will be remembered that he had been for a brief time a fellow student of Titus's at Caius College, Cambridge. On leaving the university in 1668, Elliot, in the fashion of young gentlemen of his class, had crossed the Channel in order to see something of foreign parts before settling down. In the summer of 1670 he had suffered the misfortune, while on his way home to England, of being captured by some of the pirates who at that time infested the seas. His Moorish captors took him to Sallee, where he was sold as a slave to a Jewish merchant, Hamed Lucas, who bought him solely in order to obtain a ransom, rumour stating that Elliot was a near relation of the Duke of Norfolk. Disillusioned on this point, Lucas treated his slave with great cruelty, until at length, in November, 1670, Elliot contrived to make his escape, and after many exciting adventures, got safely home to England. There he took a post as tutor at Oxford; but in 1673, after being ordained by the Bishop of London, he removed to Ireland and settled in Dublin.

Now, in this September of 1679, Elliot was sent for to London as a witness in the case of a contested will. He was about to return to Ireland after the case was over when to his dismay he learned that there was a warrant out for his arrest as a Jesuit.

What had happened was this. The unsuccessful party in the lawsuit, Lord North, happening to encounter Dr Oates at Whitehall, had poured his woes into that sympathetic ear. Titus, scenting reward, and possibly remembering youthful grudges against Elliot (for he was a man who never forgot the smallest of slights), immediately took North to the King, and to his Majesty imparted the information that this man Elliot was really a very dangerous Jesuit disguised in a parson's gown. "Oates told his Majesty, his name was Elliot, and that he knew him very well, for one of the most mischievous wicked men in the world, and that he believ'd he had more malice in him, than all the Jesuits who were hang'd; nay more, says he, he is a Circumsis'd Jesuit. God bless us, says his Majesty, What sort of Jesuit is that? a Jesuit who is no Christian but a Turk, reply'd the

Salamanca Devil."[8] Wasting no time, Oates easily procured a warrant from his friend, Justice Waller; and a constable and some soldiers were sent to arrest Elliot at the house of the Dowager Lady Grey, where he lodged.

But while Elliot, to his bewilderment, was being seized by the law, Titus was learning two most uncomfortable facts. The first was that his victim had very influential friends; the second, that North's motive of revenge in this arrest was so obvious that he would almost certainly back out of the business, and leave his would-be benefactor in the lurch. Titus, therefore, falling into a panic, hastened to Sir William Waller's house, whither Elliot had been taken for examination after his arrest, and protested that the whole thing was a mistake; this mistake had arisen, he said, through his being told by the Fathers at the Scots College in Rome (where, by the way, he had never been), of one Adam Elliot, once a member of their community, who had been seized by the Turks and probably circumcised.

"This", commented Elliot, who later wrote an account of the whole business, "was a piece of such intolerable impudence, that I could hardly refrain giving him the Lye; for he not only contradicted what he had told his Majesty the day before (as persons of the greatest Quality can attest) but he contriv'd a Story, whose every sillable was false. . . . However, I thought it was not convenient to put him out of humour by my contradiction at that time, but . . . I ask'd him if he had anything to alledge why the Constable might not be discharged farther attendance; his Doctorship was pleas'd to speak the word that he might go about his business, and so I was set at liberty."[9]

Elliot returned to Ireland; but it was not to be long ere he would meet with Dr Oates again. Meanwhile, it is interesting to notice how even this innocent parson, who was to show himself, in his later battles with Titus, a doughty fighter, dared not "put out of humour" the informer, who was fresh from his first serious defeat.

(3)

Among all those persons who, for whatever reason, were infuriated by the acquittal of Sir George Wakeman, we may be sure that the man who felt it most keenly was Anthony Ashley Cooper, Earl of Shaftesbury. He was now permanently established at his headquarters in Aldersgate Street, for the City had been always the stronghold of the Opposition, and here, at Thanet House, Shaftesbury's mansion, Dr Oates was ever a welcome visitor. On September 29th, Justice Warcupp noted in his journal: "In Fleete Streete I met Dr Oates coming from Shaftsbery. . . . He told me Lord Shaftsbery would dally no longer; he would impeach the duke [of York], against whome he had witnesses to prove high treason."[10]

Evidently Shaftesbury decided after all to dally a while longer; for instead of impeaching James, he unleashed upon a London gradually recovering from its hysteria the silly hoax known as the Meal Tub Plot. It was supposed to be one of a series of "sham plots"—that is, a conspiracy of the Papists to stifle their own Plot by suborning witnesses to swear a false one against the Dissenters. A gentleman calling himself Captain Dangerfield (he had several *aliases*, and about as much right to the military title as Oates to his doctorship), was the hero of this one; he was an old crony of Bedloe's, and the pair had shared prison together on more than one occasion. His story might have caused a sensation had it not come as something of an anti-climax after the scare of the Plot, for it had many picturesque touches; a Popish midwife, Mrs Cellier, figured largely in it; damning documents were "discovered" in a meal-tub in her house; the assassination of Shaftesbury himself was the highlight of the drama; and Dangerfield's descriptions of Mrs Cellier's attempts to slaughter his lordship with a consecrated dagger, and of Shaftesbury's too attentive eye upon his, Dangerfield's, murderous hands, were really very moving indeed. It is regrettable to have to add that Dr Oates shared London's scepticism about the whole affair; Smith, the ex-schoolmaster, visiting his old pupil one day, and enquiring his opinion of the story, was surprised to hear fall from those reverend lips the exclamation: "By the Lord they have put these Papers into the Meal-Tub themselves, and found them when they have done."[11] Yet Titus's cold welcome to this latest "King's Evidence" is understandable, for why should Dangerfield be able to produce papers of any kind when he, Titus, could not?

While his chief patron, Shaftesbury, was busying himself with such attempts to put the great Popish Plot upon its feet again, Titus himself was endeavouring by every means in his power to avenge the insult offered him by the acquittal of Wakeman. He was hatching an accusation against Chief Justice Scroggs, of which more in a moment; and on October 15th, he attacked Sir Philip Lloyd, Clerk of the Council, whose evidence at Wakeman's trial had been particularly damaging to the informer's credit. Lloyd had just given Oates an excuse for this attack by saying, apparently in private conversation, that he now believed there was no Plot at all. The time was not yet come when it was safe to say such a thing, even privately, and Lloyd was haled before the Council. After examination, he was addressed by the Lord Chancellor thus:

"Sir Philip Lloyd, you have in the triall of Sir Geor Wakeman given in such evidence as became an honest man and a good Christian; for the truth is alwaies to be spoken, but more especially when a man's life lyes at stake. Yet you have been to blame in declaring there is no plott at all, since two parliaments have voted it one. For which you are suspended till his majesties farther pleasure."[12]

In the satisfying of his spite, Titus did not, of course, neglect his old method of charging his victims with priesthood. "Last Tuesday in the Evening, the Councill sitting, and Dr Oates being at the door, he observed a Person to be in Discourse with the Countess of Powis, and taking exact notice of him, he discovered him to be one Dormer, a Popish Priest, and charging him therewith, the Countess was pleased to say, that he was no more a Priest than she was; however the contrary being made to appear by Dr Oats, he was seized and taken into custody."[13] Early in December, Titus was the means of sending a Jesuit, Father Lacy, to Newgate, where the latter died in the following March. "Yesterday His Majesty was Graciously pleased in the Gallery at Whitehall to discourse Dr Oates about this persons impudent denial of his name and knowledge of the Doctor, and to express himself well satisfied in the Doctor's Evidence."[14]

Meanwhile the Opposition, having failed to impeach the

Duke of York, since the King, in order to check the Plot madness, continued to do without a Parliament, determined at least to insult him in public. In the month of October, James, who had been given permission to remove from Flanders to Scotland, was invited by the Artillery Company to a feast at Merchant Taylors' Hall on the eve of his departure for Edinburgh. On October 20th, the night preceding this entertainment, a certain Martha Cradocke, whose husband kept the Cider House in Maiden Lane, was attending to the wants of a numerous company assembled there, the customers including Lord Howard of Escrick, Sir William Waller, Dr Tonge, Captain Bedloe, and Dr Oates. As she busied herself with replenishing mugs and tankards, she "heard them speak of going into London next day to affront the Duke of York in his passage, and she heard Lord Howard speak to the following effect, that the Duke was a great rogue, and a Papist, and that he [Howard] would go with the said company into London to affront him and added that the King was as great a Papist as the Duke. . . . And then all the company assented and said they would have no Papists to reign in England and so commanded her to withdraw as they had private business."[15]

On the following day, James duly rode into the City, and was entertained with unusual splendour. The Lord Mayor walked bare-headed before him, despite the Duke's remonstrances; there was a long table occupied by noblemen on the one side and by the Mayor and Aldermen on the other, and five or six more tables at which were accommodated the principal citizens. The streets were crowded to watch the Duke enter and return, and the welcome he received from the common people was such that he remarked to Sir Charles Lyttelton that "this was pritty well for a poore banished man but so little a while since". After the entertainment, as his cavalcade was passing beneath the balcony of a bookseller named Cockeril, there occurred the only unpleasant incident. Upon this balcony stood Lord Howard, Oates, Bedloe, and others of the same ilk, and as the Duke passed by, the two informers shouted out, "A pope! A pope!" and their friends took up the cry. One of the Duke's attendants immediately rode back, and, cocking his pistol, cried, "What factious rogues are these?" Titus and his friends faded discreetly from the balcony, and the multitude, the fickle mob of London, yelled, "No pope, no pope! God bless his Highness!"[16]

Rumour whispered that Oates had not stopped at these petty insults. "There is one sworne to-day", Sir Charles Lyttelton wrote to Lord Hatton on the same date, "that Mr Oates sayd it would never be well in England till the monarchy were elective. This, I think, is sworn to before my Lord Ch. Justice Scroggs, and my Lds Warrant is out for another who will sweare to ye same thing. When that is done, my Lord will give out his Warrant to bring Mr Oates before him; and he will commit him. Say nothing till you heare further."[17]

But the Saviour of the Nation was still too formidable to be brought down by such means; and apparently Titus was not even rebuked.

(4)

The welcome given to James by the City, the very stronghold of the Opposition, was a matter of deep concern to Shaftesbury and his colleagues; and since the Meal Tub Plot had fallen very flat, and they could not look for any more bloody spectacles at Tyburn, at least for the moment, to keep up the hysteria of the mob, they tried a new device. On November 17th there took place the first of those elaborate anti-Popery shows which, for the next few years, were to become an annual nuisance.

Ever since the Gunpowder Plot, November 5th had been celebrated with fireworks, bonfires, and guys, but this was not enough for Shaftesbury's present purpose. At the Green Ribbon Club, where he and his friends met nightly to talk over their plans, it was decided to institute another bonfire night; they chose November 17th because it was the anniversary of the accession of that great patroness of Protestantism, Queen Elizabeth, and they let it be known that they themselves would honour the entertainment with their presence. There was nothing the citizens relished more than a grand free show, and the prospect of a new one, with gaudy pageants and plenty of liquor, was received with tremendous enthusiasm. The gentlemen of the Green

Ribbon Club were excellent showmen and thorough good fellows; they were often to be seen upon the double balconies of their tavern, "with Hats and no Peruques; Pipes in their Mouths, merry Faces, and diluted Throats, for vocal Encouragement of the Canaglia below"; it mattered little to the citizens that the names of some of these gentlemen were ominously reminiscent of the Civil War—Ireton, Falconbridge, Waller, Hutchinson, Claypole, Hollis, and so on. They were generous and genial to the rabble of London, whom they called affectionately *mobile vulgus*, soon shortened to mob; and they were stout in their defence of Liberty, Property, and the Protestant Faith.

So, upon the night of November 17th, 1679, the whole of London turned out to enjoy the sport. The magistrates, who ordinarily frowned upon such night-time frolics, knowing what they entailed in theft, fire, and even murder, did nothing to hinder this particular entertainment, "and no wonder, when it is considered that the Faction . . . had the choosing of the Mayor and Sheriffs of London".[18] This first show is said to have been witnessed by two hundred thousand spectators; the principal pageant in it displayed an effigy of the murdered Godfrey, carried on a horse behind a man dressed as a Jesuit, and with the bellman walking before, chanting at intervals in mournful accents: "Remember Mr Justice Godfrey." But the most vivid description we have of these anti-Popery shows is that of 1681, given by Roger North:

"When we had posted ourselves at Windows, expecting the Play to begin, it was very dark, but we could perceive the street to fill, and the Hum of the croud grew louder and louder, and, at length, with Help of some Lights below, we could discern, not only upwards towards [Temple Bar], where the Squib War was maintained, but downwards towards Fleet-Bridge, the whole street was crouded with People, which made that, which followed, seem very strange. For, about eight at Night, we heard a Din from below, which came up the street, continually encreasing till we could perceive a Motion; and that was a Row of stout Fellows, that came shouldered together across the street, from Wall to Wall on each Side. How the People melted away I cannot tell; but it was plain these Fellows made clear

Board, as if they had swept the street, for what was to come after. . . .

"Behind this Wave (which as all the rest, had many Lights attending) there was a Vacancy, but it filled apace, till another like Wave came up, and so four or five of these Waves passed one after another; and then we discerned more numerous Lights, and Throats were opened with hoarse and tremendous Noise; and, with that, advanced a Pageant born along above the Heads of the Croud, and upon it sat an huge Pope in *Pontificalibus* on his Chair, with a reasonable Attendance for State; but his Primier Minister, that shared most of his Ear, was *il Signior Diavolo*, a nimble little Fellow, in a proper Dress, that had a strange Dexterity in climbing and winding about the Chair from one of the Pope's Ears to the other.

"The next Pageant was a parcel of Jesuits, and, after that (for there was always a decent Space between them) came another with some ordinary Persons with Halters, as I took it, about their necks; and one, with a stenterophonic Tube, sounded Abhorrers, Abhorrers,* most infernally. And lastly came one with a single Person upon it, which some said was the Pamphleteer Sir Roger L'Estrange, some the King of France, some the Duke of York. . . . When these were passed, our Coast began to clear, but it thickened upwards, and the Noise encreased; for, as we were afterwards informed, these stately Figures were planted in a Demilune about an huge Fire that shined upon them; and the Balconies of the Club were ready to crack with their factious Load, till the good People were satiated with the fine Shew; and then the hierogylphic Monsters were brought condignly to a new Light of their own making, being, one after another, added to encrease the Flames: All which was performed with fitting Salvos of the Rabble echoed from the Club, which made a proper Music to so pompous a Sacrifice."[19]

"It might be asked", observes the shrewd North, "what was the End or Intention of all this Pains and Expence? It is easy to answer it was not for meer Sport; that's too Boyish for such a noble Society, and their Drivers in secret, to design and execute with so much Application. . . . The

* The first nickname of what was to become the Tory Party.

Faction had always, upon the Tip of their Tongues, the People, and all their Routs were the People; and now they intended, by this Leviathan Mob, to shew the People in good Earnest. And then the King, if he had not known better, might perhaps have mistaken this Assembly for the People whom he was to satisfy, and whom nothing would pacify but the Exclusion [of the Duke of York] and its Dependances; and here is the Spirit of this Congregation."[20]

(5)

There was nothing that hurt Dr Oates more keenly at this time than any aspersion, great or small, upon his personal character. The acquittal of Wakeman, and the disparaging remarks made by Scroggs during his summing up at that trial, had shaken Titus's credit as a witness; an attack upon his private life, if successful, might even cast him back into that dismal state of obscurity and destitution from which a miracle had rescued him in the September of 1678. When, therefore, a few months after Wakeman's trial, a former servant of Titus's, young John Lane, brought an accusation of sodomy against him, the full force of that famous malice descended upon the luckless head of the accuser.

The Grand Jury of Middlesex returned an Ignoramus to the bill; but this did not satisfy the wrathful Titus. He immediately indicted Lane, together with another servant, William Osborne, and a certain Thomas Knox, who had been in the employ of Lord Dunblane, son to the Lord Treasurer, of endeavouring to "hinder and stifle" the Popish Plot, and to "scandalise" Dr Oates and Captain Bedloe. Osborne fled; but the other two were brought up for trial at the King's Bench on November 25th, the Lord Chief Justice presiding.

That Titus attached enormous importance to this trial is evident from the fact that he persuaded the chief Opposition leaders to grace it with their presence. *The True Domestick Intelligence* for November 28th mentions among others the Bishop of London, Lords Wharton, Grey, Howard, Halifax, and Cavendish, and last, but by no means least, Shaftesbury himself. On October 25th, Titus had written to Mr (afterwards Sir) George Treby: "I pray you to take notice that Thomas Knox hath petitioned the King to order him those papers, which the King hath not granted, but ordered his Councell to have them of you, which if you deliver them I suppose it may tend to help their memories, they haveing as I understand forgotten what they did contrive against mee. Sir I hope you will not deliver them if by any meanes you can keep them by law, for you received them not of the Councell but of the Committee of Lords. Tit. Oates."[21] There can be no doubt that Titus was well aware of the fact naïvely recorded by Luttrell—namely, that had the "conspiracy" of Knox and Lane succeeded, "it had rendred Dr Oates his testimony invalid for the future".[22]

The trial is one of the most complex and involved in the whole of this series, and the only clear fact which emerges from a reading of it is that both prisoners had been bullied and threatened in jail, and that Lane in particular, a very young man, was terrified of being put in the pillory by the order of Shaftesbury. The whole drearily ridiculous story of the Plot was yet again rehearsed, nor was the murder of Godfrey considered irrelevant by those who were anxious to draw as many red herrings as possible across the trail. The principal witness for the prosecution was Sir William Waller, but Captain Dangerfield likewise played a considerable part, possibly to the surprise of Dr Oates, who "was ignorant that he knew anything of the contrivance against him".[23] The gallant captain was in great form, and told the most intriguing story about pen and ink being thrust by Lady Powis under Lane's door in prison, in order, apparently, that the young man might write down some damning evidence for Dangerfield to see. (Unfortunately, what he had written had disappeared.) Samuel Oates junior, Titus's sailor brother, made a brief appearance as a witness for the prosecution, and must have been moved to hear his brother's description of how strict Titus was in sending his servants to prayers every morning in the chapel at Whitehall, keeping only one with him to assist him at his toilet.

"Well, Gentlemen," said the Lord Chief Justice to the jury at the end of this most complicated trial, "you need not any summing up of the Evidence, I think the thing is evident." "Gentlemen," added Mr Justice Pemberton, " 'tis a very clear Case, as clear as the Day; I think you need not go from the Bar, but do as you will." Thus addressed, the jury, without retiring, obediently returned a verdict of Guilty. "At which the People gave a great shout." Poor Knox begged to be allowed to speak one word for himself, but both he and Lane were hustled into the Marshal's custody, leaving a jubilant Titus to be congratulated by his friends. "The Honour that Dr Oates got by his last Tryal is of greater concernment than some imagine: among the rest that have lost by it are the persons convicted, and perhaps the Sheriff of Litchfield may be no Gainer, who refusing to joyn in a Commission for the Examination of a Witness in order to Dr Oates's Concerns, is sent for to the Council. . . . There is this to be added, that the next day [Oates] appeared at the Bar, and demanded Judgment against the Persons convicted; and that His Majesty has been graciously pleased to give Dr Oates an Order directed to the Commissioners of the Treasury, to reimburse the full charges of his Prosecution."[24]

Far from being out of pocket by this vindication of his character, Titus reaped a material reward. In the following January he prayed a grant of fines inflicted on the luckless couple (two hundred marks on Knox, and one hundred on Lane), "on account of his great sufferings from the said offenders", and accordingly a warrant was sent to "Samuel Astrey, the King's Coroner and Attorney in the Court of King's Bench, to levy the said fines and pay them to the said Oates".[25]

(6)

Upon December 22nd, 1679, Captain William Bedloe was married to "a Lady of a very considerable Fortune".[26] It may have been partly in order to celebrate this event that "Last Saturday several eminent Citizens of London joined together to treat Dr Oates, Capt. Bedlow, Mr Dugdale, Mr Dangerfield, and divers others of the King's Evidence, which was done very magnificently at the Three Tuns in Crutched Friars, which was intended to demonstrate their Zeal to the Protestant Interest, and to Encourage the

Witnesses to proceed undauntedly in the Good work wherein they are ingaged".[27] So far, no lady had won the heart of the prince of informers, Dr Titus Oates; but during this same month he had the happiness of a visit from his mother, who, since her husband's flight from Hastings, seems to have lived apart from her spouse.

Titus's "great and stupendous Fortune", says Schoolmaster Smith, "brought his Mother up to Town from Hastings in Sussex where she was a Midwife, to see her Son; which was a little before Christmas in 79, who lay with her Husband in York Buildings, where one day I happen'd to dine with them. Some time after dinner the old man went out, and left only me and the old woman together . . . where discoursing with me, she said thus, Mr Smith, you have known my Son Titus a great while, pray what do you think of him and this business (meaning the Plot) to which I answer'd, Very well; not thinking fit to tell her my real sentiments: The old woman shaking her head, replied, Indeed I do not like it well. Pray God bless him."[28]

But Titus was still the Saviour of the Nation, and the opinion of poor old Lucy Oates, the Hastings midwife, can have caused him little anxiety. Public affairs occupied his time; his patrons, the Opposition leaders, were working might and main to prepare men's minds for the acceptance of the bastard Monmouth as the future King of England, and Titus loyally and unstintingly aided them in this great work. Monmouth had returned to England in November, by invitation of Shaftesbury, but without the King's permission, and the Green Ribbon Club staged a great welcome for him, ringing bells and lighting bonfires, and proclaiming, in a perfect snowstorm of pamphlets and broadsheets, that his presence was necessary to preserve the King's life from the Papists, or, if necessary, to avenge his Majesty's death. Monster petitions were got up for the early sitting of Parliament (at which it was hoped to exclude the Duke of York), petitions which were thrust into the King's hands everywhere he went. All who would not sign were stigmatised as Papists, public enemies, and so forth, until Dr Titus Oates hit upon the nickname which stuck to them for ever after; he called them "Tories".

"In England about the year 1680, a Party of Men appear'd

among us, who tho' pretended Protestants, yet apply'd Themselves to the Ruin and Destruction of their Country. . . . These Men for their Eminent Preying upon their Countrey, and their Cruel, Bloody Disposition, began to shew themselves so like the Irish Thieves and Murtherers aforesaid, that they quickly got the name of Tories—Their real Godfather and who gave them the name, was Titus Oats, and the Occasion as follows: The Author of this happened to be present—There was a Meeting of some Honest People in the City, upon the Occasion of the Discovery of some Attempt, to stifle the Evidence of the Witnesses, and tampering with Bedlow and Stephen Dugdale—And among the Discourse Mr Bedlow said he had Letters from Ireland, that there were some Tories to be brought over hither, who were privately to Murther Dr Oats, and the said Bedlow. The Doctor, whose Zeal was very hot, could never hear any Man after this talk against the Plot, or against the Witnesses, but he Thought he was one of these Tories, and call'd almost every Man a Tory that oppos'd him in Discourse; till at last, the Word Tory became Popular, and it stuck so close to the Party in all their Bloody Proceedings, that they own'd it, just as they do now the Name of High Flyer."[29]

There were indeed, with the coming of the new year, 1680, the first faint signs of a counter-attack against the faction which had held sway so long. For well over a year, the King had fought single-handed; now in his battle with the Opposition he began to find friends to rally round him, timidly indeed, and in a somewhat half-hearted fashion, but ready to take heart at the first decisive victory. Contemporaneously with this, and in fact a part of it, there appeared a series of attempts to discredit the bunch of rogues dignified by the title of the King's Evidence, attempts which, if at first as unsuccessful as had been poor John Lane's, were at least sustained, and were made by persons of education and repute.

From the very first disclosure of the great Popish Plot, one man had shared King Charles's incredulity. That man was Sir Roger L'Estrange. "From the First Moment of Otes'es Plot coming into the World," he wrote, "I look'd upon it, and declar'd my Opinion of it, as a Conspiracy in

Disguise. . . . I contracted a Horror of this Villanous Cheat of a Plot, from the very Spawning of it; and, in the same Instant, an Ambition, above all things under the Sun, to have some Hand in breaking the Neck on't."[30] In this year of 1680, L'Estrange published his first attack on the credit of the informers, his witty *Narrative of the Plot*; yet, though the heat of the Terror was past, extreme caution was still so necessary that a superficial reading of this tract gives the impression that it was a defence of the witnesses. In his *Brief History*, published in 1687, L'Estrange gives some idea of the problem with which he was faced in his first attempts to shake the belief of the nation in the Plot, and to discredit Titus Oates:

"As to the Time, the Faction had the Ascendant of the Government, and the Multitude bore down all before them like a Torrent; The Witnesses led the Rabble; The Plot-Managers led the Witnesses; and the Devil himself led the Leaders: For they were to pass to their Ends thorough Subornation, Perjury, Hypocrisy, Sacrilege, and Treason. This was the State of Things when first I dipt my Pen into this Subject; and there was no Launching-out, into the Abyss of the Plot-Mystery, without certain Ruine: but Coasting, and Slanting, Hinting and Trimming, was the best Office a Body could perform, in that Season: And the Man had to be Felo de se, that should have taken upon him to Search the Ulcer to the Quick; A little Skirting now and then upon the Narratives, and Bantering, betwixt Jest and Earnest, upon the Credit of the Witnesses, gave People, by Little and Little, to Understand, as much as any man could Safely Communicate: But the Foundations of the Plot lay as yet Untouch'd; The Patrons, and the Vouchers of it, remain'd Sacred; and, for a long Time, there was no Meddling with a Vote, without burning a Man's Fingers; So that the Source of the Plot lay hitherto in the Bowels of the Earth, and (like a Consecrated Fountain) it would have been little less than Sacrilege, to Puddle and Prophane it."[31]

All doubts cast upon Titus's probity were answered, says L'Estrange, by the argument, "Where's your Record? If you can produce a Record you say something" (an exquisitely ironical question, surely, when we remember that a record of any description was the one thing Titus himself, in his accusations against his victims, never could produce). That Sir Roger did not exaggerate the idolatrous admiration still felt by a section of the people for Oates and Bedloe is proved by the fact that this very year there was published a pamphlet, *A Full and Final Proof of the Plot from the Revelations*, in which the principal informer and his lieutenant were identified with the Two Heavenly Witnesses described in the eleventh chapter of the Book of Revelation, whose mission was to prophesy for one thousand two hundred and three score days. The evidence of the informers, stated this tract, was "in Law sufficient to hang all the Subjects in England, if they are guilty". Titus and William were "Mediums and Pipes employed by the Almighty to convey the Knowledge of this Masterpiece of Villany to us. . . . If you believe not these Witnesses, Dr Oates and Mr Bedloe, the Prophets you have with you, neither would you believe one though he rose from the Dead".

(7)

On January 6th, Dr Oates diverted himself with a variation of his pastime of priest-hunting; he obtained a warrant to search a "nunnery".

In the village of Hammersmith there had existed, prior to the Reformation, a convent, which, because of its lack of endowment, had escaped the destruction of religious houses during that upheaval. In 1669, a Mrs Bedingfield, in partnership with another lady, had set up at this former convent a boarding-school for the daughters of Catholics. "Soon after its institution, the governesses and teachers having voluntarily obliged themselves to the observance of monastic rules, it obtained the name of a nunnery."[32] Now, in January, 1680, Dr Oates, possibly because he was in need of a little recreation in the midst of strenuous public duties, decided that the Hammersmith boarding-school was distinctly worth a visit.

"Information being given to Dr Oates, that [at] a House in Hammersmith, near London, several suspicious persons did usually meet, he went immediately thereupon and acquainted the Lords of the Council with it, upon which they issued out a warrant to one of His Majesties Messengers, who taking to his Assistance one of the Justices of the Peace of the County of Middlesex [Sir William Waller], and as many other officers as was thought convenient, and accompanied with Dr Oates, and his servants well armed, they went to Hammersmith, and going privately into the Town, they sent for Justice Yersby, who with a Head-Constable, and other Officers, together with Dr Oates and the Messenger, went to Mrs Beddingfield's house, who is a kinswoman of Beddingfield the Jesuit, and upon Search they found divers Children of several Persons of Quality, and three or four Women to attend them; Mrs Beddingfield her self did not appear, they being told that she was gone beyond Sea, but there was an ancient Ge[n]tlewoman in the House, who it seems was left as Governess; whom the Justice ordered to appear the next day; Upon further search several Popish Books were seized upon, with an Altar-stone; and some other Trinkets belonging to Popish Priests, which were all left in the hands of the Justice; they then proceeded to the top of the House, and there between two Houses they found an outlandish Person, who said he was a Walloon, and that he belongs to the Spanish Ambassador; This Person together with the Governess, were ordered to appear before the Council, and the Justice at the same time to attend with the Examinations taken before him; This House went under the name of a Boarding School, yet we are told that Dr Oats and some others have an Account, that under that pretence there is a private Nunnery maintained, to educate Children of several of the Popish nobility and Gentry in the Romish superstition and Idolatry."[33]

It is not a very pretty picture: the informer with his armed servants, the messenger and the justice and the constable and the "other Officers", forcing their way into a girls' school, bullying an old gentlewoman, terrifying children, and chasing a foreign servant over the rooftops; nor does a little detail added by Schoolmaster Smith make it any the more pleasant. He tells us that "to make out this formidable Discovery they found out a Discipline, which they had formerly taken among the spoils of some Popish Houses: and which Oates had a long time carried in his pocket. With this infallible demonstration of a Monastery they returned: Which Relique Oates kept afterwards in his pocket still, and I have seen him flang his menial Ganymedes with it."[34]

Such little excursions were only, however, for Titus's brief hours of leisure; the main business occupying him at this time was an attempt to ruin Chief Justice Scroggs. Sir Charles Lyttelton, in a letter to Lord Hatton on January 13th, after relating how a bunch of the witnesses and their friends had been snubbed by the King on their presenting one of the Opposition petitions for an early sitting of Parliament, adds: "To morrow, I heare Mr Oates and Bedlow are to accuse my Ld C. Justice at the Councell, or rather ye former accusation to be heard."[35] They had, in fact, appeared before the Council on the 6th, declaring their unwillingness to give any further evidence while Scroggs remained upon the Bench, and on the 10th they had exhibited articles of High Misdemeanour against him. The reason why Titus was so anxious to ruin Scroggs at this precise moment was because a new batch of trials connected with the Plot would soon be commencing, and he was not going to risk a repetition of the Wakeman acquittal if he could help it.

Yet when, on the 17th, Scroggs presided at the trial of a batch of priests who were tried for their priesthood only, he behaved exactly as he had at the Plot trials, bullying and insulting the prisoners, and defending the King's Evidence against all attacks upon their credit. One of these priests, David Kemish, was so weak that he could neither speak nor stand, and had to be sent back to prison, and another, Henry Starkey, had lost a leg in the King's service. The old gang of witnesses appeared in force, headed by Oates, and all six priests were condemned. From Titus's point of view, Scroggs' conduct was unimpeachable on this occasion; he was full of jocose insults when he addressed the prisoners—"So, he says you eat of Good Friday and Ash Wednesday, the Pope shall know of it. . . . Why don't you ask him some Questions? Why, you have not Catechisms in your Church, you don't know how to ask Questions"—and reprimanded one of the prisoners at great length for trying to "throw dirt upon the King's Witnesses". Scroggs did, however, possibly through boredom, leave the Bench some little while before the trial ended.

On January 21st, the thirteen articles exhibited by Oates and Bedloe against the Lord Chief Justice were read by the Council, together with Scroggs' answer. Among other things, the witnesses complained that Scroggs "did Brow-beat and curb" them at the trial of Wakeman; "That the said Lord Chief Justice is very much addicted to Swearing and Cursing in his common Discourse, and to Drink to Excess"; and that at the trial of Knox and Lane "in further disparagement and disparaging of the evidence of the said Dr Titus Oates and Mr William Bedloe . . . rose up suddenly after the Evidence closed by the Council [*sic*], and left the said Court abruptly, before the said Jury had given in the same."[36] Scroggs' answer to these accusations was deemed satisfactory, however, and the Privy Council left him to seek his remedy at law.[37]

But so mortally had the Lord Chief Justice offended the Opposition by his summing-up in the Wakeman trial, that he dared not bring an action against the Opposition's protégés, Oates and Bedloe; he was removed from office in the following year, possibly to save him from the impeachment which was being engineered against him by Shaftesbury. The only way in which he could retaliate against the informers was to turn upon them, during the few trials over which he was to preside in the year 1680, some of that withering scorn which hitherto he had reserved for the victims of the Plot. The admirers of Oates and Bedloe, meanwhile, to compensate them for their disappointment in failing to ruin Scroggs, addressed them in the most flattering verse. They—

> "*shall in story dwell*
> *In Heavenly Fame, like Angels that ne'er fell*
> *Whilst such as he* [*Scroggs*] *lie in oblivious Hell.*"

The King's Evidence were—

> "*Men who of right by us should honour'd be,*
> *Their Names made great to all Posteritie;*
> *And for Encouragement, and greater Grace,*
> *Their Statues set up in some Public place.*"[38]

Fortunately for "Posteritie", no public-spirited citizen came forward with funds for such adornment of the London streets.

(8)

The early months of 1680 brought Dr Oates innumerable invitations to preach and to dine, from which it is evident that, at least in the City, he was as popular as ever.

"Last Sunday [Jan.] the 25th instant Dr Titus Oates . . . preached an Excellent Sermon at St Buttolphs Aldgate, to the great Satisfaction of a numerous Auditory who were then present."[39] "We hear that on Sunday [Feb. 11th] Dr Oats Preached at Hackney Church to a numerous Auditory who came hither both to see and hear him."[40] "On the 19th [Feb.] Dr Oates preached before the Company of Working Goldsmiths, and afterwards dined with them at their Hall."[41] "Upon Tuesday the 24 instant [Feb.] Mr Godfrey (Brother to Sir Edmundbury Godfrey) an eminent Merchant in Lothbury (London) in remembrance of his dear Brother, who was so barbarously murdered for his King and Religion, invited Dr Oates and Captain Bedlow to dinner, who were both entertained very kindly, Mr Godfrey expressing his great joy in the hopes he had of his Brother's eternal happiness, who suffered so much for his Loyalty to his Majesty, and maintaining the Protestant Religion."[42] Doubtless the conversation at this dinner included a discussion of the startling rumour that "notwithstanding the Jury who sate upon Mr Bedingfield the Jesuit in the Gatehouse, and found him to be dead, and was buried accordingly; yet we have an account that Sir William Waller found him alive at Newark, and has committed him to the Gate-house by that name, but it is discoursed that this Beddingfield will prove himself but a cobler".[43]

While Sir William Waller was conducting a big priest-hunting tour in the provinces, Dr Oates nobly seconded him in London, and late in February was the means of getting one Baker *alias* Heskins sentenced to be drawn, hanged, and quartered (though the King had the impertinence to reprieve the victim);[44] just previous to this, Titus had obtained the reward for the arrest of a Catholic barber.[45] But amid these personal triumphs, his heart must have bled for his patrons, the lords of the Opposition, who, having heard the King announce that he intended to recall his brother, instantly had threatened to resign, only to hear Charles exclaim fervently: "With all my heart!" On February 24th, James arrived in London, and so fickle were the citizens that they received him with loud acclamations, and the Lord Mayor entertained him at a splendid banquet. To add to Titus's heaviness of heart, his good friend Sir William Waller was disgraced; "Sir William Waller haveing taken one Higgie out of the Gatehouse, where he was committed for treason by order of the councill, and kept him drinking all night in a tavern, his majestie has turn'd him out of commission of peace, and ordered the keeper of the prison to be proceeded against."[46]

Both Shaftesbury and his protégé Titus seem to have grown a little wild in their efforts to maintain their prestige which was threatened by the recall of the Duke of York. Shaftesbury's method took the form of putting about the fantastic rumour of the Black Box. It was given out that the Bishop of Durham, recently dead, had bequeathed to his son-in-law, Sir Gilbert Gerard, a mysterious black box containing a marriage contract between King Charles and the Duke of Monmouth's mother. But the hoax went off like a damp squib; neither the box nor the contract could be produced, and Sir Gilbert himself, examined by the Council, denied on oath knowing anything about them; "'tis thought", wrote Luttrell gravely, "to be a popish story to scandalize his majestie and the duke".[47] On April 26th, the King once again made a public denial of ever having married any woman except the Queen, and the particulars of the hoax were published in the *Gazette*.

As for Titus, "The Project for carrying and re-carrying of Letters from place to place throughout the Cities of London and Westminster, for a penny a Letter, so often mentioned in the Intelligences, is as Dr Oates says, a farther branch of the Popish Plot: for that he is credibly informed, it is the most dexterous Invention of Mr Henry Nevil alias Pain, who is notoriously known to be a great asserter of the Catholick Cause, and shrewdly suspected to be a promoter of this way of Treasonable Correspondencies; and it is to be feared, as that good Invention of Pipes hath wholly destroyed the Trade of Tankard-bearers [that is, the water-cobs], so this silly Invention will only serve to ruine the poor Porters."[48] It is only fair to add that Titus denied saying any of this; though which was the more reliable, Titus's word or the gossip of the news-sheets, it is difficult to decide.

Early in May there was a rumour that "if the season prove not too hot, and greater affairs hinder not, Dr Oats intends a progress into Scotland".[49] Scotland was destined to be denied this honour, for greater affairs did hinder, and the first of these was yet another attempt to ruin the Reverend Adam Elliot.

Elliot, who, as has been mentioned, had returned to Ireland after his narrow escape in the previous September, not unnaturally had been expressing his opinion about Oates to his acquaintance, and that in no uncertain terms. It was not safe to do this, even in Ireland, and Elliot was fined £200 and imprisoned till he paid it, for saying that if Oates "depos'd with no more truth against the Jesuits than he did against me, they died Martyrs".[50] The swift retribution which had fallen upon Elliot in Ireland encouraged Titus to finish off his enemy while he was thus laid low; and accordingly, in this month of April, 1680, Dr Oates, in the Court of Delegates, swore new informations against the tiresome parson. Since, as he often boasted, Titus was accustomed to do everything "thorough-stitch", he began right back in Elliot's college days, swearing that Elliot had robbed a study and tried to sell Titus the books, that he had gone a-deer-stealing, that his "rude, riotous, whoreing and debauch'd living" had compelled the University authorities to withdraw his maintenance, and that later, having written to the Rector of St Omers that he had been ordained (which letter Oates, of course, had seen, and equally of course, could not now produce), he had taken up his residence in Kent, where he "did lead a very dissolute debauched life, and was much given to Drinking, Whoreing, Lying, and swearing that to be true which was not so". Lastly, not only was Elliot a circumcised Jesuit, but Titus had now remembered that "as he confessed, did give poison to his Master or Patron when he was a slave".[51]

Elliot was sent for to answer these accusations, but it

was to be some while before the case came on, and meantime a greater business than the satisfying of a personal grudge was occupying Titus. On June 23rd, in the Court of King's Bench, Lord Castlemaine was tried for intriguing with the Jesuits to kill the King, and for "instructing and managing" the sixteen scholars sent over from St Omers in the previous year as witnesses for the defence at the trials of the Five Jesuits and Langhorne.

(9)

Once more the familiar scene was set; once more the broad visage and brutal wit of Scroggs presided on the Bench; once more a prisoner of importance stood charged with High Treason; once more was Dr Titus Oates to play his favourite role of King's Evidence, and with all his old comrades present to back him up. And yet, what a melancholy difference! Scroggs' insults and bullying were now equally divided between the defence and the prosecution witnesses; the victim, heartened by the memory of Wakeman's acquittal, faced his accusers with something of contempt; and Titus, conscious all the while of that unsuccessful attempt of his to ruin the Lord Chief Justice, was flustered, evasive, and even, at times, downright nervous. The following dialogue is typical:

"*Castlemaine*. I will ask him as many questions as I think reasonable, and when, my Lord, I do desire Times, and he can't tell the Times, he must tell me so.

"*L.C.J.* Mr Otes, Answer my Lord [Castlemaine] what Questions he asks you.

"*Dr Otes*. I will tell my Lord Castlemaine as near as I can remember, my Lord.

"*Castlemaine*. Mr Otes, when was it you came over [for the 'Consult']?

"*Dr Otes*. Really it was some few days before the Consult.

"*Castlemaine*. How many days do you think?

"*Dr Otes*. Really I can't remember.

"*L.C.J.* I suppose you have your Memorials.

"*Dr Otes*. Really, my Lord, no."

So great a change had come over Scroggs that he even expressed a wish that Oates would produce some of the innumerable letters of which he had talked so much. Titus was aghast. "It cannot be expected, my Lord," he cried, "that I should have them." A long argument as to whether Dangerfield, since he had stood in the pillory, was "*liber et legalis homo*" or even "*probus et legalis homo*", gave Scroggs an opportunity to declaim against the informers in general. "We have men grown so insolent," he cried, "they behave themselves with that vile insolence, that now they take upon them to speak against whole Societies of men; as if so be there were any thing in them that should render them better than their former Lives or Natures. Humility becomes penitents, and no wicked man is supposed to be a penitent that hath not that; but these carry it with that insolency, as if they were not concerned themselves, when God knows the best of them discover what they do, by being parties themselves." Often had such diatribes been heard from that mouth against the prisoners; never before had they been directed against the King's Evidence.

But when Castlemaine produced a record of the trial of young Parker at Hastings, the Bench, though on this occasion it allowed the record to be read, became cautious, and Parker himself was not allowed to give his testimony which would have discredited Oates. It was one thing to declaim against the witnesses in general; the time was not yet come when Titus could be attacked by name, for he was still the Opposition's pet, and with a large section of the populace he was still the Saviour of the Nation. Castlemaine next called the former priest, Berry *alias* Hutchinson, "a person whom Mr Otes hath since converted to be a Protestant", who admitted reconciling Titus to the Catholic Church. Despite the obvious uneasiness of the Bench, Berry gave his evidence freely and frankly. He had told Mr Oates that the latter could not be a true priest while he remained of the Church of England; he had received letters from Titus from Valladolid, and he had employed him in writing "certain things against the Corruption of the Church of Rome. He had 10s. I gave him, and this was before the Discovery he made (as he pretends) of the Plot. And he told me he would suffer no more for Conscience-sake: It is a hard thing, said he, Mr Berry, for a Man to want Bread; upon which I gave him 10s. . . . And thereupon, my Lord, in May was twelvemonth he sent for me, when I heard he had done some more mischief; and

I went to him, my Lord . . . upon that he was very kind to me, and gave me 20s. Said he, Mr Berry, you have been civil to me, and you shall never want any thing so long as I have it. Said I, Mr Otes, are these things true that you swear against the Jesuits? Said he, As I hope for Salvation they are. . . . Then, said I, Mr Otes, answer me this only thing. There are an hundred and twenty persons that saw you every day, and dined and supped with you at St Omers, and these you have recommended to me for vertuous people, and I know them to be so. He said, They are outlaw'd Men. . . . Mr Otes, speak the Truth: There is a God in Heaven."

Titus, losing his temper, flatly contradicted everything the witness had said, adding vindictively:

"And I have a charge of High Treason against that man, for seducing me from my Religion, my Lord; I will swear he turned me to the Church of Rome, and I desire it may be recorded."

At this point the Vicar of Barking stepped forward, and said that Berry had been his curate, but that the Bishop of London lately had replaced him, because he was "distracted". Mr Recorder remarking that the witness's behaviour was "a very concurrent Testimony" to that fact, poor Berry was hauled out of the witness-box.

In his summing-up, Scroggs dismissed the Parker scandal, but added concerning Oates: "You must weigh well with yourselves how probable or not probable what he doth swear is. . . . I must tell the Jury they are to weigh the natures of people among themselves, as they carry probability or not, or else the confidence of a swearer shall take away any man's life whatsoever." He reflected even more damagingly against the character of Dangerfield (who, it had emerged during the trial, had a record of no less than sixteen convictions); and finally informed the jury that if they believed Oates's testimony, but could not believe Dangerfield's, they must acquit the prisoner, since two witnesses were necessary to convict a man of High Treason. Whether the jury believed Dr Oates and not Captain Dangerfield, or vice versa, is not recorded, but certainly they could not have believed them both, for they returned a verdict of Not guilty.

Titus's disappointment at the result of this trial was sharpened by the escape of two more victims, an Irish priest named O'Cullen, and the Countess of Powis. Moreover, on June 30th, Samuel Pepys got his discharge from the Tower, having steadily refused to incriminate the Duke of York. What was even worse was that, almost certainly as a result of Castlemaine's acquittal, the pensions of the informers were very drastically reduced, and that of Dangerfield stopped entirely. Hitherto, Titus had received from the public purse ten pounds a week pension and two pounds for his diet; in modern terms, something in the nature of three thousand a year. This was now cut to forty shillings weekly. He, together with Dugdale and Bedloe, immediately appealed to the Council, and it is rather touching to find the Opposition lords offering to pay the informers a "competent allowance" out of their own pockets if his Majesty would not continue to do so.[52] The Council replied by raising the pensions of all three from forty shillings to three pounds; though whether Messrs Oates, Bedloe, and Dugdale considered this a "competent allowance" is a debatable point.

(10)

In the midst of an attempt to bring down the Duke of York by "presenting" him as a recusant, an attempt in which Dr Oates was aided by such great persons as Shaftesbury, Russell, Cavendish, and other Opposition lords, Titus's attention was distracted by a most unpleasant little incident; or, rather, it would have proved unpleasant had the principal character in it been other than the weakling he was. His name was Simpson Tonge; he was none other than the son of Dr Israel Tonge, the originator of the Popish Plot.

Young Tonge was at this time a prisoner for debt in the King's Bench Prison, living as best he could on threepence a day, and employed in making pegs for shoes. It is possible that he resented the fact that his father's son, who ought to have been caressed and cared for by the Plot managers should be left in such a miserable condition. At all events, being "Extreamly Restless, and Troubled in his Mind", he

BOB FERGUSON OR THE RAREE-SHEW

OF MAMAMOUCHEE MURTY

informed his jailers that he had a communication of the first importance to make to the King, and accordingly, in July, he was admitted to the royal presence.

Now, the whole affair of Simpson Tonge is most complicated and difficult to unravel, for, like Prance before him, he swore backwards and forwards so many times that it is impossible to discover when he was telling the truth. Yet the fact remains that he must have known something about the inner workings of the Plot, since he had been present at its birth. He had found Oates and his father together when he had come down from the university in 1677; he knew all about the drawing up of the famous *Narrative* at the Plot House in Vauxhall; and there is no getting away from the significance of the fact that Oates and his friends, when they found that Simpson had opened his mouth in this July of 1680, were at the utmost pains to shut it again. We may take it as certain, therefore, that Simpson really was in a position to disclose something damaging to the credit of the discoverers of the Plot.

What Simpson said to the King at his private audience is not known; all we have is North's statement that "he railed at his own Father so indecently, the King could not bear it".[53] The probability is that Charles, that most excellent judge of men, dismissed the fellow as one intent on revenge or reward, or both. In the following month, a rumour was circulated that young Tonge had retracted all he had said to his Majesty, and that he had declared he had been hired by the Papists to say it. When Simpson heard this, he "of his own Accord, in the Presence of three Persons, drew up a short Declaration . . . and it was attested by the three Persons there Present".[54] This declaration stated definitely that the rumour was untrue. At about the same time, while his original information was being laid before the Privy Council, Simpson was visited in prison by his uncle, Captain Tonge, accompanied by Dr Oates and a man named Stephen College; they relieved his material necessities, and seem to have suggested to him a method of making his fortune which would prove far less hazardous than that of blabbing out inconvenient truths about the Plot.[55]

It would appear that at first Simpson resisted such

temptations, for in September "Dr Oates haveing complained to the privy councill against Simpson Tongue, son to Dr Tongue, he was examined in his own defence, and severall witnesses heard; but the matters against him being very plain, he was committed by their lordships to Newgate for high misdemeanours, and endeavouring, by false accusations and subornation of perjury, to defame the king's evidence, and all the prosecutions concerning the popish plott".[56]

So there was poor Simpson, a fast prisoner, with a very dangerous accusation hanging over his head. All he had got for disregarding the advice of his uncle and the great Dr Oates was the exchanging of the comparative comfort of the King's Bench prison for the very horrible Common Side of Newgate. The Common Side of Newgate was the ideal environment for second thoughts; and Simpson had not been there long ere he decided that there was still a way out. He got hold of pen and paper and wrote a letter to Sir Roger L'Estrange, the Plot's most vigorous exposer. To him he repeated his former story, and expressed a desire of pouring further "informations" into that surely willing ear. But the ear proved not so willing. L'Estrange was suspicious of anyone bearing the name of Tonge, and, fearing a plot to trepan him, refused to have anything to do with Simpson and his informations.

In October, Sir Roger's caution was justified. On the 6th of that month, he found himself haled before the Privy Council and charged by Oates with tampering with young Tonge in order to invalidate the evidence of the Saviour of the Nation. Titus added, for good measure, that to his certain knowledge, L'Estrange had harboured priests.[57] Yet, after two full hearings, L'Estrange was acquitted, and Titus was left to seek his remedy at law; which, for reasons best known to himself, he failed to do.

The affair of Simpson Tonge did not end here, and though it entails anticipating the story, it seems best to follow it briefly to its conclusion. Though the chance to trepan L'Estrange had ended in defeat, Oates and his friends saw to it that Simpson was well provided for, since, in the words of Roger North, "some holy Secrets were in his Power, and might have been (truly) revealed". But in the following year, whether because he was not so well provided for as he deemed fitting or because he had really repented him of his weakness, Simpson again approached L'Estrange. He wrote Sir Roger that he was troubled in conscience on account of his false oath against him, and begged his forgiveness. L'Estrange, still cautious, replied tersely that he had it. In return, Simpson sent the Tory pamphleteer the copy of a petition from himself to the King, and an interesting, though nauseatingly servile, letter to L'Estrange.

"I am confident", wrote Simpson, "if you had known, how I was us'd, by my Unkle first, and afterwards by College, and Oates, to Force me to accuse you Falsly, you would sooner have Pity'd my Weakness, and Forgiven me." His petition to the King ran thus:

"Sheweth, That after your Petitioner had Declared the Truth to your Majesty concerning the Contrivance of his Father and Mr Titus Otes, your Petitioner being in great want of Necessaries, his Uncle, Captain Tonge, having sent for him was compelled to go to him for Relief; and Captain Tong made your Petitioner Drunk, and then Threaten'd and Forced him to deny the Truth, and to Sign a Paper, which the said Captain Tong had Written, your Petitioner not knowing what he did, and afterwards when your Petitioner was committed to Newgate, Colledge came to him, and by Threats and Promises forced your Petitioner to deny the Truth, for the which your Petitioner hath been ever since under great Trouble of Mind for his great Wickedness and Cowardice to deny the Truth: but your Petitioner doth protest in the presence of Almighty God, that it is very true that the Plot was contrived by my Father and Titus Otes, when he [Oates] returned the Second time beyond the Seas. . . ."[58]

The correspondence between L'Estrange and Simpson Tonge continued from December 27th, 1681, till January 11th, 1682, and the whole of it was published by Sir Roger in the latter year. In his *Observator* for May 15th, '82, he inserted the following advertisement: "*If any Man, Woman, or Child, will be so Kind and Generous, as out of an Affection to the Protestant Religion, and the Vindication of Dr Oates, to call Simson-Tonge to a Legall Account for Endeavouring to Destroy the Credit of the said Doctor, and his Evidence, by Scandalous Reflections upon Both; Roger L'Estrange doth here offer himself, out of a Zeal for the Publique Good, to furnish Authentique Papers and Materialls towards the Prosecution of the Work.*" "The Whole Party", says L'Estrange, "were as Mute as Fishes, after this Publication; which they would never have been if they durst have put the Reputation of Otes'es Evidence to the Test."[59]

(11)

On August 17th, 1680, a most extraordinary rumour diverted the coffee-houses: "Last week", wrote a news-letter writer, "Dr Oates was married to a lady, neice to Lord Shaftesbury, by his Lordship's consent."[60] The Saviour of the Nation was now thirty-one years old, and evidently his admirers considered it high time he should make some woman happy. But in fact Titus was too busy to think of matrimony; he was engaged with a branch of the Plot which for months had been occupying the attention of his patrons. Much had been said in his *Narrative* about plotters in Ireland, and since the English version had grown a little frayed at the edges, it was hoped that the Irish one would prove more promising. In Ireland there were not lacking recruits for the noble army of informers; as long ago as last December, Plunket, titular Primate of Ireland, and the Earl of Tyrone, had been arrested on the information of three witnesses; and now a whole bevy of these pleasant gentlemen were arrived in London to bolster up the declining credit of Dr Oates.

On September 16th, the new Secretary of State, Sir Leoline Jenkins (he had replaced Coventry in the spring), wrote to Sidney Godolphin: "Last night arrived in London 14 Irish priests and others, not priests, of that nation, whose business it is to prove a Popish plot in Ireland.... As soon as they arrived, Oates sent to compliment and treat them last night. Having got new shoes, which they wanted very much, they were conducted by Oates to Lord Shaftesbury to-day. I cannot hear that any of them is of any credit, some being abettors of Tories [the Irish robbers] and receivers of them, others horse-stealers, but none that I hear of any good note."[61] On September 28th, Jenkins complained to the Council that there were so many of these undesirable characters in London that he durst not walk in St James's Park, being in fear of his life.[62] Later, one of these gentry, Owen Murthy, was to depose that in August he had been persuaded by Oates and William Hetherington (one of Shaftesbury's chief agents), to swear to a paper of information written by them to the effect that he had seen Charles II at Mass, and that the Queen, the Duke of York, and the Duke of Ormonde (the latter, it will be remembered, was originally cast for the role of a victim of the conspiracy) were all in the Plot. Murthy was to have £100 if he would do his part properly. He added that Hetherington was frequently at Oates's lodging, and was wont to discourse with him for an hour in private after dinner.[63]

There was now to befall Titus a most sad bereavement. In the middle of August, Captain William Bedloe, making a journey to Bristol, was stricken with a fever, and grew very ill. It happened that the Lord Chief Justice North was on the Western Circuit at the time, and was then in Bristol for the Assizes. He was alone upon the Bench, for his brother judge, Sir Thomas Jones, having suffered a bad attack of gout, had left the Circuit before they came to Bristol. Bedloe's wife and brother, who had followed the gallant captain on his journey, now began to haunt the lodgings of Chief Justice North, endeavouring to persuade him to come and visit the sick informer. North, a staunch loyalist, for some while refused; but when assured that Bedloe's sickness was mortal, and that the informer had "great things" to communicate, the Lord Chief Justice at last complied, taking the precaution of carrying with him as a witness his clerk, who sat at the bedside and wrote down every word spoken at the interview.

It transpired, however, that Bedloe had nothing new to communicate, except that he now exonerated the Queen and the Duke of York from the design to kill the King; his object, it seemed, in bringing the Lord Chief Justice to his bedside was to inform his lordship that his sickness "was very Chargeable", and to implore him to move the King "for some Supply of Money for his Subsistence".

Bedloe added that all he had ever said concerning the Plot was true, saving only his accusations against the Queen and the Duke. Immediately upon his return to London, North laid before the King and Council the record of this interview, publishing it likewise in pamphlet form; his lordship plainly was anxious lest Bedloe's friends should give it out that North himself had arranged the interview in order to make the informer retract his evidence.

The Oppositionists were very cast down to find that Bedloe had not made any new and startling "discoveries", especially as this able lieutenant of the great Oates had now succumbed to his fever. "Even Dr Oates himself was disappointed; for soon after, on a Council Day (he diligently attended at all those Times) as the Lord Chief Justice passed through the Court, he was heard to say aloud, Maay Laird Chaife Jaistaice, whay this Baisness of Baidlaw caims to naithaing. But his Lordship walked on, not attending to his Discourse."[64]

Bedloe's funeral is thus described by an admirer: "Yesterday being Sunday [August 22nd], after he had been publickly exposed in Merchant-Taylors Hall in this City [Bristol], to the view of all Spectators; his corps was carried thence about six of the Clock in the Evening, and buried in the Mayors Chappel, called the Gaunts; the Funeral was attended by a very numerous Company of Citizens, both Men and Women. Mr Mayor, and others of the best quality being present, several Gentlemen of the Council and others bearing up the Pall. The Church was hung with Black. . . . There were Escutcheons fixed to the Hearse, with this Inscription in black Letters in a Field-Argent: *Testimonium quod vivens Exhibuit Moriens constanter Obfirmavit!*"[65]

Another admirer published this really striking epitaph:

> "*Behold his Tomb, who bravely help'd to save*
> *Three trembling Kingdoms from a Popish Grave;*
> *Who, firm to sacred Truth, and justly bold*
> *Defy'd both Reading's Craft and Danby's Gold:*
> *Who seal'd his Evidence with expiring Breath*
> *And frights the Traytors even after Death:*
> *Bedloe! a Name must live, when Rome's shall be*
> *Forgot, or cloth'd with general Infamy.*"[66]

(12)

In the autumn, the King's extreme poverty, and his fears for Tangier, compelled him at last to allow Parliament to sit; and the battle for the exclusion of the Duke of York opened in good earnest. The Oppositionists were determined to get their Exclusion Bill passed, and they were not too particular about the means they used to so noble an end. Though for some reason they do not seem to have enlisted the aid of Titus at the moment, the other members of the shoddy gang were called in and were hearkened to in solemn silence as they endeavoured to blacken the character of the Heir Presumptive. On November 11th, the Bill passed the Commons; but on the 15th, at nine at night, it was defeated in the Lords by sixty-three to thirty votes. This defeat was due in great measure to Halifax, who had trimmed at the last moment, and who, sixteen times during the day's debate, had used his famous eloquence on behalf of law and justice. The Commons immediately voted an address for the removal of Halifax, which was met by the King with a firm refusal.

On October 23rd there had been another execution; a secular priest, Thomas Thwing, was drawn, hanged, and quartered at York. His chief accuser was one Bolrun, who had embezzled money from his employer and was therefore out of a job and in need. Having studied the methods of the great Oates, he announced that for his share in the Plot (for needless to say he was, like all the rest, a repentant conspirator), he had received an Indulgence for thirty thousand years. On the thirtieth, Archbishop Plunket was brought over from Ireland and closely confined in Newgate.[67]

While these events were taking place, Titus Oates had been busy defending his character against all who dared assail it. On October 25th, he complained that the Bishop of Chichester and a Justice Bickley had reviled his evidence; a man named John Peachy swore before the Committee for Examinations that the words had been spoken by Bickley at a Sessions dinner at Chichester, the Bishop being present. The words in question seem particularly to have enraged Titus; they were to the effect that he had contradicted himself twenty-two times in the course of his evidence at the Plot trials. He therefore became spiteful. "Oates complains that the Order for Mr Bickley's attendance is given him, and not sent by the officers. He desires he may be attached as a criminal. Ordered, that Mr Snow get the order served." On November 6th, the Committee resolved to move the House of Lords to put Bickley out of all his employments.[68] On the 9th, one Shippon, for speaking disparagingly of Oates, Dugdale, and the memory of the late Captain Bedloe, was sentenced to pay a fine of five hundred marks and to lie in prison till he paid it.[69]

These and others were the victims of Oates's personal spite; but now the whole pack must draw together to hunt down a nobler quarry. The Opposition, furious at the defeat of the Exclusion and their failure to revenge themselves on Halifax, were resolved to have at least one life to satisfy their malice; and looking about them they selected one who should answer their purpose very well. This was old Viscount Stafford, one of the Five Lords who all this while had remained in the Tower without being brought to trial. Stafford was a victim fit for the purpose. He was old and infirm; he was at loggerheads with most of his relations, the Howards; he had suffered two years' confinement; and it was known that he was by nature timid. "My poor Lord Stafford", laments Ailesbury, "who, I believe upon my conscience, would have trembled at the sight of a naked sword, I know him so well."[70]

No art was neglected to terrify the victim into offering to save his life at the expense of his honour; for what the Opposition wanted from him more than anything was that he would acknowledge the conspiracy, and so put the ailing Plot upon its feet again. Hooligans were hired to yell and hoot at him as he was taken to and from Westminster Hall; the whole gang of informers was rounded up to bombard him with their lies and insults; the Oppositionists, both in the Lords and Commons, had seats reserved for them in the Hall, and so far forgot their dignity as to add their voices to those of the mob in execration; and against this one old man were ranged the most distinguished lawyers of the day, Powle, Treby, Trevor, Jones, Winnington, and Maynard. The one redeeming feature of the whole dreary business was the courtesy and fairness displayed by the Lord High Steward, the Chancellor, Finch.

In a setting strangely incongruous—the Lords in their scarlet robes, the Bishops in their rochets, the solemn procession, including Garter King-at-Arms, and Black Rod, which escorted the Lord High Steward from his house in Queen Street, the trumpeters, the ancient forms and ceremonies—was the old, old story of the Popish Plot recited all over again. Mr Serjeant Maynard argued learnedly that there must have been a plot, because so many men had been executed for it. He referred with a kind of naïve satisfaction to the murder of Godfrey: "What that Oates first made a discovery, it seems it had not that weight that we think now it will clearly have with your Lordships; and had not the Murder of Sir Edmondbury Godfrey follow'd in the neck of it, the World, as it were asleep, would have lain so, but that awaked us." On several occasions during the course of the trial did the prosecution refer to the Popish Successor, whose expected accession to the throne had encouraged the Papists to form the Plot, references which showed clearly that the trial was part and parcel of the Opposition's new attack upon the Succession.

Titus himself was in great form. He began his evidence right back in 1676, when he was in Norfolk's household and had heard the first faint whisperings of that Design of which he was the First Discoverer. He related with relish his introduction to the Jesuits: "they were the Men for my turn, because I found they were the cunning political Men, and the Men that could satisfy me". There was no hesitation on his part at this time of day in roundly accusing the Duke of York, not only of participation in the Plot, but in playing a leading role in the Great Fire of 1666, a calamity which, according to Titus, had been due to Popish machinations.

The trial dragged on from November 30th till December 7th. On the fourth day, after evading some embarrassing questions regarding his alleged degree of doctor of divinity, Titus was called upon to answer to a matter unconnected with his testimony. The Lord High Steward required the Lieutenant of the Tower to describe a scene which had taken place between Mr Lieutenant and Dr Oates the previous day.

"*Mr Lieu.* My Lords, I was desiring Mr Oates to keep the People down, because there was a great Croud; and seeing a great many People come in, he told me they were Witnesses that were to come in: said I, I believe half of these are not Witnesses; and the Door opening so often, I could keep this Place in no order, so I desired they would stand away that were not Witnesses: why, says he, you are but a Gaoler. Then I told him, if it were not for his Coat, and I were out of this Place, I would break his Head. Then he called me Rascal.

"*L. Stafford.* My Lord Steward, I desire to know whether this be a Witness fit to be believed against any Man.

"*L.H.S.* Mr Oates, this does not become you; 'tis very ill Manners in you.

"*Dr Oates.* My Lords, the Lieutenant of the Tower hath the Law; and I refer my self to the Law, if I have done him any wrong.

"*Mr Ser. Maynard.* It did not become Mr Lieutenant of the Tower to tell him he would break his Head.

"*Mr Lieu.* Why? If any Man out of this Court, and in any other Habit, should tell me I was a Gaoler, I think I should not deserve to be the King's Lieutenant if I did not break his Head."

Scarcely had his ruffled feelings subsided from this encounter than Titus heard himself challenged by the prisoner on his former statement that he was seven hundred pounds out of pocket for his services to the Government, since he had just said that at the time of his discovery he was without twopence to his name. Titus replied with dignity:

"My Lords, I will satisfy this House what I said: what Folks write after me, I am not to justify. But, my Lords, I had a Friend of mine presented me with 100. *l.* I name not his Name, but if that be questioned, he is a Peer of this House, and will justify it: I had 100. *l.* for my Narrative; I had 100. *l.* for taking some Jesuits; which is 300. *l.* I had for some other Copies that I printed, a matter of 50 or 60. *l.* And now I can make it appear, that as to those Sums which I received in gross, I have spent them all, and more, in this Service; for I have none of the Money now by me."

On Monday, December 6th, the poor old victim, who all

this while had defended himself with a spirit which surprised both friends and foes, desired to have a paper read, because his voice was grown so low and hoarse that he could not be heard. "I cannot deny to your Lordships," he added, "that what happened to me on Saturday-night, disturbed me very much. Every day since I came hither, there hath been such shouting and houting by a company of barbarous Rabble, as never was heard the like, I believe; but it was at a distance most of the time, and so it did not much concern me. But Saturday-night it was so near and so great, that really it hath disturbed me ever since; it was great to-day, but at a distance; if it were not thus, I should not offer a Paper to be read: I scarce know what I do or say, considering the Circumstances I am in."

On the morrow, before the prisoner was brought to the Bar, the peers' votes were taken and counted. Out of eighty-six, thirty-one declared the prisoner Not Guilty, fifty-five Guilty. Four Howards, his own kinsmen, were among the latter. Stafford was brought in and informed of the verdict. "God's holy Name be praised," he said. "I confess I am surprised at it, but God's will be done, and your Lordships'. I will not murmur at it." The Lord High Steward told him that it had been decided (and he might have added, in the teeth of the Opposition) to petition the King to commute the full sentence of High Treason to one of simple beheading. Then, for the first time, the old man broke down. "It is not," he murmured, "your Lordships' Justice does make me cry, but your Goodness."

Both Reresby and Evelyn witnessed the trial, and each recorded his disgust that the prisoner should have been condemned on the testimony of men like Oates. "One thing my Lord said to Oates", observed Evelyn, "which I confesse did exceedingly affect me; that a person who during his depositions should so vauntingly brag that tho' he went over to the Church of Rome, yet he was never a Papist, nor of their Religion, all the time that he seem'd to apostatize from the Protestant, but only as a spie; tho' he confess'd he tooke their sacrament, worshipped images, went thro' all their oathes and discipline of their proselytes, swearing secrecy and to be faithfull but with intent to come over againe and betray them; that such an hypocrite, that had so deeply prevaricated as even to turn idolater (for so we of the Church of England term'd it), attesting God so solemnly that he was intirely theirs and devoted to their interest, and consequently (as he pretended) trusted; I say that the witnesse of such a profligate wretch should be admitted against the life of a peere, this my Lord look'd upon as a monstrous thing, and such as must needs redound to the dishonour of our Religion and Nation. And verily, I am of his Lordship's opinion; such a man's testimonie should not be taken against the life of a dog."[71]

(13)

While Stafford lay awaiting his end, Titus was suffering another bereavement. On December 18th, there passed away, at the house (near Bridewell Ditch) of Stephen College, nicknamed the Protestant Joiner, Dr Israel Tonge. The poor old originator of the Plot had begun to say the most disconcerting things of late, and, says Burnet, to have "a very bad opinion of Oates, upon what reason I know not",[72] so he had been placed in College's care. Tradition says that he died of starvation, and was "eaten up with vermin"; at all events the King was petitioned to pay for his burial, which he did to the extent of £50.[73] In the autumn session of the Parliament, he had been recommended to Charles for the first good ecclesiastical preferment which fell in his Majesty's gift, "but the Doctor was disappointed of the Benefit, by leaving the World not long after".[74] He was interred in the churchyard of St Michael's, Wood Street, his funeral sermon being preached by the Reverend Thomas Jones.[75] *The True Protestant Mercury* of December 28th describes his death and burial in a manner befitting this Opposition organ:

"On the 18th last past dyed Ezreel Tonge Doctor of Divinity, eminently assistant to Dr Otes in the first discovery of the Popish Plot . . . he retained his Intellectuals firm to the last gasp, and with great Serenity of Mind resigned his Soul into the Hands of his Redeemer. His body on Thursday the 24th instant was conveyed from the Scotch Hall in Blackfryers to St Michaels Wood-street, attended with the Coaches of several persons of Quality, a considerable number of Divines, and other good Protestants, and there (after a Sermon preach'd) decently interr'd. . . ."

The Council ordered his papers to be seized and brought before them, but it would appear that his brother, Captain Tonge, contrived to keep back a certain number, for which L'Estrange hunted in vain for several years, since they were said to contain some secrets about the origins of the Plot. The Council on their part, whatever they discovered among the mass of manuscripts delivered to them, never made a statement on them.[76]

If Titus grieved for the loss of that patron to whom he owed so much, his sadness must have been short-lived, for he was lively enough on Boxing Day, when he dined with the Bishop of Ely. "On the 26th", wrote Sir John Reresby, "I dined with that excellent man, Dr Gunning, Bishop of Ely; the famous Dr Oates was of the company at table, and flushed with the thoughts of running down the Duke of York, expressed himself of his highness and his family, in terms that bespoke him a fool and something worse; nor contented with this, but he must rail at the Queen, his mother, and her present majesty. In this strain did he hurry on, while no soul dared to oppose him, for fear of being made a party of the plot; till, no longer able to bear with the insolence of the man, I took him to task to such purpose, that he flung out of the room with some heat. The bishop told me that such was the general drift of his discourse, that he had sometimes checked him for the indecency of his talk, but that finding he had done it to no manner of purpose, he had desisted from any further effort to set bounds to his virulence."[77]

On the 29th, Stafford was executed on Tower Hill in the presence of a vast multitude, "some hundreds of standings being taken at very dear Rates, a Guinee being an ordinary price to look out at a Window".[78] The old man died with calmness and courage, forgiving Oates by name in his speech upon the scaffold; and though the mob had made his last few weeks on earth intolerable by their execrations, they listened to him in silence, and, when he asserted his innocence, there were even some shouts of "We believe you, my lord!" Even Ben Harris, chief among the Opposition news-sheet writers, admitted that when the head was held up, the people made "no great shout or reflection"; he estimates that there were ten thousand spectators present. The malice of his enemies, thwarted by his refusal to acknowledge the Plot, expressed itself, on the very day he suffered, in a ballad, of which the following is a specimen:

> "*Where was St Dominic, asleep?*
> *Where did St Frank his Kennel keep?*
> *That on a business so emergen'*
> *They did not briskly teize the Virgin?*
> *To let his Lordship play a Prank*
> *Her Grace becoming, and his Rank?*"[79]

(14)

With the new year came the dissolution of Parliament. "Th[ey were] dissolved for acting high and doing little. Their cheife time they spent in bringing people upon their knees from all parts of the nation, that had been against pet[it]ions for the parliament to sit";[80] the dissolution saved Scroggs from impeachment (he retired to Essex and died there two years later); and it determined the Opposition either to force the King to exclude his brother or else to appeal to arms. On February 3rd, Justice Warcup noted in his journal: "Turbervile [one of the informers] told me that Shaftesbury discoursed him about raising men; and that he offred to head any men on his lordship's designe,—who answered he thanked him, but he found the damned citty to flag and fall off. His lordship further said he was sure of Wapping and Southwark and all that way, but the cittizens were for peace and flow off, and would not rise. Turbervile replyed, I am at your lordship's service, give me any men. Sh. thanked him, and told him time might come that he might make use of him."[81] The King's own conviction that the nation was on the brink of civil war is evident from the fact that he appointed the new Parliament to meet at Oxford; though the more sober citizens of London might "flag and fall off", the Green Ribbon Club and the mob it controlled were quite capable of repeating the disaster of 1641.

As March came in, the month in which Parliament was to meet, great preparations were made by these worthies. London was full of vicious pamphlets and seditious ballads, the mob prowled the streets at night, shouting for Shaftesbury and openly damning York. In readiness for their journey to Oxford, the lords and gentlemen of the Opposition gathered round them bands of armed retainers, while the King took the precaution of posting his Guards along the route. Dr Oates himself, confident that his noble patrons would gain the victory, and having every intention of sharing in the spoils, proposed to draw a bill to the tune of thirty thousand pounds upon the triumphant Parliament, in order that he might purchase for himself a country estate, none other than Bobbing Court in Kent, now owned by Colonel Edward Diggs, who had married the widow of Sir George Moore. He was actually in negotiation with Colonel Diggs for the purchase; Bobbing, he said, agreed with his health (though he had said precisely the opposite at the trial of Langhorne).[82] Lest the victory of his patrons must be preceded by a little blood-letting, he took the precaution of taking loaded pistols with him on his journey to Oxford; and also, naturally, a little ready cash. "Major Wildman, and Mr Charleton Furnished Oats at his going to Oxford to the Parliament with Forty Pound, his Collections are now gathered by Elias Best the Hop-Merchant in Thames-street."[83]

Oxford received King Charles with a tremendous ovation; "all the way the king passed were such shoutings, acclamations, and ringing of bells, made by loyall hearts and smart lads of the layetie of Oxon, that the aire was so much pierced that the clouds seemed to divide. The generall cry was 'Long live King Charles', and many drawing up to the very coach window cryed 'Let the King live, and the devill hang up all round-heads': at which his majestie smiled and seemed well pleased.—The throng and violence of people to express their affections was such that the coach was scarce able to pass. The youths were all on fire. . . . Their hats did continually fly, and seriouslie had you been there, you would have thought that they would have thrown away their verie heads and leggs. Here was an arme for joy flung out of joynt and there a legge displaced. . . ."[84]

The ageing Charles needed all his popularity if he were to emerge a victor in the coming clash. For it was plain that this time the Opposition meant business; they were going to deliver an ultimatum—the Exclusion, or civil war; and no means had been overlooked in their determination to frighten Charles into choosing the former. They brought with them to Oxford, not only bands of armed retainers, but a perfect army of lampoonists, pamphleteers, and squib-writers, whose business it was to stir up the people of Oxford as already they had stirred up those of London. These hirelings were to "hunt the Party Members in to the Question, to make themselves acceptable by being good Company and pushing Discourse, advancing Satyr and News, and to banter if any pretended to talk on the Loyal Side, to dash their Countenances with ridiculous Turns of Wit, and then come off with the Horse Laugh, and so to encourage their Party, and gain over Proselytes of as many as, by Dexterity of Courtship, Flattering, Wheedling, Lying, and Reviling, could be invited into their Measures".

Songs, lampoons, tracts, and wood-cuts were there in variety, designed to cater for all tastes, "some adapted to deceive Men of Fortune and Education, well penned, and, perhaps, in Heroick Verse; others for the Rabble, and drunken, sottish Clubs, in Ballad Doggerel, with witty Picture affixed, in Dainty Conceit and Proportion; notable Eloquence for the Eye! . . . There was also an Impression of Libel in Miniature upon Purple Ribbon, with lacker'd Tin; The Words, *no Popery, no Slavery*. These were worn by the Troops of Citizens attending their Members on the Road, and at Oxford, and were given out to be worn in Hats, and every one, that would, had his Favour; whether for any Signal, or Ostentation of Party, the Administrators best knew."[85]

On Monday, March 21st, the King opened this fateful Parliament with a speech in which, while he declared his willingness to agree to any measures against a Popish Successor which did not alter the lawful descent of the Crown, he warned them that, since he would never use any arbitrary measures himself, he would not suffer them in his subjects. The Commons retorted with an immediate re-opening of the attack on York by a new Exclusion Bill.

On the following Monday, March 28th, the day fixed for the introduction of this Bill to the House of Lords, the King walked down to the Geometry School (in which sat the peers), followed by a sedan, bearing, concealed, his robes and crown. These latter he donned in an ante-room, and, taking his seat upon the throne, dispatched Black Rod to fetch the Commons. He then briefly and tersely informed the two Houses that "we are not like to have a good end when divisions at the beginning are such", and ordered the Lord Chancellor to dissolve Parliament.

His dramatic action, which took the Opposition completely by surprise, averted a repetition of '41. Had the Exclusion Bill passed the Lords, he must have chosen between giving his assent to what amounted to an end of hereditary monarchy, and an appeal to arms. He drove straight back to Whitehall, concluded a secret treaty with Louis of France, which made him, at least for the moment, independent of supplies from Parliament, and, taking a leaf out of his enemies' book, inaugurated a vigorous campaign of pamphlets. On April 13th, there appeared the first number of Sir Roger L'Estrange's *Observators*, which were to lash the Opposition, and in particular its protégé, Titus Oates, for several years to come. Titus, cheated out of his thirty thousand pounds and his country estate, must have ground his teeth as he read the parodies on his mode of speech which fell from that witty pen:

"I remember six times what I reade; for I supply all that was left out, and yet its a wonderful thing, I cannot for my heart's blood remember Faces. I dare swear I have taken one man for another twenty times; but I am altogether for Things, and Notions, d'ye see, and such like; Countenances, let me tell ye, don't Affect me."

(15)

During the brief life of the Oxford Parliament, a great commotion had been caused by the affair of a certain Edward Fitzharris; and since Oates was to appear as a witness at his trial, it is necessary to give a sketch of it here.

Fitzharris was an Irishman, and seems to have intended

to play the part of Dangerfield, and that at the very moment when the Opposition was set upon pushing the Exclusion Bill through the Oxford Parliament. Either he or his supposed accomplice, Everard, wrote a libel entitled *The True Englishman speaking Plain English*, which incited the people to rise against a king who designed to abolish Magna Carta, parliaments, and liberty; it particularly referred to the forthcoming Oxford Parliament, and stated that if the people could get no satisfaction during its sitting, they must rise in arms. How far Fitzharris was let into the inner councils of the business is not clear; at all events, with or without his connivance, Everard had witnesses concealed to overhear their treasonable talk, and Fitzharris was arrested. The idea was that now, in order to save his life, he should become one of the King's Evidence, and "confess" that he had been hired by the Papists to write the libel and then to send copies of it to the Opposition leaders, so that, these copies being found in their possession, they could be charged with High Treason.

But the King was growing used to dealing with these "conspiracies in disguise". He refused either to grant Fitzharris his pardon in advance, or to have him impeached by the Commons. On hearing that he was being visited in Newgate by the two Sheriffs, Bethel and Cornish, and other Oppositionists, Charles had him removed to the Tower, and later tried in the Court of King's Bench. This trial took place on June 9th, and the luckless Fitzharris, having no pardon, was bereft of his designed defence—namely, the accusation of the Papists and the anti-Oppositionists who were supposed to have hired him. When asked to call his witnesses, he at once called Dr Oates, and asked him to state what he had heard Everard say about the libel since his, Fitzharris's, arrest. Everard had told him, said Titus, that he wrote the libel with a design to have it printed, and "sent about in Penny-Post Letters to the protesting Lords and leading Commoners; who were all to be taken up as soon as they had it; and, upon Search, it was to be found about them. That the Court had a hand in it, and the King had given Fitzharris money, and would give him more if it had success."

It is plain that Titus was uneasy while he gave this

evidence, nor is it difficult to imagine the reason. He had been saying what he had been told to say; "Here is the Sum", observes North, "of what the Faction, at that Time, laboured to have believed of the King; and how could it fail, coming out of so oracular a Mouth?"[86] But it was a very dangerous thing to say, because it was an indirect accusation of the King himself (indirect because Titus only said that Everard had told him this); and the King had just scored a signal triumph over the Oppositionists, Titus's patrons, by his dissolution of the Oxford Parliament. So when Fitzharris called other witnesses, Dr Oates begged leave to retire, making the excuse that "the Croud is very great". The Lord Chief Justice (now Sir Francis Pemberton) refusing permission, Titus repeated his request, which was again refused. Presently he could stand it no longer.

"*Dr Oates*. My Lord, I desire to have Liberty of going away, the Croud is so great, I cannot stand, and the Prisoner hath nothing to say to me.

"*Mr Attor. Gen.* My Lord, that may be part of the Popish Plot, to keep Dr Oates here, to kill him in the Croud.

"*Fitzharris*. Have you not something more to say, Doctor? Truly I forget, my Memory is so distracted.

"*Dr Oates*. I know not, if you have any Questions to ask me, I will speak Truth."

To Titus's relief, Fitzharris could think of no more questions, and the Saviour of the Nation was allowed to retire.

In his summing-up, the Lord Chief Justice referred somewhat disparagingly to Oates's evidence. "The first witness [Fitzharris] brings, is Dr Oates; and he does tell you, That having some Discourse with Everard, Everard should say, this was a design of the Court, and was to be put into some Lords, and I think some Parliament-Men's Pockets; and then they were to be apprehended. I think this is Dr Oates's Testimony. Mr Everard is here upon his Oath, and he testifies no such thing in the World. 'Tis easy for one to come and say, I heard a Man say so; perhaps he said it by way of Conjecture; but that is no Answer to direct Proof."

Altogether, Dr Oates's first experience as a defence witness had not been a very happy one.

Fitzharris was condemned on June 15th, and, in company with Archbishop Plunket, who had been tried on the 8th, was drawn, hanged, and quartered at Tyburn, July 1st. On the scaffold, Fitzharris retracted all he had said at the trial, and accused Lord Howard of Escrick of having been the real author of the libel; he added that his former depositions had been suggested to him by Bethel and Cornish, Sir George Treby the Recorder, and Alderman Clayton, all Opposition stalwarts. Plunket, executed for the Irish branch of the Plot, was illegally tried in England, was denied time to send for his witnesses, and was promised his life if he would "confess". Even Burnet acknowledged him to be a man of very high character.[87]

He was the last man to suffer execution for the Popish Plot.

(16)

The Plot was dying, the Opposition was at bay, the King's star was in the ascendant, and the nation, realizing how near it had come to experiencing once again the horrors of civil war, showered upon Charles loyal addresses, all expressing their abhorrence of the traitors who had tried to engineer such a catastrophe. Shaftesbury, Russell, Howard of Escrick, and the rest, in their turn trembled under the threat of impeachment, and meanwhile the King set himself to cleanse the disaffected City, their stronghold. As for Dr Titus Oates, he, thoroughly disgruntled, sought to gain consolation in petty spite and blasphemous speech.

In the previous November, his pension had been raised again to ten pounds a week; immediately, he had petitioned the House "to address the King that he may have money, 12. *l.* to diet himself as formerly, and not diet from the King. The L. Privy Seal, M. Worcester, and E. Essex undertake to move it to the Council tomorrow".[88] But in June of this year, 1681, possibly because of the part he played in the Fitzharris business, his pension was reduced once more to forty shillings weekly, though he still had his lodgings at Whitehall.[89]

In May, he had appeared as plaintiff before the Court of

the Merchant Taylors' Company, against Isaac Backhouse, Headmaster of the Company's school at Wolverhampton. His accusation ran thus: "I doe hereby attest that upon the Lord's Day, or thereabout, after Sir George Wakeman was tried, as neare as I can remember, I was walking in St James's Park, and I saw a Gentleman in the habit of a Clerke, to whom Mr William Smith did speak, who then was with me, and told me after he left him that his name was Mr. Bacchus, an Usher in Merchant Taylors' School, and meeting the said person so called, I heard him say, there goes Oates, that perjured Rogue. Witness my hand this 18th of May, 1681. Titus Oates."[90] His witnesses were "Elephant" Smith, the Opposition bookseller, and Elias Best, the hop-merchant, who, as has been seen, was a collector of contributions for the maintenance of Oates. (He was also one of the Grand Jury of London.) Both testified to having heard Backhouse disparage the King's Evidence; but it is pleasant to record that the schoolmaster was acquitted.

On June 30th, Titus tried his hand at blackmail. It may be remembered that one of the witnesses who had sworn to having seen Oates in London at the time of the "Grand Consult" was an old priest named Clay, and that Charles Howard, at whose lodgings in Arundel House they were supposed to have met, had been brave enough to appear for the defence, and to contradict Clay's statement. Now it seems that a man named Wilcox, probably John Wilcox, a Dissenter, and son of Alderman Wilcox, an associate of Oates,[91] at some time previous to this June of 1681 had approached Charles Howard with a demand for money for an unspecified service. Howard had refused to pay. Hereupon, Titus, who was to share in the spoil, took a hand in bringing pressure to bear upon the victim; the latter, losing his nerve, bleated for mercy, begged Oates a little to consider the wrongs he had suffered (again unspecified), and engaged himself to abide by Titus's decision as to the amount of the sum demanded. Titus had no hesitation in naming a good fat sum—so fat, indeed, that the victim faltered, delayed, and tried to wriggle out. Dr Oates, shocked by such behaviour, wrote him, on June 30th, the following most sinister letter:

"SIR,

"I have taken paines in yor buisness, and have not had any advantage but my labour for my paines. You may have occasion to use me in plt [parliament], when your cause may come before either lords, or commons, or both: but, if you breake yor word with mee at this rate, you will finde mee but cold in appeareing for you there, or in any other occasion. I have done you justice in this, and if you stand not to that award, you will finde mee severe in other respects: for, in plaine termes, I cannot keep friendpp with any man that values not his word: and further, let me tell you that your house will not protect you from mee. However, if you comply with your word upon honour to me,

"I will appear, Sir,
"Yor affecte. sert.
"TITUS OATES.

"June 30 in 81.
"To the Honble Charles Howard Esqr."[92]

Whether or no the victim paid up is not recorded, but the chances are that he did, for Oates's name still carried terror, especially to a Catholic, and his accusations were still listened to with respect.

It was in this summer of 1681, however, that the tables began to be turned on Titus. The Opposition, defeated in open fight, had been driven underground, and the King was not unaware that already in the City there were certain sinister and secret preparations which hinted at the possibility of a plot against the Government. A watch was kept, therefore, on persons known to be disaffected, and among them was Dr Oates. In June, an unknown correspondent reported to Secretary Jenkins: "Last Sunday I was informed of Key [Keyes] living in Angel Court, Throgmorton Street, a great Presbyterian, who yet has taken the place of churchwarden this year. He is observed to have in his house, drums, trumpets, colours, etc., his neighbours much wonder for what use. Dr Oates has been lately observed to frequent his house."[93] About the same time, a news-letter writer reported: "It's said two Irishmen have sworn that Dr Oates was at a consult, whereat resolutions were taken to swear against the Queen, Duke, etc. Dr Oates, being late at the Bowling-green at Newington, spoke very scandalously of the Court of Aldermen, of which Capt. Broomer, who was present, has given them information, and, I am told, they have summoned the Doctor to appear before them."[94]

Other informations concerned Titus's blasphemous speech. L'Estrange gives many instances of Titus's fondness for this vice: "And our Lady-day (says one) How comes that to be a festivall? I'le tell ye, says another [Oates]; some five hundred years after Christ was dead, they made her Son a God; and soon after that, they made his Mother a Goddess."[95] "The Literall, and Actuall Crucifixtion of Jesus Christ, was neither necessary nor available to the Salvation of Mankind."[96] His swearing, too, was notorious. "He is no Gamester, 'tis true: But a most Prodigious Swearer; and any man that has ever Serv'd him will tell ye that he Swears, and Curses, Night and Morning, First and Last, as if he did it by Prescription."[97]

Late in June, a rumour went round that Oates was actually to be prosecuted for blasphemy. "I am told", says a news-letter writer on the 28th, "that Dr Oates is summoned to the Council at Hampton Court and that there is an information against him for blasphemy, which, they say, will be proved against him by several witnesses." Justice Warcup, writing to the Earl of Conway, gives further details: "His Majesty last Thursday at Hampton Court told me he would know who were the witnesses that could prove the blasphemy spoken by Dr Oates. I told him I was informed they were Mr East, who formerly belonged to the Earl of Essex and has some affairs depending before the Lords of the Treasury, and Mr Cressett, a lawyer of the Temple, Capt. Cressett's son. The last tells me this afternoon that the words he could prove were his denial of the Godhead of Jesus Christ, and that they were spoken before himself, Sir Richard Corbett, Mr Mulys and myself, and I believe I was present and that those words were spoken at the Royal Coffee-house. The words Mr. East proves are as bad or worse, as I am informed, but the particular words I cannot learn, but Mr East said that, if he were called upon, on examination he would affirm the truth. I beseech you to acquaint his Majesty with these particulars, if you judge it meet."[98]

Either the Earl of Conway did not judge it meet, or else the witnesses' courage failed them at the last moment, for Titus was not called upon to answer to such charges. Meanwhile, he continued to find favour in the City:

"At a Court of Assistants held on Monday the 27th of June last at Weavers-Hall, London, it was by several of the Livery desir'd that some of the Members of the said Court of Assistants might wait on the Reverend Titus Oates, to request him that he would be pleased to take the Pains to Preach before the Company of Weavers on the 25th of this instant July, being the day of Election of the Officers of the said Company; which Proposal was taken into serious Consideration, and maturely debated, and (though opposed by several of the said Court, in regard of the trouble they should put upon the Dr) upon an Argument of a Member of the said Court that the Dr's Father was a Weaver, it was resolved that some Members of the said Court should wait upon the Dr to desire his complyance therein, which hath been performed since accordingly. The Dr was pleased to grant their request; answering, That he took it for a great Honour that he had the opportunity so kindly offered to wait upon that Society in so Solemn a manner."[99] "His Text was in Hebrews Chap. 1. the latter end of the 2nd verse. There was a very great Auditory; after which the Dr was invited to a noble Dinner in Weavers' Hall. The entertainment was the more splendid, because the Reverend Dr (upon his Father's account) had some relation to their Society."[100]

Earlier in the month, upon the 2nd, Titus himself had played host to an honoured guest, when Lord Shaftesbury had dined at his lodgings.[101] But the occasion was melancholy. The Opposition leader was in fact on his way to the Tower, having been arrested that morning. Yet he cannot have been unduly cast down; he had been in the Tower before and had got out, and he knew very well that, in the present state of the City, the King could not hope for justice in his own courts. So infatuated was the City with everything for which Shaftesbury stood that, at this precise moment, it was ordering an inscription to be engraved upon the Monument, stating that the Great Fire of London had been begun and carried on by the Papists, in order to introduce Popery and Slavery.[102]

(17)

Before coming to the death-bed of the Plot and its hero's disgrace, it is necessary to glance at a species of activity which had occupied many of the great Titus's hours of leisure during his fame—namely, his excursions into the realm of literature. "He published Books", says North, "so completely vile in Manner and Language swoln with Evil of both Sorts, and discharged upon almost all his Betters (for he spares but few) as none but he could be the Author of, and whereout Instances (to prevent the Disgrace to human Kind for owning such a Monster) are not fit to be taken and related; so who will, for me, may rake in such Merda."[103]

The first on the list is his *Narrative*, published in two tracts, *The Discovery of the Popish Plot* (which includes his examinations before the Parliament, the Lord Chief Justice, and three justices of the peace); and his *True Narrative*, published by order of the House of Lords. "It were idle", says Smollett, "to detect the falshood of an information which contains such a number of palpable absurdities",[104] and as a summary of the eighty-one articles has been attempted earlier in this work, it remains only to notice some of the finer flights of fancy contained in the dedicatory letter of the *True Narrative*, addressed to the King. In this, Titus informs Charles of the Papists' designs against his grandfather, father, and himself; he urges him to banish the vicious from his presence and to advance the virtuous; he declares (without, of course, stating the source of his information), that two Jesuits undertook to provide the reward offered by the rebels for the capture of Charles II after the Battle of Worcester; and that "above all Men, they [the Papists] Endeavour'd to Betray, and Sacrifice his Majesty into the hands of his Enemies".

Early in 1679, there appeared in print a sermon of his preached at St Michael's, Wood Street, in January; it was published, says the sub-title, "to prevent mistakes". The dedication is to Prince Rupert, whom Oates describes as one to whom under God and King Charles II "is chiefly owing a very considerable Temporal Deliverance to this Nation. For without your Highness's great Zeal and Interest, and generous Example, to several Right Noble and Willing Lords and Patriots, to support the Evidence, (and some miraculous Providences intervening) it hardly had fail'd, but that Might and Craft had quite stifled and overladen the Truth in Weak Hands. . . ." The Christian reader is informed that the sermon is published "not for any ostentation, but for general Satisfaction, upon Occasion of some Exceptions raised against it, by some open and some secret Enemies, which my present Affair hath raised against me in great numbers", and is begged to excuse any levity in the style, which is due to "my so little leisure to recollect or pen, in my present Circumstances, and multitude of other Affairs and Visits"; the Church of England is praised for her "hoary and Apostolical Antiquity"; the Dissenters ("those gone astray in Schism") are rebuked for "weakening and undermining the Protestant Interest, by their Divisions"; and the general reader is recommended to observe a greater purity and sobriety of life. The conclusion to this address was well calculated to wring the hearts of all admirers of the Saviour of the Nation:

"And lastly, It is my own humble Request to all Christian Brethren, who have a sense and compassion of the danger I am in, from so many Enemies. that they would drop a Tear in private, in my behalf, for my preservation, from the strong Lyes and Machinations of a Sort of Men, not inferior for Malice, and cruelty, and enmity to the Truth, to the Powers of the Air, and likewise as invisible (though abounding in our Air as much as the other) through their lying Artifices. . . . And that God would stand by me in my Informations and Testimony, before Tribunals and Councils, to direct and preserve me from wronging, or unjustly favouring any of them, great or small, in the least tittle, which always was, and shall be, more my fear, than the fear of Death."

The Cabinet of the Jesuits Secrets Opened, which appeared in February, 1679, does not deserve more than a mere mention; it purports to be a collection of secret rules and maxims of the Society of Jesus, the nature of which can be left to the reader's imagination. To *The Witch of Endor* (November, 1679), with its sub-title: "An Account of the Exorcisms or Conjurations of the Papists, as they be set forth in their Agends, Benedictionals, Mannals, Missals, Journalls, Portasses", etc., the same applies, except that, in the dedicatory letter to Shaftesbury, Oates makes a remark which sounds very strange at this period of his career: "As for my self, my Lord, I have had nothing but Affronts and Afflictions, and your Lordship hath vouchsafed to stoop to share with me in them; and since your Lordship hath been pleased to own me in my Sorrows and Cares, I am thereby incouraged to address my self to your Honour for your Patronage and Protection."

Two other tracts were published this year. The first was *The Pope's Warehouse, or The Merchandise of the Whore of Rome*, likewise dedicated to Shaftesbury ("The Publisher's affectionate good Friend, and singular good Lord") as an acknowledgement of Shaftesbury's favours. If my lord will continue firm in his purpose, and will encourage other patriots to buy the tract, he may "Assure your self of a lasting Repute in this Life, and of Peace at your Death, and a joyful Resurrection to the World to come". Having dropped this delicate hint, Titus turns to his readers, addressing them in that Epistle-like style so favoured by him: "To all that profess the Protestant Religion within this Kingdom of England, Grace, Mercy, and Peace. Dearly beloved brethren . . ." The modern reader recoils from the extraordinary venom, irreverence, and obscenity of this alleged "Catalogue of the Romish Lies and Cheats, many of which are, to mine own Knowledge, maintained and practised to this day in the Romish Synagogue", and from what is surely a first-hand description, horrible in its open gloating, of the execution of the Five Jesuits.

The other tract, *The King's Evidence Justified*, was written as a counterblast to Castlemaine's *Compendium*, which appeared shortly after the Five Jesuits suffered at Tyburn. The King's Evidence "are in no way concern'd" by Castlemaine's exposure of their inconsistencies; but it is only right that "such puny Extravagancies must not pass uncorrected". The method adopted by Oates for this purpose was to calumniate, with a spitefulness extraordinary even for him, the characters of his dead victims. Most of this calumny is too gross for quotation; the following are specimens of the milder variety. Fenwick was "a Parsons Son, disown'd by his Father, and by him Expelled for his Debauchery, from his House, and in a fair way to be Hang'd, till he took Sanctuary at St Omers, as Bankrupts do at Jamaica". Whitebread was "a Fisher in all Professions for Preferment. First a Jew, then a Presbyterian, then a Quaker, to whose Meetings he us'd to go in a Carters Habit; one that had more shapes to disguise himself, then a Player, as is attested by a Letter written to the Lord Mayor of London: And at last a Jew again, that is, a wandering Jesuit." Pickering is described as "a pitiful, ignorant, lying Priest"; and even poor Hill, Green, and Berry did not escape the malice of Titus's pen.

What Dr Oates's sales were, we have no means of knowing. But it is to be hoped for his own sake that his literary efforts brought him some material reward, for very soon now he was again to be a man without an income, living on the voluntary contributions of his patrons and friends.

(18)

On July 29th, Stephen College, "the Protestant Joiner", was committed to the Tower for high treason, and on Wednesday, August 17th, he was tried at Oxford, in which city the crime with which he was charged had been attempted. His trial formed part of the King's vigorous counter-attack, and a means of exposing to the nation at large how determined had been the efforts of the Opposition to precipitate civil war. It is notable for the melancholy spectacle of the King's Evidence appearing on different sides; Dugdale, Turbervile, and others of the lesser fry were called by the prosecution, Dr Oates by the defence; and the way in which this band of brothers attacked one another's personal characters during the hearing of the case was really most unedifying.

College himself seems to have been a genuine fanatic, of the type which had appeared in 1641. It was stated in the course of the evidence that he, in conversation with a witness, had justified the execution of Charles I and all the measures of the Long Parliament. That his simple fanaticism had made him a protégé of the Opposition is evident from the fact that his defence had been invented for him by the notorious Aaron Smith, Oates's tame counsel; contrary to law, papers containing all sort of objections of a legal nature had been smuggled in to him before the trial; these papers, on their being discovered, had been confiscated, and College wasted a great deal of the court's time endeavouring to have them restored to him. Aaron Smith himself was called to answer for his conduct, and his recognisance of £100 demanded of him as security for his appearance before the Bench during the sessions.

The charge against College was that he had attempted to seize the person of the King during the Oxford Parliament, and to raise a rebellion; and to this end had endeavoured to enlist the aid of several persons, including the informer Turbervile. The evidence against him was pretty conclusive; but to make things sound as bad as possible, the Attorney-General, in his opening speech, observed that if the case could be thoroughly investigated, he had no doubt that the Protestant Joiner would turn out to be a Papist in disguise, "for I think that no Protestant subject would attempt such things as we shall prove to you". He had forgotten, apparently, the happenings of the previous reign.

The defence was pitifully poor. College would not call his witnesses until he had argued for hours upon the validity of the case against him, and it became plainer than ever that he had been primed beforehand by some man of law. When at last his witnesses were summoned, it was obvious why he had been so anxious to postpone calling them; they were supposed to be there to discredit the prosecution witnesses, but a woman among them turned out to be the mother-in-law of one of these gentry, another was proved, by a king's messenger, to have perjured himself, and a third firmly refused to say what College was trying to put into his mouth; until at last the Lord Chief Justice was obliged to remind the prisoner that it was of little use to call one witness only to disprove the evidence of the previous one. It must have been with a sigh of relief that College saw stand up the great Dr Titus Oates, who, when he was at his favourite occupation of blackening a man's character, always did it "thorough-stitch".

He began on Turbervile. Dr Oates, hearing that Turbervile was to be a witness against College, had asked the former if it were so, to which Turbervile had replied that "the Protestant Citizens have deserted us; and, God damn him, he would not starve". Turbervile strenuously denying this, Dr Oates became pious. "Upon the word of a Priest, what I say is true. My Lord, I do say, as I am a Minister, I do speak it sincerely, in the presence of God, this Gentleman did say these words to me; which made me afraid of the man, and I went my ways, and never spake with him afterwards, nor durst I; for I thought he that would swear and curse after that rate, was not fit to be talk'd with." To this Turbervile retorted somewhat childishly: "I always look'd on Dr Oates as a very ill man, and never would converse much with him." Rogues were falling out with a vengeance.

Titus, having received a warning from the Bench that he must not say that witnesses had been suborned to testify against College, now started on another of the prosecution witnesses, one John Smith, known as Narrative Smith, an apostate priest and recently ordained a minister of the Church of England.

"To my own knowledge," brayed Titus, "as to Mr Smith, Mr Colledge and Mr Smith had some provoking Words passed betwixt them at Richard's Coffee-house, and Mr Smith comes out and swears, God damn him he would have Colledge's blood. So, my Lord, when I met him, said I, Mr Smith, you profess yourself to be a Priest, and have stood at the Altar, and now you intend to take upon you the Ministry of the Church of England, and these Words do not become a Minister of the Gospel: His reply was, God damn the Gospel: This is Truth, I speak it in the presence of God and man."

Next there was his old colleague, Dugdale. "I was engaged for him," Dr Oates gravely informed the court, "for 50. *l.* for last Lent Assizes, he wanted mony to go down to the Assizes, having paid some debts, and paid away all his mony; and so I engaged for 50. *l.* which he borrowed of Richard the Coffee-man. After he came from

Oxon, I called upon him to hasten to get his mony from the Lords of the Treasury, which, as near as I remember, was order'd him upon his Petition, for so I heard. And at that time, said he, Sir, I hear there is a great noise of my being an Evidence: Against whom? said I: Against several Protestants, my Lord Shaftesbury, and others: Said I, I never heard any thing of it: says he, there is no body hath any cause to make any such report of me, for I call God to witness I know nothing against any Protestant in England. After that I met with Dugdale at Richard's Coffee-house, and pressing him for the mony, and he saying he had it not just then, but would pay it in a little time: Mr Dugdale, said I, you have gone I am afraid against your Conscience, I am sure against what you have declared to me: said he, it was all along of Colonel Warcup, for I could get no mony else."

"Mr Oates," exclaimed the Attorney-General, "is a thorough-paced Witness against all the King's Evidence."

"And yet," observed Mr Serjeant Jeffreys dryly, "Dr Oates had been alone in some matters, had it not been for some of these Witnesses."

"I had been alone perhaps," haughtily retorted the Saviour of the Nation, "and perhaps not; but yet, Mr Serjeant, I had always a better Reputation than to need theirs to strengthen it."

Presently he remembered something else against Dugdale, something which seems to have been true;[105] for it must be understood that Dr Oates was never averse to speaking the truth when it enabled him to damage somebody's reputation.

"My Lord, now Dugdale is come I will tell you something more. There was a Report given out by Mr Dugdale's means, that Mr Dugdale was poisoned; and in truth, my Lord, it was but the Pox. And this sham passed throughout the Kingdom in our Intelligences; and this I will make appear by the Physician that cured him.

"*Mr Ser. Jeffreys*. That is but by a third hand.

"*Dr Oates*. He did confess that he had an old Clap, and yet he gave out he was poisoned; but now, my Lord, as to what I said before of him, I was engaged for 50. *l*. for Mr Dugdale; do you own that?"

Dugdale owned that, but stoutly denied the other charges. "Upon the Oath I have taken, and as I hope for Salvation, it is not true.

"*Mr Ser. Jeffreys*. Here is Dugdale's Oath against Dr Oates's saying.

"*Dr Oates*. Mr. Serjeant, you shall hear of this in another place.

"*Mr Att. Gen*. 'Tis an unhappy thing that Dr Oates should come in against these men that supported his Evidence before."

Part of the charge against College was that, on the occasion of a dinner given by Alderman Wilcox at the Crown tavern near Temple Bar, he had spoken treasonable words in the hearing of John Smith. College called on Titus to refute this evidence; and Dr Oates embarked upon his own version of the story with the utmost relish:

"This Summer was twelve-month, or I am sure a great while before Christmas, the Alderman invited me several times to give me a Treat, and I had not time, other business calling me off; but finding a time, I sent him word I would come to see him. He said he was a Brewer, and troubled at home with Customers, but he would give me a Dinner at the Crown Tavern without Temple Bar, that was the place fixed upon; there was Mr Smith the Counsellor,* who had been serviceable to me in several instances. . . . Colledge did tell me he was invited; said I, You shall be welcome, as far as I can make you welcome. So Colledge and I went together from the Rainbow Coffee House to the Crown Tavern: Now indeed Colledge was very pleasant and merry, and as I think the discourse betwixt the Rainbow Coffee House and the Tavern was betwixt Mr Colledge and me; for Mr [John] Smith stayed somewhat behind or walked before, I cannot tell which: When we came to the Crown Tavern we did, to divert ourselves till Dinner came up, enter into a Philosophical Discourse with one Mr Savage who was formerly a Romish Priest, but this Savage is since pardoned by the King, and is a Member of the Church of England. . . . This I remember was the Discourse

* Titus's circle of acquaintance included so many Smiths that the reader may well grow confused. This "Counsellor" Smith was a Thomas Smith, possibly a Common Councillor of the City of London. He must be distinguished from Aaron Smith, described by North as Oates's "Counsel".

HAPPY INSTRUMENTS OF ENGLAND'S PRESERVATION

before we dined till we went to Dinner, it was concerning the existence of God, whether that could be proved by natural demonstration, and whether or no the Soul was immortal. My Lord, after Dinner [John] Smith went away, I did not hear the least Discourse of any such thing as he speaks of, and Mr [John] Smith and Colledge had no discourse in my hearing from the Coffee House to the Tavern; and when we were in the Tavern we did discourse about those two Points. . . . If your Lordship please [John Smith] speaks of Mr Wilcox to be a Man that contributes Mony to buy Armes, Powder, and Shot, I think Sir George Jefferies knows Alderman Wilcox is a man of another Employment.

"*Mr Ser. Jeffreys*. Sir George Jefferies does not intend to be an Evidence I assure you.

"*L.C.J.* Do you ask him any more Questions?

"*Dr Oates*. I do not desire Sir George Jefferies to be an Evidence for me. I had Credit in Parliaments, and Sir George had disgrace in one of them.

"*Mr Ser. Jeffreys*. Your Servant, Doctor, you are a witty man, and a Philosopher."

Thomas Smith then backed up Oates's evidence, adding that during the dinner, far from indulging in treasonable talk, College had gone to sleep. With this College himself eagerly agreed. The next witness was Samuel Oates, Titus's elder brother; and he went and spoilt the whole thing. Certainly he had been at the dinner and had heard no treasonable talk; but neither had he heard the learned discussion between Oates and Savage, though Thomas Smith had just affirmed that the room was so small that the conversation must have been audible to all the guests. Jeffreys immediately pounced upon Samuel, demanding of him:

"What did they talk of?

"*Mr S. Oates*. There was nothing at all spoken of.

"*Mr Ser. Jeff*. What, did they say nothing all the while?

"*Mr S. Oates*. Nothing but matter of common discourse, matters of eating and drinking, and talking of Country affairs, there were several that had Lands in the Country and they were talking of those things.

"*Mr Justice Jones*. Were you there all the while?

"*Mr S. Oates*. Yes.

"*Mr Ser. Jeff*. Hark you, Sir, were there no Disputations in Divinity?

"*Mr S. Oates*. Not at all.

"*Mr Ser. Jeff*. Nor of Philosophy?

"*Mr S. Oates*. No.

"*Mr Ser. Jeff*. Why pray Sir did not Dr Oates and Mr Savage talk very pleasantly of two great Questions in Divinity, the Being of God and the Immortality of the Soul?

"*Mr S. Oates*. There was not a Word of that, but only common discourse."

It would be interesting to know what Titus said to brother Samuel concerning this sorry performance when the privacy of their chamber gave freedom for a little frank fraternal talk, especially in view of the fact that Samuel had forgotten his part to such an extent that, asked when it was that College had fallen asleep, he replied that College did not fall asleep at all.[106]

The Bench was very patient with College. It listened to defence witness after defence witness contradicting one another; it repeated to the prisoner, over and over again, the Law's decision on minute legal points he attempted to dispute; and it bore with his constant interruptions during the Solicitor-General's final speech. No trial during the whole period is more tedious to read, and this applies particularly to the prisoner's rambling and irrelevant defence; at one point he engaged the Bench in an interminable argument as to whether the Papists or the Long Parliament had cut off the late King's head. His objection to the prosecution witnesses is somewhat ironical, considering that they were old cronies of his: "if a Man shall be sworn against by such Fellows as these, no Man is safe."

The Lord Chief Justice summed up very shortly, and in a manner which contrasts strangely with that of his predecessor, Scroggs. The verdict of Guilty was received by the loyal folk of Oxford with great applause; and it is a significant comment upon the more healthy state of the kingdom that the court committed one of the most vociferous to jail and publicly rebuked him next morning. College made a brave end of it on the last day of August, asserting on the scaffold that he knew of no plot but the Popish Plot, though he acknowledged that "he might in heat have uttered some words of indecency concerning the king and councill".[107]

(19)

The behaviour of Oates at the trial of College had given King Charles the opportunity he had long been seeking.

That such a man as this, with his obvious falsehoods, unsavoury past, foul tongue, and murderous malice, should have lorded it about Whitehall, compelled men to address him by a title to which he had no right, eaten at the public expense, lodged sumptuously in the Palace, and appeared among the lords and gentlemen in the King's own Presence Chamber, was a crying scandal which had lasted too long. Between July 2nd, 1679, and September 2nd, 1681, Oates had received from the public purse the sum of one thousand, three hundred and sixty-four pounds, eight shillings, and tenpence,[108] and there must have been another five hundred pounds or so previous to that. The King was obliged to pay Sir Edward Cartaret sixty pounds a year for the use of his lodgings for the informer; and, as has been seen, there were all kinds of rewards and perquisites pocketed by Titus on the side. All these favours and benefits had been bestowed despite the fact that it was known that, in conversation with his patrons and cronies, Oates bit the hand which fed him and took every opportunity of vilifying, not only his royal benefactor, but the Monarchy itself.

A news-letter writer reports that, during the course of College's trial, the Attorney-General addressed Oates thus: "Your bread you have from the King, your lodging in the King's Palace, you are obliged to the King for your life, and what esteem you have amongst men is on the King's account, and now will you behave so wickedly ungrateful for all his favours and mercies towards you, as to stand here in Court in the justification of so notorious a traitor, contrary to your allegiance to the King?"[109] Whether or no this rebuke was really given (there is no record of it in the printed trial), it was certainly merited; and Titus, though it is evident that he regarded himself as immune from justice, had gone too far this time. He had made a public exhibition of himself as a creature of the Opposition's, and he had been deliberately offensive in giving his evidence, pronouncing with relish "the round Oaths and ribald Stuff that he charged others to have uttered".[110]

On August 31st, the day after College suffered at Oxford, the Lord Chamberlain's warrant was conveyed to Titus by Sir Edward Cartaret, Black Rod, commanding him to remove himself and his goods from Whitehall. The King was human enough to enjoy adding insult to injury: "The Order by which the Reverend Doctor Oates was excluded the Court, gave in Charge also, That the Officer should see that none of His Majesties Goods should be imbezelled; and a Centinel was placed at the dore whilst the Doctor removed his Goods."[111]

The news-sheets and news-letters were full of it. Some added that several of Oates's brother witnesses were come forward to give testimony against him. It was said that Bolrun, the informer attached to the Yorkshire branch of the Plot, went so far as to accuse Titus of perjury "and other High Crimes and Misdemeanours, to the great amazement of all True Protestant Dissenters, who seem to fear a further Discovery of such matters."[112] A Mr Fitzgerald "acquainted the Court that 15 persons of good repute and some of very good quality had already given in several informations of highest treason against the doctor and prayed he might be immediately committed, but we hear not as yet that he is."[113] One news-letter writer either reported or invented the King's parting speech to Titus: "Mr Oates, I am assured that you have so far forgot your duty to me as to be guilty since your pardon of several high crimes and misdemeanours against me, I will not say of treason, though I believe as much, and I have good reason for my belief, however I forgive you again and leave you above board, but, if you are any more faulty, I shall spare you no more than any of the rest of my subjects, and so they parted."[114]

Though this speech sounds very unlike Charles II, the fact remains that, for the present, Titus was left "above board". His time would come later, when the King had accomplished the defeat of the Opposition and the thorough cleansing of the City. Towards that City did the hero of the Popish Plot direct his reverend feet when, upon the last day of August, sixteen hundred and eighty-one, he left Whitehall behind him.

BOOK FOUR

THE PROTESTANT MARTYR

(1)

THERE are few trials harder to bear with patience than that of being suddenly bereft of fame in mid-career; and Titus Oates, since he could be no longer the Saviour of the Nation, was determined to remain at least a public figure. In this very natural resolve, friend and foe alike seemed determined to assist him. An admirer, indignantly replying to a squib against his idol, likened him to "a noble stag" pursued by curs. On leaving Whitehall, says this writer, "the Doctor, knowing the Malice of these Curs, and understanding the eagerness of their Hunting after him, wisely and betimes hearded himself in the City, where only the Malice of their Pens could reach him, whom, could these Blood-Hounds conveniently have overtaken, had questionless made him a Sacrifice to their Rage and Fury".[1] Luttrell considered Titus important enough to deserve two references at this time in his *Brief Relation*;[2] and naturally the Tory news-sheets (for a terrific paper battle was now in progress in that field which for so long had been occupied entirely by the Opposition), found the occasion of Titus's expulsion from Whitehall a heaven-sent target for their wit:

"The same day the Dr removed from Whitehall, a Friend of his had provided Lodgings for him in Broad-street, upon Pretence of a Minister that came newly out of the Countrey; and about 8 of the Clock the same evening, the Dr with his usual Guards, came to take possession; but the Gentlewoman of the House perceiving an attendance somewhat extraordinary, enquired who the Minister was? and was whisper'd by one of the Company, it was Dr O——; upon which so unexpected a surprise, she cried out, I am undone! undone! undone! They are all French-Merchants, Strangers, Papists, that lodge in my House; For the Lord's sake perswade the Gentleman to take another Lodging, or else all my Lodgers will be gone immediately; which the Dr soon perceiving, gravely begg'd the Gentlewoman's pardon, and found out a more convenient place, which is said to be an honest Quaker's a watch-maker in George-yard near Lombard-street, where his Friends visit him daily; Some say he may go (if the Weather permits) for Amsterdam, there being an Arch-bishoprick reserved in bank for him these many years, he never approving of the fashion of our English Lawn-Sleeves."[3]

The same writer asserted that "Since the Salamanca Dr's removal into the City, the Whigs are so generous in their Supplies, that Pigs, Geese, and Capons fly in at his Windows in as great Plenty as ever they did to Dr Faustus; nay, his Magick is so great, that it hath attracted two Infants in their Swadling-Cloaths to lie at his Door, not doubting Entertainment, since such great Plenty cannot be consum'd, without open Housekeeping. The one will be Christen'd Titus, and the other Oates." But Titus, though fallen from his high pinnacle, was still a power in the land, and the writer of the news-sheet in question, Nathaniel Thompson, in October found himself called upon to answer for his *A Dialogue between the Devil and the Ignoramus Doctor*. His news-sheet continued in circulation, however, and on October 21st, when his bill of indictment was laid before the Grand Jury, it reported that Oates, who attended the proceedings, "discoursing with some of the Jury, received a Reprimand by a worthy Justice, who told him, If he did not leave tampering with Juries, and get him out of Court he would lay him by the Heels; upon which Mr Titus gravely brush'd off."

In November, Titus was attacked by a pen far sharper than the journalistic quill of poor Nat Thompson. Upon the 17th of that month, there appeared, anonymously, one of the most famous political satires in English literature, Dryden's *Absalom and Achitophel*. Its success was instantaneous and phenomenal. "Entire lines from it passed into household words; the characters assigned to the persons introduced, clung to them for the rest of their lives; the same Scriptural titles were employed by a host of poetasters and pamphleteers; and even the clergy volunteered to give increased notoriety to their application, by bringing them into their discourses from the pulpit."[4] The feelings of

"Corah", *alias* Dr Titus Oates, must have been bitter, when he read the well-known lines:

> "*Yet, Corah, thou shalt from oblivion pass;*
> *Erect thyself, thou monumental brass,*
> *High as the serpent of thy metal made,*
> *While nations stand secure beneath thy shade.*
> *What, though his birth were base, yet comets rise*
> *From earthly vapours, ere they shine in skies.*
> *Prodigious actions may as well be done*
> *By weaver's issue, as by prince's son.*
> *This arch-attestor for the public good*
> *By that one deed ennobles all his blood.*
> *Who ever asked the witnesses' high race*
> *Whose oath with martyrdom did Stephen grace?*
> *Ours was a Levite, and as times went then*
> *His tribe was God Almighty's gentlemen.*"

All things considered, Titus's heart cannot have been very lightsome at this time. True, he was not cast back into that total obscurity from which he had arisen in his thirtieth year; but a lodging in the City, though provided by the friends who regarded him as a martyr, was not to be compared with a suite of apartments in Whitehall; and, moreover, he was estranged from many of that noble company of informers of whom he had been the leader. So bitter were his feelings against some of these gentlemen that he refused to give evidence against a batch of priests brought to trial at this time, because Dugdale was to have been his fellow-witness.[5] Again, there could be no doubt that the temper of the nation had undergone a most distressing change. The Westminster schoolboys had so far forgotten their true Protestant sentiments as to burn Jack Presbyter in place of the Pope on the Fifth of November bonfire; and, despite the most strenuous efforts of the Opposition, a loyal gentleman, Sir John Moore, had just been elected Lord Mayor of London. The Government displayed an inconvenient curiosity about the details of these efforts, and among the informations concerning them was one, by a Dr Novell, which describes Titus's own feelings on the election:

"On the day Sr John Moore was chosen Ld Mayor for the ensuing yeare I having business in Bartholomew-Lane,

I passed through the insurance office Court, intending to goe through Amsterdam Coffee-house into the said Lane; But as I pass'd along I met with one Spineage, who is call'd by some Capt. Spineage, and knowing him to be a relation of a Worthy Friend of Mine, I sate down by him and call'd for a Dish of Coffee, wch I thinke I had scarse dranke before Mr Oates came into the Room, who applying himselfe to Mr Spineage ask'd him how the Choice went? Spineage answered he had not heard, Then I immediately answered that there was no doubt but Sr John Moor would carry it. Mr Oates hastily replyed Why Sr; what make you thinke so? I answered I was informed it was his right in course, and that he had all the Church of England men of his side and many of ye Moderate Dissenters. Mr Oates replyed: Dissenters? Those Dissenters are Rascals, and so are all such, that will hold up their hands for such a Popish Rascal as Moor is. Then putting his Thumbs under his Girdle he flang away in a great passion not giving me the opportunity of answering him. I (being amazed at these irreverent an[d] undecent expressions;) told Spineage I thought he was Mad, and that he ought to bleed;* Spineage said I need not have stood up so much for Sr John Moor and those words of Mr Oates's, to wch I thought fit to give no answer, but being much Mov'd to heare so worthy a person abus'd, I related these passages immediately tho without any designe of doing Mr Oates injury having ever had a respect for everything wch I saw that was good in him, and in particular for the Discovery he made of ye Popish Plot."[6]

But on November 24th, all Titus's heaviness was turned to joy, for on that day a packed jury threw out the bill of indictment against Lord Shaftesbury. The Shaftesbury proceedings are a kind of sequel to the trial of College, and prove beyond all doubt that it had been the intention of the Opposition to appeal to arms at the time of the Oxford Parliament; but whereas College had been tried at Oxford, his noble patron Shaftesbury had the advantages of a jury of London citizens, picked by the disloyal Sheriffs, his friends' propaganda which displayed itself in another huge anti-Popery show on the 17th, and the efforts made on his behalf by his protégé, Dr Titus Oates.

* That is, be bled by a surgeon.

On this occasion, Dr Oates did not rely on evidence, since this had not saved poor College; he relied instead upon that hooliganism which had proved so effective during the Plot trials. "We all remember the time," the Solicitor-General was to observe some years later, "when Indictments were preferred, and a plain Evidence given to a Grand Jury, even to the publick Satisfaction of all that heard it; and yet they have refused to find the Bill: And not only so, but were so abetted by the Rabble, that it was scarce safe for the Judges to sit upon the Bench."[7] On the night before the Shaftesbury proceedings, "At least 40 people about 11 came down St Paul's Churchyard towards Ludgate with their swords drawn, crying No Popish Successor, No York, A Monmouth, A Buckingham, Another troop, one Harrington at their head, crying as above and God bless the Earl of Shaftesbury. . . . Prance brought a rabble into a coffee-house, railing against the Tories on purpose to make a quarrel, and Shute's nephew with a gang at another door, so that the master of the house was forced to turn them out. Oates on the rising of the Court went shouting along the streets, An *Ignoramus*. Why do you not cry out *Ignoramus*, *Ignoramous*? Shute, the Sheriff, came out of the Sessions House on pretence to discharge the rout, and said, You keep me a prisoner here too, pray depart, smiling, and immediately waving his hat, Shout, boys, shout, and they did so."[8]

Dugdale and John Smith were among the witnesses called to give evidence against Shaftesbury; Smith stated afterwards that during the time of the proceedings, Oates's servants were treating the rabble at the Fountain tavern near the Old Bailey with bottles of wine, and encouraging them to insult and ill-treat the prosecution witnesses. Smith had endeavoured to persuade Dugdale that "the rabble were but like little curs that barked but dared not approach to bite", but Dugdale knew better, and refused to give his evidence.[9] Smith and Turbervile, who were brave enough to appear, complained several times during the proceedings that they were in danger of their lives, and Smith, while under cross-examination by a member of the jury, suddenly broke off to exclaim:

"My Lord, they commanded the People to stone us to death.

"*L.C.J.* Who did?

"*Smith.* Several Persons, and when we were at the Tavern, Dr. Oates's Man came out and gave the Rabble a Bottle of Wine, and bid them knock us down.

"*L.C.J.* Do you know what the Man's name is?

"*Dr Oates.* I know nothing of it, my Lord.

"*L.C.J.* What is your Man's Name?

"*Dr Oates.* I keep half a dozen men, my Lord.

"*L.C.J.* I hope you keep no Man to affront the King's Witnesses.

"*Dr Oates.* No, my Lord, it is a Mistake, I know nothing of it, we went thither to refresh ourselves."

A few days later, Titus had the satisfaction of hearing of the death of his one-time friend, Turbervile, who had had the impertinence to appear against Lord Shaftesbury; the informer died affirming that he had told the truth in his evidence against both that lord and Viscount Stafford, which seems a little singular.[10]

On the very day of Turbervile's death, there was a startling rumour to the effect that Dr Oates, that champion of the Church of England, had preached at a conventicle in or near St Bartholomew's Lane. The rumour moved Thompson (who was writing harder than ever against Titus) to ask some pertinent questions in his *Loyal Protestant and True Domestick Intelligence* for December 22nd: "In what capacity the Dr frequents and Preaches in such Conventicles; whether only as a Spye upon the Dissenters, as formerly he was upon the Jesuits and Papists; or as a real Dissenter from the Church of England?" He added a challenge to Titus and his father to state the time, place, and officiating minister, supposing Titus had ever been baptized into the Anglican Church. Neither took up the challenge; Titus evidently considered it beneath his dignity, and his father, long returned to the sect of his youth, was naturally, one supposes, anxious to forget the almost indecent haste with which he had administered that sacrament to his offspring as soon as he himself had conformed at the Restoration.

The rumour that Titus was flirting with the Dissenters continued to circulate throughout the next few years. In 1683, he was to write to the Bishop of London: "My Lord,

I am a Minister, yea, a Minister of the Church of England, and have done her more Service than any Clergyman in England; and because I hate those Monsters that are amongst us who were bred in the Protestant Religion, and have left this religion and are reconciled to the Church of Rome, and are by that means declared Traytors to our Law, I am looked upon by our little Clergymen as a Dissenter from the Church of England. . . ."[11] Meantime, in his news-sheet for January 10th, 1682, Thompson asked a question which was to prove curiously prophetic: "That since there is no Church or Society wherein hitherto he [Oates] hath Hearded, but he hath Actually Betray'd; whether or no the Conventicles have any reason to expect any better from him; or whether in all probability they (as well as others) will not be necessiated to spew him out?"

The year 1681 ended for Titus on a note of melancholy. Not only were several condemned priests either pardoned by the King or transported instead of being hanged,[12] but Dr Oates's own brother, simple sailor Samuel, turned against him. Samuel had already, in November, given information of seditious talk among Titus's friends, and now, as if that were not bad enough, in December, in a petition to the King for employment, whether on land or sea, he spoke of his famous brother in terms which must have cut that noble heart to the quick. He himself, said Samuel, was "bred to the sea, and served in several engagements against the Dutch and Turks. Soon after the discovery of the Plot by his brother Titus, he sent for him to London, under pretence of his being preferred to some command at sea, but his brother was so backward in his solicitations, that he was only entertained as one of his servants, whereby he and his family are totally ruined."[13]

(2)

The new year brought Titus fresh troubles. To begin with, the Emperor of Morocco's Ambassador was on a visit to England, and in his train was Hamed Lucas, the identical "murdered" master of the Reverend Adam Elliot. The legal authorities had the bad taste to choose this of all moments to hear Titus's suit against Elliot, and so hard put to it was

Oates to find witnesses, that he even dragged in disloyal brother Samuel. "Lastly, to bring up the Rear of this goodly Company, comes Brother Sam. Oates . . . it was observ'd here, as also at Colledge's Trial, that this fellow had not been taught his lesson well enough. To be short, he is a mere blockhead, and will never make an Evidence worth a farthing, notwithstanding all the examples and Copies the Doctor has swore before him."[14]

On the other hand, not only could Elliot produce the very man Titus had accused him of murdering, but he could produce likewise his tutor at Cambridge and a bunch of fellow students, all of whom cleared him of Oates's accusations concerning his college days. Finally, so anxious was Elliot to establish his own innocence that he proved, "by a demonstration not altogether so consistent, I confess, with the gravity of my Profession", that he had never been circumcised. On Elliot's bringing a counter-accusation of slander, Titus was jailed; but he still had powerful friends, and was bailed after a few days' incarceration.[15] Meantime, Elliot feasted his late master, whose timely appearance had proved so welcome, and who magnanimously expressed his pleasure in having been able to disprove the lies of Titus Oates.[16]

Next, in April, Titus's younger brother Constant followed the example of Samuel junior in giving information of suspicious goings-on among the disaffected. "About 4 April last his father, Samuel Oates, senior, required him to go over to Southwark to a blind woman's house nigh Sir Richard How and to take thence a great bundle of papers or writings, relating to the public, which he did and carried them to his father's lodgings in King Street, Bloomsbury. They were about one cwt. to the best of his judgment. His father was dubious whom to employ in such weighty affairs and directed the informant to carry the bundle the back and by ways that he might not be dogged, which he did. Among these papers the informant believes there are some which relate to the actions of persons of great quality, and are of dangerous consequences and seditious to the Government."[17]

In the same month, Titus had a most humiliating adventure.

"Two honest Scotch Gentlemen having been to view the Rarities of this City, among the rest, their curiosity led them (about 7 at night) to a certain Commonwealth-Coffee-house [the Amsterdam], near the Royal Exchange, where they ask'd for an Animal formerly called the S. . . . a Doctor; and being answered he was not there, they desired the good man to send for him; which he being somewhat loath to do, they were very importunate with him; insomuch that he desired to know what they would have with him? they jollily answer'ed, To piss upon him. This pious good man being somewhat startled thereat, and fearing the Saviour of the Nation might come to some bodily harm, presently gave notice to the Quondam Doctor; who (being always in a pious fear) immediately repaired to a Magistrate, and complain'd of these two Gentlemen, very devoutly swearing (which is a Trade which he is very well acquainted with) That he was affraid of his Life, for they had Threatn'd to Pistol him; Whereupon the Gentlemen were sent for, who appearing, but no weapons found about them but their Swords; and being demanded whether they threatn'd to Pistoll him? They answered, They did not threaten to Pistoll him, but to Piss on him; But if they heard him speak against His Majesty and His Royal Highness (as he had done formerly) they would."[18]

Titus had no reason to love the Scottish nation at present, for about the same time he had another encounter, no more to his liking than the first, with a Scot, Sir William Paterson:

"I'le tell ye a Dialogue that pass'd betwixt a Knight and another man (but hee was no Dr) upon Good-Friday last. For Brevity's sake, the one shall be *O.* and t'other *P.* . . . Up comes *O.* to *P.* Sir (says he) are not you such a one? *P.* Yes. sir, at your service. *O.* You talk at Random, I hear; You hope to see me Hang'd within these six weeks, ye say. *P.* I speak my Mind freely, sir, both of Men and Things. There are a great many Rogues I wish Hang'd, and some that I hope to see Hang'd. If you'l concern yourself in't I can't help it. *O.* Y're a Rascall, Sirrah, and your Brother's a Rascall. *P.* I thank ye, Sir, for using me no worse than the best man in the Kingdom but One. *O.* What? You mean the Duke, I warrant? *P.* You may say your pleasure of mee, and my Brother; but by the Eternall God, if ye fall foul upon the Duke, I'le cut off your Ears with mine own hand. *O*. What d'ye swear for? *P*. My oaths are not so dangerous as yours. *O*. Why then, God damn you and your Nation; and y're all Rogues: But for my part, I'le ha' you order'd before you go out of the City. . . . *P*. Remember Dr 'tis Good-Friday, Be not so passionate. *O*. Why what have I to do with Good-Friday, I'm no Papist. *P*. No, nor Protestant neither."[19]

Fickle fortune seemed all out of humour with Titus at the moment. On April 29th, he was arrested at the Royal Exchange at the suit of a gentleman from Chichester, to whom he was in debt for board and lodgings (but again he was bailed by his rich City friends); and on May 4th, a news-letter writer reported that his brothers Samuel and Constant were resolved to swear High Treason against him.[20] On the 29th, during the usual Restoration Day rejoicings, he was actually burnt in effigy at Covent Garden.[21] June brought a veritable spate of informations from his brothers, some reporting mere seditious talk, others hinting at a plot against the Government. On June 8th, Samuel junior informed the authorities that Titus and Sheriff Bethel had spoken of the necessity of providing their party with arms. Samuel "has heard the Earl of Shaftesbury say to his brother, Dr Oates, at his house in Aldersgate Street, about January 1681, soon after the dissolution of the last Parliament at Westminster, there was an Association agreed on by all the protesting lords and commons to destroy all this arbitrary power and its forces in this kingdom. . . . He believes the said Earl and the City clubs withdrew his said brother from his allegiance to the King."[22] There is something rather touching in the way Samuel reiterates his belief that his brother was led astray by Shaftesbury, since it is clear that Titus was a rebel against authority long before he met his noble patron.

Constant Oates, besides numerous reports of seditious talk (which he heard, he said, because he was supposed to share Titus's political opinions), gave in a list of the Dissenters in Southwark, where he lived: Presbyterians: Ministers 10, people about 5,420. Baptists (General, Particular, and Fifth Monarchy-men): Ministers 13, people about 4,250. Many of these Dissenters were old Commonwealth-men, who had not altered their views on government when their cause had suffered defeat in 1660. Constant seems to have been accepted by Secretary Jenkins as an accredited informer on these matters; and both he and his brother Samuel continued to send in their reports during this and the following year.[23]

On June 14th, Titus was again arrested for debt, this time at the suit of a Mr Henry Oke, landlord of the Royal Exchange tavern in the Mint, for "Meat, Drink, Black-puddings, etc." He denied the debt, and once again was released on bail.[24] On the 22nd, Kearney, or O'Kerney, said to be one of the Four Irish Ruffians, was brought to trial at the King's Bench; in the previous July, he had returned of his own accord to England from France, and had surrendered himself for trial.[25] The names of the witnesses against him, endorsed on the back of the indictment, were those of Titus Oates and Robert Jenison, but neither made an appearance, and "Mr Atturney generall being called, said he had no evidence against him, so that the jury gave in their verdict, Not guilty; and so he was discharged".[26]

On July 1st, an action for slander, brought by Adam Elliot against Titus, was heard before Chief Justice North. The only defence Oates's counsel could invent was that Titus's accusations against Elliot of poisoning his master and general debauchery were spoken "only jocularly, as [one] who had no malicious design."[27] "The Dr could not justifie the words, being altogether False and Scandalous; But (for mitigation of Damages) produced some Witnesses, who testified, Oates himself had told the story to them at several times, but could not prove any thing reflecting upon Mr Elliot's Reputation, which was proved (both here and in Ireland) by sober and credible Witnesses. The Jury withdrew, and after an hours debate (in tenderness to the Dr's low condition) brought in 20. *l.* Damages, and Costs of Suit, against Dr Oates."[28]

So low, indeed, was Titus's condition at present, that a rumour went round that he had attempted suicide.[29] The fallen idol was become the butt of every man's wit; on September 26th, Thompson's news-sheet regaled its readers with a comical and highly improper story of his being accosted in Moor Fields by "a Popishly affected Gentlewoman"; and his very family joined in abusing him. Brother Constant went so far as to express his opinion that Titus was "a base, unworthy, ungrateful rogue, and was grown a most villanous and dangerous Whig".[30]

Early in November, Sir William Waller, Titus's companion in the old priest-hunting days, felt that a change of air would be beneficial to him, and accordingly sailed from Weymouth for Holland, a country peculiarly hospitable to Englishmen known to be enemies to their King. Rumour had it that both Shaftesbury and his protégé Oates had made the same trip. " 'Tis strongly reported that Dr Oats is going to recreate himself at Rotterdam, and that some Persons of Quality would accompany him."[31] "Some conclude, that upon the account of the intimacy between [Shaftesbury], and the Salamanca Doctor, he chose the Doctor to go with him as Chaplain; And in order thereunto, we hear the Doctor is preparing for a march."[32] Shaftesbury was, as a matter of fact, in hiding at Wapping at this time, and did not actually flee to Holland until November 28th. Dr Titus Oates did not accompany him. On December 10th, a Thomas Deane wrote to Secretary Jenkins that "Dr Oates of late has been often at Mr Ashurst's in St John's Street".[33]

(3)

Sixteen hundred and eighty-three seemed determined to add to the troubles of poor Titus.

His old cronies were displaying a most shocking tendency to rob him of the rewards of his plot-discovering, and on January 8th he was fain to write to the Lords of the Treasury and point out that it had been he and he alone who had disclosed the vast wealth and estates of the English Jesuits, and that John Savage and Samuel Button, who were petitioning for reward for such disclosures, "never did appeare discoverers till the year 1680, and then had information from yor petr. as to Langhorne's concernes".[34] Samuel Oates junior and brother Constant, moreover, were still acting in a most unfraternal manner (on January 18th the former wrote to Jenkins that he was "trying to smoke out a design");[35] and certain ex-servants of Titus's were following John Lane's example in accusing Dr Oates of sodomy, though with no better success.[36]

Within the space of sixteen days, Titus now suffered two more bereavements. On January 21st, there died at Amsterdam, in the sixty-third year of his age, that very remarkable politician, Anthony Ashley Cooper, Earl of Shaftesbury. And on Tuesday, February 6th, Samuel Oates senior followed him to the grave. The ex-dipper died at his lodgings above a pie-shop in King Street, and a news-letter of the day adds the grisly detail that "As I am credibly informed before he was cold his Tongue swelled and hung out of his Mouth as black and almost [as] big as those wee hang up the chimneys".[37] There seems to be no record of his funeral, and as Titus's financial condition was very low at present, it is probable that he was not able to afford to bury his revered parent in a manner befitting that worthy man. Nevertheless, he hit upon a way of showing his filial regard, a way both cheap and characteristic. He bestowed upon his father posthumous honours, proclaiming that the deceased had been a prebendary of St Paul's Cathedral.

"*Observator*. To see the Malice of people now, that will needs have his Father to have been Samuell Oates, that lodg'd at the Pye-Woman's in King-Street, Bloomsbury, the Dipping Weaver. . . . But how come you to know Titus'es Father was Prebend of Paul's?

"*Trimmer*. I had it from his own Mouth."[38]

Whatever Titus's faults, he was never easily discouraged. Plot victims might continue to be released,[39] and the scaffolds, which for four years had remained in Westminster Hall in readiness for the trial of the Five Lords in the Tower, might be taken down;[40] still Dr Oates retained his old self-confidence. The one successful venture of his life had proved so enormously successful that he could not persuade himself that his star would ever really decline. "A Friend of mine was talking with him—But I'le tell ye how it came in. Mr Oates (says this Gentleman) you are a great Friend to the Church. (Oates) The Church is a good Church an' 'twere well Govern'd. Yonder's a good Prebendship at Windsor, would poor Dr Tonge had [had] it. (G.) Why mythinks it might do pretty well for yourself Mr Oates. (O.) For Mee? I'le not give a Groat for all the Benefices in England. (G.) What would you be at then, Mr Oates? (O.) I'de have the King make Mee his Agent, and allow me Twenty Thousand Pounds a Year, whereas it costs ye now about Two Hundred Thousand Pounds a year in Intelligence; And yet ye know no more neither then what you have in the Gazette; I'de place my Intelligence so, that not a Prince in Christendom should Piss, but I'de have an Account on't; for I'de spend my whole Estate but I'de be Master of all the Secrets in Christendom."[41]

Nor had he given up hope of earning an honest penny by his old methods; he sent a report to the Lords of the Treasury that he and only he had been the discoverer of the Papist Sir John Preston's estate, and when it transpired that other vultures had smelled out this rich carrion, he wrote sharply to the Hon. Henry Guy, praying that he "may not always be oppressed by unrighteous dealings of falce pretenders".[42]

There was now to come to a head a conspiracy which for a long while had been hatching underground, as can be seen from the many informations sent into the Government (including those of Titus's brothers), ever since the dissolution of the Oxford Parliament in the spring of '81. Throughout the entire reign, the Opposition, which was the successor to the old Commonwealth party, had tried one trick after another in its efforts to bring down the Monarchy; the withholding of supplies, the attempts, continually repeated, to exclude the lawful successor to the throne, the Popish Plot, the Meal Tub Plot, the Black Box, each had been used in turn, and, thanks to Charles II's magnificent statesmanship, had failed. An open appeal to arms could not hope to succeed, because the country as a whole would not stomach civil war again. There remained but one last card in the pack; and in 1683, the Oppositionists were grown desperate enough to play it. Their stooges, the genuine fanatics who were ready to shed blood in the cause of Jehovah, were given orders to assassinate the King and his brother; when this was done, and the kingdom in a state of distraction, it should be easy enough to plant Monmouth on the throne and rule all in his name.

The deed of assassination was timed for the end of March. The King and the Duke were at Newmarket, and were due to return to London on a certain known date. It was arranged that at a convenient spot on their route—namely, at the Rye House near Ware, on a lonely stretch of road—a cart of hay should block the passage of the royal cavalcade, and that immediately the halt was made, a bunch of fanatics, hidden in a ditch, should shoot the King and his brother at close range. Waiting messengers were then to go galloping to London to rouse the disaffected City to action, and, before the nation realized what was happening, King Monmouth would be proclaimed. It was a simple and effective plan, and, but for an accident which no one could have foreseen, undoubtedly would have succeeded. On the evening of March 22nd, a careless groom was smoking in a stable in Newmarket; there was a high wind; the straw caught fire; the stable caught fire; and next morning half the town was a mass of charred rubble. Charles and his brother left immediately for London, several days before their time, and thus, unconsciously, saved their lives.

Such, very briefly, was the Rye House Plot. There remains the question: How far was Titus Oates involved in it?

It seems impossible to give a definite answer. That he would have given it, if requested, his blessing, and the benefit of his peculiar talent in lying, no one can doubt. The bloodthirsty tenets of the creed in which he had been bred remained strong within him to the end of his days, and his political opinions were always anti-monarchical. But whether or no he was let into the inner councils of the plotters, or assigned an active part in the conspiracy, remains a matter of doubt. All that can be done here is to quote the evidence for and against his guilt, and then to endeavour to sum up. First, then, the facts which seem to implicate him.

Though L'Estrange never accuses Oates of any direct part in the plot, he repeatedly emphasizes the significance of Titus's friendship with the actual assassins and their associates. "Take this along with ye too; that Titus all this while, was the very Minion of the Conspirators: And none so wellcome as they, to his Privacies, or to his Table: Hone (that was to have been one of the Assassins) frequently took a Bed with him."[43] Again, Sir Roger notes Titus's relief when Monmouth's wavering between signing a confession and forbearing to do so for fear of his fellow conspirators (for Monmouth most certainly was in the Plot) gave birth to a rumour that the plot prisoners were to be reprieved. "Oates himself began to put his Nose into the Weather; He brush'd up his Canonical Weed. . . . It is most certain, that the Doctor lay as Dead as a Swallow in a Hollow Tree, 'till the Tydings of the Gentlemen-Pris'ners going-off upon Bayl, and of Mr Sydney's forty-days Reprieve, brought him to Life again. In one Word: He was never seen so merry about the Mouth before, since the loss of his 30,000. *l.* by the Dissolution of the Oxford Parliament that should have Purchas'd Coll. Digg'es Estate at Bobbing in Kent."[44]

The plot had been made known to the King on June 12th by one of the conspirators, an Anabaptist oil-merchant named Keeling. On the 23rd, L'Estrange wrote to Secretary Jenkins: "Oates' servant was yesterday and to-day to inquire what is become of Wotton and whether he has confessed. I presume it is not unknown to you that Wotton was a servant in common to Oates and Smith. College's sister is deep in the privacy of this conspiracy, and, if Wotton says nothing of her, he does not deal candidly."[45] Next day, the Earl of Sunderland wrote to the same correspondent: "The King has intelligence that Oates, being frightened with the discovery of the late conspiracy, intends to run away and that a gathering has been made for that purpose. He would have you and the lords who meet at your office consider whether it would be proper to stop him or no."[46] On July 5th, information was given by Samuel Starkey, clerk to Aaron Smith, Oates's "counsel": "Some of the discoverers of the late plot often met [Aaron] Smith privately sometimes at his house and sometimes at the King's Head tavern and papers sealed with many seals were sometimes given to me to deliver to Smith. Some broken speeches and words I heard betwixt Smith and these men, and concluded from them that Smith directed Dr Oates and two more, whose names I have forgotten, what to say in some affairs then in agitation. Smith, being looked on as a stickler for the cause and a man of profound parts, they looked on as fittest for the purpose."[47]

So much for the evidence, such as it is, for Oates' having

been a party to the plot. On the other hand, we have the following:

Francis Charleton, a most objectionable character, and one who seems to have acted as a kind of paymaster for the Opposition, was examined before the Privy Council on August 4th, and, while mentioning Oates, made no definite accusation against him, though Charleton was ready enough to turn against his former associates in return for a pardon. "Never knew of any contribution or having given any money to any but Dr Oates. Has paid 2 or 300. *l.* to Oates for his subsistence, 80 *l.* at one time about six or seven months ago. Had 10 *l.* [of it] of Lord Shaftesbury. He [Oates] had 80 *l.* a quarter. Sir William Jones told him he might lawfully contribute to Oates' subsistence. Had no more than the 10 *l.* from Lord Shaftesbury from any. He is the rest out of purse, and they told him a parliament would reimburse him."[48] It seems clear that this money was nothing more than a pension allowed by the Oppositionists to a man who had been very useful to them in the past, and that it had nothing to do with the present conspiracy. Charleton admitted, by the way, that he had paid Oates £400 in all, and had received receipts, and he gave in a list of those willing to contribute to Titus's maintenance.[49]

On September 1st, a man named Peckham gave information concerning Titus's attitude towards Keeling, the conspirator who had betrayed the plot to the Government. "On Friday 24 Aug. being at the Amsterdam Coffee-house with my brother John and four others, Mr Oates came in and said he knew Mr Keeling, but did not like him, since he heard he had not walked orderly with the society he belonged to. Though, said he, I never belonged to the people [presumably the Anabaptists] I love to hear of persons being fair and square and to my knowledge Keeling talked treason in all companies and its said he was to have had a division of men in Wapping under his command. I believe the reason why no more men are tried for the plot is that their magazine of witnesses is almost spent. Said I, the men tried for this plot have more or less confessed the fact but the Papists denied all. Said he, because they were resolved to die with lies in their mouths. Not any of these men confessed but Hone and it's supposed he did it in hopes of pardon. It's true I believe they had treasonable talk amongst themselves. He asked me if Keeling had his pardon. I said it was granted, but he had not received it. Said he, I remember or some say there is something in the law that witnesses may be asked what benefit they receive by their evidence and there can be no greater benefit than a pardon."[50] If Titus had been seriously implicated in the conspiracy, his attitude towards Keeling would have been, one may be sure, very much more bitter.

Finally, two slightly more positive testimonies to Titus's innocence. In a squib against him, *Dr Oats's Last Legacy*, he is made to say, speaking of his Whig friends: "Rot 'em, they do not deserve all this kindness from me, because they durst not trust me with the right plot." The importance of this lies in the fact that it was written by an enemy of Oates. Secondly, there is Burnet, who, though a staunch Oppositionist, had no great opinion of the Saviour of the Nation. After stating, somewhat grudgingly, that the King "shewed some appearance of sincerity in examining the witnesses" (Charles insisted on examining them personally to prevent any suspicion of subornation), Burnet adds that his Majesty "told them, he would not have a growing evidence; and so he charged them to tell out at once all that they knew: he led them into no accusations by asking them any questions: only he asked them if Oates was in their secret? They answered, that they all looked on him as such a rogue, that they would not trust him."[51]

From the foregoing scanty and most unsatisfactory evidence, it would seem that Titus had not been told the details of the plot, but only that the King and the Duke were somehow to be ruined, and that when this was accomplished, he himself would be called upon to ply his old trade again. "Oates was to have sworn in a fit time that the King gave commissions to the Roman Catholics to destroy his Protestant subjects";[52] in other words, once the plot had been successful, Oates was to have come in and justify it by the King's secret papistry. That Oates must have known something of what was in the wind is as certain as anything can be, since many of the lesser conspirators were his bosom friends. To take one instance out of many, that villainous character, "Colonel" John Scott, twice a murderer and a rogue of the Bedloe type, was an old crony of Titus's; John Gelson, meeting Scott in Norway, whither the latter had fled after the discovery of the Rye House business, wrote Pepys that Scott "told me many particulars of their cabals and debates. That Oates did acknowledge to him he swore the King was to be killed [in the Popish Plot] merely to get a party of such as were dear lovers of the King, and to make the Papists more odious that they might the better serve their ends by them, and in a fit time would have brought in his Majesty to have given commissions for the destroying his Protestant subjects."[53] A man so frankly confiding as this expects his friends to be so in their turn; and while it is doubtful that Oates risked his precious neck by active participation in so dangerous a conspiracy, it is impossible to imagine him fraternizing with Hone and Aaron Smith and the rest of the small fry among the plotters without learning something of their plans.

(4)

Titus's prospects at this date were worse than they had ever been since his spectacular rise to fame in the September of 1678. His chief patron had died in exile; of the other Opposition leaders, Essex had cut his throat in prison, Russell had perished on the scaffold, and the Duke of Monmouth and Lord Howard of Escrick had turned King's evidence in order to save their necks. The people, shaken by the knowledge that only an accident had prevented them from losing the King and the Heir Presumptive by an assassin's bullet, were in a mood of fervent loyalty; and under Charles's personal rule, trade flourished and contentment reigned. It is understandable, therefore, that Titus (who at this time was again arrested for debt and again was bailed) was irritable to a degree which bordered on the fantastic.

The topic of the moment was the dreadful possibility of the capture of Vienna by the infidel Turk. Titus who, despite his poverty, managed still to frequent the Amsterdam Coffee-house, naturally heard a great deal of talk upon the subject, and did not hesitate to express his own opinion thereon:

"There was a dispute at the Amsterdam coffee-house last

Thursday", says a news-letter, "in effect whether the Turks or Christians were the honester men. A gentleman siding with the Christians and being a little too familiar with the Salamanca Doctor, Oates told him he was a rascal and struck him two or three blows over the head with his cane. The gentleman was wedged in on the wrong side of the table and could not make him a return, but only with a dish of warm coffee in the eyes of him."[54] "There's a Report about the Town as if Dr Oates had taken up Arms for the Turk and Advanc'd his Pastoral Staff at the Coffee-house, in the Honour of Mahomet. . . . Why I'le tell ye what he said then, upon Saturday last was Sennight, at the same Place. 'We are waiting here' (says Titus) 'to hear the Good News that the Turk has taken Vienna. I hope they get the Town, and subdue the Army.' 'What?' (sayd a Gentleman) 'Turks against Christians?' (Dr) 'Christians! Ay, the Turks are as good Christians as they. I don't believe there's any Papist in the World a Christian.' (Gent.) 'Say ye so, Doctor? That's very Hard. I believe you are turn'd Turk.' (Dr) 'Well Well! 'Tis my Opinion. You don't know 'em so well as I do. I don't question but there's a great many Honest Men of my Opinion.' "[55]

His thwarted malice found some relief in another tract, *The Devil's Patriarck*, published for him by John Dunton. The object of this new excursion into the field of literature was "to Revive the Remembrance of the almost forgotten Plot against the Life of his Sacred Majesty and the Protestant Religion", and with this noble end in view, he regaled his readers with one hundred and thirty-four pages of vigorous obscenity. One specimen of his style will suffice: "May we but be let in a little to behold the Bowels of this Grand Cheat [the Pope], and View but a little his Guts and Garbage, 'twill soon be Discerned that he is the Devil's Patriarck, bearing upon his Banner the Abomination of Desolation: The time would fail to tell, How many Families this Abominable Beast hath made Desolate: what else is the whole Cento and Fardle of Popery, but a Concatenation of Wiles to compass a Purse?"

Though his Plot might be forgotten, Titus himself was still occasionally remembered by the news-writers and lampoonists. A squib, *Vox Lachrymæ*, purported to be a funeral sermon on "the late Dr Oates"; the coffee-houses were diverted with the story of how he had chastised a gentleman only for disagreeing with him upon the question as to whether or no the streets should be cleansed till after the ice was gone (it was a hard winter); and a report was circulated that he was retiring into the country. "Pray will you tell me, if a body may ask ye: Is there any such thing as Oates's Retiring? *Observator*. 'Tis in every bodies Mouth, that he's going into Surrey; and that he has, I know not how many People at work there about Camberwell, to fitt up a very noble House for him."[56] L'Estrange's ceaseless ridicule annoyed Titus so much that he begged leave to bring the matter before the King and Council; he was told that he should apply himself either to a justice of peace or the ordinary legal authorities. This advice drew from him the following indignant letter to Secretary Jenkins:

"I thought I should never have lived to see the day, that the Plot should be called in question, which the King had owned in his several proclamations; but since it is so, I must pray your pardon, if I cannot apply myself for redress in that way and method your honour has pleased to order: For I humbly conceive, that it is the Government that is abused, and therefore in conscience and honour it is bound to vindicate its proceedings from such aspersions as are cast upon them by the said L'Estrange and his confederates. I would not use any method or way to injure the worst of my enemies but hope the Council will take my hard usage from the said L'Estrange into serious consideration, and cause the said L'Estrange to be silenced, and reparation made me. To that end, I have in this sent a petition to the King and Council, which I would have presented, if I might have had the liberty to appear at Court, in which I pray for redress. I hope God will put it into your hearts to do me right. In the mean time

"Sir, I am,

"Your honour's humble servant,

"TITUS OATES.

"My humble request is, that this petition inclosed may be presented to the King in Council, so that I may be in some probable way of having redress."[57]

L'Estrange's own comment on this appeal was that Titus's prayer that God would put it into the hearts of the King and Council to do him right was probably the only prayer in which he and Oates ever had agreed. The Government, for the moment, ignored Oates. On April 12th, he wrote an aggrieved letter to King Charles himself: "I sent a Petition to Mr Secretary Jenkins but could not be heard, and I have written to several of your Council, but can have no Effects of my just Complaints, though I am left to starve; yet I may say I have deserved better of the Government than to live in danger of being knockt of the Head as I go along the streets, and for no other Crime, but that of the 28th and 29th of September 1678; if I must perish for serving your Majesty and the Government, I humbly pray that I may perish quietly, and starve in Peace, and not be put into a Bear's Skin in order to be worried by Popish Dogs, whose Religion is nothing else but a Cistern of Immorality, and their Immorality Treason in the highest degree."[58]

Instead of writing these impudent petitions, Titus would have done better to have faded into that obscurity from whence he came. For, in this late spring of 1684, the Government took notice of him in a manner little to his liking; on May 10th, at the Amsterdam Coffee-house, he was "arrested at the suit of his Royal Highness in an action of Scandalum magnatum and carried to the Compter".[59]

He had only himself to blame. Ever since his banishment from Whitehall, he had done nothing but talk against the Government, rave against the Duke of York, and draw attention to his inbred hatred of authority. No government could continue to ignore these insults from a man who was still a public figure, and who was known to have great influence among its enemies. He was indicted under the Scandalum Magnatum Statute of Richard II, as being a "devisor of false news and of horrible and false lies . . . whereby great peril and mischief might come to all the realm, and quick subversion and destruction of the said realm"; and surely no man in history was more guilty of this crime. How could any self-respect be maintained among a people if a man like Oates were allowed to say with impunity the things he said of a prince they were prepared to accept as their future king?

After two days in the Compter, he was transferred to the King's Bench Prison, where he was affronted by persons unknown; "blows ensued, for which they were bound over".[60] He was ordered to plead within three or four days, but he chose to let judgment go by default, and a writ of enquiry for damages was requested. On June 18th, an enquiry was held in the Court of King's Bench, in the presence of the High Sheriff of Middlesex; it was the business of the jury to assess the damages the plaintiff had sustained. Even Luttrell admits that "the words were proved very fully, being very scandalous";[61] and the jury, without retiring, awarded full damages of £100,000 with twenty shillings costs.

The official account, *The Account of the Manner of Executing a Writ of Enquiry*, which bears the imprimatur of the Lord Chief Justice (now Sir George Jeffreys), is full of interesting evidence of Oates's malice against the Duke of York. On one occasion, after receiving the Sacrament either at Easter or at Whitsun, Titus, at the Bishop of Ely's dinner-table, called the Duke a traitor, and, on being rebuked for it, summoned his two servants ("his Mirmydons, that used to be always with him and follow him up and down"), and flounced out of the room; the witness who related this incident, a Mr Penniston Whaley, told how he had apologized to the Bishop for the heat with which he had rebuked Oates, but "says the Bishop to me, I thank you kindly for it, none of us dare talk with him". Another witness described how Oates, after preaching at Foster Lane church, was invited by the churchwardens to dinner, "but then he asked them, If ever any of them had dined with James Duke of York at any of the Feasts of the City where the Duke used to come sometimes? To which they none of them answering a word, he replied, He would not dine with any Man that had eat with the Devil: And so would not go to dine with them, and went and dined at a private Brasiers by London-Wall."

Justice Warcup (he was now Sir Edmund Warcup), was among those who gave evidence, and in his journal records what he said: "I swore that Mr Heron tooke me by the hand into a room parted by a hangeing from that where Sir Wm Jennings and others with Oates were; that Heron began the duke's health; 'here's a health to James D. of Yorke and God confound his enemies'. After we had dranke it round, I went into the other roome where the gent. told me Oates had said the duke had betrayed the nation and wished, if the devill had a hotter place in hell than other, that he would reserve it for the duke. I met Oates afterwards, and asked him why he should speak such undecent words of the duke, whome he knew to be the King's brother and as virtuous a prince as trod on the earth. His answer was; he is a traitor and in the plot, and you are a Yorkist and I'le remember you for it."[62]

Oates himself did not appear at the enquiry, and when the Lord Chief Justice asked if there was anyone present in court "to offer anything to lessen the damages", nobody replied. Addressing the jury, Jeffreys stated that the case had been given all possible publicity "in order to satisfie all People what a sort of Fellow this Defendant is, who has been so much adored and looked upon with an Eye of Admiration, courted with so wonderful an Affection, and so, I had almost said, Hosanna'd among People that have been Factious and Tumultuous to the Government". By choosing to absent himself from the enquiry, the Saviour of the Nation escaped hearing these near-profanities; but his cup of bitterness was already full to overflowing. There he lay in prison, not to come forth till he had paid the uttermost farthing; and here he heard the news that the residue of the Popish Plot victims had been discharged.[63]

But worse, far worse, was to follow.

(5)

In the middle of June, there was an ominous rumour. "It has been very hotly discoursed about town that there are informations taking by Mr Justice Guise and Mr Justice L'Estrange of high treason against Mr Oates, and that he would be indicted thereon the next Sessions."[64] When, on June 19th, his two servants were committed on this very charge, the rumour seemed to be true. But the Government chose to make the charge against Oates one of perjury instead; and it quickly became known that a bill of indictment for that crime was to be brought before the Grand Jury of London in the late autumn.

In the meanwhile, Titus was kept in comfort by his friends, and had the consolation of their frequent visits. "Oates spends his time merrily in the King's Bench. He has hung and furnished his Chamber, keeps a good table, where his daily messmates are Braddon, Aaron Smith, and others of the same stamp, who for their twelve pence a piece come in for their ordinary, and the Doctor pays the rest. He seems well pleased with his lodgings; but 'tis believed by the next sessions he must move his quarters."[65] On November 12th, a news-letter writer reports, a bill of indictment "was found against Titus Oates for perjury in the Guildhall, London, and on the 13th he was arraigned at the King's Bench Bar, where he pleaded 'Not Guilty'. He then desired Emparlance, which the Court told him after a plea could not be; but that he should see that he should no way be surprised; he should, if he desired it, have time to next term for trial. And upon his request it was granted. He then desired that he might have Counsel, To which the Court told him that except the King's, he should have any Counsel in England. He then asked liberty to go to them, but was told that being prisoner in execution that could not be granted, but that any Counsel might have liberty to go to him."[66]

It is clear from the fact of his desiring "Emparlance", that is, a demand of one day in order to see if he could end the matter without further suit, that Titus treated the charge against him as frivolous. That he, who had sent so many men to their death, should come to stand in a court of justice in the role of prisoner must indeed have seemed to him unthinkable. Yet, by December 12th, he had had reason to consider the matter in a more serious light. His two servants, Robert Nicholson and William Dalby ("the only Servants that ever he stuck to", says L'Estrange), had been tried and convicted for speaking scandalous and seditious words against the King, the Duke, and the Government; and probably it was this, to him, unexpected condemnation of his minions, that induced Titus to attempt an escape from prison. At all events, when he was brought up to the Old Bailey to answer to a second indictment for perjury, he was fettered, and to his request that his irons be removed he was answered that "an information had been given that he designed to break gaol, and so he was ordered to be kept in safe custody".

The new term began on January 23rd, and on that day the Duke of York wrote to his nephew, the Prince of Orange: "I have little news to return you, only that that villain Oates was this morning brought to the King's Bench bar, being the first day of term, to answer to the two indictments of perjury against him, and tomorrow fortnight appointed for his trial for the first of them."[67] But Titus was destined to be spared for the moment, for during that fortnight there occurred a most unexpected and tragic event. Early in the morning of February 6th, King Charles the Second succumbed to an attack of apoplexy, and the whole nation mourned the most popular king in history. Yet absurd rumour followed Charles to the grave; "some apprehended that the Popish Plot was executed upon him", wrote the Baptist minister, Calamy, "and that he perished by violent means. They said he was carried off by poisoned chocolate, to make way for his brother. . . ."[68]

On February 9th, Titus, who, if he had no reason to join in the mourning for Charles the Second, certainly had none for rejoicing at the accession of James the Second, pleaded Not Guilty to the two indictments for perjury, and had three counsel assigned him, Sir George Treby, Mr Wallop, and Mr Freak. He began straightway to busy himself with his defence. "He has resolved to produce Copies of the Lords Journals, the King's speeches and votes and resolutions of the commons".[69] Already, on January 30th, he had written to Treby: "I must pray you to consider of what letters you have of Mr Coleman's, to the end that I may make use of them att my tryall. I must interest you to show me what favour you can. It is my right to be preserved by all and every of those whom I have faithfully served. I have no more but assure you I am your affectionate ff and servant Titus Oates."[70]

With this broad hint, which almost amounted to a threat, and armed with records never permitted to his victims in the like predicament, Titus awaited his great ordeal. The fact that Jeffreys, whom of late he had so often and so gratuitously insulted, was to be the presiding judge, far from discomposing him, seems to have determined him to provoke as much as possible that famous temper, in order, presumably, to arouse the sympathy of the spectators on his own behalf. But in this he failed. Whatever may be said against Sir George Jeffreys, there can be no doubt that at the trial of Titus Oates he was extraordinarily and most scrupulously fair.

(6)

Upon the eighth day of May, 1685, Titus was brought into the Court of King's Bench to be tried on the first indictment against him—namely, that he had sworn he was at the "Grand Consult" in London when, in fact, he was at St Omers. Scarcely was the court in session than that braying voice, which had brought death and terror to so many, made itself heard. "My Lord," intoned Titus, "I am to manage my own Defence, and have a great many Papers and things which I have brought in order to it, I pray I may have Conveniency for the managing my own Tryal." "Ay, ay," replied the Lord Chief Justice; "let him sit down there, within the Bar, and let him have Conveniency for his Papers."

Titus then proceeded to challenge the majority of the jurymen, though without, as he himself admitted, any particular cause; Ailesbury, who was present, asserts that they were all men of good reputation in their wards and parishes.[71] Probably the prisoner's aim was to waste as much of the court's time as possible, for he now asked that he might have three condemned prisoners brought from jail to testify for him; and the Clerk of the Crown having read the indictment (which was of enormous length), Titus demanded to have it read all over again in Latin. It was done; but scarcely had Mr Phipps opened the charge, than the prisoner interrupted to say that there was an error in the indictment. This error, it seemed, turned upon one Latin word, and he was told that he would have proper time to argue the point later on. Undismayed, he insisted that the entire record of Ireland's trial, just produced by the Attorney-General, be read to him; patiently the court complied.

"*Mr Att. Gen.* Now this long Record in Latin is read, I would fain know whether it be to any great purpose, but only to spend time.

"*L.C.J.* Nay, I think it has not been very edifying to a great many; do you think, Mr Otes, that the Jury, who are Judges of the Fact, do understand it?

"*Otes.* I cannot tell, may be they may, my Lord.

"*Mr Jus. Withins.* Do you understand it yourself, Mr Otes?

"*Otes.* That's not any Question here; but to oblige the Court and the Jury, I desire it may be read in English too."

When the time came for Titus to make his defence, it became evident that he was still resolved to waste the court's time and try its temper. He maintained, for instance, that since Ireland had been convicted and condemned on his evidence, that evidence must have been true; and he desired that counsel might be called upon to argue this singular hypothesis. But the Lord Chief Justice disposed of it in a few crisp sentences. "God forbid, if a Verdict be obtain'd by Perjury, that that Verdict should protect the perjur'd Party from being prosecuted for his false Oath. There were no Justice in that; nor is it an Averment against a Record, for this is not a Writ of Error in Fact that will reverse it, but the Record remains a good Record and unimpeached still: But tho' it be a good Record, yet it is lawful to say this Verdict was obtain'd upon the Testimony of such an one, that forswore himself in that Testimony, and for that particular Perjury he may surely be prosecuted."

Compelled at last to make some serious attempt at a defence, Titus laid his case under three heads. (1) It was six years since he had given evidence against the Five Jesuits, and the witnesses against him were the same, or at least their testimony was the same, now as then. That testimony had not been believed at the former trial; why, therefore, should it be at this one? (2) Whitebread and Fenwick, being remanded to prison, had heard, while in the dock with Ireland and the others, all the evidence against them, and so had had six months in which to provide themselves with fresh testimony "to asperse me". (3) It was very hard that after his evidence had been accepted by "the King and Kingdom, four successive

Parliaments, all the Judges of the Land, and three Juries", he should be now, after the lapse of so many years, called to account for it. "If at that time my Evidence was true, it must be true still; for Truth is always the same; and if it were then true, and I can prove it to be true, 'twill be thought a hard thing without all doubt, that this should be put upon me."

It is impossible not to admire the way in which Titus put the legal profession on trial with him, and also the vigour of his defence. He pointed out that the king's counsel now against him were formerly for him, and he asserted that his trial was but another attempt to stifle the Popish Plot. He waxed eloquent upon the insult offered to the nation. "Can any thing, my Lord, more plainly tend to destroy and subvert the Methods of Justice, to frighten all Witnesses from henceforth for ever appearing to discover such Conspiracies? And does it not tend to expose and vilify the known Understanding and Justice of the late King of ever Blessed Memory, to arraign the Wisdom of His Privy Council, His Great and Noble Peers, His Loyal Commons in three successive Parliaments, His Twelve Judges, and all those several Juries that were upon those Tryals?" He quoted Scroggs' congratulation to the jury which had brought in the verdict against Ireland; he boasted that he was content to stand the test of a new attack by "Popish adversaries"; "And then, to conclude all, I shall shew the Court, That 'tis in vain for the Popish Party to expect and think to wipe their Mouths, with Solomon's Whore, and say, they have done no wickedness: No, I question not but thousands of Protestants in this Kingdom are fully satisfied and convinced of the Truth of the Popish Plot, all and every part of it."

In reply to these preliminary fanfares, the Lord Chief Justice pointed out that the question was, not whether there had been a Popish Plot or a "Grand Consult", but whether Oates himself had been at that Consult, since the prosecution had brought witnesses to testify that at the time he was in fact in Flanders. Titus fell back on the credit his evidence had had at the time of the Plot. He had the impudence to ask the Lord Chief Justice whether his lordship would consent to be sworn as a witness, since he wished to mention certain things spoken by Jeffreys when the latter was Recorder of London. To this Jeffreys replied with suitable gravity that it was unnecessary, because he was willing to admit to anything he had said at former trials. Oates, nothing daunted, proceeded to read from the records of these trials a great many of the remarks made by the then Lord Chief Justice and his brother judges, until Mr Justice Withins, either embarrassed or merely weary of it, complained: "We are got into an endless Wood of Sayings of People, I know not where and when; and when all is done, it is to no purpose." "What my Lord Chief Justice Scroggs said at any of those Tryals," added Jeffreys, "or what I said, or any other Person, that either was of Counsel, or a Judge on the Bench, said as our opinion, is but our opinions on the Fact as it occurred to our present Apprehensions, but is no Evidence nor binding to this Jury."

Then, said Oates, if he could prove that the late Ireland had been a priest and a Jesuit, and had been engaged in a design against the King's life, surely that would "render me of Credit sufficient". He was answered in the negative. "If the Jesuits and Priests did plot, that is nothing to make your Evidence true, if you swore that which you did not know of your own knowledge." Nevertheless, Titus called Miles Prance to testify that Ireland had been a priest and a Jesuit; but Prance did not appear. Jeffreys, keeping his temper with what must have been considerable difficulty, advised the prisoner that he would do far better to call witnesses to prove where he was in April, 1678; and this, at long last, Titus consented to do; when it immediately became apparent why he had tried to avoid having to call them.

For Sir Richard Barker sent a message to say he had had a bad night and begged to be excused; William Smith the schoolmaster had long since retracted the evidence he had given for Oates at the Plot trials; old Clay had owned himself suborned; and Mrs Mayo the housekeeper and Butler the coachman were led by the Solicitor-General into flatly contradicting each other. When Titus loudly protested against this treatment of his witnesses, he was reminded of the case of Susanna and the Elders. Mrs Mayo, a pious matron, became very annoyed. She spoke nothing, she asserted, but what she spoke in the presence of God. We are all in the presence of God, the Lord Chief Justice blandly reminded her. "And," rejoined Mrs Mayo tartly, "shall answer before Him for all we have done and said, all of us, the proudest and the greatest here."

As for poor old William Walker, the minister, he was plainly sick of the whole business. Asked when and where he had encountered Oates in London during the spring of 1678, he replied: "My Lord, I have been interrogated in former times upon this Point, six or seven Years ago, and I do confess I did see the Man, and met him between St Martin's Lane and Leicester-fields; and truly, my Lord, I think I may say it was my unhappiness to meet with him; for I have had a great deal of Trouble by it since, Subpœna upon Subpœna, Trouble after Trouble, that I am even weary of it; for I am an old Man: But I do say I did meet him at that end of the Town, between St Martin's Lane and Leicester-fields in a strange Disguise; he was just like a vagrant, a very Rascal, and that's true, I believe, my Lord." Pressed as to the time, he replied that he would not take his oath upon it; the elm-trees were in bud, he remembered, and by this he guessed it was between Lady-day and the latter end of April; but in what year, he was now quite unable to say.

"*L.C.J.* Was it 77 or 78?

"*Walker*. Truly, my Lord, I never thought it worth so much taking notice of, to fix the particular time in my Memory.

"*Otes*. Whether was it that Year the Plot was discovered or the Michaelmas [*sic*] following?

"*Walker*. I cannot tell when the Plot was discovered, or whether it be found out yet or no.

"*Otes*. But was it the Year before you were examined?

"*Walker*. To answer you, Mr Otes, when it was exactly, I cannot say; truly I would give you the best Satisfaction I could, and do you as much Right as I would do my self; I think if that time when I was examined, were in 77 or 78, it was near a Year and a quarter before I did see you."

This was most unsatisfactory, to say the least, and after wasting some more of the Court's time in demanding records and notes he knew very well could not be allowed him, Titus called certain august personages to testify that he had reported the business of the "Grand Consult" to the Council. It did him more harm than good, for these, his one-time dupes, the Duke of Devonshire, the Earl of Clare, Mr Williams, formerly Speaker of the House of Commons, and many other of his old admirers, were either suffering from a sudden loss of memory, or else were only anxious to excuse their former credulity. Even that stout Whig, Compton, Bishop of London, joined in the general trimming; and the Earl of Huntingdon was positively insulting.

"I do believe, my Lord," remarked Huntingdon solemnly, "Mr Otes's Discovery found a good reception in the House of Lords; but it was grounded upon the opinion, that what he said was true, and that he was an honest Man: For so the House then accounted him to be; and upon this it was their Lordships gave Credit to his Testimony. . . . But since that time it being apparent there were so many, and great Contradictions, Falsities, and Perjuries in his Evidence; upon which so much innocent Blood hath been shed, I believe a great many Persons who were concerned in the Tryals of those unfortunate Men, are heartily afflicted and sorry for their share in it: And I do believe most of the House of Peers have altered their Opinion, as to this Man's Credit; and look upon his Evidence, as I do, to be very false."

Titus's retort to the tergiversations of his noble friends was to say stoutly: "My Lord, I am not at all concern'd at this; I value my self more upon my own Innocency and Integrity, than any Man's good or bad opinion whatsoever."

(7)

The trial continued.

The Attorney-General, constantly interrupted by the prisoner, produced further evidence. If Titus based his defence on his having been believed at former trials, then it was only fair to show the records of those at which he had not been believed, as those of Wakeman and Castlemaine; "and not only so, but we shall actually prove that he was perjur'd in them; that what he swore against them was utterly false, and you will hear that this is not the first time that he had sworn false; for in an Accusation that he gave at a Tryal at Hastings, we shall prove he swore Buggery upon a Person which was prov'd false." He then turned his attention to Oates's witnesses, and in particular to the suborning of Clay and William Smith. When the Plot broke out, Clay was a prisoner in the Gatehouse. Three or four days before the trial of the Five Jesuits, when Oates was desperately anxious to find witnesses to swear he had been in London at the time of the "Grand Consult", he had visited Clay in prison, and had told him that, unless he would agree to swear that he had seen him during this period, Titus would bring evidence against him to hang him with the other priests. The case of Smith has been given earlier on in his own words. When asked why he had perjured himself, he had replied, said the Attorney-General, "I must have died for it, if I had not done it, 'twas only a mistake in point of Time: But he threatened me, and so did others too, that he would have me hang'd for being in the Plot, if I did not comply with him, and swear this for him."

Both Wakeman and Castlemaine were called upon to state what Oates had testified against them at their respective trials, and to swear that his evidence had been false. Titus, in a manner reminiscent of Scroggs in the latter's bullying of the St Omer witnesses, immediately demanded of Castlemaine of what religion he was; and here, for the first time, Jeffreys lost his temper. It was a matter of surprise to all who knew him that he had not done so before. "Knowing well the Chief Justice Jefferies' unlimited passion", says Ailesbury, "I expected he would show himself in his true colours, but I was greatly surprised at his good temper, and the more because such impudent and reviling expressions never came from the mouth of man as Oats uttered."[72]

"*L.C.J.* We all know what Religion my Lord is of, you need not ask that question.

"*Otes.* That's not the point, my Lord, I must have it declar'd in Evidence.

"*L.C.J.* I wonder to see any Man that has the Face of a Man, carry it at this rate, when he hears such an Evidence brought in against him.

"*Otes.* I wonder that Mr Attorney will offer to bring this Evidence, Men that must have Malice against me——

"*L.C.J.* Hold your Tongue; you are a shame to Mankind.

"*Otes.* No, my Lord, I am neither a shame to my self or Mankind. . . . Ah! Ah! my Lord, I know why all this is, and so may the world very easily too.

"*L.C.J.* Such Impudence and Impiety was never known in any Christian Nation.

"*Otes.* But this will not do the work to make the Plot to be disbelieved; Things are not done by great Noises: I will stand by the Truth."

Yet Jeffreys continued to be scrupulously fair to the prisoner. When the Attorney-General called on Smith the schoolmaster "to acquaint my Lord and the Jury, how you came to swear at the former Tryal; by whom you were perswaded, and how you varied from the Truth", the Lord Chief Justice immediately intervened.

"*L.C.J.* That is very nauseous and fulsome [*sic*], Mr Attorney, methinks in a Court of Justice . . . if he did forswear himself, why should he ever be a Witness again?

"*Mr Att. Gen.* 'Tis not the first time by twenty that such Evidences have been given.

"*L.C.J.* I hate such Precedents at all times; let it be done never so often. Shall I believe a Villain one Word he says, when he owns that he forswore himself? . . . Pray call some other Witnesses, if you have them, to contradict him; but do not offer to bring a Man to swear that he did forswear himself before." Despite all the arguments of the Attorney-General and the Solicitor-General, Jeffreys persisted in his refusal to admit Smith as a witness, and the prosecution had at last to give way.

Concerning the suborning of old Clay, a Laurence Davenport was call'd.

"May it please you, my Lords and Gentlemen of the Jury, Mr Otes came to the Prison, I being then a Prisoner at that time in the Gatehouse at Westminster myself, and having no other Employment I had the Government and Care of some of the Prisoners for a Livelihood, being in Custody; and at that time Mr Otes, as I said, when old Clay was in Prison, did come there to visit this Clay at several times; and coming there to visit this Clay, up stairs he went to his Chamber, and desired to speak with him; and I did desire your Worship, Mr Otes, that you would go in to him, and you did go into his Chamber, and there these words you did speak to him before the Tryal of the five Jesuits, That if he did not swear what you put to him, he should be prosecuted as a Priest, which you did believe he would die for." Oates, added the witness, was accompanied by Sir William Waller, and old Clay agreed to do what they told him, if he might have money, for, said he, "he had been a Rogue before, and he could not say what he might do". Another witness testified that he had been told by Clay himself that Oates and Waller had said to him "That he must swear that Mr Otes dined at Mr Howard's House such a Day of the Month, and Mr Clay did say he knew nothing of the Matter; but then Sir William Waller and Mr Otes did reply to him again, here's your Choice; if you will not swear this, we will try you for a Priest, and hang you, and so Clay agreed. . . ."

This more or less concluded the case for the prosecution, and Titus was called upon to answer it. His defence was necessarily feeble. He obtained permission to have two passages from the *Lords' Journals* read in order to show what credit his testimony had received in the Upper House; he solemnly affirmed that all he had said regarding the "Grand Consult" was true, "and I resolve by the Grace of God to stand by it and confirm it with my Blood, if there be occasion"; he objected against the St Omer witnesses because they were Papists (though one of them was, in fact, a Church of England parson); and he then repeated the testimony of his own witnesses, adding most unwisely that he had expected William Smith to be examined. The Bench immediately offered to have this done; "it was to do you right that he was refused to be sworn before". Titus, hastily changing the subject, went out of his way to insult the lords and gentlemen he had called to testify for him; he had found, he said, "either the distance of time has wrought upon their Memories, or the Difference of the Season has chang'd their Opinion, so that now they disbelieve that which they did believe before, and perhaps for as little Reason as——"

"As they believed you at first," interrupted Jeffreys dryly.

After a further brush with the Bench, and a diatribe

against Sir George Wakeman, Titus wound up in the melodramatic fashion he loved:

"But, my Lord, since I have not the liberty to argue those things that were most material for my Defence against this Indictment, I appeal to the Great God of Heaven and Earth, the Judge of all; and once more in his Presence, and before all this Auditory, I avow my Evidence of the Popish Plot, all and every part of it, to be nothing but true, and will expect from the Almighty God, the Vindication of my Integrity and Innocence."

He added a complaint about the conditions of his confinement. "My Lord, I lie under very great Affliction with the Stone and the Gout, and besides that, I have lain in Irons these twenty-one Weeks; I beseech your Lordship, that this Cruelty may not be inflicted on me." In reply, Jeffreys reminded him that the reason why he was fettered was because of "the abundance of attempts made for your Escape", and the Marshal was called on to testify that only the previous night "Ropes were brought into his Chamber, on purpose to give him means to Escape, and here are the Bundle of Ropes".

Titus did not hear the remainder of the proceedings, for, having asked leave to retire because he was weak and ill, he was allowed to go, a privilege never accorded to his unfortunate victims. The former credulity of the nation, of the Parliament, and of themselves, was referred to with regret both by the Solicitor-General and the Lord Chief Justice; the Popish Plot, said Jeffreys, had nearly succeeded in masking a genuine plot against the Government, "that black and bloody Conspiracy, from which it hath pleased God lately to deliver us". By a strange piece of irony, the Lord Chief Justice advanced as a reason why Oates was not to be believed, the very self-same argument proffered by Oates's victims—namely, that the Papists must have been devoid of all sense and reason if they had trusted such a man with secrets so weighty and so dangerous.

The jury, after an absence of fifteen minutes, returned a verdict of Guilty.

(8)

Luttrell described Titus's demeanour during his trial as "very confident";[73] and on the second day, despite his condemnation on the first indictment, he was as bumptious as ever. Witness after witness was called by the prosecution to testify to Ireland's whereabouts on every day between August 3rd and September 14th, 1678, when Oates had sworn the Jesuit was in London, and their evidence formed so complete a record of Ireland's movements between these dates that the Lord Chief Justice was moved to remark that surely the prisoner must be concerned by it. "Not at all, my Lord," retorted Titus. "I know who they are, and what is the end of it all." "Upon my Faith," exclaimed Jeffreys, awestruck by such impudence, "I have so much Charity for you, as my Fellow Creature, as to be concerned for you." "'Tis not two straws matter," snapped Titus, "whether you be or no; I know my own Innocency."

Called on to make his defence, he complained bitterly of the hardship of having to make good the words he had sworn six years previously, and he pretended to be puzzled by the fact that the majority of the prosecution witnesses had not appeared at Ireland's trial, though one of them, a servant named Fallas, had just related how the mob had threatened to knock him and his companions on the head on that occasion, crying, "Knock them down, hang them Rogues; do they come to be Witnesses against the Saviour of the World?" As for the alleged perjury, Titus dismissed it as a mere trifling mistake in time and place. Ireland, he said, had been convicted of plotting against the King's life, and therefore it was hard and unreasonable to "tye up Witnesses that come to discover Plots and Conspiracies, to speak positively as to Circumstances of Time and Place; and every little Punctilio in their Evidence to bind them up to such Niceties in the Delivery of their Testimonies. . . . It is usual to speak with Latitude, as to such kind of things." He quoted Scroggs' savage denunciations of Ireland and his companions; he offered notes of Ireland's trial to prove that Bedloe had backed up his evidence, and desired that he might offer Jenison's evidence also, that informer having absented himself. (This was admitted as a special favour, on condition that Oates would consent to the prosecution offering in evidence a letter of Jenison's owning that he had been "mistaken" in the whole matter.) Lastly, having called a number of witnesses who did not appear, he said he would sum up everything else he had to say in "two or three words"; and proceeded to do so in about fifteen thousand.

Much of it was a mere repetition of what he had said the previous day; some of it was exceedingly insulting to the Bench. Now he whined; now he threatened; now he preached. The whole catalogue of Popish crimes, beginning with the Gunpowder Plot, was rehearsed anew; and finally he requested that counsel be assigned him to argue the legal errors in yesterday's proceedings. He was told that "We did assign you Counsel before; you may have who you will for Counsel." Titus's only reply was an appeal for leave to retire from the court, "because I am not well". The request was granted, and again the trial was concluded in his absence.

"The Chief Justice", says Ailesbury, "summed up with more sedateness than I expected from one I knew so well, and (loving to do every one justice) he was quite another man that day, than ever I knew him before or after."[74] Jeffreys spoke solemnly, even with emotion, of the "Mischiefs and Inconveniencies we have run into, if the Testimony given this Day in this Cause against Otes prove true", of the innocent blood which had been shed, and of the wickedness of an age which had caressed and rewarded such a man. "Good Lord! What Times do we live in? Surely, 'tis an Age as was never known, from the Creation of the World, to this Day." The crime of Oates, if crime it was found to be, was worse than common murder, even as parricide was worse than common murder. As for Ireland himself, Jeffreys revealed to the court the late King's reluctance to permit the execution of that priest, and his remorse for it afterwards, a remorse which "continued with him even to his dying Day, as the Business of my Lord Strafford did with his Royal Father". Lastly, let the jury weigh all the evidence with the most scrupulous care, "For, Gentlemen, because it is a Matter which is not only publick here, but all the World over, we must have the Justice of the Nation vindicated, and its Dis-reputation wiped off".

The jury took half an hour to decide upon their verdict of Guilty.

(9)

Two days later, on May 11th, Mr Wallop, Oates's counsel, moved that his client be given until Saturday, May 26th, to make his exceptions to both indictments. This was allowed. Accordingly, on the 26th, the prisoner was brought into court once more, and straightway complained that his counsel had not had sufficient time in which to examine various records. Jeffreys replied that Oates himself had had all the vacation in which to examine them, and that a longer time than ordinary had been allowed since his trial. Wallop himself, asked if he had anything to say, replied in the negative. Titus then offered four exceptions, culled from his defence against both indictments; they were pitifully trifling and irrelevant, and the Attorney-General had no difficulty in disposing of them in a short, pithy speech.

A solemn moment had now arrived. Jeffreys spoke at some length on the history of the penalties incurred by the convicted perjurer. Originally this crime was punished by death, later by the removal of the tongue. "Since that time," continued the Lord Chief Justice, "our Ancestors have yet been more moderate, and have not extended the Judgment to Life and Member; but by the unanimous opinion of all the Judges of England, whom we purposely consulted with upon this Occasion, It is conceived, that by the Law, crimes of this nature are left to be punished according to the Discretion of this Court, so far as that the Judgment extend not to Life or Member." Mr Justice Withins then pronounced sentence.

Oates was fined one thousand marks upon each indictment. He was to be stripped of his canonical habit, and to stand in the pillory at Westminster Hall Gate the following Monday for one hour, with a paper round his head stating his crime; this upon the first indictment. Upon the second, he was to be pilloried for one hour on Tuesday at the Royal Exchange, on Wednesday to be whipped from Aldgate to Newgate, and on Friday from Newgate to Tyburn. And as annual commemorations of his perjuries, in order that so long as he lived they might be recalled to the people, he was to stand in the pillory at Tyburn opposite the gallows for one hour every April 24th, in that at Westminster every August 9th, and on the 10th and 11th of the same month at Charing Cross and Temple Gate respectively. Lastly, he was to be pilloried at the Royal Exchange for one hour every September 2nd. "And I must tell you plainly," added Sir Francis Withins, "if it had been in my Power to have carried it further, I should not have been unwilling to have given Judgment of Death upon you: For, I am sure, you deserve it."

Of Oates's trial, the gentle Ailesbury wrote: "And I do repeat and declare it also before God, that the prisoner had the most just and fairest trial that ever had been in any Court of Justice";[75] no one who will take the trouble to read that trial in its entirety can differ from his verdict. But on the subject of Oates's sentence, controversy has raged from that day to this. Certain Whig historians have gone so far as to hint that his punishment was a piece of private vengeance on the part of James II, and even Echard considered that "the King of England shou'd have disregarded the Injuries that had been offer'd to the Duke of York".[76] But Oates was not being tried for his libels against James; he had been convicted on this charge, as we have seen, in 1684, and sentenced to a heavy fine. His trial in May, 1685, was for perjury, perjury which had been the direct means of sending at least eleven innocent men to die by the most horrible form of execution ever invented. King James left Oates to the Law, which was precisely what King Charles had done in the case of Oates's victims; but whereas Charles knew those victims to be innocent, James was convinced that Oates was guilty. And it must be remembered that, apart from the shedding of innocent blood, enormous damage had been inflicted on the very fabric and foundations of English society by the lies of Titus Oates, and that an example had to be made of him.

That he justly deserved punishment cannot, surely, be disputed. Two questions, then, remain: Was his sentence in accordance with the law of the land? And was it of unusual severity?

In regard to the first, the point to be borne in mind is well summed up in the words of a contemporary: "His Sentence, though it seem Severe is much less than he deserves; our English Law-makers, as never imagining the possibility of so unexampled an offender, having provided no Punishment equal to the Demerits of such unprecedented Villany."[77] This was precisely the difficulty; there was no precedent for so complex and heinous a crime, and therefore no formulated punishment. Before pronouncing sentence, Mr Justice Withins had said to him that a man was hanged for killing or intending to kill another, "But when a Man shall draw innocent Blood upon himself by a malicious, premeditated, false Oath, there is not only Blood in the Case, but likewise Perjury, corrupt, malicious Perjury. I know not how I can say, but, That the Law is defective that such a one is not to be hanged." It seemed particularly defective to the men of that age, in which robbery on the highway or picking a pocket meant the gallows. Ailesbury complained that "even in the Kingdom of Scotland, at least before the Union, perjured persons were subject to the same death as those executed on their false evidence, which in French they term *la Loi de talion*".[78]

A modern authority, who, while he recognized the falsity of Oates's evidence, entirely believed in the Popish Plot, thus describes the legal aspect of the sentence:

"There was a statute of Elizabeth's reign which declared what was the least penalty for perjury, and subornation, but the power of the judge to exact a greater was expressly reserved. It was the unanimous opinion of the judges that they might proceed as they did. Fine, imprisonment, the pillory, and whipping were all recognised engines of the law in cases of misdemeanour, and it would be difficult to prove that there was any recognised limit to their application. . . . A few centuries before, he [Oates] would have been treated as an approver—a person who, confessing himself to have been implicated in some felony or treason, gives up the names of his associates. When an approver of earlier days failed to obtain a verdict of guilty against any person accused, he was hanged without further ceremony; and this would have been the fate of Oates when Wakeman was acquitted, had the proceedings been in the form of the ancient appeal. But if Oates was not to be punished as a false appellor, it followed that he must, if punished at all, be punished, as in fact he was, according to the analogies to be detected in other cases of misdemeanour . . . there was no punishment for him as a perjured witness, except such as might be provided by the Act of Parliament, which expressly gave discretionary powers to the judges."[79]

Secondly, was Titus's punishment unusually severe? Those writers who insist that it was without precedent are in error. A song of the period expresses surprise that he was not subjected to some form of mutilation, and it is a fact that the sentence for false accusation almost invariably included either branding or tongue-boring, or both. Mr J. G. Muddiman quotes the sentence on a Sarah Waite, convicted of perjury in 1619: " 'Fined at £500, committed to the Fleet and from thence one day to be whipped to Westminster and another from the Fleet to Cheapside and there to be burned in the face with an A. and an F. for False Accusation, and from thence to Bridewell, there to remain all her life.' This was an even worse punishment than that of Oates, for the poor woman was liable to be continually whipped at Bridewell."[80] To take only one other example of seventeenth-century severity in punishment, there was the case of that unfortunate fanatic, James Naylor, who was sentenced by one of Cromwell's Parliaments to be pilloried for two hours and then whipped from Westminster to the New Exchange, where he was to stand in the pillory for a further two hours, a couple of days later to be whipped from Newgate to the Old Exchange, there to be branded in the forehead and to have his tongue bored through, then to be sent to Bristol and whipped again, and finally to be confined in Bridewell and kept at hard labour during the pleasure of the Parliament. This sentence was inflicted for blasphemy; unlike Oates, Naylor had not been the means of shedding innocent blood.

(10)

On Monday, May 18th, Titus was led from prison, wearing round his hat a paper with the inscription: "Titus Oates, convicted upon full evidence of two horrid perjuries."[81] In accordance with a clause in his sentence, he was led round all the courts in Westminster Hall before being set in the pillory at the Gate; here, having desired the

Lord Chief Justice to see that he was protected from the rabble, "he said that they might there see the late King, the Lords, and three Houses of Commons standing with him upone the pillory. He was well pelted with eggs, and bore all with invincible impudence."[82] A ballad-writer took the liberty of imagining Titus's reflections on this occasion:

"From three prostrate Kingdoms at once to adore me
And no less than three Parliaments kneeling before me;
From hanging of Lords with a Word or a Frown,
And no more than an oath to the shaking a Crown:
From all these brave Pranks
Now to have no more thanks,
Then to look thro' a Hole, thro' two damned oaken Planks.
Oh! mourn ye poor Whigs with sad lamentation,
To see the hard Fate of the Saviour o' th' Nation."[83]

Next day, however, when he was pilloried in the City, he was given a more kindly reception. "This day . . . the rabble were very disorderly upon the Pilloring of Oates. They are apprehending them."[84] Another ballad-monger thus describes the scene:

"At City Exchange next day he appears,
Where Whining Phanaticks saluted his Ears;
Their Pillory'd Prophet they boldly defend,
Who can't save them, nor himself, in the end.
His throne they pull'd down,
To the City's Renown,
The Relicks on Shoulders they bore up and down:
But tyr'd with Procession, 'twas Judg'd for the best,
In Prison these Zealots should take up their Nest."[85]

On Wednesday, the 20th, Titus was stripped to the waist, tied to the cart's tail, and whipped according to sentence from Aldgate to Newgate; "he made hideous Bellowings, and swooned several Times with the greatness of the Anguish".[86] Henry Muddiman, the news-letter writer, witnessed this first whipping, and recorded that "the opinions of the bystanders about its severity differed according to their political bias [and] answered the question of how severe the punishment was by saying that in such

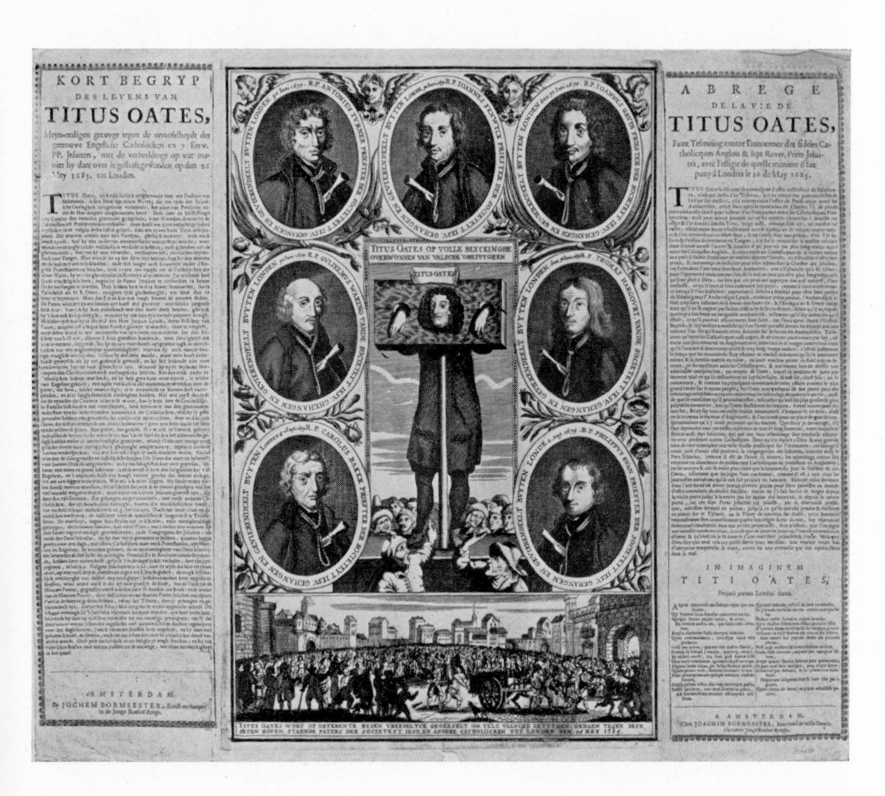

TITUS OATES IN THE PILLORY

matters the hangman was the best judge, and that he told him that 'He did one day, as he might another.' "[87]

On Friday, the 22nd, he was "placed on a sledge", says Evelyn, "being not able to go by reason of so late scourging, and dragg'd from prison to Tyburn, and whipt againe all the way, which some thought to be very severe and extraordinary; but if he was guilty of the perjuries, and so of the death of so many innocents, as I feare he was, his punishment was but what he deserv'd. I chanc'd to pass just as execution was doing on him. A strange revolution!"[88] The Baptist minister, Calamy, who likewise witnessed this second flogging, says that the victim's back "miserably swelled with his first whipping, looked as if it had been flayed. . . . Dr Oates was a man of invincible courage and resolution, and endured what would have killed a great many others. He occasioned a strange turn in the nation, after a general lethargy that had been of some years continuance. By awakening us out of sleep, he was an instrument in the hand of God for our preservation. Yet, after all, he was but a sorry foul-mouthed wretch, as I can testify, from what I once heard from him in company."[89]

The statement of L'Estrange that Titus was placed on a sledge because he had made himself so drunk he could not stand may be dismissed as a piece of uncharacteristic spite on the part of the Tory pamphleteer. But as for the over-severity or otherwise of Titus Oates's punishment, one cannot but observe the curious fact that, in every age, a certain section of public opinion is always more moved by the punishment of the criminal than by the fate of his victim.

(11)

Titus was not alone among the King's Evidence to have a richly deserved sentence passed upon him at this time. Dangerfield, who had fled on the arrest of Oates, had been captured in March and committed to Newgate. On May 30th, he was tried and convicted by a Middlesex jury for "writing and publishing a scandalous libel called his Narrative", and an indictment for perjury was then preferred against him. On June 29th, he received a sentence very similar to that of Oates, except that his fine was in the sum of £500. On July 4th, after his second whipping, "In the returne from Tyburne, as he came in a coach, guarded with the Sheriff's officers, in Holborne, one Mr Francis, of Grey's Inn, came to the coach side to see and speak to him, with whome yet he had no business nor acquaintance. He askt Daingerfeild 'how he liked his race, and how he did after his heats'; to whome Daingerfeild reply'd, 'You are the sonn of a whore.' Francis thereupon, haveing a small caine in his hand, thrust at him, which rann into his eye, and he died next day. Francis was indicted of murder at the Old Bailie, was found guiltie, and was hanged. It may well be presumed Francis had noe designe of killinge, for he had a sword by his side, which was a more likely thing to kill him then that little caine, indeed, the smallest that ever I see used, and without any iron ferule or anythinge at the end; and Francis his wife was by too. But Daingerfeild was under protection of the Kinge and his officers, and had suffered the law, and that was a great aggravation of the crime, I suppose, for certeinly there was noe intent to kill him."[90] We hear of no complaints from the Whig writers that Francis in his turn was left to the Law.

In April of the following year, Miles Prance voluntarily surrendered himself, and retracted all he had sworn concerning the murder of Sir Edmund Berry Godfrey.[91] On May 14th, he pleaded Guilty to an indictment for perjury in connection with the evidence he had given at the trial of the three unfortunates hanged for that crime. On June 15th, he was sentenced to be pilloried and whipped; "Prance owned his guilt, and said he was sorry for what he had done".[92]

Meanwhile, the First Discoverer of the Popish Plot, the great prince of informers, lay almost forgotten, save for his periodic appearances in the pillory. In August, 1685, he was removed to the King's Bench Prison in Southwark, and here he remained for over three years. He himself has left us several descriptions of his life in prison, varying from the pathetic to the complacent. Sternly addressing King James (after the Revolution) in one of his tracts, he says that "by your own Command I was loaded with Irons of excessive weight, for the space of one whole Year without any intermission, and of your Princely Compassion they were not suffer'd to be taken off even when my Legs were swoln with the Gout. Nay, that I might appear to partake of the utmost of your Mercy, I was by your order shut up in the Hole, or Dungeon of the Prison, whereby I became impair'd of my Limbs and contracted Convulsion Fits, to the hazard of my Life".[93]

On the other hand, Titus was able to boast that, while many of his old friends had deserted him in his distress the Almighty had "raised up new ones who have not without Difficulties preserved me from Perishing in my Afflictions, Feeding, and Cloathing me; many of whom were Persons who were better acquainted with my Cause, than my Person, who escaped the being deluded by that Infamous Race of the Babylonish Strumpet".[94] It is not difficult to guess the identity of these persons, when it is remembered that Titus was imprisoned during the reign of James the Second, a reign during which the Opposition which had seemed to die in the early 'eighties, became very much alive again, and was working away merrily underground for the destruction of hereditary monarchy.

Despite the awful conditions of his imprisonment, as described by himself, Titus does not seem to have been entirely incapacitated. If rumour lied not, he found consolation in the gentle sex. Gossip reported the appearance of a bastard child borne of his bed-maker in the King's Bench Prison;[95] and Ailesbury states definitely that he went so far as to marry "a Lady Baltinglass, a heap of flesh and brandy".[96] Whatever the truth of these rumours, it is certain that Titus found the strength to write several tracts, including his *Sound Advice to Roman Catholicks*, which later was to take an honoured place among his published works.

The assurance that the world had not forgotten him may have been a comfort to Titus during these trying years, for he seems to have viewed a return to obscurity as the worst of all evils. The street-hawkers cried new and yet newer songs concerning the late Saviour of the Nation, *There was a Doctor of Antient Fame*, *Oates well Thrashed*, *Hail to the Prince of the Plot*, *Once on a Time the Doctor did Swear*, *A Hue and Cry after T. Oates*, and so on. Moreover, the greatest humorous writer of his day, Tom Brown, deemed the fallen idol worthy of his wit, and wrote some excellent satire in his honour, *Advice to Dr Oates, not to be Melancholy.*[97] Better still, as the years wore on the people who came to view his periodic appearances in the pillory accorded him a new respect, and, according to the Venetian Ambassador, even went so far as to present him with money on these occasions. For times were changing once again; the balance shifted; and the Glorious Revolution loomed like a sun through the dark clouds of Popery and Arbitrary Power. The Good Old Cause, beloved of Titus's father, was due to come into its own again, as Titus himself, if we are to give credit to a tract of which he was part author, had foreseen. Despite the dreadful conditions of his imprisonment, we are told, "he bore up . . . with so strange and almost miraculous a Patience, that during his four years Imprisonment, he was never once heard to sigh, or manifest any impatience under his condition. He refused all offers of the Jesuits, who even after this had the Impudence to propose to him his recanting his Evidence. He had still a strong Belief that he should see better times, and get his freedom again, which he had in that General Gaol-delivery, granted all England by the then Prince of Orange's Heroick Undertaking."[98]

One cannot but regret that Titus and his collaborators spoiled the effect of these noble words by adding their assurance that the Revolution Parliament "would appoint him Rewards suitable to his Sufferings and Merit".[99]

BOOK FIVE

THE DUTCHMAN'S PENSIONER

(1)

ON November 1st, 1688, four days before William of Orange landed at Torbay to seize the throne of England at the invitation of the Opposition, Titus Oates felt confident enough in his own future to pen the Epistle Dedicatory to a tract he had been writing in prison, *A Discourse of the Unlawfulness of Praying to Saints.* This Epistle he addressed to "All True Protestants", and he signed himself "Your Brother and Servant, in the King's Bench Prison, for the Testimony of a Good Conscience, Titus Oates". After treating his readers to a hair-raising description of his sufferings for the Good Old Cause, he informed them that his enemies had intended, by their sentence upon him, to murder him, "that I might not Communicate to the World, those Particulars relating to the Popish Conspiracy, carried on by that Wicked Party, for the Murther of the Late King, and the Subversion of the Protestant Religion . . . which I shall do, when it shall please God, and the King that now is, that a Parliament shall meet, and sit, and Redress our Crying Grievances, and Heal all those Wounds which the Devillish Hellish Popish Crew have made against us".

Towards the end of the following month, with King James the Second gone overseas and King William the Third settled on the throne as a puppet monarch, Titus issued forth from the King's Bench Prison, put on his canonical garb again, donned his doctor's scarf,[1] and, while waiting for the first Revolution Parliament to set aside his sentence and reward him in a suitable manner, sent round the hat to the great ones of that faction which had triumphed after all. One token of their remembrance of his past efforts in their cause remains to us: the eccentric Duke of Bolton sent him a cheque for fifty pounds, which is still in the possession of Child's Bank. Incidentally, we have it from his own mouth that, during the whole period of his imprisonment, "several Noblemen and Gentlemen, Citizens and others contributed 400 *li.* p' Ann. for his support and maintenance";[2] so, despite the pathetic accounts by him of the horrors he suffered in prison, it is not really surprising that Henry Muddiman should see him, in the month of January, 1689, walking through St James's Park, looking "very fat and trimme".

He was, it seemed, as outspoken as ever. "He had the impudence to go to Lambeth, to Archbishop Tillotson, and that prelate was so weak as to admit him to his table, and, the King and Queen's health going about, he impudently cried, 'My Lord, I will see first what King William and Queen Mary will do for me before I drink their healths!' "[3] The reinstatement of himself as a public idol was now his main objective, and with this end in view, in January he "petitioned the lords and commons, setting forth the sad condition he hath lay'n under, and how hardly he hath been used".[4] On March 31st, he forwarded to the Lords a second, and very long, petition for redress.

The Lords gave him leave to bring in a writ of error, and on April 9th his petition was read in the House; it was ordered that "this House will hear Counsel on the said Writs, on Thursday the 18th of this instant April, at Ten of the Clock in the Forenoon; whereof the said Titus Otes is to cause timely Notice to be given to Their Majesties Attorney General for that Purpose".[5] The hearing was, however, three times postponed,[6] and it was not until April 26th that Oates's solicitor, Thomas Bales, was sworn, his counsel heard, and ordered to set down in writing their arguments and exceptions against the judgment in his trial, and next day to deliver them to the Lord Chief Justice. Rather naturally, no counsel appeared for the plaintiff to defend the judgment.

On the 27th, orders were sent to Sir Richard Holloway and Sir Francis Withins, who had shared Jeffreys' Bench, to attend the House on May 4th, there to give in their reasons and grounds for their judgment against Oates; but again the hearing was put off, from May 4th to the 6th, from the 6th to the 7th, from the 7th to the 11th, from the 11th to the 13th, and from the 13th to the 17th, when at long last the defence of the two judges was heard. They defended their judgment with many precedents; after hearing them, the House ordered all the judges to attend next Friday, "upon the Occasion of Tytus Otes's Case upon the Three Writs of Error depending in this House".[7]

But on May 24th they were still putting off till the morrow what they should do to-day, and poor Titus, scraping along on his miserable four hundred a year, was getting decidedly impatient. This was not the way in which he had been accustomed to be treated by Parliaments, and so great was his resentment that he applied himself to the Commons, presenting a paper which contained a lengthy description of his wrongs, together with a slightly revised version of the old Popish Plot. The Commons, deeply moved, ordered "That the said Mr Otes, and his Counsel, be heard at the Bar of this House this Day Seven-night in the Forenoon".[8]

Two days later, Titus was sent for by a very wrathful House of Lords. Not only, said their lordships, was it a breach of privilege to petition the Commons after petitioning the Lords, but it was reported that Mr Oates had said that "if he could not have justice in the upper house, he hop'd to have it in the lower".[9] It was ordered, therefore, "That the Gentleman Usher of the Black Rod attending this House, his Deputy or Deputies, do forthwith convey Tytus Oates in safe Custody to the Prison of the King's Bench, there to remain during the Pleasure of this House";[10] and thus did the indignant Titus find himself back in jail again.

On May 30th, he was brought into the Lords' House once more, "and having kneeled, was told, 'There were Exceptions taken at his stiling himself D.D. in his Petition'. He said 'That he is a Doctor of Divinity, and had his Degree at Salamanca in Spaine'. Then he was commanded to withdraw. The House, upon Consideration, called him to the Bar again. And he was told 'That the House required him to strike out the title D.D. in his Petition'. He said 'He could not do it, out of Conscience'. Upon this, it is ordered, That Titus Oates be, and is hereby, remanded to the Custody of the Marshal of the King's Bench."[11] Next day, the first of Trinity term, "the Judges gave their opinions in Mr Oates case, unanimously, that it was an extrajudicial judgment, and unpresidented; but after a long debate the lords divided, 23 were for reversing it, and 35 for affirming it, notwithstanding the judges opinions; so he was thereon remanded to the kings bench prison".[12] It is painful to imagine Titus's feelings; really it almost seemed as if he were going to be made a martyr twice over.

Relations between the Houses, already strained, now threatened to grow dangerous. On June 4th, the Commons ordered the Clerk of the Crown to attend the House on Thursday with the records of Oates's conviction, and appointed a committee to inspect the *Lords' Journals* in relation to the proceedings against him.[13] On the 7th, the Lord President informed the House of Lords that the King had given order for issuing a pardon for Oates; and on the 11th, the Commons voted that the judgments against Titus were "cruel and illegal", and ordered a Bill to be brought in to reverse them.[14] This Bill was passed on July 6th, and sent up to the Lords, who immediately showed their intention of diverting it by means of amendments. "The Lords house have sat thes 3 dayes very close and long on ye bill for reversing ye judgmt agt T. Oates. It hath been caryed agt generall clauses in ye bill only by 2 votes, ye Ld Devonshire and Dr B[urne]t of Salisbury. The freinds of T.O. will have ye judgmt wase erroneous. Others say ye divesting him of his ecclesiastic orders wase erroneous, for yt lay not in their power to doe, Yt ye rest of judgmt wase not erroneous but too severe. Tomorrow ye sages of ye law are to deliver their opinion whither one branch of a judgmt being erroneous, doth not render ye whole judgmt soe."[15]

On the 13th, "The lords and commons haveing had a conference about the lords amendments . . . each returned to their own house, and, upon debate, the commons adhered to their bill without amendments".[16] Reminders, conferences, and disagreements continued to the end of the month, and relations between the Houses grew more and more acrimonious. A very stiff message was sent to the Lords from the Commons on August 13th, in which the Lower House made the case of Oates the basis for a lecture on their own rights and privileges. On the 20th of the same month, William prorogued Parliament, just in time to prevent a crisis; this entailed an order for Oates's release from jail, though, since the judgments against him had not been reversed, he remained a convicted perjurer, and as such his testimony was invalid in any court of law.

It is always pleasant to record an act of gratitude, more especially, perhaps, when it is performed by a royal person. The Parliament had done little for Titus Oates, but William of Orange knew his friends, and recognized the instruments which had helped him attain the ambition of his life, the throne of England. The Popish Plot, though it had seemed to fail as a weapon of the Opposition, had re-awakened to an intense degree the hatred of Popery long smouldering in the heart of the ordinary Englishman, and this hatred had gone far in making the Revolution possible, since the rightful King was a Catholic. As he was presently to promote the officer in charge of the Massacre of Glencoe, so now did William reward the hero of the Popish Terror. "Sept. 19. Hampton Court. Present: all my Lords. The King came in. . . . Ordered by his Majesty that 10 *l.* a week be paid to Dr Oats out of secret service in answer to the address of the House of Commons."[17]

It is most regrettable to have to add that Titus, far from being grateful in his turn, "was very wrath; for Charles gave him 600 *l.* [per annum] and sure, said he, William will give me more."[18]

(2)

Once again in receipt of a royal pension, Titus took a house in Axe Yard, Westminster, and prepared to keep himself well in the public eye. He had been the Saviour of the Nation, and he had been a martyr, and no one was going to be allowed to forget either role. A pack of "Orange-cards", brought out by the same enterprising firm which had manufactured the Popish Plot playing-cards, included Dr Oates's whipping among the incidents which had caused the Glorious Revolution; but Titus was not at all content with such trifling mementoes of his sufferings. In this same year of 1689, he produced the first part of his magnum opus, *A Display of Tyranny; or Remarks upon the Illegal and Arbitrary Proceedings in the Courts of Westminster and Guild-hall London.* This masterpiece, which runs to three hundred and forty pages of close type, gives us the advantage of Titus's impressions of the trials of Knox and Lane, College, the Rye House plotters, and many others; and naturally includes yet another re-telling of the story of the Popish Plot.

Charles II was dead, James II in exile, and therefore could Titus speak with the utmost frankness about both these monarchs. Charles, he informed his readers, was always a Papist, "but upon his Restoration, that the Duke's turn might be served, he must not then declare". (The meaning of this statement is obscure, to say the least of it.) The Popish Plot began in 1660, but after failing to take proper advantage of their success in starting the Great Fire, the Papists had postponed further action, apparently until they had confided their secrets to Dr Oates, who, in 1678, "by the Providence of the Almighty", detected their machinations. There followed Titus's version of the history of the reign of Charles II, after which he got down to the business of his own trial. Anonymity made him able to dispense with all false modesty. "Dr Otes, the first discoverer of the Popish Plot, being no way shaken, but bearing with most undaunted Courage and Constancy, innumerable Reproaches and Slanders from the Pulpit and Press, nay, and from the Stage also, Hell itself seemed to be engaged to discredit and batter down the belief of his Evidence." The carping reader might find the repeated references to this "undaunted Courage" of his a little tedious.

Early in 1689, probably in January, an anonymous writer, who was almost certainly Dunton, had issued a small tract of sixteen pages entitled *The Protestant Martyrs: or, The Bloody Assizes*. The success of this sensational broadsheet induced Dunton to publish a second edition, *The Bloody Assizes: or, A Compleat history of the life of George, Lord Jefferies*. In the meantime, Tutchin had produced *The Dying Speeches, Letters and Prayers of those eminent Protestants who suffered in the West of England*, the Protestants in question being the Monmouth rebels, and the bulk of their "speeches" shameless fabrications. But they were clever fabrications, for Tutchin was an expert at that sort of thing.[19] In the autumn, these two writers were joined by a third, no less a person than Dr Oates, and, pooling their talents, the three of them collaborated in *A New Martyrology: or The Bloody Assizes now exactly methodised into one volume.*[20] The interesting point to be noted is, that the contemporary historians, White Kennet, Echard, and Oldmixon, mention no other authority for their accounts of the Monmouth Rebellion trials and executions than this tract; so that our knowledge of what has come to be known as the Bloody Assizes rests largely on the testimony of Titus Oates and his two disreputable friends.

Among the martyrs listed we find, of course, Dr Oates and Mr Dangerfield, "whom all means possible, fair and foul, had been used, to make 'em turn Villains, and deny their Evidence; but to their eternal Praise, they still continued firm to their first Testimony, to the Rage and Confusion of their Enemies". As for the punishment inflicted on Titus, "we'll safely defy all History to shew one Parallel of it either on Man or Dog, from the Creation of the World to the year 1685".

If this tract were interesting for nothing else, posterity would be indebted to it for the character it draws of one of its co-authors, the subject of this biography: "His Firmness and Courage, even perhaps to a Fault, have been visible through these mentioned, and all his other Actions since he appear'd on the publick Stage: his Passions are lively and warm, and he's the worst made for a Dissembler, an Hypocrite, or a secret Villain of any Man in the World. Nor have all his Sufferings much sunk him, tho he be a little alter'd in this particular. He's open and frank, and speaks whatever he thinks of any Persons or things in the World, and bearing himself justly enough, on his Services to his Country, is not careful to keep that Guard which others do, on his Words and Actions. He has Wit enough, a pleasant Humour, and sufficiently divertive to those he knows, and his Learning is far from contemptible. He has a good Library, is no mean Critick in Greek, and well acquainted with the Schoolmen and Fathers. He's owner of as much Generosity as any Man, and as much Tenderness to any in Misery, scorning to strike at those below him; an example of which very remarkable there was in his inhumane Judge's Fall, he being almost the only Person who has been heard to pity him; tho' one would have thought he should have been the last. In a word, as this present Age has begun to do him Justice, so 'tis not doubted will make an end on't, and those succeeding joyn with it in making honourable mention of his Name and Services to the Protestant Religion."[21]

One other work of Titus's appeared this year, his *Sound Advice to Roman Catholicks*, published by Janeway, the Whig printer. As in his *The Devil's Patriarck*, so here, he regaled his readers with juicy descriptions of the characters of the Popes: "Gregory VII caused a fellow to put great stones, right over the place where the Emperor Henry used to pray, in St Mary's Church, to knock him on the Head, by an ingenious contrivance; whilst he was at his Devotion, he Cursed, and Excommunicated him, without occasion, and took his Crown from him without any just cause. . . . Nicolas III begot a Bastard Son, that had Claws and Hair like a Bear. . . . Clement VI caused to poyson the Emperour Lewis, without any Cause but Pride, Covetousness, and desire of Superiority. . . ."

No man made less of inconsistency than Titus, and, having asserted constantly during the Plot period that he embraced the Catholic Faith solely in order to unearth Popish conspiracies, he confesses in this work that "I my self was lulled asleep, by the allurements of the Popish Syrenes, and the bewitching sorceries of the Man of Sin (as by the impetuous current of Babel's streams) driven headlong to the brink and shore of the See of Romish Abominations. But as Joseph was sold to Egypt, for the Preservation of his Brethren, so was I laid aside, by the permission of Divine Providence, for the safety both of my King and Country." Titus, who was fond of comparing himself with Biblical characters, presently informed his readers that he was like St Paul, "who was once a Persecutor". He was full of the most graphic similies. The Scriptures, he says, are like "a River, wherein an Elephant may swim, and an Insect wade and drink".

Having given "Sound Advice" to the Papists, Titus added "a Word to the People called Quakers", in which he explained to them their errors and set their feet upon the right path.

(3)

Sixteen hundred and ninety is almost a blank so far as Titus is concerned, unless we count the publication of the second part of his *Display of Tyranny*, from which we learn that, in March, he had attended the parliamentary elections in Essex. Subscriptions for the book do not seem to have come up to his expectations, and he complains that "some Men are too zealously intent and busie in their private affairs, to be publick-spirited". The work contains the first hint of his future line of action. There is no longer, he explains to his readers, the danger of a Popish Plot, but most assuredly the country is in peril from a Franco-Jacobite conspiracy, and "That we have such a Race of Animals [i.e. the adherents of King James] walking, and that with no more than two Legs apiece, amongst us, is too well known to be denyed or dissembled".

His manner of life during this period is sketched by North thus: "It was observable of Oates, that, while he had his Liberty, as in King Charles's Time, and King William's, especially the latter, he never failed to give his attendance in the Court of Requests and the Lobbies to solicite hard in all Points, under Deliberation, that might terminate in the Prejudice of the Church, Crown, or of any Gentlemen of the Loyal or Church of England Party. And it was not often, if ever, he was seen there, but upon some such Occasion, and when he might shew his Constancy, by zealous abetting on the ill-natured factious Side: So that he was looked upon as a Screech Owl, ever boding Mischief. . . . He was never seen to hold Dialogues with any but the rankest Party Men, unless it were to rascal them over, as he would liberally bestow if he so thought fit, which was not seldom."[22]

At his house in Axe Yard these "rankest Party Men" were always sure of a welcome, and at this time his closest friends were Aaron Smith, John Arnold, John Tutchin, and John Dunton. Of Smith's origins very little is known, but as early as 1677 he was mentioned in a proclamation as a seditious person. A cunning lawyer, he knew all the tricks of the trade, and especially how to cover his own tracks. He had been in the Rye House conspiracy up to the neck, and yet, when arrested in July, '83, so little could be proved against him that the Law had been forced to let him escape with a fine of £500 and two hours in the pillory. On April 9th, 1689, King William had acknowledged Smith's services to the Good Old Cause by making him solicitor to the Treasury, with which he combined the post of public prosecutor.

John Arnold, a Welsh justice of the peace, had been a zealous priest-hunter for some years before 1678, and during the Plot period had distinguished himself in a very singular manner. "This vile fellow perceiving that about the year 1680, That this forged plot was sinking, that the eyes of the nation began to be opened, he passed a razor over his throat, enough to bleed, and lay in that condition on the ground in Jackanapes Alley leading to Chancery Lane, a great passage for people on foot especially. The first that espied him took compassion and asked him the circumstances, he answered that one Giles, an Irish Papist, had committed that fact, and on the strictest search after that man it was proved on oath that the said Giles was that very day in Gloucester or thereabouts, and that he had not been in London for some time. This I know to be true to a tittle."[23] Nevertheless, Giles was tried and convicted of attempted murder, and on his first appearance in the pillory was nearly stoned to death by the mob.

John Tutchin had started his career by being expelled from school for theft. He had narrowly escaped hanging for his share in the Monmouth Rebellion, and, since the Revolution, had become the chief pamphleteer of the Whigs. His literary efforts were not, however, sufficient for his needs, and in 1692 he was given a clerkship in the Victualling Office to help him pay his way. From this post he was dismissed in '95, for having failed to prove his accusation of embezzlement against the Commissioners. John Dunton, his collaborator in many a Whig pamphlet, was much more comfortably situated. He had had the sense to live abroad during the reign of James II, and now had a prosperous bookshop at the sign of the Black Raven in the Poultry. He was always unbalanced; became certifiable in 1697; and remained stark mad till his death.

To these choice friends of Titus's, there was now to be added another, a man young in years, but old in iniquity, passably handsome, prodigiously plausible; "he had not only so many fair words at pleasure, but likewise that innocent Face, that it was hard to suspect him a Counterfeit".[24]

Since he was also resolved to advance his fortunes by fair means or by foul, it will be understood why he was a fit candidate for the patronage of Titus Oates.

This William Fuller was born in the year 1670, and possibly was the bastard of one of the Herbert family; certainly that family interested themselves on his behalf even when he became notorious. Later, when he and Oates had quarrelled, the latter "said at Will's Coffee House in Scotland-Yard, our Man of Quality's Father was a sorry sort of Butcher, and his Mother a poor Servant-Maid to a Husbandman at 40s. a Year Wages".[25] Whatever the truth about his parentage, by the year 1687 Fuller had a stepfather whom he decided to blackmail; taking french leave from his master, a "Coney-wool Cutter" in Shoe Lane, London, the young man trudged down to his home in Kent for the express purpose of accusing his stepfather of having murdered his mother. Failing most lamentably to advance his fortunes by this means, Fuller returned to his master, who was indulgent enough to receive back the runaway apprentice; but in the following year, the youth played truant again, turned Catholic, and obtained the post of page in the household of Lord and Lady Melfort, faithful servants of King James. It has been seen that young Fuller was plausible and had an innocent face, and when, at the Revolution, he retired to France with the exiled Court, his master and mistress were so far deceived by his manner and appearance as to employ him in the carrying of letters and messages between themselves and their Jacobite friends in England.

On one of these trips, Fuller was recognized by a member of the Herbert family, who whispered in his ear the suggestion that he turn his coat, and by doing so, make his fortune. In his autobiography, Fuller lets us into the secret of how he solved the problem of whether or no to make a change of masters. He decided to "put two Names, James and William, into a Book, to Blindfold my self, and then lay the Book down, afterwards walk three times round the room, then take the Book up and shake it, and that Name which fell nearest me, that King would I serve".[26] Blind chance having laid at his feet the name of the reigning monarch, the young man immediately handed over his letters to the Government, was formally thanked by the King, and settled down to enjoy a royal pension. By April, 1690, he had become quite the gentleman, called himself Major Fuller of Lord Sydney's Regiment, and in the summer went off to Ireland in the train of King William, where possibly he witnessed (though, one suspects, at a safe distance) the Battle of the Boyne.

But treachery, though a paying game, was not quite so lucrative as to be able to provide for Major Fuller's expensive tastes. Returning from Ireland in the late summer of 1690, he was arrested for debt and thrown into a sponging-house; he managed to free himself by giving "security", or, in less polite terms, a bribe, to the Marshal, and took lodgings in Axe Yard, Westminster, which, being within the Verge of the Court, secured him from the attentions of the bailiffs. It was now that he struck up an acquaintance with a gentleman much older than himself both in years and treachery.

"Whilst I lodged in Ax-Yard", says Fuller, "I became acquainted with Dr Oats, who had seen me often before, as I had him, puffing about the Court, but now being Neighbours, we began to grow very intimate; he invites me to his House to Dinner, and there I met with Mr John Tutchin, and a great many that talked mightily against King James. . . . They preached up Liberty and Property, and spoke very despiscably [*sic*] of all Kings, not sparing him on the Throne. . . . These things startled me at first, but some considerable Men, as John Arnold Esq., John Savil Esq., and others it is not fitting to name, appearing amongst them, and saying the same things, telling long stories of what they had done to serve and save the Nation . . . made me look on them as Saints, and mighty Patrons for the publick Good. In a short time the Reverend Doctor invites me to come and lodge in his House, and having his first Floor very handsomely furnished, I accepted his offer, and had room for my Servants also: We had a good Table provided, so I agreed with him to pay fifty shillings per week for my Diet and Lodging, and the same for two servants, only I was to find my own wine, and if a Friend or more came with me, I was to allow as he thought fitting, by which means, after seven weeks, I became Debtor to him about nine Pounds; I paid him some Money, but was not strictly careful to discharge all, by reason the Dr pretended an unspeakable love for me; and having afterwards some urgent occasions, the Marshal of the King's-Bench calling upon me for a fresh Bribe, I borrowed about 5 *l.* of the Dr."

There was a limit to the doctor's "unspeakable love", and shortly after this, he set the Marshal on Fuller's tail. If the rumour reported by a news-letter writer was true that in March Titus's pension had been withdrawn,[27] there was some excuse for this harsh conduct, though Dr Oates's fall from the royal favour, if it took place at all, must have been of short duration, for on April 28th another news-letter writer reports that "a great many Court officers are to be promoted, that is . . . Sunderland, Secretary of State, who with Dr Oates kissed the King's hand on Friday or Saturday last at Kensington".[28] Fuller escaped to Holland, and there for a while he lived on credit in the manner of the deceased Bedloe; but in November he was unwise enough to return to his native land, was again arrested for debt, and again was consigned to the King's Bench Prison.

Here he had leisure to reflect on all the good advice given him by Dr Oates and his friends; here the tales of their past services, so valuable to the State and so profitable to themselves, returned to a mind attuned to meditation by his sad plight. The result of such meditation was a letter to the Dean of St Paul's, an old patron, informing that reverend gentleman that the writer had a Jacobite plot to disclose. The Dean refusing to take any notice, Fuller applied himself to an assembly which had shown itself refreshingly credulous in the past; he wrote to the House of Commons, which straightway ordered his release, and addressed the King for a pardon for him. His Majesty replied by granting the hopeful discoverer thirty shillings a day pension; and, evidently determined to profit by the expert advice of the First Discoverer of the Popish Plot, Fuller, nobly allowing bygones to be bygones, returned to lodge at the house of Dr Oates.

But by the spring of 1692, the young man's stories had grown so crude that even the Commons began to look upon him coldly, a fact which brought down upon his devoted head the wrath of his model and patron:

"When I was in [Oates's] House, he, and his Friend Tutchin, (whom he almost kept) with the rest of the Gang, prevailed with me to let them see a Copy of my information to the King, of the whole Plot; and when they had read it, they shook their Heads, blessing themselves, said, what pity it was, that so good a Plot should be so mangled and spoiled, and no better used. Godzooks, says the Dr, I would not be served so, you are a fool Fuller, and a Coxcomb, God's Life I could beat you for having no more Wit: Why I would go to Charles, and tell him his own, nay swear he was in the Popish Plot himself, only he knew not that part designed against his own Life, I made him afraid of me; and his Lords, Lotherdel [*sic*], and the rest, I called them Rogues to their Faces, but you are afraid to speak to them. At this kind of rate was I baited by him and his Crew, until to avoid them, I returned to my former Lodging over against him, for I could not bear his continual foul Language; besides, I had a good Pretence for this, for Mr Aaron Smith, seeing the Dr and I together one day, at a Tavern in the City, he fell a swearing at me, for being with the Dr in publick; Look you, Mr Fuller, the Dr is a good and an honest Man, he saved his Country, and deserves well from all good Men, but there be many at Court who hate him, and so they will you, if you keep him Company; besides, the Jacobites will say he tutors you . . . so you must leave off being seen publickly in his Company, or I shall complain of you to your damage. I was not sorry for all this; and tho' I left the Doctor's House, yet he would visit me frequently, as did his Retainers, until I began to be as great a Whig as the rest of them, being easily deceived by their specious Pretences and Professions of Vertue, of which too late I find, they had not one Grain."[29]

While thus engaged in giving advice to Fuller on a Jacobite "plot", Titus was assisting Mr Robert Ferguson in vilifying the Government, and even in dispensing copies of a proclamation by King James that his Queen was again with child, a proclamation intended to refute the Whig libel that Queen Mary had been for some years incapable of further child-bearing and therefore was not the mother of James, Prince of Wales. This Robert Ferguson, known as the Plotter, had been one of Shaftesbury's protégés, a notable Rye House conspirator, and the man who had drawn up Monmouth's absurd "Manifesto" on the eve of Sedgemoor. Oates must have come into frequent contact with him during the reign of Charles II, when Ferguson had been a most valuable tool of the Opposition, and the author of some of the most vicious pamphlets against the then Duke of York. Lack of any great reward at the Revolution had led him into temporarily changing his coat, and on May 5th, 1692, both he and Oates were examined "for reflecting on the government and dispersing king James letter about his queen being with child".[30] Ferguson was sent to Newgate charged with High Treason, but for some mysterious reason he was never brought to trial. Titus escaped scot-free.

But when, in November, William Fuller was tried and convicted as an impostor, cheat, and false accuser, the Government gave his reverend patron a strong hint to leave meddling with plots of all varieties. Titus's pension of ten pounds a week was reduced in this month to a miserable two.[31] Dr Oates himself, in a petition of much later date, says that it was so reduced from Lady-day, but the accounts in the Treasury Books contradict him; he enjoyed his full pension until July 21st at least.[32] In May of the following year, 1693, he was drawing but two hundred per annum; and, for a gentleman accustomed to keep a good table, and to the enjoyment of his friends' society at the coffee-houses (not to speak of the necessity to support his aged mother, if we are to believe his own statement to that effect), things were desperate indeed.

So in August, 1693, Titus took the plunge he had long resisted, sacrificed his freedom, and entered into the bonds of matrimony with a lady worth two thousand pounds.

(4)

This most unfortunate young woman (the application for the marriage licence gives her age as twenty-three),[33] was Miss Rebeccah Weld, the daughter of a wealthy draper of Bread Street, in the City. She was married "with the consent of her father" to the middle-aged Saviour of the Nation at St Mary Magdalen's, Old Fish Street, on August 17th.[34] The only detailed account of this match is the highly improper but exceedingly amusing squib, Tom Brown's *The Salamanca Wedding*. Whether Brown purposely misled his readers in calling the bride Margaret when her name was Rebeccah, and in describing her as a widow when she was actually a spinster, it is impossible to determine. In all probability the details he gives of the ceremony are equally erroneous, yet his pen is so lively that some of the less improper passages are well worth reproducing.

The squib purports to be a letter to a gentleman in the country, and is dated August 18th. "Sir, The only news of importance I have to communicate to you at present, is That the famous and never-to-be-forgotten Dr O——ts was married the beginning of this week." The writer then expresses his astonishment, in the frankest possible terms, that a man of Titus's unnatural habits should enter into matrimony. Brown goes on to say that perhaps "this was the surprising Revolution which most of our Almanacks both at home and abroad threatned us with in the month of August. I remember I happen'd to be at Garraway's, when a Gentleman came in, and told us the News. Immediately all other discourse ceased, East-India Actions, the price of Pepper, and rising of Currants; not a word of our Army in Flanders, or the Siege of Belgrade, the Turky Fleet, and the Battle of Landen were not mentioned in two hours after. Nay, the Duke of Savoy, who is now working miracles for us in Piedmont, was wholly laid aside. Every body stood amazed, and it was a considerable time before they could recover themselves out of this astonishment."

After speculating (in unprintable fashion) upon the reasons which had induced Dr Oates to marry so late in life, Brown goes on to describe the selection of the bride. "At last an Independent Minister advised him to Mrs Margaret W—— of Bread Street (whose former husband was a Muggletonian, and she continued of the same Persuasion) urging this Argument on her behalf, that . . . she being no Charmer, and consequently would not equip him with a pair of Horns, which she knew the [Dr] abominated, as being Marks of the Beast, and all together Popish. The D. liked the Proposal, and at the first interview, was so extremely smitten with the Gravity and Goodness of her Person, that he could neither Eat (which was much) nor Drink (which was more) till the business was concluded." Then we have some "marriage-articles", including a promise by Oates to hang up a picture of the Destruction of Sodom in his bed-chamber, and to teach his children to swear as soon as they could speak; and finally there is an account of the wedding itself:

"On the 17th of this present August the Dr was new Washed and Trimmed, with a large Sacerdotal Rose in his Hat, and all his other Clergy Equipage, came to the House of an Anabaptist Teacher in the City; where in the face of a numerous Assembly, consisting of all sorts, divisions, and sub-divisions of Protestants, he was married to Mrs Margaret W——. The Dr was observed to be very merry all Dinner time, and the largest part of his Face, meaning his Chin, moved notably. There stood right over against him a mighty Surloin of Beef, to which he shewed as little compassion, as he did to the Jesuits in the Reign of the Plot. . . . But Madam Salamanca (for so we must now call her) . . . looked very Disconsolate and Melancholy. One of the Sisterhood asked her why on a day of Rejoycing she expressed so much Sorrow in her looks? To which Madam O. after two or three deep sighs, answered, That she very much doubted (like the Staffordshire miller that mounted King Charles after Worcester Fight upon one of his sorry Horses) whether she should be able to bear the weight of the Saviour of three Nations."

For writing this scandalous lampoon, Brown was arrested in Cheapside on August 29th,[35] and on September 7th the Grand Jury of London found a true bill against him.[36] There seems to be no record of his trial. On September 15th, the new Mrs Oates was received at Court: "Dr Oates wife yesterday kist the queen's hand."[37]

A bare six months after his marriage with this heiress, Titus was again in a destitute condition. That he had run through two thousand (or as we should say, ten thousand) pounds in so short a time, when he was likewise enjoying his full pension of ten pounds a week again, almost looks as though he were being blackmailed. At all events, on the first day of March, 1694, he wrote to the President of the Council this brief and piteous note: "My Lord, what evill have I done the King, yt I am thus severly used. I have a Peticon that lyes before the Councell six months and cannot gett it read. I beseech Yr Lpp to obtein the favour that it may now be read and answered yt I may not perish in Prison for debt and that I may not starve for want of bread. I am Yor Lpp's humble Servt, Titus Oates." At the foot of this appeal is the following memorandum: "5 times presented to K. by Ld President and enclosed returned for answer."[38]

Two months later things were even worse. On May 14th, Titus wrote to Sir William Trumbell, principal Secretary of State:

"RT HONBLE SIR

"Was not my condition so deplorable as tongue cannot express it I would not at this time have given you the trouble of this Scribble and if I should tell you Sir the particulars of my case you would not believe mee but let truth bee spoken and reason in the first place. Sr I protest I have been so long oppressed that I have not one whole shirt to my back wch I never wanted in K. James his reigne. I have not one shilling to buy my poor Wife and family bread. I am in debt 508 *li*. and must the latter end of this month go to prison for the same and I have not a Bushell of Coles in the house to dress a little meat wn God shall send it. I have not bought a ragge of clothes these 4 years and those I have are very [word illegible] and threadbare. Sr I am a gentleman that hath been a long sufferer and had not the mallicious counsell of Sr Edward Seymour taken place I should not need to have told you this sad story. I am sure if his Matie were made sensible of my condition hee would not thus leave me to perish. I beg of your Honr upon my knees to lay my sad condition before the king this day. I have not a whole pair of stockins to put on and onely one pair of shoes wch a shomaker lett me have of much pitty. My spts [spirits] are sunk to death. I will say no more but tell your Honr that there is no poor wretch you [word illegible] is in so miserable a condition as I am at this time but above all I have a Hogr [?] of Bailiffs pursuing me which hath put my poore wife into such frights that have occasioned the death of two children.

"I am Rt Honble
"Your Honrs humble Servt
"TITUS OATES.

"in a few days time I shall have all my goods distrained for ten pounds I ow for a years rent that I keepe my poor aged mother who I am obliged to maintaine."[39]

Towards the end of July, the King gave him one hundred pounds:[40] but this did not satisfy Titus. Like Oliver Twist, he asked for more, regularly petitioning the King, and complaining bitterly of his sad condition, the hard winters, his aged mother, and so on. He was for ever requesting advances on his pension, and sometimes managed to get the full pension as well, though at other times he was not so lucky. "July 10 [1695]. Forenoon. [My lords order] Mr Tailor to pay Dr Oates 150 *l.*, but to tell him it must be in part allowance of 200 *l. per an.* and must be defalked therefrom by degrees."[41] By this it would seem that, for some reason unknown to us, his pension had again been reduced.

In June of 1695, William Fuller was released from prison, and renewed his acquaintance with Titus. He now had an allowance from Mr Charles Herbert (who possibly was his father), and could live in modest comfort again; to supplement this income, he set to work to libel the exiled King and his family in pamphlets, a safe and profitable hobby in which he was ably assisted by Oates. Especially did he revive the old Warming Pan story, the tale of a suppositious Prince of Wales, adding new and spicy details. Despite several spells of imprisonment for debt, this game served him well on the whole for a number of years, his pamphlets being "improved" by the more expert pen of John Dunton.

Towards the end of 1695 there is what may be the first hint that Titus was again meditating a change of religion. On the other hand, it may have been nothing more than that hasty temper of his which caused him to strike a Mr Green, chaplain to the Archbishop of Canterbury.[42]

(5)

By the summer of 1696, Dr Titus Oates had decided definitely that he would seek a new spiritual home. The Church of England had shown a most shocking lack of gratitude towards this stout champion of hers; where he had looked for a bishopric at least, she had given him absolutely nothing, and he was quite disgusted with her. There remained the Dissenters; and here at least was a more hopeful field of activity, for the Dissenters were favoured by King William, himself at heart a Puritan, and Titus had many friends among these people. Out of the large number of sects in existence at the time, he chose, not unnaturally the one in which his father had been a burning and a shining light, though it had shortened its name and become more respectable. The tale of his approach, initial rebuffs, and final reception into the Baptist fold is told in a contemporary tract, *A New Discovery of Titus Oates*, quoted at large by Crosby in his *History of the Baptists*. The original tract, written in 1701, informs its readers in a postscript that "nothing contained in these Papers, is any ways design'd to lessen the credit of the true Popish Plot"; Crosby only mentions the affair in order to exonerate his sect from the folly of admitting Oates, and to show the caution it displayed before it would do so. Neither writer, therefore, can be numbered among the opponents of the Popish Plot and its managers.

Some time in June, 1696, a conference took place between Titus and a deputation from a Baptist congregation, in order that the latter might discover from the former his motives in seeking to change his religion. On July 7th, a deacon, one Brother Burroughs, wrote to Titus, telling him that, while the conference had been satisfactory so far as it went, the brethren would like Oates to give them an account in writing of his "grievous apostacy", re-conversion, and the present state of his soul. Titus replied on the 24th; it is interesting to note the contrast in style between this and subsequent letters to the brethren, and his begging letters to the Government. With the Baptists he is pious, unctuous, and slightly patronizing; "Dearly beloved Brethren", he begins; and ends: "Brethren, the

Grace of our Lord Jesus Christ be with you all, Amen. I am your affectionate Brother in our dearest Redeemer, Titus Oates."

Some long while ago, says Oates in this first letter, he had held debate with a certain Brother Lamb with a view to seeking re-admittance to his father's sect. (The original Brother Lamb, of Bell Alley, Coleman Street, at whose conventicle Samuel Oates had disputed and held forth in the good old days, had died in 1672,[43] but as he had had eight children, the "brother" to whom Oates was referring may have been one of the young Lambs.) Soon after Titus had approached him in the manner aforesaid, this Brother Lamb likewise had been gathered to his fathers, and "so the matter fell: for I then knew none, or very few of the Church, excepting our Sister T——, and old Sister M——". As for the state of his soul, if his friends could behold it through the fleshly screen they would find it "as sincere as becomes a Man that professeth the Gospel of Christ". There might be, however, one minor difficulty. "I know, my Beloved, there is one thing that may give you great offence, and that is my Habit, which I must by no means leave off: It will neither be safe for me, nor of any advantage to the Church of Christ . . . you being satisfied that I may walk as becomes a Minister of the Gospel amongst you, I trust you will not refuse me for this or that sort of Garb." The Brethren must have been taken aback by so odd and unusual a condition; but, in fact, the explanation was a very simple one. Titus Oates, D.D., in his silk gown and scarf, was a national figure; and a national figure he was determined to remain to the end of his days.

His next letter is dated September 14th. He had met the brethren the previous day for another conference, "and although I knew the faces but of a few of you, yet I love you in the truth, even for the sake of that truth, that dwelleth in my Soul". He trusts in future to be a comfort to the sect "from which I have withdrawn my self these twenty Seven Years". (His arithmetic was a little faulty; he had been withdrawn by his father in 1660.) But he must make it plain that he cannot possibly agree to print, or allow to be printed, anything about his original apostacy; to do that "I must tell you will by no means be convenient:

and that for this one unanswerable reason, because the great adversaries that I have may construe it a receding from my Testimony and certainly will expound it so; which I am sure will tend highly to the Dishonour of God and the publick Truth, in which I have been engaged, and for which I have so severely suffered, and of this I am sure great care must be taken". As for his turning Papist, he had already explained, on more than one occasion, that he did it only that he might "the better be enabled to see and understand the bottom of that Design". He is a little hurt by their not immediately and without question welcoming him into their fold; the late Brother Lamb had been ready to do it, and if there really were any difficulties at present "it is high time I knew them", so that they might all partake of Communion together in the same spirit "as the Church had when the Blessed Apostle Paul was joyned to the Church at Jerusalem". He prays for wisdom for them in making their momentous decision, and concludes: "The Grace of our Lord Jesus Christ be with all those that love him in sincerity. I am, Your Affectionate Brother and Servant, whose Soul longeth after you, Titus Oates."

On October 3rd he writes in haste to correct an error. Encountering a Sister D—— at the Admiralty Office, he has learned from her that "a certain Woman" has told them that he designs to attend some other meeting-house than theirs in Virginia Street. This is untrue; it is only that "in the case of bad Weather, I would go to the Meeting at Covent-Garden. . . . I do declare to you, though you are at a distance from me, if it be the Will of the Lord that I may sit down with you, that I shall not seek for any other resting Place, but will walk in close Communion with you as long as I live: therefore let that be no hindrance." But on the same day he writes to Brother Burroughs (his "Beloved Brother B."), that he begins to doubt whether they have any serious intention of admitting him; "if the next time you break Bread I sit not down with you, I shall esteem it a final rejection". He again laments the loss of "my dear Lamb", who, he adds with what seems to have been unconscious humour, "knew how to bring home a strayed Sheep in the Spirit of Meekness and Love".

These letters are described by Crosby as being "full of

seeming sincerity and sanctity, and earnest pressing desires".[44] Nevertheless, the brethren seem to have suspected that a wolf might lurk beneath this strayed sheep's canonical garb, for they still delayed, conferred, evaded, and questioned, the while Titus's holy impatience moved him to write them almost daily. He trusts they have the Lord before their eyes in their debates about him; for his part, he is "willing to do any thing that may give you the satisfaction that becomes a Person that hath been for many Years on the public Stage of the World". He is so upset by their constant delays, that "on the Lords Day at Night I thought I should have died with the very anguish of my Soul". A Mr A. (who may have been John Arnold) has hinted to him that the reason why they will not receive him is because he has been heard to swear and to talk obscenely at table.

For the first, "unless it were before a Magistrate, I never swore in my Life; but I may have repeated other Men's Oaths in my Discourse of them. For the talking obscenely, I protest, in the Presence of God, it is a Lye." If the whole accusation could be thoroughly investigated, it "would prove neither better nor worse than a Trick to keep me from the ways of the Lord". He tells Brother Burroughs that he has written a final letter to the brethren, "and will conclude with that of the Disciples when they could not prevail with Paul not to go up to Jerusalem, they ceased their Requests, and said, The Will of the Lord be done".

(6)

In intervals of this pious correspondence, Titus was writing some more tracts. *The Picture of the Late King James*, which appeared in May, 1696, was dedicated, in a letter of great length, to King William; the author's statement that "to discant on the Misfortunes of a Person that is fallen from so high a Dignity, and is reduced to a state that is next to Death, is neither a thing that I coveted or designed", is contradicted by the obvious relish with which he abuses James in the text. Among other crimes, he accuses him of attempting to poison his brother at the Restoration, and of succeeding in doing so in 1685. He implies that either

Charles or James poisoned their sister Henrietta; and he is careful to be as insulting as possible to the wives of both these monarchs. Of Catherine of Braganza he says that "what she wanted in Understanding to be a Counsellor, she had made up to her, in the blessed Gifts of Malice, and Treason, and Revenge, which she exercised to the utmost"; Mary of Modena is "your Italian pugg". Naturally, a large part of the tract is devoted to yet another account of Titus's sufferings, a gentle hint, perhaps, to the royal dedicatee. Nor does it seem to have been altogether wasted; several sums were advanced to him on account of his pension this year.[45]

The second part of the same work appeared in the autumn, from which a single quotation, the author addressing his subject, will suffice: "Well, Sir, you may wipe your Face, for I suppose by this time you are got into a fine breathing Sweat. And what think you of all this? Are you not as black as Hell, tho the Prince of Orange, our present King, had not said one word to blacken you? But there is yet more Matter behind, that will shew you in your true Dress: But its time you go and acquaint my old Landlady, your Italian yoke-fellow, with what I have said; and it's high time for me to forbear raking your stinking Kennel, for it even turns my Stomach."

Sixteen ninety-six witnessed the publication of one more of Titus's works, though this appeared anonymously, *A Tragedy called the Popish Plot Reviv'd*. The "Plot" in question is "The Secret League between the late King James and the French King, The Popish Conspiracy to Murder His Present Majesty King William, And the wicked Contrivance for adulterating the Coin of the Kingdom: With many other Hellish Practices"; but the pamphlet is, in fact, vague upon all these conspiracies, and for the most part concerns itself with a re-telling of Oates's own trial, a "brief extract" from his original *Narrative*, a tedious something he calls his "Further Narrative", and a collection of letters he claims to have written to Charles II and his brother, all tending to display Titus's "undaunted, and never to be shaken stedfastness in adhering to and avowing the Truth of his Discovery, his plain Dealing with those Princes, his gallant Resistance of the highest Temptations, and his just Regard to the Interest and Rights of his Countrey".

There can be no doubt that the majority of these letters are spurious. One cannot seriously imagine Titus presenting Charles II, in the November of 1678, with the following piece of insolence: "For your Majesty knows that to be true, that you were reconciled to the Church of Rome, by Father Richard Huddliston, that was Uncle to John Huddliston, who is excepted in all your Majesty's Proclamations that are issued out against Papists and Priests. And also, 'tis not unknown to some, that your Majesty receiv'd the Sacrament according to the Usage of the Church of Rome, in the Dutchess of Portsmouth's Lodgings, by the Hands of Father Ireland, and I my self served then at Mass; which I have not made publick, because I would preserve your Majesty's Reputation."

In the following year there appeared a very mild counterblast to Oates's tract *The Picture of the late King James*. Whoever was the author was at pains to inform his readers that this, *The Picture of Titus Oates, D.D.*, was written and published by those who "are true and unshaken Friends to the present Government; and as real Abhorrers and Detestors both of the Romish Superstition and Interest, as the deepest Gall of even Titus his Pen can write himself". The writer concurs in much of Titus's criticism of the last two reigns, "But, Sir, in all the true Strokes you have made in the Picture, you have notoriously flatter'd the Painter. For in drawing of King James and his Brother, both at full Length, you have here and there dasht in some few Lineaments of your own, *viz*. Your Virtues, Innocence, Services to the Nation; together with a lamentable outcry of Wrongs, Oppressions, Suffering for Faith and a good Conscience, and what not; when there are Thousands in the World, that believe not one of these Qualifications, Graces, Merits, Pretensions or Titles, belong to you." Titus had chosen to publish his tract anonymously; but "Truly, Doctor, to do you Right, I believe the whole Draught (by a peculiar bold stroke all the way throughout it, *viz*. of Railing and Beroguing at every shadow and Dash of your Quill) to be truly your own. That singular Master-Touch of yours is so conspicuous all through the Rough Painting, that without the Subscription of your Name, every common Eye may find whose Pencil-Work 'tis; for he that reads but Three Pages, may plainly see the *Delineavit Titus*."

Titus could afford to ignore such carping critics, for his own endless petitions to King William were bearing fruit. Sums varying from forty shillings to fifty pounds were being paid him at frequent intervals from the public purse,[46] and he was not without hope of obtaining something more substantial from a monarch who owed him so much.[47] Buoyed up with these hopes, he continued to take the keenest interest in public affairs. "A small book has been published here", wrote J. Vernon to Sir Joseph Williamson, "inveighing against the standing Army, which is now the most debated argument, and Dr Oats has lately written to the Duke of Bolton in these terms (as is said and believed):—The Court Whigs have a mind to keep an army of 30,000 men, to enslave the nation, but I hope those two rogues, Seymor and Musgrove, who never did a good thing, will oppose the motion and save the nation."[48]

(7)

But what of the Baptists all this time? It must not be imagained that either literary labours or preoccupation with the sordid question of his income would cause Titus to forget the care of his soul. The fact that no letters to the brethren survive between October 13th, 1696, and March 6th, 1697, can be explained, perhaps, by the spate of authorship then occupying him; at all events, on the latter date we find him still clamouring for admittance, still lamenting the loss of his dear Lamb, who with tears had implored him to come in, and now alas! the door is shut, still imploring Brother Burroughs to ensure that, instead of mourning with the turtle, his latter days be made comfortable.

There follows an even longer interval of silence; the next letter is dated July 26th, 1698. It is not unlikely that part of this time was spent by Titus in prison, for in one of his petitions to the King he says he has been arrested for debt, and speaks of other creditors threatening him. On July 26th he wrote two letters, one to the brethren in general, reminding them of all the past conferences and correspondence, and of how, on November 10th, 1696, at a church meeting, he was told that he must exercise patience a little while longer. He has now exercised it for some twenty months, and obviously it is growing a little thin. The other letter is to Brother Burroughs. It has come to Titus's ears that the reason for all this delay in admitting him is because Brother Burroughs and another have been against it from the first (Titus stored up this rumour in his malicious and retentive memory, as will be seen). He makes, therefore, a personal appeal to Brother Burroughs; and he adds that he has some good news. If by any chance his debts have been a hindrance to his admittance, the brethren need hesitate no longer, for the King has now granted "to me and my poor wife" a pension of three hundred pounds per annum for ninety-nine years "if we both or either of us so long shall live", and five hundred pounds to pay his debts.

For once he spoke the truth. Throughout the early part of this year of 1698, sums amounting to one hundred and ten pounds had been paid him by the Treasury, but only on account of his pension; this unsatisfactory state of affairs terminated on July 15th, when Titus was called before the Commissioners and informed "that pursuant to the King's commands he is to have 500 *l.* to pay his debts and 300 *l.* per an. from midsummer last during his life and his wife's life out of the revenue of the Post Office; and he is to expect no more out of secret service money. Ordered that the said pension commence from Lady day last."[49] *The Post Boy* made the good news known to the public in its issue of July 30th to August 2nd, and Luttrell duly noted it in his *Brief Relation*. Not only this, but late in August, Titus prevailed with his father-in-law, John Weld, to buy from him, for the sum of one hundred pounds, a piece of ground in the City; the wording of the deed of sale (now in the Bodleian) inclines one to the belief that this ground had formed part of Mrs Titus Oates's dowry. Thus was Titus in comparative affluence once more.

Either the improvement of his financial condition overcame the brethren's scruples, or else, as Crosby puts it, "the seeming sincerity of his religious protestations, not only contained in so many letters, but also in his daily converse with them, in the end gave them some hopes of his integrity and true reformation";[50] in any case, in this late summer of 1698, the strayed sheep was received back into that fold of which his father had been, so to speak, a bellwether.

For a time, all went well; "his visible Sobriety and Moderation" greatly impressed the congregation, and in a few short months he was even accepted as a preacher among them. The imagination boggles at the extraordinary spectacle of this man, wearing the canonical garb of the Church of England, claiming a degree bestowed by a Catholic University, and holding forth in a Baptist meeting-house. But there can be no doubt that he was a popular preacher. Succulent tales of Romish abominations, of which he had been an eyewitness, enlivened his sermons; and, sober and moderate as he may have appeared, he had not by any means discarded the habit of boasting which had distinguished him in youth. As he had informed his fellow students at Valladolid and St Omers of the great preferments he had sacrificed for the sake of the Catholic faith, so now he regaled his Baptist friends with tales of even greater temptations offered him in order to keep him in the Church of England once he had found his way back to her in '78; "he might have had a Bishoprick twenty times, but his Conscience would not give him leave to accept of it; particularly his Majesty once offer'd him a Bishoprick then vacant; to which the Dr made answer in these express words as an excuse for his Refusal; viz. He could not hold Communion with Belial, and Fellowship with Devils". In fact "the very Door of the House of Lords no less than twenty times opened for his Entrance, and the Drs disdainful Backside as often turned upon it".[51]

On the other hand, the Pope had wanted to make him a cardinal, and on Titus's visiting Rome, had begged him to sit at his right hand, so great a fancy had his Holiness taken to "the sweet Face of little Ambrose". But neither kings nor popes had succeeded in seducing this free spirit; coming one day "to make a civil Visit to the Pope, he happen'd to see Six Men, in grey Hats standing at a Stair-Head, in the Pallace, not far from the Popes Apartment, ready to be consecrated Bishops; and truly receiving some dislike against their Persons, and some other small Disgust, he pickt a Quarrel with them and kickt four of them down stairs".[52]

Thus happily and harmoniously did Dr Oates and his Baptist friends dwell together; until the fatal day arrived when the wolf threw aside the sheep's clothing, and disclosed his true character in the really shocking affair which may be called The Case of the Rich Old Lady.

(8)

In the month of June, in the year 1688, one Hester, widow of Mr Thomas Moore, had married a Mr Anthony Parker. She was not young, but she was rich; and very shortly after her second marriage she began to suspect that Parker had married her for her money, for he was "a Person not answerable in Fortune to hers". On the advice of her friends, therefore, she settled a certain sum of money on her husband, reserving her right to leave the bulk of her fortune elsewhere. This so infuriated Parker that he began to ill-treat her, with the result that she separated from him.[53] Now, Mrs Hester Parker was a member of the Baptist congregation honoured by the presence of Dr Oates, a congregation to which he was wont to hold forth "to the great Satisfaction of his Auditors", as was still occasionally reported in the news-sheets.[54]

Titus, who should have been wary of the very name of Parker, was anxious to become better acquainted with the rich old lady, and prevailed with a mutual friend to get him invited to her dinner-table; but for some strange reason Mrs Parker took a dislike to him, going so far as to vow that he should never enter her house again. In the October of 1699, the old lady fell sick, and, fearing that her end was near, sent for her lawyer and altered her will, for the near relation to whom she had left the bulk of her fortune was recently dead. In this new will, "after the Disposal of some Considerable Legacies, she constituted two intimate Friends, both Members of her own Communion, her joynt Executors, bequeathing the rest of her Estate to be equally divided between them, dying three days after; and possest at her Death of her whole Effects, including three Hundred Pounds Debts whether good or bad, according to due and legal Estimate and Examination made, of about 1200 *l*."[55] One of these fortunate executors was a Brother Reynolds; the other was no less a person than Brother Burroughs, Titus's own "Beloved Brother B."

Dr and Mrs Oates were not invited to the funeral; obviously, the late Mrs Parker's friends would have thought it indecent to have invited a man so much disliked by the deceased. There then arose the question of the funeral sermon, in those days a most important ceremony, usually preached on the Sunday following the burial. "The heads of the Church appointed a minister, much esteemed by the deceased, to preach her funeral sermon. He waited on the doctor [Oates], who seemed very well pleased, and readily gave his assent to the choice; but to the surprise of the congregation, on the Lord's day, the doctor got into the pulpit half an hour before the usual time, on purpose to prevent the intended funeral sermon."[56] This was Titus's delicate way of intimating his displeasure at not being invited to the funeral or given a mourning-ring.

The scene must have been almost farcical. Here was Dr Oates, in all the glory of his Church of England garb, popping up in the pulpit half an hour before sermon-time, and preaching to his dismayed auditors "on a general Discourse, without the least Syllable or mention made of the Deceased". There was nothing to be done about it at the moment, short of removing the preacher by force, so the congregation "submitted to the rudeness and obstinacy of the doctor, and appointed the funeral sermon to be preached next Sunday following". This so enraged Titus "that with much passion, and unbecoming words, he told the officers of the church, that from that day forwards, he would never preach more amongst them. In answer to which, they told him, that they would take him at his word; for the church had made an entry in their church-book, that he never should preach more amongst them. From this unexpected answer, joined with the aforementioned resentments, we may presume the doctor premeditated revenge."[57]

We may indeed presume so. Never yet had Titus let the most trifling insult pass unavenged; and an affront of this magnitude stirred to the depths that old savage malice of his. His first retort was deceptively petty. At his admittance to this Baptist congregation, he had presented it with a pulpit-cloth, table-cloth, and cushion, which were worth, by his calculation, fifteen or sixteen pounds. He now sent a messenger demanding the immediate return of these gifts, which accordingly were sent back to him. But this was only a warning growl; the bite itself was to follow.

For three or four months Titus kept away from the meeting-house, and it is possible that it was during this period that he frequented the Baptist conventicle at Westminster, of which Calamy was afterwards minister.[58] But he had not forgotten his former brethren in Virginia Street. He was busy insinuating himself into the confidence of the very disgruntled widower, Anthony Parker, and it was not long before he had persuaded that gentleman that, by insisting that his late wife was *non compos mentis* when she had drawn up the will, he might be able to get it set aside in his favour. Encouraged by his energetic and reverend friend, Mr Parker had the case brought up in Doctors Commons; and, largely through the testimony of Dr Oates, obtained a verdict invalidating the will. The two executors, Brothers Reynolds and Burroughs, naturally dismayed at finding their lawful inheritance thus snatched from under their noses, appealed against the verdict, and the case was removed to the Court of Arches for a new hearing.

It was at this precise moment (in February, 1700), that Dr Oates suddenly reappeared in Virginia Street, bearing with him his pulpit-cloth, table-cloth, and cushion. He professed himself distressed beyond measure at the return of his gift; it was his wife, not he, he said, who had demanded it back. He would have returned them to the congregation himself, the very next day, had it not rained. A member of the congregation had the bad taste to enquire whether it had rained for three or four months on end,[59] but Titus was not to be put out of temper. He was penitent; he was bewildered; he was hurt; he applied himself to the church officers, desiring to know wherein he had offended them. In a word, he was the old plausible Titus, the dog who knew so well how to wag his tail at the right moment. Nor had he lost the art. When he entreated his beloved Brother B. to explain to him the whole case of the contested will, "as imagining he might have received it before from the Adverse Party delivered a little too favourably on his own side", Brother B. wasted no time enquiring into the reasons for this volte-face, but poured forth into that sympathetic ear the tale of his grievances. When it was ended, Titus went into raptures of joy at hearing the truth at last, following this up by torrents of grief at the thought of the injustice done to his dearest Brother. After a good deal of this, he lapsed into horror at the idea of so much good Christian money being wasted in arguing the case in the Court of Arches, that "vile remains of Popery", presided over by a "damned Crew of Rogues and Rascals".

What, then, enquired simple Brother B., should he and his co-executor do? The remedy, replied Titus, was both cheap and easy. Let them appoint some good Christian Brother as an arbiter, and so save their labour and their money. In other words, let them submit their case to the judgment of Dr Titus Oates.

Brother Burroughs was simple, but not quite so simple as all that. He argued, evaded, demurred, and, driven into a corner by Titus's eloquence, insisted on certain conditions. There must be two arbiters, of whom Oates could be one; and there must be no lawyers present, "for that if they left the Law, they would not be concerned with Lawyers".[60] But Titus was one too many for his beloved Brother B., even in such reasonable conditions. He objected vehemently against each proposed fellow arbiter, till at last he "made a shift to shuffle the whole Arbitration into his hands"; and when, bonds being sealed, both parties in the case appeared at his house with their witnesses, the executors were dismayed to find their opponent, Mr Parker, backed by three lawyers, Porter, Lovell, and Jeffreys, who "rudely behaved themselves against the Respondents and their Witnesses, but palliated the manifest Contradictions of the Appellant's Witnesses".[61] Finally, Dr Oates announced that he would, after due consideration, inform them of the award.

His due consideration took him fifteen days ("not but half Fifteen minutes would have done the Business as well, considering how little the Award had any Relation to the Matters discuss'd by the Witnesses"), and at the end of that time he pronounced sentence as follows: "That the Executors the First day of the then Term shall stand obliged to pay 1500 *l.* at the Drs own House, for the Use of the Husband [*sic*]; and also to give up all the other Effects already in their Hands, Bonds, Bills, Chattels, Moneys: Sum total, all the Husbands."[62] Not, of course, quite all; in view of Titus's efforts on behalf of Anthony Parker, the former was fully entitled to half the booty.

"The Dreadful Thunderstroke of paying 1500 *l.* more than ever they received, besides 300 *l.* more Laid out for funeral Charges and on the Estate, gave no little Shock. . . . But . . . the Drs all inexorable: He makes 'em a short Answer: Rest themselves contented. He'll stand and fall by his Award."[63] But Brothers Burroughs and Reynolds were by no means inclined to rest contented. Now thoroughly disillusioned about Dr Titus Oates, they exhibited a bill in Chancery for relief against the award, and expressed themselves as determined to fight it to the last gasp. Faced with a situation which threatened to become awkward, Titus fell back on an old game. His memory suddenly improved; he recalled that the deceased herself, but a fortnight prior to her death, had acquainted him with the fact that Brother Burroughs had above two thousand pounds of hers in his hands, and, in proof thereof, she had shown him two bonds, the one for fifteen hundred pounds, the other for five hundred.[64]

This was indeed the old Titus; but alas! times had changed. The patents, the commissions, the letters which had caused the deaths of so many innocents during the Popish Terror had been accepted on Titus's bare word; the two bonds must be produced; and they appeared not. On the other side, the executors were able to bring witnesses who testified to the late Mrs Parker's extreme dislike of Oates, and who swore that, at the very time when he was begging Burroughs and Reynolds to leave the matter to his arbitration, "he declared in other company, that he was angry with them for not inviting him or his wife to the funeral, and for preventing his preaching the funeral sermon, and putting a boy over his head, who had been a doctor in divinity twenty years".[65]

"It was likewise proved, that soon after the affair was committed to his arbitration, he said, with an air of joy and triumph, to two gentlemen of the executors' acquaintance, that he had then a rod in his hands, with which he would scourge the person above-mentioned [Burroughs] (whom in his letters he had called his dear friend) that he would swinge him with it, and when he had worn it to the stumps, he would lay it by; that before he had done with him, he would ruin him, and make him fly his country, and not leave him worth a shilling. And being told that he ought not to seek revenge, but leave it to God, he replied, that vengeance was indeed God's sweet morsel, which he kept to himself; but that he was often long before he executed his vengeance; and that when the Jews refused St Paul, he turned to the Gentiles. To which being answered, that though St Paul did turn to the Gentiles, yet he did not wage war with the Jews; he replied, that tho' Paul's teeth were grown, his nails were not. And further it was proved, that in discourse after the award, Oates declared there never was any reconciliation between himself and that executor; that though he went to the same meeting with him, he had an end in that; and that he believed he had done his business."[66]

In November, 1701, the award was, by a decree in Chancery, condemned and set aside as "revengeful and partial"; and Dr Titus Oates himself was spewed out of the Baptist fold.

(9)

The years which had witnessed this lamentable affair were otherwise uneventful so far as Oates was concerned; only an occasional notice of him shows that he was not entirely forgotten by the people who once had hailed him as the Saviour of the Nation.

In September, 1699, Luttrell notes: "One Edwards, a printer, is to be tryed this sessions at the Old Baily, for printing a dialogue between Dr Oates and Collonel Porter, wherein are many atheistical expressions, and ridiculing the late conspiracy."[67] In the same year was published a sermon, supposed to have been preached by Oates at Wapping, but it is obviously a squib, and the text, "Faith is the evidence of things not seen", is used by the writer as a satire on Oates's past. From this text, Titus is made to draw four propositions: "First, That Faith is an Evidence. Secondly,

If Faith is an Evidence, that an Evidence consequently ought to be believed. Thirdly, That there are many things talked off [*sic*] in the world, that were never seen. Fourthly and lastly, That an Evidence and through him any Nation, may, nay ought to believe in things not seen." This "Sermon" has a cut of Titus in the pillory, on the title-page, and must have hurt the poor doctor's feelings not a little.

In the following year, 1700, *The London Post* reported that the "nunnery" at Hammersmith, once raided by Titus and his armed servants, had at last been suppressed, notwithstanding the petitions of some of the local inhabitants, who protested that "the Nunnery was no such thing as represented, but only a School to breed up Gentlemens Children, and that the putting down thereof, would be very prejudicial to the Neighbourhood, who get a good Livelyhood by them, but this availed them nothing".[68] This news-sheet, in its issue for December 21st-24th, advertised a new set of playing-cards, wherein was "the Memory of the Popish Plot revived, in a lively representation of the several particulars relating to that horrid piece of villany".

This year of 1700 witnessed a happy event in the Oates family. On October 3rd, there was baptized at St Margaret's, Westminster, Rebecca Crisp Oates, Titus's daughter and destined to be his only legitimate child.[69] According to a pamphleteer, "the Doctor's Lady is a High Episcopal", and when the time arrived for christening the infant, "the Doctor sent one Day for an Elder of the Baptists to give it the Customary Benediction according to his own Church, and the next Day sent for a Minister of the Church of England, and with all suitable Ceremony Christen'd it a Member likewise of his Spouses Communion".[70]

In December Titus lost an old friend, Sir George Treby, latterly Lord Chief Justice of the Common Pleas; and in the same month *The Post Boy* published a malicious advertisement concerning another of Oates's former cronies. "The late famous William Fuller, by Original a Butcher's Son of Kent, by Education a Coney-Wooll-Cutter, by Inclination an Evidence, by Vote of Parliament an Imposter, by Title (of his own dubbing), a Colonel, is now removed from his Walks in the Verge of White-hall to the Rules of the Poultry Compter, at the Grocers-Arms, where he may be seen for a Three-half-Penny Pot of Ale." A paper warfare continued to be waged between the Tory *Post Boy* and the Whig *Flying Post* anent the true character of Fuller; in December, 1701, it was demanded of Fuller that he prove certain statements he had made in his *Original Letters of the Late King James*, in which he had implicated some of the leading lights of the Government in Jacobite plots; he failed to do so; and in the following May, was sentenced to pay one thousand marks, to be whipped at Bridewell, thrice pilloried, and kept at hard labour till he could produce his fine. Not being able to do so, he remained in prison till his death in 1720, representing himself, perhaps with justice, as the tool of John Tutchin and Titus Oates.

Soon after Titus's expulsion from the Baptist fold, there was published the tract, mentioned above, which contains an account of his dealings with that sect, *A New Discovery of Titus Oates etc*. An exposure so damaging to his reputation could not but be resented by Titus, and from the following advertisement it would seem that he meditated a counterblast: "The beginning of next Week will be publish'd, The History of the Five last past Years of Dr Oats's Life, wherein the Calumnies and Aspersions of a certain Dissenting Party are entirely wiped off, and the Doctor's Veracity, Virtue, Integrity, and Innocence fully clear'd and Vindicated." Unfortunately for his biographer, this "history" either was never published at all or has not survived.

In 1702, Titus was again in trouble connected with an old lady. This Mrs Eleanor James was a printer's widow; she was eccentric, and had written several crazy tracts. Dryden had paid her the compliment of mentioning her in his Preface to the second edition of *The Hind and the Panther*, and she was well known in London as a harmless crank, for it was her boast that she had catechized no less than five successive sovereigns on the subject of their eternal salvation. Upon more than one occasion, Mrs James had been affronted by hearing Dr Oates vilify religion in general and the Church of England (of which she was a devoted daughter) in particular; and at last, meeting him one day in the Court of Requests, she took advantage of the encounter to enquire of him why, being an Anabaptist, he presumed to wear the canonical habit. Titus straightway lost his temper, lifted his cane, and struck her "in a violent and riotous manner" on the head. He was going on to repeat this performance when he was prevented by the bystanders.

On Thursday, July 2nd, he was brought before the Quarter Sessions in Westminster Hall on a charge of "assaulting and scandalising" the said Mrs James, and, being convicted, was ordered to pay a considerable fine. But "upon the doctor's acknowledging the crime, and promising to refrain from such like scandals for the future, and withal acknowledging he was above a thousand pounds in debt, and consequently incapable to pay a large fine, but must be obliged to lie in prison all his life for its payment; and upon his engaging that he would never affront, scandalise, or assault Mrs Eleanor James, or any other person whatsoever, in the like nature any more, he was only fined six marks and dismissed the court, but not without a severe check for acting so irreverently and unbecoming his profession".[71]

Mrs James petitioned the House of Lords (apparently without result) that Titus should be forbidden to wear his canonical garb, that his cane be burnt, and his pension reduced to £300, the remainder to be given to "poor ministers widows". This brings us to the vexed question of his pension in general. We have seen that, in 1698, William III granted him £300 a year for life out of the Post Office; yet in July, 1702, Mrs James asks that it be reduced to that sum. Most writers have assumed that Oates enjoyed his pension to the end of his days, but there is no mention of his name in the Treasury Papers of the reign of Queen Anne, and Ailesbury states that, when Anne ascended the throne in March, 1702, she stopped his pension altogether. "Since Oats' time, when false evidences swarmed, this reign [William III's] exceeded that if possible, and the Secretary's Office swarmed with them, because the hungrey Dutch aspired to all our estates, the rich as well as the poor ones . . . on the death of her [Queen Anne's] brother-in-law, those rogues were all kicked out of doors, Oats' pension taken from him . . . and one given to that honest Platt that saved her father's life at Feversham by receiving a blow on his arm which might have knocked the King her father down."[72] "I may mistake, but I have an idea of what follows, that the Queen on looking over the pensions erased out the names of Titus Oats and George Porter. . . ."[73] Ailesbury's remarks, taken in conjunction with the absence of Oates's name from the Treasury Papers of the reign, argue the strong probability that, some years before his death, Titus ceased to enjoy a royal pension.

In the year 1703 there is a last appearance of brother Samuel Oates. He petitioned for either employment or superannuation, and added a brief statement of his case. He had served, he said, forty-five years in the Navy, was on board the fleet which brought King Charles II home in 1660, received several wounds which had now grown grievous with advancing years, and by reason of his lameness had been forced to lay down his commission in the *Edgar*. But he was now able and willing to serve, though he feared the anger of the Prince Consort's Council, because of his having resigned his commission. He added that he had four sons in the Navy, two in the West Indies, one in the East Indies, who was cast away in the *Harwich* frigate "at China", and one serving in the *Triumph*. The petition was referred to Prince George's Council, but history is silent as to poor old brother Samuel's fate.

At the end of the year 1704, Titus Oates heard news which must have pleased him. On Monday, December 11th, there died, in the eighty-eighth year of his age, the great exposer of the Plot hoax, the man with a pen like a rapier, Sir Roger L'Estrange. But Titus had little time left for gloating on the departure of old enemies; for his own end was upon him, suddenly, while yet in middle life.

(10)

Long, long ago, L'Estrange, in one of his *Observators*, had speculated on the nature of Titus's death. "I could tell ye too, that there's no great Danger of Bloud, in the case, neither; For his dead Father, that was little less than a Wizzard, foretold in a Publique Coffee-House, that his Son would come to Dye a Dry Death. I believe (says he) they will Hang the Boy at last."[74] They did not hang the boy at last; they did something far worse: they ignored him.

Two diarists of the day, Luttrell and Hearne, noted the death of Titus Oates, in mid-July, 1705, in a fashion so perfunctory as to be worse than not noting it at all.[75] Moreover, they disagreed about the actual date. Abel Boyer, the historian of Queen Anne's reign, mentions the event without a date, and adds a very brief, uncomplimentary sketch of Oates's career and character.[76] The rest is silence; the most patient research among all the news-sheets of the day has failed to find so much as one bare mention of Titus's decease. There was no admirer left, it seems, to write down his last words; no patron survived to bury him in fitting splendour; no fashionable divine wrung the hearts of London with a funeral sermon. We know not where he died, of what sickness, in what religion, and in what circumstances; only that the administration of his estate, such as it was, was granted to his widow on August 16th.[77]

This, then, was the Nemesis which overtook Titus Oates. For seventeen years he had managed to keep himself in the public eye, though latterly it was only by such petty crimes as those of striking an old lady and endeavouring to cheat his Baptist brethren out of the benefits of a will. But even this notoriety was something to a man who feared obscurity as much as did Titus; even an occasional sneer at him in a news-sheet kept him on the national stage, albeit in the background. It cannot have been very long before his death that Tom Brown's witty pen had thought him worth a line or two: "Having seen the famous brass monument in Westminster, I went in the next place to see Dr Oates, whom I found in one of the coffee-houses that looks into the Court of Requests. He is a most accomplish'd person in his way, that's certain. The turn of his face is extremely particular; he has the largest chin of any clergyman in Europe; by the same token, they tell a merry story how he cheated a two-penny Barber by hiding it under his cloak."[78]

But it seems they told no stories, merry or otherwise, when Titus came to die. The news of his forthcoming marriage had caused a sensation in the coffee-houses as late as 1693; the news of his death in 1705 was not considered worth a mention by a single news-sheet. This man had shaken a throne, he had threatened a nation with civil war, he had played a not inconsiderable part in bringing about the Glorious Revolution, a part acknowledged by the Revolution's hero with a royal pension. He had been the companion of kings, the protégé of dukes and earls. Parliament had set aside the business of the kingdom to listen to that voice braying out its stories. He had loosed on England to prey on society the worst criminals of the underworld, so that in the King's Presence Chamber, in the lobbies of Westminster, in the fashionable coffee-houses, rakehell footmen, confidence tricksters, forgers, and murderers had mingled familiarly with the highest in the land.

To great men like the Five Lords, as to humble men like Stratford and Medburne, his bare word had brought death, imprisonment, or ruin. But for him, Lord Stafford would not have lost his head on Tower Hill, nor would Archbishop Plunket have endured the anguish of the quartering-block at Tyburn. Through his agency, hundreds of loyal Englishmen had been driven into exile, thousands of families had lost their livelihood, numberless innocents had succumbed to the filth and fetters of a jail. His voice, that peculiar, affected voice, uplifted in accusation had instituted a period of terror unparalleled in the history of a great and ancient people; judges had listened to it in respectful silence; men high and low had trembled to hear it; honest men like poor Schoolmaster Smith had perjured their souls rather than have it accuse them of crimes of which they were as innocent as the babe unborn. But now it was silent for ever; and no man noticed its absence.

Like a meteor, which owes its luminosity to a collision with the atmosphere of the earth, so was this small, malefic star named Titus Oates. He had shot up suddenly out of obscurity, colliding with the peculiar political conditions of the day, so that, for a brief space, the eyes of England were blinded by him. But the star descended; the light went out; and in the end of it there was but a small mass of matter, a little dust. Somewhere in an unknown grave, buried by an unknown hand, fortified by belief in some unknown religion, there has lain for nearly two hundred and fifty years the dust of him who once was adored as the Saviour of the Nation.

AUTHORITIES CONSULTED

CONTEMPORARY TRACTS, NEWS-SHEETS, PAMPHLETS, BALLADS, ETC.

A Breif Account of many memorable Passages of the Life and Death of the Earle of Shaftesbury. (Undated.)

A Brief History of the Times. Sir Roger L'Estrange, 1687.

A Collection of One Hundred and Eighty Loyal Songs. Nathaniel Thompson. 4th Edition. 1694.

A Compleat and True Narrative of the Manner of the Discovery of the Popish Plot to His Majesty. By Mr Christopher Kirkby. 1679.

A Dialogue between Doctor Titus and Bedlow's Ghost. 1684.

A Dialogue between Two Porters, upon Dr O——s's removing from White-hall into the City. 1681.

A Discourse of the Unlawfulness of Praying to Saints and Angels, etc. By Titus Oates, D.D., A Presbyter of the Church of England. 1689.

A Display of Tyranny; or Remarks upon the Illegal and Arbitrary Proceedings in the Courts of Westminster, and Guild-hall, London. 1689.

A Faithful Account of the Sickness, Death, and Burial of Capt. William Bedlow. 1680.

A Full and Final Proof of the Plot from the Revelations: whereby the Testimony of Dr Titus Oates and Mr Will. Bedloe is demonstrated to be Jure Divino. By E. C. Doctor of the Civil Law. 1680.

A Further Discovery of the Plot. Dedicated to Dr Titus Oates by Roger L'Estrange. 1680.

A Hue and Cry after Dr T. O. 1681.

A Letter from a Friend in London to Another at Salamanca. 1681.

A Modest Vindication of the Hermite of the Sounding Island: In Requital for the Modest Vindication of the Salamanca Doctor from Perjury. By Bartholomew Lane Esq. 1683.

A Modest Vindication of Titus Oates the Salamanca Doctor from Perjury. By Adam Elliot, M.A., 1682.

A New Discovery of Titus Oates: Being a Collection of his Letters to the Church of the Baptists, with Remarks upon them. 1701.

A New Martyrology: or, The Bloody Assizes. 1689.

A Reply to some Libels Lately Printed against the Earl of Danby, Together with some Observations upon Dr Oates his Narrative concerning the Conspiracy of Knox, Lane, and Osborne. 1680.

A Sermon preached at St Michaels Wood-street, at the request of some Friends; and now Published to prevent Mistakes. By Titus Oates, D.D., 1679.

A Sermon preached in an Anabaptist Meeting in Wapping on Sunday the 19th of February, by the Reverend T. O., D.D. 1699.

A Tragedy, Called the Popish Plot. Reviv'd etc. By a sincere Lover of his Countrey. 1696.

A True Narrative of the Horrid Plot and Conspiracy of the Popish Party against the Life of His Sacred Majesty, the Government, and the Protestant Religion. By Titus Oates, D.D. 1679.

A True Narrative of the Late Design of the Papists to Charge their Horrid Plot upon the Protestants, etc. 1679.

A True Narrative of the Sentence of Titus Oats for Perjury, 1685.

A Vindication of Dr Oates from that Scandalous Pamphlet called an Hue and Cry. 1681.

A Vindication of the English Catholicks from the Pretended Conspiracy, etc. 1681.

An Exact and Faithful Narrative of the Horrid Conspiracy of Thomas Knox, William Osborne, and John Lane, to Invalidate the Testimonies of Dr Titus Oates and Mr William Bedlow, etc. Published by the Appointment of me, Titus Oates. 1680.

Anti-Fimbra, or An Answer to the Animadversions uppon the Last Speeches of the Five Jesuits. By A.C.E.G. 1679.

Articles of High Misdemeanour Humbly Offer'd and Presented to the Consideration of His Sacred Majesty, etc. against Sir William Scroggs, Knight, Lord Chief Justice of the Kings-Bench. By Dr Titus Oates and Mr William Bedloe. 1680.

Concerning the Congregation of Jesuits held at London April 24. 1678. Which *Mr Oates calls a Consult.* (Undated.)

Discovery upon Discovery. . . . In a Letter to Dr Titus Oates, by Roger L'Estrange. 2nd Edition. 1680.

English News-letters and News-sheets, 1641–1705. Burney Collection. British Museum. (Titles given in the text or in the Notes.)

Florus Anglo-Bavaricus, etc. 1685.

Gangraena: or a Catalogue and Discovery of many of the Errours, Heresies, Blasphemies and pernicious Practices of the Sectaries of this time, etc. Thomas Edwards. 1645.

Gangraena. The Second Part. 1646.

Gangraena. The Third Part. 1646.

Intrigues of the Popish Plot laid open. William Smith, M.A. 1685.

L'Estrange's Case in a Civil Dialogue Betwixt 'Zekiel and Ephraim. 1680.

L'Estrange's Narrative of the Plot. 3rd Edition. 1680.

Massinello: Or, A Satyr against the Association and the Guild-hall-Riot. 1683.

Memoires of the Life of Anthony late Earl of Shaftsbury; with a Speech of the English Consul of Amsterdam concerning him, etc. 1683.

Miracles Reviv'd, In the Discovery of the Popish Plot, By the late Reverend Dr of Salamanca. (Undated.)

Mr Tonge's Vindication, In Answer to the Malicious and Lying Aspertions thrown upon him by Thomson and the Observator. 1682.

Song upon Information. 1681.

Sound Advice to Roman Catholicks, etc. By T. O. 1689.

Strange and Wonderful News from Southwark, Declaring how a Sham Doctor got two Aldermen Students of the same University with Child. 1684.

The Account of the Manner of Executing a Writ of Inquiry of Damages between His Royal Highness . . . and Titus Oates. 1684.

The Answer of Sir William Scroggs, Kt, Lord Chief Justice of the Kings-Bench to the Articles of Dr Titus Oates and Mr William Bedlow. (Undated.)

The Auricular Confession of Titus Oates to the Salamanca Doctor, his Confessor. 1683.

The Cabinet of the Jesuits Secrets opened. . . . In part begun by Dr Oates from an Italian Copy; But now more largely discovered, from a French Copy, printed at Colon, 1678. 1679.

The Case of Humphrey Burroughs and George Reynolds, Respondents; Upon the Appeal of Anthony Parker, Appellant, Touching an Award made by Dr Oates, and set aside in Chancery. To be heard on Wednesday, the 27th of January, 1702.

The Character of an Ignoramus Doctor. 1681.

The Compendium: or, A Short View of the Late Tryals in Relation to the Present Plot against His Majesty and Government. 1679.

The Counter-Rat, or Oats Sifted and Sack't up in the Counter. 1684.

The Devil's Patriarck, or A Full and Impartial Account of the notorious Life of this Present Pope of Rome Innocent the 11th. Written by an Eminent Pen. 1683.

The Discovery of the Popish Plot, being the several Examinations of Titus Oates, D.D. before the High Court of Parliament, The Lord Chief Justice, Sir Edmund-bury Godfrey, and several other of His Majesty's Justices of the Peace. 1679.

The Fanatick History; or An Exact Relation and Account of the old Anabaptists and new Quakers. Richard Blome. 1660.

The Kings Evidence Justifi'd; or Doctor Oates's Vindication of Himself and the Reality of the Plot, etc. 1679.

The Life and Errors of John Dunton, Late Citizen of London. Written by Himself in Solitude. 1705.

The Life of Titus Oats from his Cradle to his first Pilloring for Infamous Perjury. 1685.

The Life of Wm. Fuller, alias Fullee, etc. 1701.

The Melancholy Complaint of Dr. Otes, of the Black Ingratitude of this present Age towards him. 1684.

The Memoires of Titus Oates. Written for Publick Satisfaction. 1685.

The Picture of the Late King James drawn to the Life. By Titus Oates, D.D. 2nd Edition. 1696.

The Picture of the Late King James Further drawn to the Life. Part II. By Titus Oates, D.D. 1697.

The Picture of Titus Oates, D.D. Drawn to the Life, 1697.

The Pope's Ware-house, or The Merchandise of the Whore of Rome. By Titus Oates, D.D. 1679.

The Salamanca Doctor's Farewell, or Titus's Exaltation to the Pillory, upon his Conviction of Perjury. 1684.

The Salamanca Wedding; or, A True Account of a Swearing Doctor's Marriage with a Muggletonian Widow in Bread-street, London. 1693.

The Shammer Shamm'd: In a Plain Discovery, under young Tong's own Hand of a Designe to Trepann L'Estrange into a Pretended Subornation against the Popish Plot. By Roger L'Estrange. 1681.

The Whole Life of Mr William Fuller. . . . Impartially writ, by Himself, during his Confinement in the Queen's Bench. 1703.

The Witch of Endor; or the Witchcrafts of the Roman Jezebel. Titus Oates, D.D. 1679.

Vox Lachrymae. A Sermon newly Held Forth at Weavers-hall, upon the Funeral of the Famous T. O. Doctor of Salamanca. By Elephant Smith, Claspmaker, an unworthy Labourer in the Affairs of the Good Old Cause. 1682.

OTHER WORKS

A Brief Historical Relation of State Affairs. Narcissus Luttrell. 1857 Edition.

A Collection of the State Papers of John Thurloe Esq. 1742.

A Compleat Collection of State Tryals. 1719.

A Complete History of England. T. Smollett, M.D. 1757.

A History of Crime in England. Luke Owen Pike, M.A. 1876.

A Hundred Years of Quarter Sessions. Sir William Searle Holdsworth, O.M. 1932.

Admissions to the College of St John the Evangelist in the University of Cambridge, Jan. 1629/30–July 1710. Ed. Professor John E. B. Mayor. 1893.

An Account of the Life and Conversation of the Reverend and Worthy Mr Isaac Milles. 1721.

An Appendix to the Three Volumes of Mr Archdeacon Echard's History of England. By the same Author. 1720.

An Historical Account of my own Life, With some Reflections on the Times I have lived in. By Edmund Calamy, D.D. Ed. John Towill Rutt. 1829.

An Impartial Examination of Bishop Burnet's History of his own Times. By Mr Salmon. 1724.

Annals of Dover. John Bravington Jones. 1916.

Autobiography of Sir John Bramston, K.B. Camden Society. 1845.

Baker's Chronicle (continuation of). 1733.

Biographia Navalis; or Imperial Memoirs of the Lives and Characters of Officers of the Navy of Great Britain from the Year 1660 *to the present Time.* John Charnock, Esq., 1794.

Brief Lives, chiefly of Contemporaries, set down by John Aubrey, between the Years 1669 and 1696. Ed. Andrew Clark, M.A., LL.D. 1898.

Burnet's History of his own Time. 1838 Edition.

Calendar of State Papers. Domestic Series. Ed. F. H. Blackburne Daniell, M.A.

Calendar of Treasury Books, preserved in the Public Record Office. Prepared by William A. Shaw, Litt.D. 1931.

Calendar of Treasury Papers, 1556–1606. Preserved in Her Majesty's Public Record Office. Prepared by Joseph Redington, Esq., 1868.

Chaplains of the Royal Navy, 1622–1903. A. G. Kealy.

Correspondence of the Family of Hatton. Camden Society. 1878.

Diary of the Times of Charles the Second. Hon Henry Sydney. 1843 Edition.

Dictionary of National Biography.

Ecclesiastical History of England. "The Church of the Restoration." John Stoughton, D.D. 1870.

Espionage. The Story of the Secret Service. M. G. Richings. 1934.

Evelyn's Diary. Ed. William Bray, F.S.A. The "Chandos Classics."

Examen: or, An Enquiry into the Credit and Veracity of a Pretended Complete History. Hon. Roger North. 1740.

Hastings Past and Present: With Notices of the most remarkable places in the Neighbourhood. M. M. Howard. 1855.

Historical Manuscripts Commission Reports.

Index Expurgatorius Anglicanus. W. H. Hart, F.S.A. 1872.

Journals of the House of Commons.

Journals of the House of Lords.

Key to the Ancient Parish Registers of England and Wales. Arthur Meredyth Burke. 1908.

King Charles the Second. Arthur Bryant. 1931.

Lives of the Chief Justices of England. John, Lord Campbell. 1849.

Lives of the Queens of England. Agnes Strickland. 1888.

Lives of Twelve Bad Men. Ed. Thomas Seccombe. 2nd Edition. 1894.

London Past and Present. Henry B. Wheatley, F.S.A. 1891.

London Sessions Records, 1605–1685. Catholic Record Society. 1934.

Memoirs of Great Britain and Ireland. Sir John Dalrymple. 1790.

Memoirs of James II. James Stanier Clarke. 1816.

Memoirs of Missionary Priests and other Catholics of both Sexes that have suffered Death in England on Religious accounts from the year 1577 to 1684. Bishop Challoner, V.A.L. 1803.

Memoirs of Sir John Reresby. 1831 Edition.

Memoirs of Thomas, Earl of Ailesbury, Written by Himself. Roxburghe Club. 1890.

Memorabilia Cantabrigiae: or, An Account of the Different Colleges in Cambridge. By Joseph Wilson Esq. 1803.

Merchant Taylors' School Register. Ed. Rev. Charles J. Robinson, M.A. 1882.

Moneys Received and Paid for Secret Services of Charles II and James II. Ed. John Yonge Akerman. Camden Society. 1851.

Original Papers; containing the Secret History of Great Britain, from the Restoration to the Accession of the House of Hanover. James Macpherson. 1775.

Poetical Works of John Dryden. Ed. Robert Bell. 1854.

Probation Book of Merchant Taylors' School.

Public Order and Popular Disturbances, 1660–1714. Max Beloff. 1938.

Records of the English Province of the Society of Jesus. Henry Foley, S.J. 1879.
Registers of the English College at Valladolid, 1597–1862. Catholic Record Society. 1930.
Reliquiae Baxterianae: or, Mr Richard Baxter's Narrative of the Most Remarkable Passages of his Life and Times. 1696.
Remarks and Collections of Thomas Hearne. Ed. C. E. Doble, M.A. Oxford Historical Society. 1885.
Samuel Pepys. The Years of Peril. Arthur Bryant. 1935.
Savile Correspondence. Camden Society. 1858.
Shaftesbury (The First Earl). H. D. Traill. 1886.
Somers Tracts. 2nd Edition. 1814.
Stonyhurst College Centenary Record. Rev. John Gerard, S.J. 1894.
"Tercentenary Handlist of English and Welsh Newspapers, Magazines and Reviews." *The Times*. 1920.
The American Historical Review. Vol. XIV. 1908–9.
The Bagford Ballads. Ed. J. W. Ebsworth. Ballad Society. 1878.
The Bloody Assizes. J. G. Muddiman, M.A. 1929.
The Diary of Henry Teonge, Chaplain on board His Majesty's Ships . . . anno 1675 to 1679. 1825 Edition.
The English Historical Review. Vol. XXV. 1910.
The English Recusants. Brian Magee. 1938.
The Environs of London. Rev. Daniel Lysons, A.M., F.S.A. 1792.
The First Whig. Sir George Sitwell, Bart., M.P. 1894.
The General Biographical Dictionary. 1815.
The History and Antiquities of the Castle and Town of Arundel. Rev. M. A. Tierney, F.S.A. 1834.
The History and Antiquities of the County of Rutland. By James Wright of the Middle Temple. 1684.
The History and Antiquities of the Town and Port of Hastings. W. G. Moss. 1824.
The History and Topographical Survey of the County of Kent. Edward Hasted, F.R.S. 1798.
The History, Antiquities, and Topography of the County of Sussex. Thomas Walker Horsfield, F.S.A. 1835.
The History of England during the Reigns of the Royal House of Stuart. By Mr Oldmixon. 1730.
The History of England from the First Entrance of Julius Caesar and the Romans to the Conclusion of the Reign of King James the Second. Laurence Echard, A.M. 3rd Edition. 1720.
The History of England from the First Invasion by the Romans to the Accession of William and Mary in 1688. John Lingard, D.D. 5th Edition. 1849.
The History of the English Baptists. Thomas Crosby. 1739.
The History of the English General Baptists. Adam Taylor. 1818.
The History of Great Britain. David Hume. 1754.
The History of Merchant Taylors' School. Rev. H. B. Wilson, B.D. 1814.
The History of the Reign of Queen Anne, digested into Annals. Abel Boyer. 1703–13.
The King's Journalist. J. G. Muddiman, M.A. 1923.
The Law Quarterly Review. XI.
The Life and Times of Anthony à Wood, Antiquary, of Oxford, 1632–1695, described by Himself. Ed. Andrew Clark, M.A. 1892.
The Lives of the Norths. Hon. Roger North. 1826 Edition.
The Month. Vol. CII. July–December, 1903. Vol. CXX. July–December, 1912.
The Murder of Sir Edmund Berry Godfrey. John Dickson Carr. 1936.
The National Review. Vol. LXXXIV. September, 1924–February, 1925.

The Popish Plot. A Study in the History of the Reign of Charles II. John Pollock. 1903.

The Privy Council of England in the Seventeenth and Eighteenth Centuries. Edward Raymond Turner. 1927.

The Roxburghe Ballads. Ed. E. W. Ebsworth. Ballad Society. 1883.

The Royal Navy: A History from the Earliest Times to the Present. Wm. Laird Clowes. 1898.

The Rutland Magazine and County Historical Record. Vol. III.

The Victoria History of the Counties of England. Rutland. Ed. Wm. Page, F.S.A. 1908.

The Works of Mr Thomas Brown. 8th Edition. 1744.

Titus Oates. C. M. Clode. 1890.

Who killed Sir Edmund Berry Godfrey? Alfred Marks. 1905.

NOTES AND REFERENCES

BOOK ONE

1. Seccombe's article on Titus Oates in *The Dictionary of National Biography* states that he was the son of Samuel Oates, Rector of Marsham in Norfolk. This cannot be correct, because every contemporary writer speaks of Samuel as being a weaver. (See Wood 2, 417, *Brief His.*, 1, 116. *The Life of Titus Oates from his Cradle etc. The Character of an Ignoramous Doctor. etc., etc.*). Moreover, not one of these writers, in mentioning his conforming to the Established Church in 1660, remarks upon a former apostacy. A long controversy raged in the Sixth Series of *Notes and Queries* regarding Titus's parentage, the conclusion reached being that which I have given in the text.
2. *Discovery upon Discovery*, 18.
3. Probably Thomas Lamb, whose correspondence with Richard Baxter is given in *Reliquiae Baxterianae*.
4. *Gangraena*, 2, 173.
5. *Encylopaedia Britannica*, Article on Anabaptists.
6. *The Fanatick History*, 17.
7. *Gangraena*, 1, 78.
8. Ibid., 93-4.
9. Ibid., 92.
10. Ibid., 93.
11. Ibid., 2, 146.
12. When he went to St Omers in 1677, her son Titus adopted the name of Sampson Lucy. It is just possible that this was his mother's name transposed.
13. *Intrigues of the Popish Plot*, 22.
14. *Gangraena*, 1, 67.
15. Ibid., 3, 189.
16. Ibid., 1, 120, Appendix.
17. Ibid., 1, 182.
18. Ibid., 2, 3, 4.
19. Ibid., 146.
20. Taylor's *History of the General Baptists*, 1, 116.
21. *Brief History*, 1, 116.
22. Wood says that she was "a woman great with childe and neare her time of delivery" (2, 417).
23. *Gangraena*, 2, 146–8.
24. Wood, 2, 417.
25. *Gangraena*, 3, 31.
26. Ibid., 105.
27. Ibid., 105–6.
28. His. MSS. Com., Appen. to 5th Report, 390.
29. Ibid., 397.
30. Ibid., 403.
31. Ibid., 397.
32. Ibid., Appen. to 6th Report, 215.
33. Ibid., Appen. to 7th Report, 26.
34. *Rutland Magazine*, 3, 158.
35. *Intrigues of the Popish Plot*, 22, 23.
36. *Florus Anglo-Bavaricus*, 200.
37. *Intrigues of the Popish Plot*, 23.
38. *The Life of Titus Oats from his Cradle etc.*
39. *A Dialogue between Two Porters.*
40. Taylor's *History of the General Baptists*, 1, 135–6.
41. *The Perfect Diurnall*, January 8th–15th, 1655. *Severall Proceedings in Parliament*, January 11th–18th, 1655. *Thurloe Papers*, 3, 66.
42. *Mercurius Politicus*, March 1st–8th, 1655.
43. Echard, 3, 66.

44. *The Life of Titus Oats from his Cradle etc.*
45. Crosby, 3, 169.
46. Taylor's *His. of the Gen. Baptists*, 1, 240–1.
47. Moss, *History of Hastings*, 108.
48. J. M. Baines, *Hastings and Its Harbours.*
49. Parish Registers of All Saints'. At some fairly recent date, this entry has been inked over, using modern ink. Apparently before this it was almost illegible, which no doubt led the writer of *A Handbook of Hastings and St Leonards* into the ludicrous error of giving the date of Titus's birth as 1619. *The Horsfield History of Antiquities* (1, 453) makes the same mistake, which was repeated by various contributors to *Notes and Queries*.
50. *The Life of Titus Oats from his Cradle etc.*
51. *Intrigues of the Popish Plot*, 25. Also *Examen*, 221.
52. In Titus's admission to St John's College, Cambridge, it is stated definitely that he went to Sedlescombe (*Admissions to the College of St Johns*, 2, 20). The entry in the admission book of Gonville and Caius is more vague: "Titus Oates, son of Samuel, Clerk and Rector of Hastings, in the County of Sussex, born at Oakham in the County of Rutland, instructed in literature by Master Mackmillan, in London, for one year, and under other preceptors for two years, more or less . . ." (His. MSS. Com., Appen. to 2nd Report, 117).
53. *A Modest Vindication*, 1, 2.
54. Warner's *Historia Persecutionis*, 45.
55. Ibid.
56. Echard, 3, 945.
57. *Compendium*, 80.
58. *Observator*, October 25th, 1682.
59. So say both Wood and North.
60. *A Tragedy of the Popish Plot Reviv'd.*
61. Hasted's *Kent*, 6, 203.
62. Ibid., 198–9.
63. *A Modest Vindication*, 32.
64. *Examen*, 221–2.
65. Burnet, 282.
66. Vestry Book of All Saints. On June 4th, 1674, the accounts of Jacob Fautley and Richard Levett, Surveyors of the Highway, were passed and signed by *inter alia* "Titus Otes Curate".
67. *The Life of Titus Oats from his Cradle etc.*
68. Moss, *His. of Hastings*, 102.
69. Wood, 2, 417–18.
70. *C.S.P.D.*, March 1st, 1675–February 29th, 1676, 68–9.
71. Wood, 2, 418. *The Life of Titus Oats from his Cradle etc. Brief His.* 1, 81. *Observator*, 2, No. 61.
72. Hastings Town Records.
73. Kealy, in his *List of Chaplains of the Royal Navy*, gives the year, and as he obtained his information from original papers in the Public Record Office, it would seem to be correct. L'Estrange tells us the name of Oates's commander (spelling it Ruth), and both he and Titus himself mention Tangier as the port of destination.
74. Charnock's *Biographia Navalis*, 1, 28–9.
75. *The London Gazette*, April 12th–15th, 1675.
76. *C.S.P.D.*, March 1st. 1675–February 29th, 1676, 85.
77. *Diary of H. Teonge*, 7.
78. *Brief History*, 1, 81.
79. *A Modest Vindication*, 33.
80. *Florus Anglo-Bavaricus*, 201.
81. *Observator*, 2, No. 120. See also Burnet, 282.
82. *The London Gazette*, July 22nd–26th.
83. *A Tragedy of the Popish Plot Reviv'd*, 36.
84. *His. of the Gen. Baptists*, 1, 241.
85. *C.S.P.D.*, September 1st, 1680–December 31st, 1681, 351. Statement of Archibald Gledstanes to the Council.
86. *Intrigues of the Popish Plot*, 4.

87. *Notes and Queries*, Series 3, Vol. XI, 415.
88. *The Life of Titus Oats from his Cradle etc.*
89. *Intrigues of the Popish Plot*, 4, 5.
90. Ibid., 5.
91. Article on Oates in the *Catholic Encylopaedia.*

BOOK TWO

1. Madden's *The Penal Laws*, 152, *passim.*
2. *Roxburghe Ballads*, 4, Pt. I, 235.
3. Carte's *Life of Ormond*, 4, 583.
4. *A Vindication of the English Catholics*, 52.
5. *The Picture of Titus Oates, D.D.*
6. Quoted by Traill, 135.
7. *A Tragedy of the Popish Plot Reviv'd*, 35.
8. Sussex Record Society, *Cal. of Sussex Marriage Licences*, *Archdeaconry of Chichester*. The licence is without date, but belongs to the period 1671–6.
9. *Lives of the Norths*, 1, 325.
10. *Intrigues of the Popish Plot*, 5.
11. For accounts of this plot, see Lingard, 9, 278–80; Wood, 2, 337–8; Strickland's *Lives of the Queens of England*, 4, 559.
12. Burnet, 282.
13. Lingard, 9, 347 n.
14. *Vindication of the English Catholics*, 51.
15. Foley, quoting from a collection of papers made by Lord Arundell when in the Tower, says that " 'On Ash Wednesday, 1677, Mr Oates pretended to be converted by Mr Keynes in London' " (p. 837), but this must be a mistake. Oates himself, possibly because he felt that to acknowledge his reception at the hands of the mad Berry belittled his dignity, says that he was received by Father Langworth, S.J., Norfolk's chaplain (*A Tragedy of the Popish Plot Reviv'd*).
16. *A Tragedy of the Popish Plot Reviv'd*, 36.
17. Aubrey, *Brief Lives*, 2, 261.
18. Lingard, 9, 347.
19. Wood, 2, 417.
20. *State Trials*, Trial of the Five Jesuits.
21. An alternative suggestion, which I make here rather than in the text because there is no real evidence either way, is that some of these witnesses saw, not Titus, but his father, Samuel. At the trial of the Five Jesuits, the defence put this forward as a probability, but the Lord Chief Justice would have none of it. A woman in court stood up and offered to speak, but Scroggs cried: "The thing is done. What further evidence do we want?" (Foley, 61, quoting from the Stonyhurst MSS.). This passage was suppressed in the printed trials.
22. Narrative of Fr Alexander Keynes, S.J. Original in the P.R.O., Brussels. Quoted by Foley, 967.
23. See the trials of the Five Jesuits, Langhorne, and Oates himself in *The Compleat Collection.*
24. *Observator*, 2, No. 56.
25. *Vindication of the English Catholics*, 85.
26. MSS. in the archives of the English College at Valladolid.
27. His. MSS. Com., Lords, 98.
28. *Compendium*, 83.
29. *A Tragedy of the Popish Plot Reviv'd.*
30. Pamphlet among the Harleian MSS., quoted by Foley, 65, 6.
31. *C.S.P.D.*, September 1st, 1680–December 3rd, 1681, 602.
32. Ibid.
33. Ibid, 1678, 544–5, 551.
34. Pamphlet among the Harleian MSS., quoted by Foley, 65.
35. Attestation of Richard Duelly. *Vin. of the Eng. Catholics*, 75.
36. Foley, 838. From a collection of papers made by Lord Arundell.
37. His. MSS. Com., Lords, 98.

38. *C.S.P.D.*, September 1st, 1680–December 3rd, 1681, 602.
39. *A Modest Vindication, etc.*
40. *The Shammer Shamm'd*, 39.
41. *Brief His.*, 1, 103. Information of Christopher Kemble and James Morton, laid before the Secretary of State in August, 1681.
42. *Examen*, 225.
43. *Florus Anglo-Bavaricus*, 93.
44. "Titus Oates at School." Article in *The Month* by Fr Gerrard, S.J.
45. Trial of Oates, *Compleat Collection.*
46. Attestation of the Rector of Watten, *Vin. of the Eng. Catholics*, 81.
47. *The Life of Titus Oats from his Cradle etc.*
48. Trial of Oates, *Compleat Collection.*
49. Ibid.
50. Evidence of Thomas Billing. Trial of the Five Jesuits.
51. Trial of Oates.
52. *Florus Anglo-Bavaricus*, 94.
53. Trial of the Five Jesuits.
54. *Florus Anglo-Bavaricus.*
55. Echard, 3, 945.
56. *Vin. of the Eng. Catholics*, 46.
57. *The Life of Titus Oats from his Cradle etc.*
58. *A Modest Vindication*, 33.
59. *Intrigues of the Popish Plot*, 6.
60. *Vin. of the Eng. Catholics*, 81.
61. *Brief History*, 1, 103.
62. *C.S.P.D.*, 1679–80, 628.
63. *Vin. of the Eng. Catholics*, 55.
64. Ibid., 63.
65. Letter of Father Coniers. *Vin. of the Eng. Catholics*, 90.

BOOK THREE

Part I

1. Kirkby's Narrative.
2. Echard, 3, 946.
3. *C.S.P.D.*, 1678, 359.
4. Echard, 3, 946.
5. Lingard, 9, 352. Strickland, 4, 458.
6. *C.S.P.D.*, 1678, 466.
7. *Examen*, 172–3.
8. Lingard, 9, 350.
9. Clarke, 1, 517.
10. Lingard, 9, 351 n.
11. *Observator*, 2, No. 75.
12. Letter of Fr Coniers, February 26th, 1680. *Vin. of the Eng. Catholics*, 90–1.
13. *Intrigues of the Popish Plot*, 6.
14. There was no rain until the 9th. See Wood, 2, 415.
15. Kirkby's Narrative.
16. *Brief History*, 1, 108.
17. Ibid., 130–1.
18. *Intrigues of the Popish Plot*, 6–7.
19. Kirkby's Narrative.
20. Hume, 2, 277.
21. *Examen*, 277.
22. Clarke, 1, 526.
23. *Observator*, 2, No. 75.
24. Kirkby's Narrative.
25. *Examen*, 172.

26. Kirkby's Narrative.
27. *C.S.P.D.*, 1678, 426.
28. Ibid., 427.
29. Lingard, 9, 355.
30. *C.S.P.D.*, 1678, 432.
31. Clarke, 1, 518.
32. *C.S.P.D.*, 1678.
33. Clarke, 1, 519.
34. *C.S.P.D.*, 1678, 433.
35. Hume, 2, 280. Smollett, 3, 471.
36. See also *C.S.P.D.*, 1678, 454.
37. Foley, 19.
38. Echard, 3, 945.
39. *Absalom and Achitophel*, Pt I.
40. *Examen*, 95. See also Dalrymple, 1, 171; Burnet, 290; Lingard, 9, 360.
41. *Memories of the Life of Anthony late Earl of Shaftesbury*, 3.
42. *C.S.P.D.*, 1678, 418.
43. *A Tragedy of the Popish Plot Reviv'd*, 39.
44. *C.S.P.D.*, 1678, 434.
45. Clarke, 1, 534.
46. Treby, *A Collection of Letters . . . relating to the horrid Popish Plot.*
47. *C.S.P.D.*, 1678, 453.
48. Burnet, 284.
49. Echard, 3, 947.
50. See the examination of Robinson and Mulys in *Commons' Journals*.
51. *Examen*, 199.
52. Ibid.
53. Lingard, 9, 360–1. Strickland 4, 459–60. Luttrell, 1, 1–2. Baker, 688. etc.

Part II

1. *C.S.P.D.*, 1678, 466. Dalrymple, 1, 257.
2. *The King's Evidence Justified*, 37.
3. *Intrigues of the Popish Plot*, 8.
4. *Examen*, 204.
5. Lingard, 9, 362.
6. *C.S.P.D.*, 1678, 472.
7. Ibid., 465–6.
8. Ibid., 471.
9. Ibid., 466.
10. *Commons' Journals*, 9, 519.
11. Ibid., 520.
12. *C.S.P.D.*, 1678, 481.
13. Echard, 3, 950. See also *Commons' Journals*, 9, 519, 520; Baker, 690.
14. His. MSS. Com., Lords, 6.
15. *Lords' Journals*, 13, 309.
16. *The First Whig*, 49–50.
17. *Intrigues of the Popish Plot*, 30.
18. *Observator*, 2, No. 58.
19. *Lords' Journals*, 13, 311.
20. Ibid.
21. Ibid., 312.
22. His. MSS. Com., Lords, 53.
23. See also *Intrigues of the Popish Plot*, 8–14.
24. His. MSS. Com., Lords, 121.
25. *Lords' Journals*, 13, 332.
26. *C.S.P.D.*, 1678, 514.
27. *Lords' Journals*, 13, 360.
28. Ibid., 362.
29. Ibid., 364.
30. Echard, 3, 951.

31. Lingard, 9, 373 and n.
32. *C.S.P.D.*, 1678, 495.
33. Ibid., 506.
34. Ibid., 508.
35. Lingard, 9, 375. See also Burnet, 157–8; Echard, 3, 951.
36. Bramston, 194.
37. The case of Samuel Atkins is described at length by North in his *Examen*, who saw the account written by Atkins himself.
38. Clarke calls her Mrs Elliot, 1, 529.
39. *C.S.P.D.*, 1678, 519.
40. Ibid., 539.
41. *Lords' Journals*, 13, 389.
42. His. MSS. Com., Appen. to 4th Report, 723.
43. Information of John Lane. *An Exact and Faithfull Narrative . . . of Knox etc.*, 11.
44. The first pardon was granted November 15th; the second, covering homicide, on November 22nd. *C.S.P.D.*, 1678, 521, 535.
45. *Commons' Journals*, 9, 549. Lingard, 9, 380–1.
46. *Lords' Journals*, 13, 386.
47. Ibid., 13, 389.
48. *C.S.P.D.*, 1682, 245–6.
49. Lord Keeper North's Memoranda. Quoted by Dalrymple, 1, 391–2.
50. *Lives of the Norths*, 1, 327.
51. *Examen*, 567–8.
52. Ailesbury, 1, 36.
53. *C.S.P.D.*, 1678, 554.
54. Challoner, 192, 3, quoting Higgons, 691.
55. Burnet, 287–8.
56. North gives a most graphic account of this trial in *Examen*, 179.
57. Challoner, 195. Luttrell, 1, 4–5. Echard dismisses as a malicious rumour the report that Coleman's last words were "There is no faith in man", supposed to refer to a broken promise of pardon by the Duke of York.
58. Wood, 2, 426.
59. Echard, 3, 955.
60. *C.S.P.D.*, 1678, 548–9. *Commons' Journals*, 9, 551.
61. Luttrell, 1, 5.
62. His. MSS. Com., Lords, 49.
63. Baker, 693.
64. *Intrigues of the Popish Plot*, 16.
65. Echard, 3, 962.
66. *C.S.P.D.*, 1678, 586–7.
67. Ibid., 592–3. See also *Malice Defeated: or a Brief Relation of the accusation and deliverance of Elizabeth Cellier etc.*
68. *Intrigues of the Popish Plot*, 25.
69. *C.S.P.D.*, 1678, 596.
70. His. MSS. Com., Lords, 16, 17.
71. Ibid., 18, 19.
72. *Examen*, 121–2.
73. Ibid., 573.
74. *A Further Discovery of the Plot*, 24.
75. Foley, 35 n.
76. *Examen*, 176.
77. Ibid., 195.
78. *Account of the Manner of Executing a Writ of Enquiry.*
79. *Lords' Journals*, 13, 530–1.
80. *Observator*, 2, No. 79.
81. *Examen*, 223.
82. *Intrigues of the Popish Plot*, 15.
83. *A Sermon Preached at an Anabaptist Meeting etc.*
84. *A New Discovery of Titus Oates.*

85. To give one instance out of many, John Gerrard was thrown into the King's Bench Prison on December 4th, 1678, only because Titus had said he believed he had seen Gerrard's face at the altar. His. MSS. Com., Lords, 70.
86. *Examen*, 205.
87. *C.S.P.D.*, January 1st, 1679–August 31st, 1680, 3.
88. Ibid., 21.
89. Challoner (p. 197) reproduces it in its entirety.
90. *C.S.P.D.*, January 1st, 1679–August 31st, 1680, 57.
91. Luttrell, 1, 8.
92. Echard, 3, 966.
93. Challoner, 210.
94. Echard, 3, 970.
95. Ibid., 971.
96. Reproduced in *Observator* for June 21st, 1682.
97. Reresby, 226–7.
98. *Lives of the Norths*, 1, 349–50.
99. His. MSS. Com., Lords, 98–9.
100. Savile Correspondence, 93–4.
101. Lingard, 9, 408.
102. *Lords' Journals*, 13, 595. Temple, 2, 504. Reresby, 96. Lingard, 9, 424.
103. Challoner, 197–8.
104. His. MSS. Com., Lords, 145.
105. Ibid.
106. *Intrigues of the Popish Plot*, 17.
107. Ibid., 19.
108. Ailesbury, 1, 140.
109. *Examen*, 272.
110. Challoner, 203.
111. Ibid., 205–6.
112. Ibid., 208.
113. Ibid., 209. See also Lingard, 9, 440.
114. *Savile Correspondence*, 112.
115. *Domestick Intelligence*, July 17th.
116. Quoted in full by Challoner, 211.
117. *Domestick Intelligence*, July 17th.

Part III

1. Wood, 2, 456. Luttrell, 1, 18, 19, 20. Challoner, 213–28.
2. Evelyn, 409–10.
3. *The English Intelligence*, August 9th.
4. *The Domestick Intelligence or News etc.*, August 12th.
5. Ibid., September 12th.
6. Wood, 2, 465.
7. *Domestick Intelligence or News etc.*, September 30th.
8. *A Modest Vindication*, 22.
9. Ibid., 24.
10. Warcup's Journal, *E.H.R.*, 40, 244.
11. *Intrigues of the Popish Plot*, 21. For a good account of the Meal Tub Plot see the "Memorial" quoted in *Examen*, 265–9.
12. Wood, 2, 464–5. See also Luttrell, 1, 23.
13. *Domestick Intelligence or News etc.*, November 7th.
14. Ibid., December 9th.
15. Information of Martha Cradocke, *C.S.P.D.*, September 1st, 1680–December 31st, 1681, 556.
16. Wood, 2, 466–7.
17. *Hatton Correspondence*, 1, 197–8.
18. *Examen*, 574–5.
19. Ibid., 577–8.
20. Ibid., 576–7. For a minute description of the show of 1680, see *London's Drollery: or The Love and Kindness between the Pope and the Devil. Rox. Ballads*, 4, 221–4.

21. His. MSS. Com., Fitzherbert, 21.
22. Luttrell, 1, 29.
23. *Domestick Intelligence or News etc.*, November 28th.
24. *Mercurius Anglicus: or The Weekly Occurrences Faithfully Transmitted.* November 26th–29th.
25. *C.S.P.D.*, January 1st, 1679–August 31st, 1680, 380.
26. *Domestick Intelligence or News etc.*, December 23rd.
27. Ibid., December 26th.
28. *Intrigues of the Popish Plot*, 22, 23.
29. Defoe's *Review*, 7, 297. Quoted in *The First Whig*, Appendix.
30. *Brief History*, 1, 167, 8.
31. Ibid., 164–5.
32. Lyson's *Environs of London*, 2, 420.
33. *Domestick Intelligence or News etc.*, January 13th. (The title of this news-sheet was changed on the 16th to *The Protestant* (*Domestick*) *Intelligence etc.*). See also *The True News: or Mercurius Anglicus*, January 7th–10th.
34. *Intrigues of the Popish Plot*, 22.
35. Hatton Correspondence, 1, 215.
36. *Miracles Reviv'd etc.*, 1, 2.
37. See *The Answer of Sir William Scroggs, Kt., etc.*, 1680. Also Luttrell, 1, 31–2.
38. *Rox. Ballads*, 4, Pt. I, 175, 176.
39. *The Protestant* (*Domestick*) *Intelligence etc.*, January 27th.
40. Ibid., February 24th.
41. *The Currant Intelligence* (later *Smith's Currant Intelligence*), February 21st.
42. *The Protestant* (*Domestick*) *Intelligence etc.*, February 24th–27th.
43. Ibid., February 10th.
44. Ibid., March 2nd.
45. *The True Domestick Intelligence*, January 6th.
46. Luttrell, 1, 39.
47. Ibid., 42.
48. *The Currant Intelligence*, March 30th–April 3rd.
49. *The True News: or Mercurius Anglicus*, May 5th–8th.
50. *A Modest Vindication*, 25.
51. Ibid., 27.
52. *C.S.P.D.*, January 1st, 1679–August 31st, 1680, 536.
53. *Examen*, 271.
54. *Observator*, 2, No. 153.
55. *The First Whig*, 30.
56. Luttrell, 1, 56.
57. His. MSS. Com., Lords, 169.
58. Reproduced in *Brief History*, 1, 113.
59. *Brief History*, 1, 38–9.
60. *C.S.P.D.*, January 1st, 1679–August 31st, 1680, 608. As I can find no other mention of this, it must have been a rumour. It is to be hoped that it was, for otherwise, in 1693, Titus added bigamy to his many crimes.
61. Ibid., September 1st, 1680–December 31st, 1681, 24.
62. Ibid., 43.
63. Ibid., 623–4.
64. *Examen*, 254. See also Wood, 2, 494; Echard, 3, 989; *The Examination of Captain William Bedloe, Deceased, Relating to the Popish Plot.*
65. *A Faithful Account of the . . . Death . . . of Capt. William Bedloe*, 1680.
66. *Rox. Ballads*, 4, Pt. I, 174.
67. Luttrell, 1, 58. Challoner, 234. Lingard, 9, 465–7.
68. His. MSS. Com., Lords, 146.
69. Luttrell, 1, 56.
70. Ailesbury, 1, 28.
71. Evelyn, 424–5.
72. Burnet, 337.
73. Akerman, *Secret Service Moneys*, 22.
74. Echard, 3, 991.
75. Aubrey's *Lives*, 2, 261.

76. *The Shammer Shamm'd*, 31. Aubrey, 2, 262. *Observator*, 2, No. 16. Luttrell, 1, 128.
77. Reresby, 239.
78. *The Protestant (Domestick) Intelligence etc.*, December 28th.
79. *Rox. Ballads*, 4, Pt. I, 233–5.
80. Wood, 2, 513.
81. Warcup's Journals, *E.H.R.*, 40, 249.
82. *Observator*, 1, No. 399.
83. *Intrigues of the Popish Plot*, 28–9.
84. Wood, 2, 526.
85. *Examen*, 100–1.
86. Ibid., 289–90.
87. Lingard, 10, 8–10, 13, 14. Luttrell, 1, 104–5. Challoner, 239. *Examen*, 272–303.
88. His. MSS. Com., Lords, 148.
89. Akerman, *Secret Service Moneys*.
90. C. M. Clode, *Titus Oates*, 3.
91. See *Publick Occurrences Truely Stated*, February 28th, 1688.
92. Original among the Norfolk Papers, No. 435. Tierney, 2, 539–40 n.
93. *C.S.P.D.*, September 1st, 1680–December 31st, 1681, 380.
94. Ibid., 307–8.
95. *Observator*, 1, No. 12.
96. Ibid., 1, No. 40.
97. Ibid., 2, No. 81.
98. *C.S.P.D.*, September 1st, 1680–December 31st, 1681, 350–1. See also Warcup's Journals, *E.H.R.*, 40, 256.
99. *The Loyal Protestant and True Domestick Intelligence*, July 16th.
100. Ibid., July 26th, Luttrell, 1, 112.
101. *The Currant Intelligence*, July 2nd–5th.
102. Luttrell, 1, 115.
103. *Examen*, 224.
104. Smollett, 3, 473.
105. Luttrell, 1, 136–7.
106. William Smith the schoolmaster was present at this dinner, and in his *Intrigues of the Popish Plot* (p. 27) describes the discussion between Oates and Savage on the existence of God, etc. He says that College, far from falling asleep, "was often interrupting them with his Quibbles and Rhime-doggrel, for which Otes rebuked him".
107. Luttrell, 1, 120.
108. Akerman, *Secret Service Moneys*. (The records of the Secret Service moneys do not begin earlier than the first-named date.)
109. *C.S.P.D.*, September 1st, 1680–December 31st, 1681, 411.
110. *Examen*, 590.
111. *The Loyal Protestant and True Domestick Intelligence*, September 3rd.
112. Ibid., Also Luttrell, 1, 121.
113. *C.S.P.D.*, September 1st, 1680–December 31st, 1681, 411.
114. Ibid., 439.

BOOK FOUR

1. *A Vindication of Dr Oates from that Scandalous Pamphlet etc.*
2. Luttrell, 1, 125, 126.
3. *The Loyal Protestant and True Domestick Intelligence*, September 10th.
4. Introduction to *Absalom and Achitophel*.
5. *C.S.P.D.*, September 1st, 1680–December 31st, 1681, 574.
6. *London Sessions Records*, Cath. Record Soc., 344–5 n.
7. Trial of Oates, *Compleat Collection*.
8. *C.S.P.D.*, September 1st, 1680–December 31st, 1681, 583.
9. Ibid., 162–3.
10. Luttrell, 1, 152. Burnet 337.
11. *A Tragedy of the Popish Plot Reviv'd*.
12. Luttrell 1, 153.

13. *C.S.P.D.*, September 1st, 1680–December 31st, 1681, 604.
14. *A Modest Vindication etc.*, 47.
15. Luttrell, 1, 159. *Observator*, 1, No. 93.
16. *The Loyal Protestant and True Domestick Intelligence*, February 18th.
17. *C.S.P.D.*, 1682, 217.
18. *The Loyal Protestant and True Domestick Intelligence*, April 25th.
19. *Observator*, 1, No. 125.
20. *C.S.P.D.*, 1682, 199.
21. *The Loyal Protestant and True Domestick Intelligence*, June 1st.
22. *C.S.P.D.*, 1682, 236–7.
23. Ibid., 228, 351, *passim.*
24. *The Loyal Protestant and True Domestick Intelligence*, June 17th.
25. *Savile Correspondence*, 203–4.
26. Luttrell, 1, 196. Also *The Loyal London Mercury*, June 21st–24th.
27. *A Modest Vindication etc.*, 43.
28. *The Loyal Protestant and True Domestick Intelligence*, July 1st.
29. Ibid., July 27th.
30. *C.S.P.D.*, 1682, 496.
31. *The Loyal London Mercury*, October 6th–10th.
32. *The Loyal Protestant and True Domestick Intelligence*, October 7th.
33. *C.S.P.D.*, 1682, 573. See also Warcup's Journals, *E.H.R.*, 40, 259.
34. *Cal. of Treasury Papers*, 1, 10.
35. *C.S.P.D.*, January 1st–June 30th, 1683, 9.
36. Luttrell, 1, 248.
37. MSS. in a private collection.
38. *Observator*, 1, No. 365.
39. Luttrell, 1, 247, 259.
40. Ibid., 260.
41. *Observator*, 1, No. 365.
42. *Cal. of Treas. Papers*, 1, 10.
43. *Observator*, 2, No. 147.
44. Ibid., 1, No. 455.
45. *C.S.P.D.*, January 1st–June 30th, 1683, 336.
46. Ibid., 340.
47. Ibid., 44.
48. Ibid., 255.
49. Ibid., 274, 275.
50. Ibid., 349.
51. Burnet, 359.
52. *C.S.P.D.*, January 1st–June 30th, 1683, 390. Information of John Gelson.
53. Bryant's *Pepys*, 2, 399–400.
54. *C.S.P.D.*, January 1st–June 30th, 1683, 351–2.
55. *Observator*, 1, No. 399.
56. Ibid., 2, No. 20.
57. *Somers Tracts*, 8, 380.
58. *A Tragedy of the Popish Plot Reviv'd*, 56–7.
59. *C.S.P.D.*, May 1st, 1684–February 5th, 1685, 11.
60. Ibid., 30–1.
61. Luttrell, 1, 310–11.
62. Warcup's Journals, *E.H.R.*, 40, 260.
63. Luttrell, 1, 308, 313.
64. Ibid., 311.
65. Letter from a Jesuit in London, Original in P.R.O., Brussels. Quoted by Foley, 76, 7.
66. Muddiman's *The Bloody Assizes*, 155 and n.
67. *C.S.P.D.*, May 1st, 1684–February 5th, 1685, 294.
68. Calamy, 1, 115, 116.
69. *C.S.P.D.*, May 1st, 1684–February 5th, 1685, 293.
70. His. MSS. Com., Appen. to 13th Report, 25.
71. Ailesbury, 1, 140, 143.
72. Ibid., 138.

73. Luttrell, 1, 342.
74. Ailesbury, 1, 140.
75. Ibid.
76. Echard, 3, 1055.
77. *The Memoires of Titus Oates*, 14.
78. Ailesbury, 1, 137.
79. Pike's *History of Crime*, 233–4.
80. Muddiman's *The Bloody Assizes*, 156.
81. Luttrell, 1, 343.
82. Letter from a Jesuit in London. Original in P.R.O., Brussels. Quoted by Foley, 76–7.
83. *The Salamanca Doctor's Farewell.*
84. Letter from Sir Henry Beaumont, M.P., to the Mayor of Leicester. His. MSS. Com., Appen. to the 8th Report, 440.
85. *Perjury Punish'd, or Villainy Lash'd.*
86. Echard, 3, 1054.
87. Muddiman's *The Bloody Assizes*, 155–6.
88. Evelyn, 478.
89. Calamy, 1, 120.
90. Bramston, 194–5.
91. Luttrell, 1, 374.
92. Ibid., 380.
93. *Picture of the Late King James*, Preface.
94. *A Discourse of the Unlawfulness of Praying to Saints, etc.*, Preface.
95. Wood, 3, 274.
96. Ailesbury, 1, 144.
97. Tom Brown's *Works*, 4, 242–3.
98. *A New Martyrology*, 123–4.
99. Ibid.

BOOK FIVE

1. Ailesbury, 1, 144. *Hatton Correspondence*, 2, 125.
2. *Cal. Treas. Papers*, XLIX, No. 32.
3. Ailesbury, 1, 144.
4. Luttrell, 1, 498.
5. *Lords' Journals*, XIV, 172.
6. Ibid., 180, 184, 191.
7. Ibid., XIV, 213.
8. *Commons' Journals*, X, 145.
9. Luttrell, 1, 537.
10. *Lords' Journals*, XIV, 221.
11. Ibid.
12. Luttrell, 1, 540.
13. *Commons' Journals*, X, 165.
14. Ibid., 176–7.
15. *Hatton Correspondence*, 2, 135.
16. Luttrell, 1, 563.
17. *Cal. Treas. Books*, IX, Pt. I, 53.
18. *Examen*, 224.
19. Muddiman's *The Bloody Assizes*, 7, 8.
20. Ibid., 9.
21. *A New Martyrology*, 124–5.
22. *Examen*, 225.
23. Ailesbury, 1, 30.
24. *The Life of William Fuller, alias etc.*, 9.
25. Ibid.
26. *The Whole Life of Mr Fuller*, 42.
27. Wood, 3, 356.
28. *C.S.P.D.*, Will. and Mary, 2, 350.
29. *The Whole Life of Mr Fuller*, 62–4.

30. Luttrell, 2, 443.
31. Wood, 3, 410.
32. *Cal. Treas. Books*, IX, Pt. IV, 1479, 1512, 1531, 1659, 1665, 1733.
33. Harleian Society, Vol. XXX, 1, 266.
34. Ibid., Vol. XXX, 1, 266. See also Luttrell, 3, 94.
35. Wood, 3, 430–1.
36. Luttrell, 3, 173, 179.
37. Ibid., 187.
38. His. MSS. Com., Appen. to 9th Report. Morrison MSS., 463.
39. Unpublished letter, reproduced in *Notes and Queries*, 7th Series, Vol. 1, 186.
40. *Cal. Treas. Books*, X, Pt. II, 713, 722.
41. Ibid, Pt. III, 1393.
42. Luttrell, 3, 563.
43. Taylor's *History of the General Baptists*, 1, 341.
44. Crosby, 3, 172.
45. *Cal. Treas. Books*, XI, 57, 68, 72.
46. Ibid., 356, 389; XII, 55, 77; XIII, 18, 29, 44.
47. See two of his petitions reproduced in *Notes and Queries*, Series 2, Vol. 2, 281. Also *Cal. Treas. Papers*, XLIV, No. 60.
48. *C.S.P.D.*, 1697, 484.
49. *Cal. Treas. Books*, XIII, 103.
50. Crosby, 3, 169.
51. *A New Discovery of Titus Oates etc.*
52. Ibid.
53. *The Case of H. Burroughs etc.*
54. *The Post Boy*, February 21st-23rd, 1699.
55. *A New Discovery of Titus Oates etc.*
56. Crosby, 3, 174.
57. Ibid., 174–5.
58. Calamy, 1, 120–1.
59. Crosby, 3, 175.
60. *The Case of H. Burroughs etc.*
61. Ibid.
62. *A New Discovery of Titus Oates etc.*
63. Ibid.
64. Crosby, 3, 178.
65. Ibid., 179.
66. Ibid., 179–80. See also *The Case of H. Burroughs etc.*
67. Luttrell, 4, 558.
68. *The London Post*, June 28th–July 1st, 1700.
69. *Key to the Ancient Parish Registers of England*, 32.
70. *A New Discovery of Titus Oates etc.*
71. *Somers Tracts*, 2, 369–71. See also Luttrell, 5, 190.
72. Ailesbury, 1, 279.
73. Ibid., 2, 441.
74. *Observator*, 3, No. 41.
75. Luttrell, 4, 572. Hearne, 1, 8.
76. *History of the Reign of Queen Anne*, 4, 285.
77 Act Book, 1705. Folio 29. Commissary Court of Westminster.
78. Brown's *Works*, 1, 214.

INDEX